GOLD, VIOLET, BLACK, CRIMSON, WHITE

DAVID HEWITT

Matador
Unit E2 Airfield Business Park,
Harrison Road, Market Harborough,
Leicestershire. LE16 7UL
Tel: 0116 279 2299
Email: books@troubador.co.uk
Web: www.troubador.co.uk/matador
Twitter: @matadorbooks

ISBN 978 180313 316 4

British Library Cataloguing in Publication Data.
A catalogue record for this book is available from the British Library.

Printed and bound in the UK by TJ Books Limited, Padstow, Cornwall
Typeset in 11pt Minion Pro by Troubador Publishing Ltd, Leicester, UK

Matador is an imprint of Troubador Publishing Ltd

For Edith and Mary,
who saw all this the first time round.

1

Gold

A moon over water

A boat is coming into harbour.

It is a long boat, with two masts, and a single funnel trailing smoke.

A man is standing in the prow –

A virile man of twenty-eight in whom the joy of life is well pronounced.

(That is what the words on the title-card say.)

Up closer now, the man's dark eyelids flicker and the wind blows his dark hair across his forehead.

His name is Lonsdale. He is wearing a loose suit with a white handkerchief spilling from the breast –

With his friend, he is in search of a pretty girl to act as model for a picture he is about to paint.

The friend is wearing a blazer and a nautical cap. He speaks to Lonsdale –

If you'll come ashore with me, you shall have tea with the prettiest girl you've ever seen.

The two men are on land now, walking through crowded streets, between rough wooden houses.

One house has something painted in Oriental letters on the door: 'The Sitka Tea House' –

Be careful, old boy, she is married.

*

Inside the house, Lonsdale and his friend go from one room into another, through a low door with a thick curtain.

The tracery around the door is also Oriental.

There are young women milling about, and when the men sit down, it is at different tables.

Two of the young women jump onto the friend's knees, and they hug him and canoodle with him, giggling all the while.

Lonsdale talks to the women, seeming quite at home.

Then a bell is rung and another young woman pulls aside the curtain and comes into the room –

Suzee, the tea room keeper's wife.

She is young and supposed to be Chinese, with large eyes that dart from-side-to-side, taking everything in, missing nothing.

Suzee is wearing a silk tunic, loose trousers – also of silk – and soft slippers that make her feet seem tiny.

There is a small cap on her head, and what little can be seen of her own dark hair ends in a fringe just above her thin, curved eyebrows.

Her eyelids are shaded, her pupils dark, and a black line has been drawn out from the corner of each eye. She has strong cheekbones, a full mouth, and lips that are themselves dark.

Lonsdale seems startled by Suzee – startled, but also fascinated – and he asks her for tea.

She leaves the room and goes next door to prepare the drink.

Someone else is there – an old man, also Chinese.

The man is wearing a hat that looks like a bowler, and he has a thin pigtail dangling down his back.

He embraces Suzee and kisses her, and then he disappears –

Hop Lee takes leave of his wife.

Back in the tea room, Lonsdale has a large sketch-book and he begins to draw.

His hand moves quickly, and his eyes flicker towards Suzee's face as she brings in a tray and sets it down on the table –

Almost a child in outlook on the world, she had a woman's vanity. His interest pleased her.

His eager admiration made flattering contrast with the careless disrespect she met with from the Americans in Sitka and brought a wild desire for friendship.

Lonsdale stops drawing and holds up the sketchbook, showing a page to Suzee.

He does this proudly, thinking she will like what she sees, but she recoils.

Her head and body snap back, and she flings her arm out – the hand turned against him, the fingers splayed.

Suzee covers her face with her other hand, but she goes on watching Lonsdale from underneath her heavy eyelids.

An image from the book fills the screen.

It is a sketch of a woman reclining on a couch.

She is wearing a thin shift, and though her leg is drawn up, her thigh is visible below the hem.

The image disappears as quickly as it came.

*

The old Chinese man is in a railway station.

He searches his pockets, growing more and more alarmed, and then he hurries out of the station –

Hop Lee has left his purse behind him.

*

In the tea house once again, Suzee has pulled up close to Lonsdale and is crouching in front of him where he sits.

He is looking at the trinkets around her arms and neck.

He is inspecting the trinkets closely, and then Suzee is stroking his face with the back of her hand –

If you come upstairs, I will show you my other jewels.

She leads Lonsdale from the room by his sleeve.

The room they go into is sumptuous, with rugs and deep couches, and tapestries all over the walls.

Suzee pushes Lonsdale down onto one of the couches, and plump cushions spill onto the floor.

She kneels in front of him again, but his interest in her jewels now seems to annoy her –

Husband very cruel. You don't believe? Look!

She pulls up her sleeve and there is a mark above her elbow.

Lonsdale is frowning.

Taking hold of Suzee's arm, he lifts the sleeve higher still – and there he finds a bangle which seems to match the mark exactly.

Lonsdale pushes Suzee away, shaking his finger at her.

She leaves the room, only to return with a casket in her hands.

She lifts the lid of the casket, revealing yet more jewels, and she presents them to him.

Suzee sits down beside Lonsdale with her knees raised.

She strokes his face again, and he puts his arm round her waist and pulls her towards him.

Lonsdale kisses Suzee.

They hold the kiss for what seems an age, then, still locked in their embrace, they roll over together on the settee.

Suzee pulls Lonsdale onto her –

Hop Lee returns.

The Chinese man parts the curtains and peers into the room. He sees what Suzee and Lonsdale are doing. And she, seeing him, is startled –

My husband!

Suzee pulls away from Lonsdale, but Hop Lee is furious. He throws back the curtain and marches into the room.

He comes right up to Lonsdale and the two men start to tussle, the younger one still seated on the couch, the older one standing over him. Each has the other's shoulders in hands.

But then they part and Lonsdale's hand goes to his pocket. He pulls out a pistol and points it at Hop Lee.

The Chinese man pulls back, kicking away cushions. His weight is suddenly on his back foot, his arms held out in front of him, the palms upturned. He is shaking his head.

Suzee has turned away from this, fearing what will come. Her hands are up to her head and all her face is in view.

Hop Lee speaks –

Why do you come here to rob an old man of all that he has got in the world? Swear to me that you will not see her again.

This seems to do the trick –

Hop Lee spoke of his age, and the toil he had endured to buy this playful wife, whose lively moods were to brighten the autumn of his life! In moving terms, he begged the Englishman to leave the house and yield to him the most treasured of his many gems, his pretty child-wife Suzee.

And Lonsdale, touched by the old man's plea, felt ashamed of the conditions that beset him. Disgust overwhelmed his interest in the treacherous creature's beauty, and prompted him to go, first promising Hop Lee to hold no further converse with the girl.

Lonsdale and Suzee are seen from the back now, each raising a hand as if making a solemn oath. Then, they are walking out of the room, with Hop Lee close behind.

Downstairs, Lonsdale meets his friend and collects his sketchbook.

Giving money to the two girls who ran up to them first, the men leave the tea shop and go out onto the street.

*

Lonsdale is back on board the boat, talking to his friend in a cabin.

He yawns and seems tired, and then he is lying in a bunk, wearing pyjamas.

5

He pulls the bedclothes over him and draws the curtains closed.

*

In the tea house again, Suzee is with Hop Lee. He is very angry.

He drags her along a corridor and pushes her through a door, locking it behind him.

The room she finds herself in is small, with wooden furniture – a chair, a bench, and a table with a lamp that is lit.

Suzee is holding a corn-cob pipe, which she fills with some sort of powder before setting it down on the table –

The drugged pipe.

Hop Lee comes into the room and sits facing Suzee, on the bench.

She offers him the pipe, but he doesn't want anything to do with it at first.

He lifts his hand and shakes his head.

Suzee, however, is persistent, and she offers him the pipe again.

Hop Lee relents, and Suzee puts the lip of the pipe into his mouth and lights the bowl.

He lies down on the bench and begins smoking the pipe, with Suzee watching him intently all the while.

Before long, the pipe drops onto the floor – and then Hop Lee does the same, apparently in a stupor.

Suzee picks up the pipe and puts it on the table. Then, leaning over her husband for a moment, she blows out the lamp before making for the door.

She is in another room now, tearing down a curtain, tying one end of it to a table, and flinging the other end out of the window.

Suzee lowers herself from the window – down the roof and the side of a building – onto the ground below.

Then, she is running along a dock, her clothes billowing in the wind.

She comes alongside a boat that is tied up there, and she has a good look at it.

And then Suzee is walking up the gangway and onto the deck of the boat.

She is dropping through a hole in the deck and into a small cabin – and she is standing next to a bunk whose curtains are closed.

It is Lonsdale's bunk.

Suzee pulls the curtains aside, to reveal Lonsdale in the bunk, fast asleep.

She pulls back the bedclothes, leans over the bed, and touches his face.

Lonsdale opens his eyes and – startled – jumps up, sending bedclothes spilling onto the floor.

Then, he is sitting on the edge of the bunk, his legs dangling down.

Suzee embraces Lonsdale, and then she kisses him.

But he is wary of her and pushes her away.

Lonsdale gets out of the bunk, his mouth drawn into a short, firm line, his dark eyes half-closed.

Then, looking down at Suzee, he raises his arm and points his finger, and he makes it plain that he wants her to leave.

Suzee is crouching in front of him, in her silk clothes and cap, and she lifts her arm to his chest imploringly, the fingers of her hand slightly splayed.

She really doesn't want to go.

The sleeve of her tunic has fallen to her elbow, exposing her bare arm. Where the arm crosses Lonsdale's body, the dark of the gown contrasts with the white of his pyjamas.

Suzee stands, takes hold of Lonsdale, and begins to kiss him passionately. He returns her kisses at first, but then the screen goes black.

7

*

Sailors are making ready to sail away, and then the scene is the cabin once again.

Suzee leaps into the bunk Lonsdale vacated, but he takes her in his arms, and her little feet can be seen lifting into the air.

Then, she's dangling down his back.

Lonsdale carries Suzee along a narrow passageway, her fists thumping, her feet pedalling against his torso.

He carries her past his friend and one or two of the crew, and they turn and laugh as he goes by.

He carries Suzee along a deck, down the gangway, and off the boat. And then he sets her down on the pier before going back on board.

The gangway is removed, and the boat begins to depart.

Lonsdale is standing in the stern.

He raises his arm and waves the handkerchief he has taken from his pocket.

On the edge of the pier – seen as if from the boat, the wind again in her clothes – Suzee grows smaller and smaller.

She doesn't wave back –

The gold night passed over and melted into a new day.

2

The subject of the tea house in Sitka, and precisely what kind of place it was, came up in court.

The witness was being asked about the behaviour of the women who had leaped onto the man's knees.

'Is that an ordinary thing in human life?'

'If you have travelled much you will have seen a lot of it.' This reply was not satisfactory.

'You think, no doubt, that people should not object to these Chinese customs being exhibited to the young men and women of Lancashire.' Then, the key question. 'Tell me, Mr Stott, is a tea house a thing which is commonly known by another name in England?'

'No,' the witness replied, as firmly as he could. 'I don't think so.'

Walter Stott's many business interests included the renting out of films, and lately, he had found himself caught up in a controversy. People had taken exception to one of the films, and they hadn't been shy of making their feelings known. The Chief Constable of Preston had been particularly forthright, and Walter and his partner, Fred White, now alleged that they had been defamed by him. So iniquitous did Walter and Fred consider the Chief Constable's words, and so great the losses the words had caused, that they claimed damages of £5,000 – a sum equivalent to a third of a million pounds today.

The trial would be about what had been said as much as what had been seen.

Five Nights had been creating a stir for weeks.

'Probably no film yet produced has been more talked of than this,' a newspaper said. And when journalists who had reported every detail of the film's making were presented with the finished article, they could barely contain themselves. 'Magnificent!' one of them said. 'This is a great and wonderful film.' The costumes, photography and acting were praised. Special mention was made of 'the coloured effects in five different hues.' And if the praise was sometimes fulsome – a critic called *Five Nights* 'the greatest film the world has ever seen' – no one seemed to mind. 'The book has been read by five million people,' a headline trumpeted. 'The film will be seen by ten million.'

There was a similar reaction in Preston itself, with everyone concerned being commended for their enterprise. 'It is indeed a triumph for the King's Palace management to have secured this film,' the *Preston Herald* announced, referring to the theatre where *Five Nights* was to be shown. Outside that place, on a poster the Chief Constable will have seen as he came up to the doors, the film was proclaimed:

A fascinating reproduction of the world's most beautiful love story, embodying all the sensational incidents that made Victoria Cross's enthralling novel the most popular romance of the century.

The foyer had a mosaic floor, tiled walls, and a bow-fronted pay box. Oak and brass were abundant. And the steps that led into the auditorium might have been made of marble.

The King's Palace theatre stood close to the centre of Preston, on a piece of land wedged in between Tithebarn Street, Bishopsgate, and Old Vicarage. The Town Hall and the police station were close by; the museum, art gallery, free library, and ornate new shopping arcade only a few steps further away.

This was, however, a clamorous, fractious quarter, whose

workplaces, inns, beer shops and music halls were confronted by terraces of small, dark houses. People were forever being apprehended here – for larceny, battery, drunkenness and worse – and forever being carted off to the police court, which also stood close by.

A brewery loomed over the quarter, its outbuildings cradling the old tithe barn which had given the street its name. There were cotton mills and an ironworks, a sawmill, a cigarette factory, and livery stables. Pigs could be bought here every Saturday. Sparrows had once been shot for prizes of flour and bonnetless girls plied their trade. A man had performed the very first striptease here to rapturous applause. And the Waggon & Horses, hoping to raise the tone, had applied to change its name to the King Edward.

The theatre had been put up in place of a roller-skating rink, but though, from the outside, it was bare and irregular, the inside was a riot of the baroque. Columns reared up from either side of the stage, supporting a great arch with a bulb-rimmed tympanum filled with ripe plasterwork. Caryatids leaned out from the walls. There were cornices, curved boxes, and domes in the ceiling. The seats and curtains were of the deepest plush. And high above everything there hung a painted panel depicting a classical scene: ample women and cherubs, every last one of them – and this would be impossible to miss – unclothed.

Such a woman was the star of the first film shown in Preston. *The Lady Who Would Take a Bath* turned up at the height of summer, in a cheerful wooden booth outside the Town Hall. The first proper picture house, meanwhile, was the old Temperance Hall, where *Saved from Cannibals* and *A Trip to Niagara to Gamble for a Woman* could be seen. And the Palladium was the town's first purpose-built cinema. That place opened one Christmas, to the dismay of an alderman who had spoken out against 'establishments that are simply designed for enjoyment and recreation.' It stood close to the Empire Theatre, which also had a touch of the baroque, and close to the Prince's Theatre as well, and they all stood in plain sight of the King's Palace. Films were also on show at the Theatre Royal, where Franz Liszt had once performed, and Professor Blezzard had explained how to devour an oyster with aplomb. Portraits of Milton and Racine adorned the walls of that place. The ceiling had been done in the style of Van Dyck. And the manager, Leslie Knight, had lately put together a special band of musicians.

The Queen's and the Coronation Hall were less gilded places, the Alexander too, yet each found an audience of its own, at least for a little while. The Imperial had once been a malt house. The 'Embee' took its name from the Merigold Brothers, who owned the garage upon which it sat. The Marathon was still being used as a rink after films had started being shown. And everyone called the Picturedrome the 'Brackie', because it stood in Brackenbury Place. This hall looked like a Dutch barn from the outside, and had private boxes inside whose curtains were never drawn back. The Electric Theatre stood in the old Ebenezer Chapel, and people called it 'Fleckie Bennett's' in honour of its owner, while the Cosy, on the very next street, was run by Fleckie's sworn rival. The doorman there was Elijah Waddilove, who sold his home-made lemonade for a penny a jar.

The man who owned the King's Palace lived twenty miles away from all this, in a large house overlooking the sea, in the town of Blackpool, where he had recently been mayor.

William Henry Broadhead was a builder by trade, who had moved to the coast for the good of his health. His sons had followed him into the business, and now, his empire was at its height. He owned a score of theatres, and if most of them were to be found in and around Manchester, one could be found in Liverpool, and there was even a second one in Preston. The Hippodrome there was also red and plush inside, and it too had exhibited films. One of six of his halls to share that name, it took its place with the King's Palace alongside a King's, an Empress, a Crown, and a Royal Osborne, two Pavilions, an Olympia, a Junction, a Metropole, and a Winter Gardens.

Mr Broadhead lived by the motto 'Quick, clean, smart and bright,' and he made sure his theatres were built so they could be converted into factories if times turned bad.

The next thing to come up in court was the sketch Lonsdale showed to Suzee.

'Semi-nude, with the knee up. The knee is up, there is no doubt about that?' This was the Chief Constable's barrister.

'No,' Mr Stott replied. 'There is no doubt about that.'

'It is not exactly a pleasant position, is it?'

But it was the shenanigans upstairs, on the plump cushions, that most exercised the court at the beginning of the *Five Nights* trial. The courtroom was cold and austere, and that doubtless made the soft furnishings seem seductive. But when the subject came up, the judge couldn't help but intervene. 'If these items are to be gone into,' he said, 'I shall ask all ladies to please leave the court.'

Men had been conscripted into the Army for the first time in recent days, and German Zeppelins had almost reached Wales.

3

James Watson's rise had been striking. He was barely forty years of age, and the fifty other men he had beaten to the post of Chief Constable included many with more experience than he could claim. But when, at a special ceremony inside Preston police station, Mr Watson was presented to his constables, the Mayor told them he came with a reputation as a strict disciplinarian, which would be good for the town. For his part, the new Chief Constable vouchsafed a motto he said had always served him well:

Be straight, be good, do good, and good will come of it.

The force he was to command had grown twenty-fold since its creation a century before (the population the force served having grown five-fold in the same period). It now included plain-clothes detectives among its members, and before long, it would even include some female constables. His salary would be £400 a year, which might, with increments, rise to £500.

His predecessors included a number of military men. One of them had distinguished himself in the Gulf of Mexico and the Caribbean Sea – pacifying the Yucatan, commanding a fort in Jamaica, blockading the South during the American Civil War – while the most recent of them had spent two decades as a soldier. John Unett had won both plaudits and medals in the South African war. He had served at Biddulphsberg and Hout Nek, stormed a *koppie*, taken the surrender of many thousands of Boers, and been awarded the DSO. Shortly after his appointment to the Preston force, Captain Unett visited the

Theatre Royal to watch a film of the town's recent Whit Monday procession. He had taken part in that event himself, and each time he came up on the film he received a hearty cheer from the audience in the hall.

Mr Watson was not a local man. He had been born in North Wales to parents who were Lowland Scots, and after living for a while with his grandparents, he was reunited with his mother and father in the Pennine town of Skipton. He would complete his formal education at the grammar school there, and then be put to work at the post office, sorting letters and operating the telegraph machine. James joined the West Riding Constabulary when he was twenty-two, and worked as assistant to the Chief Constable before moving to Oldham and becoming a detective. Appointed an inspector in Barrow-in-Furness, and chief inspector in no time at all, it was in Peterborough that he was first made Chief Constable, and from there that he went to Preston. His last two predecessors had served for less time than any others, and a promise was therefore extracted from him that he wouldn't use his new post as a stepping stone to something better.

He first appeared before the Preston magistrates only a few days after his appointment, and he used that opportunity to make a short speech. A tall, fresh-faced man, the newspapers reported, with hazel eyes, a firm chin, and a straight nose, he was also by now the possessor of a fine moustache. His neat brown hair was going grey at the sides, and he will have cut a distinguished figure as he rose to his feet in his dark blue uniform. It would be his earnest endeavour, he said, to present all cases with absolute impartiality. He would try to work amicably with everyone, including lawyers and officials of the court. The inhabitants of the town could rest assured that they would receive fair and equal treatment from the police. He trusted that they would always have the most pleasant associations.

The plan at the King's Palace was to show *Five Nights* twice nightly, with houses at 6.50pm and 9pm, matinees on Monday and Thursday. Customers would be charged tuppence for a seat in the pit, a penny more for the pit stalls. It was fourpence for the grand circle, and sixpence for the orchestra stalls. And if a box was required, it could be had for a shilling.

The usual films had been shown in the month just gone – films about outlaws, stray bullets, escapes from asylums, neglected wives, and blind men who are struck by lightning and plummet into the sea; films where disaster might come in the form of a burst dam and a flooded valley, or a fire in a theatre and the terrible, fatal panic which ensues. There were the latest escapades of familiar characters – Curley, Ambrose, Fatty – and audiences had also been treated to *Tommy Atkins*, in which a couple of soldiers fight for the love of a beautiful woman. This was an old story, originally set in the Sudan, but the film comes to its own terrible conclusion on the Western Front. In some places where it was shown, men were given the chance to enlist without even leaving the picture house, military bands would strike up, or women in khaki would sing patriotic songs. In Exeter, 200 men of the Devon Regiment marched through the streets to the Theatre Royal.

But William Broadhead provided Preston with much more than films. Across town at his Hippodrome theatre, singers, comics, mimics, conjurers, acrobats and jugglers had all made an appearance; eccentric dancers, sleight-of-hand performers, a 'Hebrew humourist' and an equestrienne. Corporal Morris had played the post-horn, and Edna Latonne had sung 'We're Getting On Nicely, Thank You' dressed in the uniform of an artillery officer.

The last few days had been busy ones there, with the artistes also being called upon to give a performance for soldiers at a local barracks. But it was members of the theatre orchestra who had been busiest of all. Not only had they too been required to play twice nightly, but they had also taken part in a grand charitable garden party – an event which had occupied not one but two of the town's parks, and which had taken up not just Thursday afternoon, but much of the evening as well.

Several thousand Prestonians had attended the event, making the most of a perfect summer's day, and they had been joined by people from neighbouring towns and the country districts. A good proportion of the quality was among them, even though Lord Derby, whose idea the fête had been, cried off at the last minute. The Mayor was there, with the Mayoress by his side. There were aldermen, councillors, and countless esquires, each accompanied by his wife. And some of the wives manned stalls selling flowers, sweets, minerals, fruit, and ices under canvas. Blooms in the municipal beds had been arranged into the flags of friendly nations, and they were now co-mingled with the colourful dresses of ladies promenading around: greens and yellows, oranges, and pinks; the red, the white and the blue. There were sideshows, Pierrots, tableaux, a military tattoo, and tea on the lawn. Patriotic films were exhibited from the back of a motor van, with Corporal Weir attempting to elucidate the more martial scenes, and the crowd gave a hearty cheer when someone familiar appeared on the screen.

Everything culminated in an Empire Pageant of 400 children, which snaked between marquees and hydrangea bushes with a band of Scotch pipers at its head. Rehearsals had gone on for weeks, the sewing of the costumes too, but when the children finally came to a halt, they did so erratically, before a raised stage near the fountain, where a woman got up as Britannia sat in glory amid her faithful Colonies. Ditties were sung, in duets and quartets. There was jocosity, jocularity, a danseuse, and a magician. Miss Snape, the Misses Hodgson, and Miss Iddon gave 'The Flag That Never Comes Down'. And, as the soldiers present saluted and other men bared their heads, the Broadhead musicians struck up 'God Save The King'. Everyone then filed out and the parks were left empty, before the whole show was begun again only an hour later.

The auditorium was in darkness when Mr Watson came in, and the newsreel soon appeared on the screen. 'The latest news in pictures from all parts of the world,' it promised. There is a line of invalids being shown to the top brass, some Army athletics in which Lieutenant Moncrief RE wins three cups, and a crowd bidding '*Au revoir!*' to the Thirteenth East Surreys. The lifeboats of the *SS Arabic* can be seen in a little Irish harbour, knocking into each other on the swell. And there is more about young Eileen Lee and her long swim up the Thames.

Charlie, when he appears, is in his usual get-up, with the bowler hat the Americans call a derby. He looks dusty and fidgety, and when he finds a cane, he can't stop twirling it about. Inside a nickelodeon, people are watching a film when Charlie comes in and causes a commotion, standing on toes and sitting in laps as he tries to find a seat. It's crowded in there and people are angry, and he punches one man and then another. Then, Charlie gets upset at what's being shown. He begins to cry, and dabs his eyes with a sock, but he cheers up and starts clapping madly when the girl comes on the screen. She blows a kiss and Charlie flutters his eyes. He thinks all this is real.

Once the audience in the King's Palace had settled down again there will have been precious little to disturb the fug, hanging on the warm air, suspended over the curved backs of the sixpenny seats, a skein of cigarette smoke freighted with perspiration and perfume, and the tang of apples, oranges, peppermints, mothballs. A title-card came on the screen that referred to the Censor, and when James Watson looked around, he saw several hundred people, many of them girls and boys. It wasn't just the sketch that made him cross: Suzee kissing Lonsdale did that too; her breaking

18

her solemn oath just after she had sworn it; his fight with Hop Lee; and the pulling out of that pistol.

The manager of the King's Palace couldn't be found when he was sent for, so a brisk letter was promptly dispatched…

4

Chief Constable's Office,
Preston.
30th August 1915

Sir,

I have this day witnessed the exhibition of the picture entitled *Five Nights*, and in the opinion of the police the picture is considered an objectionable and offensive exhibition, and contrary to the terms of your licence.

Please note the exhibition is not approved of by the police and after this notice, if again shown, it will be my duty to bring the matter before my local authority.

I am, Sir,

Your obedient Servant,

JPK Watson
Chief Constable

5

By the time William Boyle started reading the Chief Constable's letter, the doors of the King's Palace had been opened once again. This, he would later say, had not been the best of days. The film had arrived late, for reasons that were still unexplained, and he hadn't been able to watch it through before the first house began.

Mr Boyle had been working in theatres since he left school, and working for William Broadhead for the best part of two decades. He had been a prop boy at the Royal Osborne, a call boy, and a stagehand. He had been employed at two of the Broadhead Hippodromes – as stage manager, assistant manager, and finally manager – and when he left the second one, it was so that he could come to the King's Palace. The Mayor, no less, had presented him with a purse of gold coins to mark the occasion.

Billy, as everyone knew him, was familiar with *Five Nights*, and also with the novel upon which it was based. He had even been made aware that the police would be visiting the theatre, though he hadn't given that possibility much thought. But after watching the film with everyone else, he felt obliged to concede that the Chief Constable had a point. 'I should certainly have cut certain parts of it out,' he would say, 'as I do not think they were suitable.'

The commotion will have discouraged him not one jot. He was a robust young man, energetic and determined, famed for his conviviality and for keeping the ends of his moustache properly waxed. He too had won plaudits and medals in South Africa – at Colesberg, Norval's Pont, and Bloemfontein – where Boer interlopers had been repelled, a railway bridge replaced, and the first concentration camps set up. 'He had heard the whirr of lead,' the *Preston Herald* recalled, and in the pit stalls of the King's Palace he will have apprehended no danger whatsoever.

Drawing apart the thick curtains and walking towards the edge of the stage, at the beginning of what should have been the second house, Billy Boyle made an announcement:

> Owing to the Chief Constable having objected to the showing of *Five Nights*, I regret to say that it will not be shown.
>
> The film was passed by the censor in the ordinary way and booked by me in the normal course of business, and the objection has come as a terrible shock, because I always take great care in my selection of films.
>
> In fact, I consider myself the severest censor in Preston, as all the patrons of the King's Palace will know.

There was no dissent as he made his exit. Moments later, he spoke to William Broadhead, the owner of the hall, who had a significant interest in the day's events. And a telephone call was then made to the Chief Constable.

'Good evening, Mr Chief.'

'Good evening, Mr Broadhead.'

'What about this picture and the letter you have sent about it? You have placed us in an awkward position by stopping it, and the time being so short, we cannot replace it. Had we known sooner we could have arranged something.'

'Pardon me, Mr Broadhead, but I haven't stopped the picture.' (Watson was emphatic about that.) 'You can please yourself entirely whether you continue to show it or not. I saw it this afternoon, and in my opinion, it is objectionable and an improper picture to show. I'm sorry for your inconvenience, but I have a public duty to perform, and if the picture is shown again as it was shown this afternoon, it will be my duty to bring the matter before the council...'

But Mr Broadhead had already put down the phone.

6

Among the many people in the King's Palace that afternoon were some who did not enjoy the film, and who were not shy of making that fact known. One of them was Edward Bennett, and he too singled out the drawing Lonsdale had shown to Suzee. It wasn't fit to be seen by the young, he said.

Edward had a vested interest in the matter, of course, given that he was young himself, and also Fleckie Bennett's son, and the projectionist at the Electric Theatre to boot. But that striking image was also mentioned by Margaret Buck. 'I considered it to be very indecent,' she said, 'both in the position of the woman and the suggestion it made to one's mind.'

Mrs Buck worked in a cotton mill and had married the boy next door. She lived just around the corner from the King's Palace, in one of the small, dark houses that confronted the place, and she said she went to picture houses four or five times a week:

> I have seven children and am not easily shocked and like
> a bit of fun. But if I had known the sort of picture it was,
> I would not have gone to see it on any account, for I did
> not enjoy it, but was absolutely disgusted with it.

Frederick Daggers also had seven children – 'four of them daughters,' he said – and he too found the sketch objectionable. He was in his forties and had joined up to fight before almost everyone else. He quickly became a corporal, but then, soon after arriving in France, he was hit by shrapnel and had to be sent home. He had been visiting the King's Palace with a friend, another soldier, whom he had met in hospital.

There was one man who expressed himself with particular force. William Patrick Meagher had travelled the best part of five miles across Preston to see the film, and even after it was over, 'the impression created upon my mind was a very painful one.'

Mr Meagher was older than Corporal Daggers, and an auditor by profession. He had run a clog business and a business making toilet soap, and he had been a moneylender. He had made a home close to the church named for St Ignatius, and gone round collecting money for the school named for St Vincent. And, though he didn't mention it now, he had five sons, each of whom was a priest. 'It is horrible to think that men and women can degrade themselves and prostitute their talents in acting in a play which is the negation and antithesis of Christian morality,' he said. 'After it, the deluge.'

But William Meagher had fallen on hard times. His work had all but dried up and he had found himself being sued by a woman he met at church. After she won her case, bankruptcy seemed the only option, for he had more than £1,000 of debt and only £6 to his name.

The woman said Mr Meagher had promised to prevent her falling into dishonest hands, as there were so many rogues about. But money she gave him on deposit ended up in the clog business, or maybe the soap business, and none of it could now be found. She wasn't the only one to allege fraud, and when William was finally brought to court, the lawyer who questioned him did not hold back. 'I see a large number of women have been your prey,' he said.

7

Before long, the telephone in James Watson's office rang again, and this time he found himself talking to a reporter.

'Is it true that you have banned *Five Nights* at Preston?'

'No.'

The Chief Constable was emphatic. 'I have not banned *Five Nights*,' he said. 'I viewed the picture at a matinee, and at the conclusion I decided I could not approve it, because of its objectionable features.'

Its 'objectionable features'; he would be hearing those words again.

'Is it true what's being said – that you treated Mr Broadhead discourteously?'

'No. Let us have no misapprehension about the matter at all. After the performance I did what I could to find the manager, Mr Boyle. Then, at about six o'clock, I caused a letter to be sent in order that he may be informed in time that if the film was shown again in the evening, it would be my duty to bring the matter before my local authority.'

This was an accurate account, in so far as it went, but what it provided wasn't the whole truth. Mr Watson was correct to say that hadn't banned *Five Nights*: he did not have the power to do that. But the letter he sent to the King's Palace will nevertheless have had much the same effect. William Broadhead will have known that, if he exhibited the film at the theatre again, he would place his licence, and his livelihood, at risk.

Later, standing in the witness box, answering questions from Walter Stott's barrister, James Watson would concede that giving the interview had not been a proper thing for him to do. However, he said, his motive had been to promote the welfare of Preston, and to do his duty as Chief Constable. And, he added:

> I wanted to disabuse any misapprehension that might get abroad about the action of the police. It is my duty to protect the police.

What James Watson told the reporter quickly made its way into the national press. It would, indeed, appear in the *Daily Sketch* the very next day. This was Britain's first tabloid, with its headquarters in Manchester, and the newspaper would waste no time in involving itself in this fresh, local controversy.

Alongside the Chief Constable's opinion there was printed a statement from Barker Motion Photography Limited, the company which had made *Five Nights*. Barker was prominent in films at the time, and its spokesman felt able to take a pugnacious line. The story of Lonsdale, Suzee and the others could only appear indecent to a mind that was already unclean, he said, and he seemed to have a particular mind in mind:

> If the Preston Chief Constable were appointed censor of art generally, what would happen to many of the beautiful pictures in our national art galleries?

The *Daily Sketch* was famous for its photographs, which it often chose to emblazon right across the front page. Captain Scott had appeared there alongside his benighted comrades, and the *Titanic* as it began its final voyage. There had been terrible scenes from the Battle of Mons. And recently, the paper had printed a photograph of a man, woman and child climbing out of a first-floor window to escape a baying mob. The headline was unambiguous:

> Clear Out the Germans, Say the People…

Several pages were now taken up with images from *Five Nights* – images printed nice and large to make them easy to inspect; images no doubt provided by the Barker company itself.

Among other men interviewed in the newspaper was George Redford. He was the Censor already spoken of by Billy Boyle, the manager of the King's Palace, and the man who decided that *Five Nights* was fit to be shown to the public. 'In my opinion,' Mr Redford said, 'it is perfectly decent.'

I have read the book, and the film can be in no way compared with it. There is no suggestive conversation in the film, while the dressing of the characters taking part in the piece is entirely different from the original.

Mr Redford had been Examiner of Plays for the Lord Chamberlain, and therefore the chief censor of the stage. And in his new role, he claimed to inspect every film himself, even if it meant watching two or three films side by side in order to get through them all. His colleagues considered him a courteous and tactful man, but on this occasion, he was keen to tell the *Daily Sketch* what he thought of Mr Watson's opinion. 'I consider it a very narrow-minded view to take,' he said, 'and do not hesitate to express in strong words that view, for the Chief Constable's action is a reflection on myself.'

The last man quoted was William Broadhead, the owner of the King's Palace. He too was unhappy with James Watson. 'I never object to any man who has the courage of his convictions, whether I agree with those convictions or not,' he said, 'but the facts in the Preston case are that we were not treated with ordinary courtesy.'

A day later, the large, clear photographs that had been printed in the *Daily Sketch* appeared there again. They also appeared in several other publications, with local papers taking their lead from national ones. And the *Preston Herald* now addressed the matter in detail, with an editorial that went so far as to quote John Ruskin:

> Let me at least clearly assert this – that whether novels, or poetry or history be read, they should be chosen not for their freedom from evil, but for their possession of good.
>
> The chance and scattered evil that may here and there haunt or hide itself in a powerful book never does any harm to a noble girl.

The same, it was said, should now apply to moving pictures, and in a forceful piece, the editor argued that people such as the Chief Constable, who had sought to suppress *Five Nights*, 'at the moment seem to be prone to namby-pambyism.'

> We want to see more common sense and more toleration in these matters.

There was much in the *Preston Herald* that had already appeared elsewhere, including George Redford's comments and those of the Barker company. There was also, however, a brief interview with one of the female stars of *Five Nights*.

Eve Balfour had been born in New Zealand and educated in a convent. She had appeared in the West End, and then on screen, and she did not take kindly to the suggestion that what she had now taken part in was an improper production. 'If the film had been like the book, I should not have been surprised,' she said, 'but it is much milder.'

> I call it a milk-diet film. All the while we were acting it, Mr Barker kept on insisting that everything should be done with one eye on the censor, and everything was.

The woman who had written the book got to have her say as well.

8

Victoria Cross was a great success by now, even if she had chosen that pseudonym to annoy the late Queen. She had produced nearly a score of novels, with *Five Nights* merely the latest to be turned into a film. Its predecessor had been about a governess who runs off to marry a rancher in Arizona, only to abandon him, and their child, for a rich Englishman. The film of the book played to packed houses, but was lost in a fire, while the book itself makes an appearance in *Five Nights*, with Lonsdale reciting passages from it during the long voyage to Alaska.

She was a daughter of the Raj, whose father knew Kipling's. He had joined the British Army as a boy and served everywhere from Karachi to Assam, with Rawalpindi, Lahore, Nepal, Tibet, and Bhutan in between. A man with literary ambitions of his own, he published epic poems and a book, *The Eastern Menace*, which warned about the ambitions of Imperial Russia. He lived through the Mutiny and was decorated for his part in the capture of Lucknow, and when he left the Army to become a journalist, it was with the rank of Colonel. His first child, a son, perished in infancy, while two of his daughters – Victoria's sisters – would die by their own hands. One of them became a journalist like her father, while the other, prone to depression and fond of passing herself off as a man, wrote poems of Sufism and doomed love that impressed Thomas Hardy.

What Victoria Cross wrote about was elemental passion, unconventional women, bewitched men, and sex for nothing but its own sake. She seemed to believe, one critic complained, that 'life means love-making,' and she was compared to DH Lawrence – though not by him. The eroticism of her books is frequently mixed with exoticism, her stories playing themselves out in Africa, its deserts and dark places; in British India, Italy, and the Klondike; on board ship in the middle of the Indian Ocean. Egypt is the setting for a story in which a woman with a moustache puts on male clothes to pursue her lover, while another tale unfolds in the thirtieth century.

The heroines of these tales are beautiful, educated, spirited, artistic, discriminating. One of them sells a picture she has painted for £500, to fund a sailing trip down the Nile. Another, discovering that her husband cannot consummate their marriage, elopes with a much younger man. When they aren't rejecting men out of hand, these women are taking up with outlaws, cowboys, lion-hunters, and inmates of insane asylums. And they turn their backs on motherhood, even when they are mothers themselves. There is transgression here and fantasy, the great supposed licence of the East, the sting of the whip and the broken taboo.

Her novel *Anna Lombard* was mentioned by Katherine Mansfield. Its heroine loves two men: a high-ranking British civil servant, and a Pathan by whom she has become pregnant. After he dies of cholera, the woman kills their child to please the Briton, who has already contemplated taking an eleven-year-old girl as his mistress. 'No man should read this book immediately before dinner,' a critic said, 'unless he wishes to lose his appetite.' It would go through more than thirty editions and remain in print for a quarter of a century.

Miss Cross can seem liberated from assumptions of her time, and to anticipate later attitudes towards men, women, empire, and the natural world. But just as she opposed vivisection, so did she vaccination, and she displayed a firm inclination towards eugenics and notions of racial purity. She was also a snob. Ezra Pound, no stranger to that vice himself, or to outright bigotry, disparaged her. Lending libraries scorned her. And the critics were scathing, one saying that she belonged to the 'charnel-house school' of literature. Yet Victoria Cross was published in the pages of the *Yellow Book*. Aubrey Beardsley designed one of her covers. And Oscar Wilde was heard to say she would have improved Thomas Hardy's women. He might have been carrying one of her stories when he was arrested in the Cadogan Hotel.

She had light, soft hair, a delicate nose, and a gentle smile, but she was hard-headed and supremely self-confident. After one row with her publisher, John Long, she took a van to his offices and removed piles of her unsold books. And when he made changes for a cheap edition of *Five Nights*, she complained:

> He has turned my beautiful style into that of a shopman and made my story rubbish; put in his own intolerable trash and given it to the public as mine.

Victoria Cross never married, but she did form a close association with her maternal uncle. She even claimed to have been bequeathed to him in her father's will, and sometimes, she took his surname as her own. He had made a fortune in Colorado – mining for silver and gold, buying and selling land – and the two of them would live together for decades. The hero of the book she dedicated to him is a strong, silent Englishman, who himself runs a mine. And the heroine is once again beautiful and bold. She dances and gambles and, in the middle of a fight in a saloon, she throws herself into the path of a bullet meant for him.

'I am simply amazed,' Victoria Cross wrote, 'that anyone can object to the film of my novel *Five Nights*.' This was in a letter published in the *Preston Herald* just after the film had been withdrawn, and the author's supreme self-confidence came shining through:

> I absolutely deny that there is anything in the book or

the film to harm or injure anyone. Its teaching must elevate and improve all who see it. There is nothing in it that a child cannot see, and much that would teach and benefit all girls and young women.

The editor of the newspaper declared himself satisfied by this. Anyone reading Miss Cross's letter, he wrote, in a column running alongside it, 'will agree that it breathes a spirit of moral freshness that helps one to dismiss aspersions upon her work.'

There was also a statement from her publisher, who had found it within himself to overlook her earlier excoriation of him. John Long said he was surprised to hear what had happened. 'If a local authority can exercise such power, then what is the use of a censor?' he asked. 'Surely the thinking people of Preston will not take the matter lying down.'

Mr Long knew whereof he spoke, for in the year in which he published *Five Nights*, he had been prosecuted over another, equally controversial book. *The Yoke* was about a middle-aged woman who embarks upon a passionate affair with a much younger man, who happens to be her adopted son. The book outraged something calling itself the National Vigilance Association, which had once locked horns with Émile Zola's English publisher and seen to it that he was imprisoned for indecency. Now, the Association alleged that *The Yoke*, too, was obscene, and gross and indecent to boot. When the matter came before the Marlborough Street police court, John Long agreed that all remaining copies of the book might be destroyed.

If Mr Long wasn't entirely disinterested in the matter of *Five Nights*, his opinion was shared by other people who wrote to the *Preston Herald*. One man, who signed himself 'SM', said that steps could have been taken to ensure that the film wasn't seen by children, and that it could certainly have been shown to adults. SM hadn't had the benefit of seeing *Five Nights* for himself, but he had spoken to people who assured him that 'sensualism' was entirely absent from the film, and that it provided 'such a faithful representation of foreign street-life as to justify the title of a travel picture, pure and simple.' He signed off much as Mr Long had done:

> Surely the public of Preston are capable of discriminating between good and bad.

A third correspondent – 'A Traveller' – *had* seen the film, and he wrote that he now felt 'a sense of deep disappointment over the action taken by the Chief Constable.' This man, too, was impressed by what he described as 'the marvellous reproductions of the various phases of life of foreign cities.' The film 'is quite an education in foreign life,' he concluded, 'and brings a real treat into the lives of those who are unable to leave their native town.'

The newspaper also, however, made space for people who supported James Watson. 'A Churchman' was the most direct of them. He had daughters who liked to go to picture shows, he wrote, and he was therefore 'delighted to think the Chief Constable has the courage to put his foot down when he sees anything which may be, shall we say, questionable.' The fact that he hadn't seen the film, nor even read the book, was neither here nor there:

> It is sufficient for me to know that a man of the world like Mr Watson considers it undesirable that the picture should be presented to the public. Good luck to him!

And one last correspondent was commendably clear:

> Our amusement atmosphere must be kept pure.

Two days later, at a meeting in the Town Hall, the councillors of Preston were told of a new development. Walter Stott and Fred White had issued a writ against the Chief Constable, alleging that he had defamed them and claiming damages for the loss they had incurred. This news wasn't unexpected and the councillors conferred only briefly, before issuing a declaration that the proceedings must be defended. For its part, the *Preston Herald* informed its readers that no further correspondence would be accepted on the matter.

It was a perilous course for the two men to take, no matter how affronted they might have been by what James Watson told the reporter and wrote in the letter that was opened by William Boyle. A writ, and a trial in the High Court with all the trappings, might easily draw the attention of the world to words that would otherwise have gone unnoticed.

An explanation for their actions would be provided in court. On the morning of the first day, as he opened the case for Stott and White, their barrister claimed that they were the victims of 'a most malicious and unjust attack' – of behaviour, indeed, that was truly 'wicked'. Their writ was motivated by fear – the very basic fear that anyone who found out what the Chief Constable had said about *Five Nights* would conclude that their business was not high class. And if that happened, the lawyer said, Walter and Fred would be ruined – their reputation would be gone and they would no longer be able to find anyone willing to rent their films.

But Walter Stott and Fred White didn't always behave as expected, or even in ways that were considered acceptable. For proof of that you only have to look at what one of them did later, and at what the other had done already.

9

Will Barker was the head of the film company which bore his name, and it was he who spoke on the company's behalf during the controversy over *Five Nights*, not least in the interviews published in the *Daily Sketch* and the *Preston Herald*.

He had started out as a salesman, and become so successful that he was able to indulge his true passions. He travelled to the Shetland Isles, Canada, Norway and Africa, taking a camera with him wherever he went, and collecting footage he would later exhibit as *Return to Civilisation from the North Pole* and *From the Cape to Cairo*. The latter film was exhibited in the West End, in what Mr Barker would claim to be the first show arranged exclusively for the trade. He then produced a daily newsreel in London, and while that had to be abandoned when fog came down, the films he made of great public events quickly found an audience. They covered such things as the Derby and the Grand National, and he worked so quickly that they could be shown to a paying audience before the day was out.

Bisley, the Boat Race and countless balloon races were Will Barker's subjects; Henley, Cowes, Punchestown, Goodwood. There was the state opening of Parliament and the Australians at Lord's, the wedding of Prince Gustavus, and the visit of King Haakon and Queen Maud. But he also produced more modest pieces, showing a busy day in a soap works, or a trip upriver to Eel Pie Island. In *Herring Harvest at Yarmouth* there are drifters and ketches coming along the Yare, and luggers with all their oars out, and seagulls can be seen swooping on swills set out to receive the catch.

The company was based in Ealing, and it was there, on the

Green, in the grounds of his own house, that Will Barker put up a large studio with glass walls. A bold man, he wanted to be able to make films whatever the weather. A reckless man, too: he chose a bulldog as his mascot and used a leather whip to settle disputes. He had taken his camera to the procession for Queen Victoria's Diamond Jubilee, but when her successor, King Edward, died and Will tried to film from the steps of the Royal Exchange, he was given a fine. Then, four years before *Five Nights*, he produced a film that would change everything.

Henry VIII was his version of a play that was being performed at His Majesty's Theatre in the Haymarket. It wasn't the whole play, in fact, merely a selection of five scenes, and filming was completed in a single winter afternoon. Fifteen lorries were used to carry scenery out to Ealing Green, and to carry it back to the West End in time for curtain-up. And the completed film was shown at midnight, after the curtain had fallen once again, with the cast and crew gathered together on the stage.

The piece had been put together by Herbert Beerbohm Tree, who was also the star, and Will Barker paid him a fee of £1,000 (which would be worth close to £100,000 today). He also paid the composer Edward German fifty guineas for sixteen bars of music. The finished film was copied twenty times. Each copy was then tinted amber, blue, green, brown, and yellow. And Mr Barker announced that, in a departure from usual practice, the copies would merely be rented, and not sold, to a distributor. Half of them would be shown in London and half in the provinces, and after six weeks, they would all be brought back to Ealing. This would ensure that audiences would be presented with only top-quality stock; that there would be little chance, as the trade journal the *Bioscope* put it, 'of a worn and rainy film, kept together by the aid of thread and pins, being shown on the screen of a tenth-rate theatre.' It would also ensure that the film made a greater profit, if not for the exhibitor, then certainly for producers such as Mr Barker.

It was a great success. 'Words fail me to adequately describe this great triumph of the kinematographer's art,' one critic wrote. 'The picture is without doubt the greatest that has ever been attempted in this country, and I am almost tempted to say in any other.' Sir Herbert had made Cardinal Wolsey the centrepiece of his production, and because that was the role he had taken himself, he was a constant presence in the film. There was particular praise for a scene in which Wolsey is seen lamenting his own awful fate.

Within days, all twenty copies had been booked up and picture houses were full to bursting, even though ticket prices had in some places been doubled. Audiences were 'more than pleased by the fine entertainment afforded them' in Folkestone. There were long queues and people turned away in Highgate and Shepherd's Bush, in Camberwell at the Bijou, and everywhere else as well, from Plymouth to South Shields. The Harrow Cinema ran a special advertisement. 'Seats may be reserved at a shilling each,' it read. 'Our patrons who find it inconvenient to arrive fairly early are strongly recommended to adopt this course.' The film was retained for another fortnight in Leicester, while in Luton it was accompanied by a juvenile choir. And in Harringay, it was 'not only drawing local people, but those from distant parts.' The Premier Electric Theatre there was a triangle of light-coloured stone, its roofs steep and its gable curved. The pavilion on the front had the hint of a *chhatri* at the corner, betraying an influence Victoria Cross might have appreciated, while in the vestibule, there were more than enough palm trees.

All sorts of films were popular at the Premier, at least until Saturday night. But then the place started opening on Sundays, and it found itself had up in court and fined two guineas. When a formal ban was introduced across a large portion of the capital, there was a protest from many picture house managers. Chief constables in several towns had 'all testified to the improvement in the condition of the streets,' the managers said, 'and to the reduction which has taken place in the amount of drunkenness on Sunday evenings since cinematograph theatres have been allowed to open on that day.' The Chief Constable of Preston was singled out for special mention.

As the summonses kept coming, the defences grew more ingenious. A near-neighbour of the Premier was the Electric Coliseum Cinema, and when that place too was had up, its barrister certainly earned his fee. All that was forbidden on a Sunday was the showing of *inflammable* films, Mr Bodkin told the court, and no evidence had been produced that his client's films were of that kind. The case was dismissed.

A diligent man, from a family of lawyers, Archibald Bodkin was often briefed in picture house cases. While some of those cases were about Sunday opening, others were about music, and whether it should be restricted to what could be played on instruments. When Mr Bodkin asked that singers be permitted as well, he conceded that a limit might be placed on the number of songs they sang. That was sufficient to carry the day for the Majestic in Clapham, but when other places made a similar request, the stakes were raised. This would surely create conflict with the music halls, Archibald was told. He pointed out that the music halls had been showing films for years.

Popular though showings of *Henry VIII* might have been, the acclaim was not universal. In one picture house, a man perhaps more used to seeing theatre in a theatre leaped to his feet. 'I say!' he shouted, 'You know we can't hear a word!' Then, on Maundy Thursday, an extraordinary event took place in Will Barker's spacious grounds – on the grass, just far enough from the glass walls, in front of an invited audience of film people and press.

With ceremony befitting the man and the studio, the prints of *Henry VIII* that had been returned to Ealing were brought out one by one in wheelbarrows, carried to the appointed place, and solemnly counted out by members of staff. Then, Will Barker climbed to the top of a ladder with a megaphone in his hand. 'Get at it, boys!' he shouted, and the films were unwound onto an iron sheet and heaped into a coil that was said to be eight miles long. The whole loose, rustling lot was then set alight.

It was Mr Barker himself who applied the fatal match. There was a great roar, a plume of flame shot into the air, the grass caught light, and spectators ran for their lives – backwards, so as not to miss a thing. Streamers of scorched celluloid spiralled down the breeze, and in no time at all, what he had made was ashes.

Ever the showman, Will Barker had arranged for the great event to be filmed, but like the one whose destruction it records, his film is now lost.

10

At the beginning of the year of *Five Nights*, the Barker company was in the ascendant. After *Henry VIII*, there had been films showing the Cup Final Replay, the Trooping of the Colour, and the great Delhi Durbar. And the company's feature films were growing longer and more elaborate.

Sixty Years A Queen was the most celebrated Barker film so far. It offered an intimate portrait of Victoria and her era, and while it did so languidly and dutifully – the subtitle proclaiming her 'Victoria the Good' – it was also graceful and diligent. Five hundred actresses had been auditioned for the title role. Ealing Green had been transformed not only into Westminster Abbey, but into Khartoum and Sevastopol as well. And rather more care had been taken re-enacting the Queen's Coronation than had been accorded the actual event. The cost of all this was something the press invariably mentioned. There was disagreement as to the precise figure, but £8,000 was confidently reported to have been spent on wages alone, with another thousand on costumes and wigs.

The film invariably arrived at picture houses that had been decorated with patriotic bunting, whose staff had been given patriotic clothing to wear. Musicians had invariably been engaged, and teachers exhorted to bring along their students. Sixty Chelsea Pensioners turned up at a showing in the West End. There was a procession of Boy Scouts in Harlesden. Speeches were given by mayor after mayor. And all of this had the desired effect. *Sixty Years A Queen* did tremendous business across the realm, not least at the Albert Hall in Sheffield and the Albert Hall in Stafford. It was kept on for another week in

Newcastle, while in Liverpool, it could be seen at 2.00, 3.15, 4.30, 5.45, 7.00, 8.15 and 9.30. Will Barker liked to describe himself as 'a patriotic republican', but this most royalist of films would provide a threefold return on his outlay.

The company had also, in fact, produced the first British feature film.

Its length was what was invariably mentioned about *East Lynne*. There was disagreement as to the precise duration, but audiences were told they would have to remain in their seats for an hour or more. There were also the title-cards to contend with. The novel upon which the film was based was as complex as it was melodramatic, and the explication the film was felt to require – the 'letterpress between the pictures', one critic called it – was more detailed and more intrusive than people had come to expect.

But the Barker company and its exhibitors approached the problem with imagination and vigour. Key scenes from the film were reproduced on lantern slides and in photographs sent to the press. A luxurious brochure was put out, containing colour illustrations and even more photographs, sandwiched between covers of gold. And in Whitstable, the Palais de Luxe offered 'chocolate for all school children' at the Saturday matinee. Musicians were engaged again, singers and dancers too, and at the Olympia in Cardiff, a comedy cartoonist was provided for the sake of additional explication. At the Eglinton Electreum in Glasgow, the 'elocutionary accompaniment' of Jack Carlton Baker was said to have 'considerably enhanced the enjoyment.'

Nor did Will Barker's involvement end when shooting was complete, for he too had a part to play in promoting the film. On the first night at the Empire in Bedford, Mr Barker was invited to deliver a short address to the audience. Stepping out in front of the screen, halfway through the proceedings, he said he 'had taken great pains to see that all the actions, dresses, furniture and wallpaper were early-Victorian.' He also revealed, however, that 'an error had crept in,' and, with a feel for the dramatic that was wholly characteristic, he promised to give a sovereign to the first person who could tell him what that error might be.

The film was praised for its patriotism, the *Bioscope* calling it 'the outcome of British enterprise, carried out by British brains, capital and labour, and enacted by British artists.' And it was even said to be instructive. In Whitby, a newspaper said it would be 'a regrettable and educational loss to the community if they fail to witness this film,' while in Tunbridge Wells, the *Courier* explained:

> One is able to appreciate the inner meaning of the story in a way impossible to those dependent on the book alone.

This wasn't, though, the only *East Lynne* doing the rounds at the time. The play of the book had been popular for years, only recently making a return to Preston, and now, there were two film rivals for the version put out by Will Barker. They had been made in New York and Brighton, and the owner of the Prince's Theatre in Preston claimed to have one of them to himself.

Will Onda had left a job in a factory to become an acrobat, only to have to retire from the stage after falling from an omnibus. Now, he showed films not just at the Prince's Theatre, but at the Brackie and the Temperance Hall; and not just in Preston, but in Lancaster and Morecambe as well. He described what he offered as 'pictures and turns,' and sometimes, he went so far as to offer a 'mammoth boxing entertainment' on a Saturday afternoon.

But if some picture houses weren't clear about which version they had, other picture houses were very clear indeed. The Midland Electric Theatre in Derby announced it was showing 'the correct version' of the novel. In Harrow, an advertisement read:

Please Note – this is not one of the cheap, short copies that is being offered the public under this title, but Barker's All-British masterpiece.

And in Lancashire:

Notice of importance to our picture patrons. A local impression may be held that *East Lynne* has already been shown in Wigan, but the film on this subject, to be seen at the Pavilion... is the One And Only Picture depicting in its entirety...

The year of *Five Nights* would prove particularly momentous for Will Barker, not least because it saw him direct a feature film for himself.

The film was *She*, adapted from Rider Haggard's famous novel. It too was expensive to make and gorgeous to look at – the sets decorated with elegant furniture, the actors festooned with real jewels – and the reviews were excellent. 'Everyone must see this,' they said. 'One of the great masterpieces of stage-craft and film acting':

Nothing more weird and beautiful has ever been screened.

The task of adapting the novel had fallen to a young woman named Nellie Lucoque. She was a native of Bath, where her husband ran the Vaudeville Electric Theatre. He was a confectioner, who had only recently been spelling his surname 'Lucock', and this, Nellie's first foray into film, had been his idea. It was the product of an association with Rider Haggard that he hoped to parlay into a new career as a director and producer. Although Nellie would go on to produce a number of film adaptations, she would say 'she doubted if she had met one which gave her so much hard thought and trouble' as this one.

The effort, though, was surely justified, for *She* was another huge success. Not only did the film receive ecstatic reviews, it was also said to have brought in two million customers in the first few weeks, and to have prompted the sale of several million postcards. In Sheffield again, after a hold-up on the railway and the cancellation of showings at the Star, a notice appeared in a local paper: '*She* has arrived and is being shown daily from 2.30.' Continuous performances were suspended in Portsmouth, so the film could be shown at 6.00 and 8.00. It was shown at three, seven and nine in Dumfries. And in Coventry, at yet another Star, it could be seen at three, five, seven and nine.

So successful was *She* that other rival versions of the book began appearing again in picture houses. One of them originated in Preston, and it made Rider Haggard angry – so angry that he took out an injunction against its owner. When the matter came to court, Will Onda claimed that his version of the film had been destroyed. He had, however, been hawking it around for months, and he had rented it to a cinema in Southampton only a few days before.

The year also saw the release of *Jane Shore*, a film based not on a novel, but on an old play about a mistress of King Edward. It too was long, and it was epic in other ways as well. Will Barker claimed to have assembled a cast of 6,000, with 300 horses, eight tons of armour, and thirteen hundredweight of make-believe snow. In one scene, shot in the Devil's Punchbowl, the extras included inmates of a local prison. The film shows high walls being scaled and wanton women confined. A woman betrothed to one man becomes mistress of another, while a man solicits a woman who is by no means his wife. And letters are put up on the screen in which lovers declare that they have gone away for the sake of honour.

Like many Barker films, this one was the product of a collaboration between director Bert Haldane and writer

Rowland Talbot, both of whom had been with the company for three years. Bert, the older man, was a native of Warrington, where they knew him by a different name, and he had *Sixty Years A Queen* and *East Lynne* to his credit as well. Rowland, meanwhile, had produced almost a hundred scripts. The two men, who would shortly collaborate on *Five Nights*, had already been responsible for *Mary of Briarwood Dell*, the very first film to be passed by the Censor, and *Their Only Son*. That film, one of the first to be set on the Western Front, features a young man who enlists in the Army after being disowned by his father, and who, when he is injured, finds himself being nursed back to health by the woman who had once been his wife. 'War, with all its horrors, has its bright side,' the film's poster proclaimed:

Our story deals with a young man's downfall and his ultimate redemption through war's cleansing fire.

Jane Shore was also notable for its colour, with the tinting that had helped make *Henry VIII* so distinctive again being used to mark different phases of the story: yellow, orange, turquoise, red, blue, purple, mauve. The *Scotsman* praised the 'painstaking care' the Barker company had taken, 'the gorgeous scenes, the pageantry of the streets,' while *Variety* pronounced it 'an excellent picture – judged by British standards.' There was another special brochure, together with an array of postcards and posters. A note was circulated, containing suggestions as to music that might complement the action. And Will Barker found himself stepping out in front of the screen once again. He was closer to home this time, at the Kinema in Ealing – a forbidding sort of place, built on the site of an old cottage hospital, whose pilasters did little to enliven an otherwise bare façade. The promotion there had again been vigorous. 'This film represents the most colossal achievement of the world's film trade,' an advertisement said. 'A Tremendous Panorama of Spectacular Magnificence.'

There was one scene in the film that attracted particular comment –

A young woman rises from her bed to greet the dawn.

She is seen from behind, her long, long hair trailing down her back.

She sways a little as, barefoot, she approaches a large window and spreads her arms out wide.

As the woman opens the shutters the sun streams in, revealing the silhouette of her figure through a very thin gown.

11

The making of *Five Nights* began in the spring, within the glass walls of the Barker studios on Ealing Green, which had this time been transformed into Alaska, and into several other places besides. The task wouldn't be Will Barker's responsibility alone, as funding for the film had been provided by an outside investor – International Exclusives Limited, a thrusting new concern, whose headquarters were to be found in the heart of the capital. It was to that company's executives that the unenviable task had been given of doing a deal with Victoria Cross.

The actual shooting of the film could, however, be left to Mr Barker. It proceeded with a minimum of fuss and was completed by the early summer. Editing and tinting then had to take place. Title-cards had to be inserted, and the requisite number of prints made and checked. The approval of those executives had to solicited. And then, *Five Nights* was ready to be released. It was sent to the Censor, George Redford, who promptly passed it for showing to the general public, stipulating only that any child who went to see it should be accompanied by an adult.

Mr Redford liked it to be thought that his word was final, but that simply wasn't the case. His office might also have been in the heart of the capital, high up in a baroque-style building with tiles on the front and a lovely bronze window, but he had insurance agents and theatrical agents for neighbours; a china dealer and a religious healer. And despite his lofty title, he was nothing more than a creature of the trade, his post funded by the £2 a reel he charged for every viewing. Local authorities could permit a film he had passed to be shown, but they could not be compelled to do so. And councillors might ban a film, even though it had been given one of his certificates. In the case of *Five Nights*, that is precisely what many councillors did.

There had been a number of Barker films already that year, and many of them had something to do with the war. *Tommy Atkins*, shown at the King's Palace in Preston just before *Five Nights*, was directed by Bert Haldane. He and Rowland Talbot were responsible for *Your Country Needs You*, as well as *Their Only Son*, while the films the latter wrote for the company also included *The Looters of Liège*, *By the Kaiser's Orders*, and *The Call of the Motherland*. In *A Hero of the Trenches*, another one of his, a seamstress who sends a shirt to a soldier ends up marrying him. *The Dead Past Recalled* sees a man lose his memory when rescuing a nurse, only to recover it when saving his own father. And the heroine of *A Daughter of Belgium* avenges the killing of her father, and also of her lover, before being rescued by members of a Highland regiment. Those men, with their distinctive dress, were celebrated in another Barker film – *Bravo, Kilties!*

Rival companies also made films along these lines. There were *A Daughter of France*, *A Son of France*, *Called to the Front*, *Lest We Forget*, *The Bells of Rheims*, and *The Road to Calais*. In *Wake Up! or A Dream of Tomorrow*, a pacifist Home Secretary is reformed when he imagines that the country has been invaded. This finds an echo in *Bringing It Home to Him*, where the invasion is real enough, but has been staged by a man's friends. And in both *For the Empire* and *An Englishman's Home*, a reluctant man decides to fight after foreigners actually move into his house.

The redemptive power of war was something these films often stressed. There are wastrels, slackers, or shirkers of one kind or another in *England's Call*, *His Reformation*, *For King and Country*, *Proving His Worth*, *Making a Man of Him*, and *So Much Good in the Worst of Us*. And what finally brings them to their senses is something as simple as a dying child or the love of a good woman, or portraits of Nelson, Wellington and General Gordon that suddenly come to life.

Crime was another favourite subject for the Barker company, featuring in films such as *Rogues of London*, where innocents are preyed upon, a woman is saved from the Thames, and a maid is compromised under swinging Chinese lanterns. *In the Hands of the London Crooks* was followed by *Darkest London* and then *The Lights o' London*, while *The Debt of Gambling* marked the screen debut of Thomas H MacDonald. He was paired with Tom Coventry in that film, and the two men would go on to appear together in *Jane Shore*, and then in *Five Nights*, in which they played Lonsdale and Hop Lee, respectively. They had both been stage actors before they ventured onto the screen, and neither had made a film for anyone except Will Barker.

To go with its war films and crime films, the Barker company was also putting out melodramas. *The Lure of London* features a surgeon who becomes estranged from his daughter. She is adopted by a drunkard and becomes a dancer, but when she has an accident and needs an operation, the man who saves her is her father. *As a Man Sows* again starred Thomas H MacDonald, and *Younita – From Gutter to Footlights*, was again directed by Bert Haldane and written by Rowland Talbot. The subject of that film is also a dancer, who is shot by the jealous lover she had persuaded to kill the Neapolitan organ-grinder responsible for her first becoming famous.

Another film made in the capital featured Sybil de Bray, the actress who played Suzee in *Five Nights*.

Though still young, Ms de Bray had already enjoyed success in drawing-room farces in the West End. 'A charming *ingénue*,' one critic called her; 'fascinating, pretty and clever' another. She had been photographed wearing a huge hat at a garden party in Chelsea, gone as a concubine to the Arabian Nights Ball, and flitted briefly across the *Kinemacolor Fashion Gazette* as one of a number of actresses and society ladies shown modelling lovely gowns.

Lately, she had also appeared on screen in *The Life of a London Shopgirl*, a film about the son of an Earl, who is disowned and becomes a greengrocer, and then finds a diamond belonging to his father in the middle of an orange. 'Miss Sybil de Bray fills with acceptance the principal part,' the *Scotsman* wrote. The *Tatler* announced that she was 'a bewitching little actress' whose 'daintiness and personal charm ensure for her a big reception.' She appeared on the cover of the *Illustrated Sporting & Dramatic News*, and in a humorous sketch in the *Sketch*. And when that magazine printed a large photograph of her, it did so under the heading 'A New Beauty Come to Town'.

Journalists were falling over themselves to interview her. 'I find aviation awfully alluring,' she told the man from the *Era*, while 'reflectively puffing her cigarette.' And, as if to prove the point, she allowed herself to be filmed for a newsreel ascending into the sky over Battersea –

At first, Sybil is smiling a lovely, broad smile, her cheekbones again prominent, her chin well defined, and her lips full. Her dark eyes are kinder, though, than her *Five Nights* make-up will make them seem. She is wearing a large overcoat with a collar that is unmistakeably fur, and there is another huge hat, this time with a bow at the front, and this time pulled low over her brow.

Sybil says something and seems to repeat it nervously. Then, she is scooped up by a good-looking man in a hat and deposited in the basket of a hot-air balloon. He, it turns out, is a famous aviator.

There are six men standing around her in all, equal numbers inside the basket and outside, and all of them seem to be clawing at ropes.

Seen now from a distance, the balloon begins to lift gently

into the air, Sybil at the basket's edge, keeping a tight hold of the aviator.

The balloon rises and the camera tips back to reveal the sky, and Sybil gives a decorous wave. Then another. Then a third.

Too soon, though, she is gone – lost with her companions in the haze, the great balloon and its little basket all that can be seen, becoming ever fainter and taking up less and less of the screen.

She found it, a title-card tells us, 'much warmer in the clouds than on the earth.'

12

Here are some characters, titles, and situations of popular film melodramas of the time:

A woman. A young woman. A hypnotised woman. *The Girl Who Played the Game*. A businessman. A toff who has lost his memory in an assault. A sleeping Jew. An artist's wife. His destitute wife. A bargee's ejected wife. A squire's disowned son. A squire's nephew's illegitimate son. A Chinaman. A drapery assistant. *One Fair Daughter*. A selfish actress. A sculptor's wife. Women who hope to become fashion models. A steward. A Jewish student. An abducted heiress. A doctor. A girl. A squire. An Earl. A fisher-girl. *Mary the Fishergirl*. A jealous Spaniard. A missionary's daughter. A Jewish gambler. An unwanted baby. A blinded officer. A jester. A peer. An admiral's daughter, who poses as a Turk. Her crooked husband. A drunkard's wife. The miller's daughter. A heroic mine manager. Her debauched husband. A rich artist. A Christian slave. A widowed lady. A gambler, who has been framed and disowned. The squire who has abandoned his sweetheart. A captain's secret wife. *Another Man's Wife*. A wastrel in his new family. The son of the King of Ruritania. A squire's daughter. The mother of a stillborn baby. A peer's daughter. *The Lady of Lyons*. The poor artist. An actor. A rich man's wife. The city girl to whom he is engaged. *Her Nameless Child*.

The Little Minister. Beware Your Sins. London's Yellow Peril. In the Grip of Death. In the Hour of His Need. Love on a Yacht. Time the Great Healer. In the Grip of Spies. The Drawn Blind. Wild Oats.

In the Shadow of Darkness. Money Works Wonders. The Power to Kill. Shadows. Creatures of Clay. The Dancer's Romance. A Park Lane Scandal. A Chinese Vengeance. The Lord Gave. His Choice. His Second Chance. Morphia, the Death Drug. The Fulfilment of the Law. The Kiss of Clay. The Cloister and the Hearth. Through the Valley of Shadows. The Price of Fame. Her Hour of Retribution. A Cinema Girl's Romance. A Fishergirl's Folly. The Heart of a Gypsy Maid. The Port of Missing Women.

She kills herself. He promises his mother he will remain single, only to fall for her nurse. He is bitten by a snake. He is mistaken for a camper. She is blinded in the car crash which kills her fiancé. She embarrasses her father. She stuffs her lover's mouth with clay. He is transformed from a man by the father of the woman he loved. She stabs her film-star lover. He saves a friend from the card sharp who killed his father. She elopes to London. He loves two women. He is posing as a thief. She poses as a gypsy and falls in love with the new minister. She is disowned by her husband. He is saved by a squire. She is abandoned by her lover, who dies in a fire. He dies in the wreck of the *Birkenhead*, trying to save his wife and the soldier who loves her. He fights a duel in the dark. She refuses the treatment that would cure her blindness. She is saved from drowning by a vicar after she has fought with a jealous rival. He has been wrongly convicted and escapes jail in time to save his sweetheart's father from being drowned by someone else. She is jealous to make him give up a dancer. She commits bigamy and is blackmailed until she learns of the death of her husband. She helps her brother escape a murder charge. He leaves a sick princess to perform surgery on a destitute girl. He teaches her to beg. She robs her father to pay for her wedding and becomes the mistress of a morphine addict. She is deserted by a peer but saved from a fire by her ex-fiancé. He recovers his sight in time to see that he is being poisoned by his assistant. She poisons him when he goes mad. He grows up to avenge the murder of his father. She fetches British sailors to save a girl from the sultan. She is wooed by a Londoner. He changes his name and denies his father. She weds her cousin's lover. He is saved from a fire. She returns to her husband after being led astray. She fetches a framed lieutenant to save the Smyrna consulate from a German spy. He is saved from suicide. He gains redemption on the North West Frontier and sees his horse win a classic race. Sacked, he becomes destitute. He elopes with a sergeant's wife, kills her, and then dies saving the life of the sergeant. He kills him when he plans to elope with the Jew's wife. He saves an emperor's secret papers. He dies in a duel. He goes mad in Paris. She is revealed to be an heiress, who has been abducted. He lets his girl wed his friend. He rescues a naval code from a Chinaman who is a crook. She does it so that the artist she loves might succeed. She does it to save her sister from shame. He is deserted by his mistress. He becomes a priest. She does it in order to secure an inheritance for her weak brother. He dies in a fire. He rides a race to win a bequest. She becomes a dancer and falls in love with a blackmailed earl. He rescues some secret plans from a Chinese secret society. He takes the blame to stop her eloping with a cad. She doesn't do it, because it would require her sister to become the mistress of a lord. She poses as a spinster. She leaves her rich lover. He saves a man from suicide. She has a baby. She saves him from suicide when he takes to the bottle. He poses as a captain. He gives an unwanted girl to a Jewish crook. He wins a sweepstake and the Victoria Cross. He secretly weds. She feigns drunkenness to repel an amorous peer. She kills her brother in a duel. She is cured of brain fever by the doctor who is her husband. He makes a curate believe his wife is in love with an artist. He is arrested after he has put on the coat of a dying highwayman. He is killed. He can only be woken by the jingling of coins. He deserts her. She tries to sell herself to her employer. He frees a woman from an Oriental den. She is last seen dying in church as he marries someone else. She is sold into slavery.

13

The first Chinese woman to live in Sitka was named Mary.

That mossy, wooden port had once been Russian, taken from native people by merchants whose adventuring turned murderous when the Tsar's troops arrived. Bombardment from the sea was followed by the paying of ransoms and the putting up of palisades, before the ground could be secured and a settlement established. A cathedral was then erected and an Orthodox bishop installed. And a church was put up, too, for all the Lutherans the merchants brought in their wake. When Alaska became American, at a price of barely thirty cents an acre, Sitka was made its first capital. Mary might even have been the first Chinese woman anywhere in the territory.

She had come from the water herself, born on a sampan in Shiqi in the far south-east, where it seems they knew her as Sing Deuh-Ah Fuh. She ran off at the age of nine, she said, and made her way to Canada, finding her own money for the journey. She worked as a maid – as a prostitute, some people said – in Victoria, near Vancouver. And at the age of fifteen, she met and married Ah Bong, a man more than forty years her senior. He owned a bakery and restaurant in Sitka, and Mary went there with him, attracted, she would later say, by the fact that he was a citizen. She was living and working in Sitka on the day *Five Nights* showed Lonsdale making his visit.

Here is an early photograph of her. She is sitting in a portrait studio, in front of a plain background, on a hard, dark chair. The photograph is formal and stylised, and looks like ones taken of countless other new immigrants, with the purpose of being placed before someone in authority. Mary seems conscious of that. She is sitting, in fact, on the very edge of the chair, her back straight, her legs crossed at the ankles. The chair is embellished with leaves and fruits picked out in paint or gold, and Mary's right arm rests on a table, which is also embellished. There is a vase on the table, full of small flowers with long stems, and a pot with a few sticks of incense. Her left hand rests on a book lying open in her lap. She has been interrupted while reading, this seems to suggest, so she cannot be unlettered.

Mary's costume is dark and loose, and so extensive that only her head and neck, her feet and her elegant fingers can be seen. There is a ring on one of the fingers that she may have wished to display. The costume is also silky and rather fine, decorated with a line or two, some swirls and stars. Mary's hair, also dark, is uncovered, pulled back to reveal a broad forehead, and gathered behind in a simple bun, just visible because her head is slightly turned. Her face bears no trace of make-up, and her pupils are dark beneath the merest hint of eyebrow, as she looks out of the photograph, off to the left.

What is striking, though – more than the flowers, the open book, or the chinoiserie – is the straight line of Mary's mouth, and her calm, level gaze. She will have had to endure a great deal as she left her home in China and travelled across the Pacific Ocean. There will have been discomfort, indignity, forced accommodations, and worse. Yet none of that is to be seen here, in Mary's round, smooth, still young face.

Nor will the indignity have come to an end with landfall safely made. Canada will have demanded a great deal from its new arrival: patience, tact, forbearance. There will have been much she had to shake off, to pretend she did not see or hear. And she will have understood the importance of always seeming composed. That Mary was equal to the task is evident from what she became, but it is also obvious from this image, the one she chose to present of herself.

She was Mary Bong when the photograph was taken, even if people insisted on calling her 'China Mary'.

14

Violet

A hot, mysterious night of summer

In Charing Cross, a mass of people is going this way and that.

And at the station, from beneath one of the arches, two men positively stride into the light –

Back in London.

It is Lonsdale and his friend again, and they are quickly on the move.

The motor car is all metal and hard, black rubber, with a running board, big wheels, and mudguards that finish it with a flourish.

The top is down and the inside is all buttoned leather.

*

In a drawing room, two new people – a man and a woman – are sitting at a piano, side-by-side –

Lawton and Viola compose an opera.

Viola is playing the piano, glancing up every now and again to look at Lawton.

He leans towards her as he tries to keep up with the score.

She has dark hair, parted down the middle, swept in halves across her forehead, and collected in loose bunches over her ears.

Her complexion is pale, her brows and lashes dark, her eyelids deep-shaded.

Then, it's the inside of some kind of studio –

Lonsdale vainly seeks an ideal model for his next masterpiece.

There are paintings on the walls, and pieces of sculpture on shelves – antique heads and torsos.

There is a window with open curtains and, on a stool, a palette over which someone has thrown some brushes.

Young women come in one by one and Lonsdale looks them up and down.

He seems dissatisfied, however, and when each woman leaves, her head is bowed.

Lonsdale paces around the studio, as if deep in thought, before sitting in an armchair with his back to the door –

Viola visits her cousin.

Another young woman has come into the room, and she is creeping towards Lonsdale.

It is the woman who was playing the piano, and he doesn't see her at first.

Viola is wearing a plush, dark cloak that touches the floor, and a broad headband, which sits just above her eyes and shows off her bunches of hair.

She seems happy, playful even, and when she reaches Lonsdale, she puts her small hands over his eyes.

Lonsdale takes Viola's hands away and looks at her over his shoulder. The sight of her seems to cheer him up –

You come like a glorious sunset to a gloomy day.

He stands up and embraces her –

I have searched for weeks for a perfect model. I would give anything to find one.

Viola thinks she has the answer –

Let me be your model.

But Lonsdale shakes his head –

No. I cannot let you stand as a model before me.

In another room, two more young women are shown to him and dismissed by him.

When he returns to the studio, his cousin is as determined as before –

Viola again asks to be his model.

And without waiting for a reply, she rises to her feet, looking around.

What is she going to do?

Viola opens her cloak to Lonsdale.

She is wearing a fine gown – the arms cut high, the neckline low.

Around her throat, on a thin chain, there is a jewel that catches the light.

Lonsdale's eyes flicker, up and down –

I know I ought not to accept your offer, but the temptation is so great I cannot refuse.

He leads her towards a door and hands her some clothing.

Viola is taking off her gown.

When she goes back into the studio, the cloak is around her shoulders again, trailing on the floor.

She steps onto a pedestal.

Lonsdale is sitting on a low chair, and Viola is looking down on him, her eyes fixed on his.

She lets the cloak fall from her right arm, which is suddenly bare, and holds it away from her body, as if to complete the pose.

Then, the cloak falls to the floor.

Viola is covered now only by the flimsy gown, which fits her so closely that the shape of her body and thigh can be seen.

The discarded cloak stretches towards Lonsdale.

He seems astonished, and drops backwards onto the heels of his hands.

Then, he hands Viola down from the pedestal, embracing her as he does so, and the picture suddenly disappears.

*

Viola is next shown returning to Lonsdale's studio, dressed as she was before.

He meets her and they embrace.

She goes out of the room, and when she comes back, she is wearing her velvet cloak.

Viola quickly throws off the cloak, to reveal the flimsy gown once again.

Lonsdale puts her in a pose and hands her a string of pearls.

Seen from behind, she is looking over her shoulder.

One hand is holding the beads out, the other is raised right up to her breast.

The gown fits her so closely that each of her legs can be seen, and something of the shape of her behind.

Suddenly, she lurches forward –

Viola is overcome by the unaccustomed strain of posing.

Lonsdale leaps up and catches her in his arms.

Then he kisses her.

They kiss and kiss, he leads her out of the room, and the picture again disappears.

*

Viola is shown going into Lonsdale's studio a third time.

Then, she is posing in the same thin gown, and he is standing at his easel, apparently painting.

Before long, though, he has put down his palette and brushes and is walking towards her.

Viola relaxes her pose, steps down from the pedestal, and comes to meet him.

Lonsdale takes Viola in his arms and leads her to a couch near the fireplace.

When she sits down, he kneels in front of her and puts his arms around her neck.

They embrace, and then they kiss and kiss again, even more passionately than before.

When they separate, they are deep in conversation –

Lonsdale asks Viola to marry him.

'I cannot marry you. Artists should never marry.'

Viola is leaving the studio.

*

In the drawing room once again, Viola is playing the piano and Lawton, leaning over her, is looking at the music.

But then she rises from the piano stool, goes over to the telephone, and picks it up.

Lonsdale is seen, talking into his own telephone.

He seems excited –

I have reserved a table at the little place where we always sit.

Suddenly, hurriedly, Viola is putting on evening dress.

Then, she is stepping into a low, horse-drawn carriage and driving away.

Lonsdale arrives outside a restaurant in the motor car, and he takes his seat at a table. He too is in evening dress.

When Viola arrives, she steps down from the carriage and hurries inside.

She shakes Lonsdale's hand and they are shown dining together, apparently in silence.

But each time she looks up he is looking at her, and they smile sweetly, one to another.

There seems to be something on Lonsdale's mind –

Lonsdale urges his suit.

He opens his mouth, but thinks better of it, before speaking anyway.

Hearing what he says, Viola turns away, shaking her head, raising her hand to her face –

'Artists should not marry. It destroys artistic temperament.'

This seems to upset Lonsdale –

'If you do not marry me the picture will be ruined. I shall not – I can-not – finish it.'

*

Their meal ended, Lonsdale and Viola rise, and he puts the cloak around her shoulders.

Outside the restaurant, the carriage and the motor car stand facing each other.

Lonsdale and Viola embrace, and he hands her into the carriage, but as he opens the door of the motor car, she is standing by his side once again.

She takes his hand in hers –

The picture... Let us go back to it, dearest.

The two of them go to Lonsdale's house, and then into his studio.

He is still in evening dress, his tailcoat dark, his tie as bright as his collar and shirtfronts. And a white handkerchief spills from the cuff of his sleeve, like the one at his breast when he first met Suzee.

Viola is wearing a long, loose velvet coat with fur at the cuffs and the neck.

She kisses Lonsdale passionately again, and he responds by drawing her to him, his arm around her waist.

She rests her head against his lapel, and gazes up at him, while he, seen only in profile, looks down at her. The top hat is still on his head.

Then, they can be seen leaving the studio for a different room –

Could there be a keener joy, a deeper delight, than they had known in the shadows of that first violet night?

64

15

'What did they go back to the studio for?'

The barrister was leaning forward, but the witness remained impassive.

'Is it conceivable to your mind, Mr Stott, that anybody going there, with the cleanest mind in the world, must necessarily draw an inference from that scene that something was going on in that studio?'

'Certainly not.'

It was the events of the evening that were now in issue.

'What I want to get at is this. Isn't it the fact that after they have had this little dispute whether she is to show her figure to him, and after they have been kissing and embracing, they go to a café and have supper? And then after supper does not Lonsdale hand Viola into a brougham?'

'Yes.'

'Kiss him?'

'Yes.'

'Viola steps away from the carriage and gets into the motor car?'

'Yes.'

'And they are shown arriving at a house which they enter together?'

'That is so.'

'Then they are shown entering in the studio?'

'Yes.'

'Where they kiss and embrace?'

'Yes.'

'They come back late at night to the studio, are shown going

into another room together under a title called *The Violet Night.*
Now do you think that objectionable at all for young people to
see – young women entering on womanhood and young men
entering on to manhood? Do you think that is an objectionable
thing to show them?'

'No.'

'You think nobody could object?'

'No, not with a clean mind.'

'Does everybody who goes to these places have a clean
mind?'

'Well—'

'They ought to?'

'They ought to.'

'Have you ever known clean minds perverted by what they
see?'

'No.'

'Never?'

'No.'

'Is it conceivable to your intelligence that they may be
perverted by what they see?'

'No, not particularly.'

'You cannot conceive that young men and young women
who may see this thing may have their passions improperly
aroused?'

'No.'

'Nothing of that kind?'

'No.'

But Mr. Watson's witnesses did not like this scene. One
called it 'extremely suggestive,' while for Charles C Charsley,
it was 'highly suggestive and objectionable, and appeared to
idealise illicit sexual intercourse.' (Mr Charsley was the Chief
Constable of Coventry, and he had become involved in these
proceedings after causing something of a stir in his own
right.)

'He cannot find a model?' (Mr Watson's barrister again, to Mr Stott.)

'Yes.'

'He cannot find anybody with beautiful enough limbs?'

'That is quite correct.'

'He wants somebody to show the limbs and the body so that he can paint a picture, and this woman is in love with him?'

'Yes.'

'And he is in love with her?'

'Yes.'

'Then they meet alone in the studio?'

'Yes.'

'She wants to become his model?'

'Yes.'

'And he objects.'

'He refuses.'

'Why should he object?'

'I don't know.'

'What do you think? May I suggest the answer to you? He objects because it is not a decent thing for a man to ask his cousin to stand naked, or nearly naked, before him. That is the answer, is it not? And that is in the book, is it not?'

'It may be.'

'And is not that what is meant by the film when the man says "No, I cannot let you stand as a model before me"?'

'Well, it says that in the title-card.'

'Exactly. Then ultimately he consents?'

'He consents after she has persuaded him.'

'And she becomes his model?

'Yes.'

'Is not that picture of the woman – Viola – standing there, with the little drapery she has on, almost worse than the picture of a nude woman in its suggestiveness?'

'Certainly not.'

Mr Meagher and Margaret Buck objected to this episode – to the kissing, but also to what Viola was wearing. He called it a 'strange scene' and she said, 'She is dressed in very light attire, and you could easily see her figure through it. It looked to me like chiffon, but it was very thin.' The actress playing the part, however, took a very different view. 'I wear a Greek costume,' she said, 'not of transparent material, but of heavy silk, and besides my face only one shoulder and arm are bare':

I would wear that costume in any restaurant in London, and then I should have more on than many of the women there in ordinary evening dress.

Eve Balfour had already been quoted in the *Preston Herald*, and now she appeared in the *Daily Sketch*, which was still talking about *Five Nights* as autumn approached. The newspaper carried four photographs of her, printed nice and large again, and headed, 'A *Victoria Cross* Heroine – Filmed in *Five Nights*'. The dress Ms Balfour is wearing in the photographs is thin, close-fitting, and not at all heavy. Her arms and shoulders are bare, and a good portion of her breast is exposed. The dress is not particularly Greek, and it isn't the one she wears in the film. Nevertheless, the caption to the photograph reads:

Banned at Preston, Produced in London – Miss Eve Balfour, Now a Cinema Star.

Walter Stott was still doing his best.

'Then these words appear on the screen: "Could there be a keener joy, a deeper delight, than they had known in the shadows of that first violet night?"'

'That appears on the screen, yes.'

'That appears on the screen?'

'Yes.'

'Is not that suggestive?'

'Certainly not.'

'Those words are put upon the screen and the rest is darkness?'

'The rest is darkness.'

16

Many early films were made in the capital – in Shepherd's Bush, Walthamstow, Muswell Hill, and Crystal Palace. And not just in Ealing, but in Isleworth, Richmond, Twickenham, and Walton-on-Thames as well – places threaded delicately onto the river as if they were jewels on the sumptuous costumes of a Will Barker epic.

And on Eel Pie Island, films were made in the middle of the Thames itself.

Outside London, they were made in Bushey and Borehamwood, Brighton and Hove, and Shoreham-by-Sea. They were made in the West Riding of Yorkshire – in the solid cities of Bradford and Sheffield, and in the small Pennine town of Holmfirth.

That undulating, cobbled place stands at the meeting of two irrepressible rivers, and while it was known for its quarries and mills, it was also known for the floods that swept it down the valley every now and again. Films were made there in a tall stone building on Station Road, which was the studio of James Bamforth, who had been turning out lantern slides for years.

Mr Bamforth was the son of a painter and decorator, and had followed that trade himself before he picked up a camera and started making portraits of local worthies. His pictures brought him great success, featuring, as they did, earnest aldermen and clergymen, wool and worsted men, worships and worshipfuls, whiskered and waistcoated men with watch chains, and the odd glowering woman in a long, striped gown.

When James Bamforth turned to the slides, and then to postcards, it was inevitable that he would use what he called 'life models'. They were relatives, now: his wife and sons, his daughter Lizzie and granddaughter Mary. And they were people he found around him: friends and neighbours, employees, even his dog, Nipper. They were local policemen, who could be relied upon to turn up in uniform, and who were so much more biddable than local firemen. They were schoolchildren volunteered by their headmaster, and drinkers from the bar of the Druids Hall just down the road.

Mona Coldwell was already working for Bamforth's when she became a life model, and Annie Hinchliffe was the daughter of the man who gave James his tuppenny haircut. Emily Lodge was a weaver at Washpit Mill, while old Thomas Settle, whose long white beard decorates many of the postcards, had been a sergeant in the 7th Regiment of Foot. He had fought at Balaklava and been wounded at Sevastopol, and he claimed to have been nursed by Florence Nightingale herself. When little Marion Leake was invited along, she came with her father and was paid threepence for her efforts. Edith Baker had just had her tea when she was brought, and the Fleming children were cast as waifs because that is just what they were. Hannah Hinchliffe was already a teenager when she first went to the Bamforth studio. She too was a weaver, out at Bottoms Mill, while Fred Bullock was a blacksmith. He lived close to Station Road and could make himself available at a moment's notice. Fred is the young man seen canoodling with his sweetheart on a postcard entitled 'On the Benches in the Park'.

James posed his models in front of backdrops he painted himself, in a room that ran across the top of the building. It had long windows and a glass roof, and the sun, when it shone, came pouring through. The walls were painted white to make the most of the light. There was an iron stove for warmth and an old bench for ease. And the hillside was terraced from the studio right up to the house, with a fountain and a *loggia*. One visitor, perhaps getting carried away, spoke of shady walks and leafy dells.

71

The slides James Bamforth produced were barely three inches square, but they certainly spoke for themselves. Lusciously painted, usually forming part of series of ten, twenty or even more, they told sentimental tales, brought popular hymns to life, and delivered cautionary messages – *Abide With Me, Annie Laurie, Christians Awake, Don't Go Down The Mine Dad, Why Should England Fear?* Hannah Hinchcliffe appeared in *Lead, Kindly Light* and *Nearer, My God, To Thee.* Sergeant Settle featured in *My Ain Folk.* And Marion Leake, who starred in *Abide With Me,* also starred in *Daddy.* So popular was this series, which saw Marion pictured alongside her father, that she was often asked to make an appearance when the slides were being shown, and to sing along to the words of the song. But while Marion was willing to do that, her father was not, and the paternal knee from which she delivered her performance invariably belonged to another 'Daddy' altogether.

As the backdrops became larger and more elaborate, and began spilling out across the studio floor, James took his camera and models into the lanes round about. He went over to the burial ground and up to the station, where he found the manager most accommodating. He visited Mark Bottoms and Beaumont Park, and he hired a wagonette to take everyone to the Hope Bank Pleasure Resort, where there was a bandstand, a boating lake, and a hall of mirrors that could be photographed.

Before long, he had two million slides in stock and a catalogue that ran to 400 pages, and he felt able to proclaim himself 'The Largest Producer in the World'. He did that on the strength of the office he had opened in New York, a stone's throw from 5th Avenue, Broadway, and the brand-new Flatiron Building. The 'The Lost Chord' series of postcards is credited to 'Bamforth & Co' of 'Holmfirth and New York'. It too features Hannah Hinchliffe, and when James Bamforth became involved in a copyright dispute in the city, it was Hannah he sent there to give evidence on his behalf.

When he started making films, that was only to be expected. They depicted festivities and shenanigans, and had themes borrowed from the slides. There were rough seas, men coming out of a factory, a gardener getting soaked by his own hose, and playground antics.

Gradually, though, the high jinks gave way to proper stories. One of them sees a tramp inveigle his way onto a park bench. Another, about a tramp who steals a baby's bottle, features a negligent governess once again played by Lizzie Bamforth. And the star of a third story, about a conjurer who tries to produce a coin from his wife's nose, is Fred Bullock, the blacksmith. Fred plays the wife, not the conjurer, and he wears a dress and headscarf to do so. The husband is shown tugging at the wife's nose for all he is worth, but the coin won't come and the wife gets angrier and angrier. A rolling pin is soon deployed and a fearful thrashing administered. The husband is beaten on his arms and legs, across his back, over his head. A table gets overturned and Fred's scarf comes off. At the end, the two actors fall, still grappling, to the floor.

James Bamforth's films were shown in halls around Holmfirth, sometimes in tents or booths, and there was no standing on ceremony. In one village, the *Huddersfield Chronicle* reported, at the annual treat for the aged poor, 'the living pictures which were thrown up on the sheet excited much wonder and admiration, and were intensely amusing to the whole company.' The films were also shown at the town's first proper cinema, the Picturedrome on Dunford Road, where an accompaniment might be provided by Charlie Senior. A confident, not to say cocksure, musician, Mr Senior would read the evening newspaper while playing along on his piano, pausing only to take bites from a large pork pie when each tune was done.

Often, films were shown, and even made, in places that had once been roller-skating rinks.

The pastime had become a craze under King Edward, and it was thought to be deserving of a title of its own. 'Rinkomania' was suddenly evident everywhere: in big places, but in small ones, too. Aspatria, Pentre and Portrush all had rinks; Inverurie and Hessle; Cupar and Chard. Spare, tenuous structures in the main, they nevertheless boasted of their perfect, true wooden floors, and of their Oriental cafés, fairy lights, and recherché restaurants. And in Yarmouth, the Olympia boasted that it had a hundred boys to help with the putting on and taking off of skates. Proprietors were paying dividends of a hundred per cent. Factories were turning out 15,000 pairs of skates a week. And in Preston, William Broadhead was content to let less adventurous patrons pay sixpence just to promenade around the edge of the rink.

Everyone did what they could to keep it going. Fast skating was banned, or positively encouraged, or permitted for ten minutes in the hour. Ladies' balloon races were held, and people turned up in evening dress. There was a 'Topsy-Turvey Night', a great 'China Night' and a 'Ragtime Fun Night.' 'Miss Bertha Doud Mack, the World's Premier Lady Skate Dancer' was booked to make an appearance. And any profits were promised to the Guild of Hope or the victims of the Titanic. To make all this possible, there were bands galore: Hanney's Band, Signor Pelligrini's Red Viennese Band, the Famous Zingari Military Band, the Band of the Royal Irish Constabulary. The band in Ballsbridge was brought down from the balcony so that everyone could see it. And the rinks of Burnley had taken on so many musicians that the Temperance Brass Band had all but given up.

Here is a postcard with a tinted photograph on the front. It shows a young woman sitting on the floor of an almost empty rink. She is fashionably dressed – in green, with a big feathered hat – but she too is glowering, with her hands on her hips. Her legs are splayed, one of her arms is in a sling, and the caption reads, *If this is Rinking, I've done.*

The postcard was published by James Bamforth, and it is one of many bearing his name that reflect the pleasures and the perils of rinking. Others show equally fashionable people, in ochres and maroons, pale yellows and blues, russets and pinks. The people are in groups, in couples, or on their own. They spoon with each other, wave to each other, or keep tight hold of each other. But they are always in, or approaching, a state of disequilibrium…

Remember, you skate on your feet, not your head.
You go to the rink to skate, not to wrestle.
It's nice to have something soft to fall on.
Hold me tighter, Willie dear!

Not everyone could see the funny side. 'Rinking, in my opinion, is an invention of the devil,' one man told a newspaper, while someone else said rinks were, 'picking up shops, at night at any rate.' A Wimbledon man obtained a divorce from his wife, who had left him for her skating instructor, and the daughter of a Glasgow merchant caused a scandal when she eloped with an instructor she had engaged while on holiday in Ayr. The White City rink in Newcastle banned all Brazilians, after some unsavoury business with local girls. And the press gleefully reported the tale of the rabbi's daughter, who said she had been drawn into prostitution by a man she met on skates. 'Up to that time I had been a good girl,' she told a court.

The music too could be controversial. It was like trains hurtling through a station, neighbours complained, or the sound of big guns at the Front. Trumpets were banned in Bolton, cornets too, and people living next to a rink in Kingston were awarded damages for what they had had to endure. It had come from an organ, drums, a megaphone, and a siren, and from the skaters going round and round. The metal roof was said to have made things worse. And in Mansfield, a monumental mason complained that the din from a rink had caused him to make some very costly mistakes.

The press spoke of tumbles, fractures, and robbery with menaces. Gold watches were said to have been stolen, and fights to have broken out between troops of different, ostensibly friendly, nations. In Chichester, a man was fined for assaulting someone who had bumped into him at the Olympia rink. An instructor at a rink near Telford was convicted of indecently assaulting a young woman in a cloakroom there. And in Barnsley, a man was sent to prison for what he did to a young woman he had met in a rink. Precisely what that was only came to light later, after the woman had been hauled out of a canal and charged with attempting to kill herself, and after what she had intended to be her suicide note was read out in court.

And then, suddenly, the craze was done. Rinks succumbed to snowfall or gales, and often they burned to the ground. That happened in Hawick, Pudsey, and Penzance; at the Princess rink in Nottingham and the Princess Royal in Peterborough. In Northampton, it happened just after a company of Pierrots had moved in. And in Dunfermline, the culprit was perhaps fortunate to be committed to an asylum. The jury found him to be insane, but the place had been failing for months and he was one of its shareholders, and witnesses had heard him say that he had no intention of losing all his money.

Sometimes, the rinks were victims of declining interest, and sometimes mismanagement, or worse, was to blame. One in Brixton went under just after another huge dividend had been declared, and in Maida Vale, the owner found himself up before the bankruptcy court. Louis Napoleon Schönfeld had once boasted that his rink was the most luxurious in the world, but the takings there had plummeted and he could now offer only £500 against the £11,000 he owed. A bandsman at the rink in Holland Park asked for a reduction in the maintenance he paid his wife. 'If he can keep another woman, he can keep me,' she replied, but the man said he had had no work for a fortnight.

A new use was found for some premises. A rink in Perth advertised 'One Hour's Pictures, Two Hours' Skating.' In Windsor, at the Windsor, it was 'Skating by Day, Pictures by Night.' And in Longton, where customers had recently been offered 'The Latest Combination – Skating and Pictures', the rink was soon replaced by the Panopticon. In Bath, one proprietor now wished to concentrate solely on films. 'Rinking is a thing of the past,' he told magistrates, before turning his place into the Coliseum Pictures. The same thing happened in Aberdeen, Arbroath, Bootle, and Finchley, and in Worthing, where the Elite rink became the Cinema Elite. The new concerns often retained some vestige of the old. Sydenham called its new cinema the Rink; St Andrews had its Skating Rink Pictures; and there was a Rink Picture Palace everywhere from Elgin to Wincanton, Scunthorpe to Tralee.

And burglars who got into the Royal Rink in Earl Shilton could find nothing to steal but a film projector.

17

The films were often made by people working beyond established studios, in the open air and sometimes far, far from home –

In Cornwall. Amid the waterfalls of Wales. On a ride under the Alps. At Saint-Malo. At Netley Abbey. In Jamaica. In the Watersmeet Valley. In Bognor Regis. On the River Meuse. At Guildford. In the fjords of Norway. In Morecambe. Off Newfoundland. At the Convent of Mercy. From Montreux to Rochers-de-Naye via Territet. In Luton. At Saint Moritz. From Malta to Gibraltar. In Cologne. Around Conway and Betws-Y-Coed. On St Kilda. In Belgrade. In Cheddar Gorge. In North Borneo. In Lulworth Cove. On the Zuyder Zee. In Egypt and the Sudan, and especially on the Nile. In Italy. In Canada. Along the Wye Valley. Among the Bretons. Carnarvon. On a trip to the Gornergrat. On a trip to Bananaland. At Nice. In South Africa. In Coventry. Ascending the Matterhorn. At the Grand Saint Bernard Hospice. Going down into Vesuvius. On the Bernina railway. In the Borromean Islands. On a trip up Mount Salvatore. In picturesque Berne. At a pageant at Zurich. In historic Oxford. At the White Farm at Crichel. Through Brittany's Hills. On the Côtes-du-Nord railway. On the Dart. In Newfoundland. On Lake Como. At Saint-Brieuc. At Chepstow Castle. At Barrow-in-Furness. In the Highlands. In Tokyo. At Irthlingborough.

The cliffs near Flamborough Head in East Yorkshire are dark and brutal at the best of times, and the sea never quite quits the shore. In that place, many miles from its studio in London, one film company made *Cliff Climbing* –

There's a 'climmer' – that's what they call them here – dangling on a rope, kicking off from the sheer rock face, and swinging back in time after time. He is trying to get at the eggs of sea-fowl – kittiwakes, guillemots, razorbills – which smack of fish but are as valuable as coal. They have been doing this for 400 years.

Out he swings, what must be twenty feet and more. He dangles and spins and then swings in again, dancing off the rock as birds wheel about his head. He is wearing a pith helmet, but his arms are bare. He can be seen stowing the eggs in satchels at his waist. He might take a couple of hundred of them in a day.

Back on the cliff-top, the climmer is kneeling in the grass, still wearing the helmet, which has a crest on the front. He pulls eggs two at a time from a great mound and places them carefully in a basket. He keeps looking up towards the camera – for direction perhaps, or approval. He takes off the helmet to wipe his brow with the back of his wrist and smooth down his hair. Then, he puts it back on again, drawing the chinstrap into his full, ragged beard. His loose corduroy trousers are held up by braces. His arms are still uncovered. And the great rope is still wound round and round.

Suddenly, he pulls a guillemot from the sack at his right side and a puffin from the sack at his left. He holds the birds up, a thick fist around each one's throat, and he waves them around, their beaks raised up and kept shut; their wings flapping madly; their useless feet waggling.

He seems to want to make the birds dance, and at the end, he pushes them together. There's more flapping and useless waggling as each is made to confront the other; to pluck at its feathers and to peck at its beak.

18

This was the world into which Winky emerged, at the beginning of the last summer before the war, and for a little while, the Bamforth company would have him to put alongside its picture postcards and decorous slides. James Bamforth was dead by now, but Winky could dance a funny little jig, and the smile he smiled was the broadest anyone could remember.

The man who played him went by the name of Reggie Switz, and the company – which had, after all, made *Why Should England Fear?* – knew just what to say. A cartoon Winky appeared in the trade press, dressed as a Boy Scout, waving a huge Union Flag. 'The World's Greatest Empire,' the advertisement proclaimed, 'and Winky, the Empire's Greatest Picture Comedian.'

This would be a new and very different life for Mr Switz, who had spent the last few years on the legitimate stage, going from one decorous theatre to another. Operettas and musical comedies had been his forte: *The Earl and the Girl* and *The Arcadians*, *The Blue Moon* and *A Waltz Dream* – entertainments which were undoubtedly popular, but which had been unfavourably compared with the Savoy operas of a generation before.

He had performed in front of audiences from Paisley to Portsmouth, Cardiff to Camden, giving them his bosun, his lovelorn Private, his doleful jockey. He was a trainer of performing dogs, masquerading as a lord. He told jokes, played drunk, pulled faces. And his fine baritone voice won him encore after encore. *Mother* and *The Crocodile* were his songs; *Pit-a-Pat* and *Woolloomooloo*. ('Double-you, double-oh, double-el, double-oh, em, double-oh, el, oh-oh.') He was declared to be 'a comedian of infinite resource' in Burnley, 'a button-busting business all the time he occupies the stage' in Eastbourne. And in Dundee, he was 'a nimble-footed dancer, who danced himself into the good graces of the audience.' He was feted in the West End and invited to tour South Africa. But he had always been 'Reginald' Switz until now.

The welcome from the picture house trade was generous, even if it did linger a little too long over the question of his origins. He was 'a joyously funny personage,' the *Bioscope* announced, in its review of his first film, *Winky Learns a Lesson in Honesty*, before offering a few truths of its own:

> Winky is thoroughly and essentially British, and so is the class of humour which he so liberally dispenses. He is eminently well suited, therefore, to entertain British audiences, who are so often compelled to content themselves with rather unsympathetic foreign humour, through lack of sufficient native talent.

After that, the films came thick and fast, and in less than a year, Winky had made nearly fifty of them. They show him confusing wine with poison, putting cheese in someone's pocket, getting all puffed up and then being punctured, frightening people with a stuffed leopard, tangling with a boxing champion, arguing about a garden hedge, setting the house on fire, becoming the father of triplets, diddling a hawker, causing a smallpox panic, getting accused of an 'orrible crime, cleaning a chimney with hens, pretending to be a dwarf, waggling a wicked widow, using flypaper to catch criminals, taking a dose of liquid electricity, causing havoc in a hotel, whacking a band of German musicians.

His clothes and make-up change from one film to the next, or even from one scene to the next, and sometimes, what he puts on aren't his clothes at all, but petticoats, a constable's tunic, the robes of a raja, or a gorilla suit. He has a widow's peak that never goes away, though, and he always ends up smiling that same broad smile, and looking into the camera and giving a cheeky wink. Then giving another wink. And then a third.

Perhaps it was the novelty of film that persuaded Reginald Switz to step off the stage, or perhaps the prospect of regular work in what had become an uncertain time. But the broad comedy now demanded of him was something he hadn't seen for quite a while. And if it had little to do with the hymns and ochre postcards of the Bamforth company, it had even less to do with *A Waltz Dream* or *The Merry Widow*. He could, though, take comfort from the band of companions that had settled in around him.

Winky was often teamed up with Alf Scott, and with Alf's real-life wife, Lily Ward, both of whom had come from music hall. She, in particular, would prove to be a natural at all this. An acrobat and dancer, with a lovely voice, she was said to be clever and charming, and 'a saucy minx.' It is Lily who helps Winky whack those Germans, and she is the floozie he disappears into the woods with, before his wife finds out and he gets his backside kicked. Lily embarked on a series of her own after that, playing a character with the same name, who looked just like her. She is a Chinese juggler. She puts on boys' clothes. She expands to ten times her normal size. And in *Crazy for Charlie*, she imagines that absolutely everyone is Mr Chaplin. Lily is the girl Winky and Alf fight over, in what would be their last appearance together.

These films were also made in the stone studio in Holmfirth, and in the lanes and parks roundabout. And when they were shown for the first time it was to cheers and whooping in a small hall at the bottom of the hill.

The Holme Valley Theatre stood above a furious weir at the place where the River Ribble meets the River Holme. It was green, yellow and white inside, with a ceiling of pressed tin. And at the end of the evening, when it was time to go home, the management chose not to play 'God Save the King', but simply to put up a slide made by the Bamforth company up on Station Road. The slide featured little Marion Leake, in a long nightdress and a nightcap, poised at the bottom of a flight of stairs with a candlestick in her hand. 'Good Night,' it said.

There were other series to go with the ones Winky and Lily made, and some of them were equally popular. They too consisted of short, simple films, with exaggerated characters getting up to all kinds of japes, capers and monkeyshine.

Joe Evans featured in many of these films. He too had come from the music hall, but his characters often had other people's names. 'Archibald' eats an egg, tries to be a chauffeur, and catches a lion. 'Piecan' appears with his wife, played by Joe's real-life spouse. He is woken from his slumbers by the Demon King, and comes to grief flirting with the maid, who is really a man. And 'Joey' dreams he has the power to kill anyone he doesn't like. Joe's uncle, Will Evans, also appeared in films. He could sing, dance and tumble with the best of them, and he can be seen as a jockey in the 2.30 race, taking the long way round and winning the 4.30 race instead.

This was often a family business. Two of the teenage 'Hurricanes' were siblings, and both 'Inkey & Co' and 'The Happy Dustmen' were brothers named Egbert (who also appeared as 'The Brothers Egbert'). The music-hall stars Sam and Will Poluski made films together, as well as performing for the King and touring South Africa themselves. And Sam Poluski also had a character of his own – 'Nobby' – who himself had a series of films. As well as being a star in his own right, Joe Evans was one half of the 'Terrible Two', whom audiences could see on the mash, the warpath, the twist, and the wangle. The other half was James Read, and he also appeared as 'Lynxeye' in the series of that name, and in the 'Arabella' series that featured the French actress Little Chrysia. A crook on that occasion, he would also encounter her as 'Sergeant Lightning'.

83

These series contained a great many policemen. There were Constables 'Nabbem' and 'Coppem', 'Platt', 'Buttercup' and 'Jawlock Jones'. There was 'Detective Finn' and 'Roland, the Defective Detective'. And there were military men in the form of Lieutenants 'Pie', 'Geranium' and 'Lily', together with 'Lieutenant Rose' and 'Lieutenant Daring', who were for a while played by the same man. Between them, they take on thieves, counterfeiters and kidnappers, tramps, anarchists, and suffragettes. And someone invariably ends up being scooped into a moving train, quelling the Boxer Rebellion, or saving a pretty woman from a noisome opium den.

Although 'Hawkeye' began as a policeman, he was soon roller-skating after a train and faking his own death for the insurance money. 'Bumbles' always managed to enrage someone, get chased, and end up in the river. 'Jack Spratt' became not one Prussian, but two. And 'Coney' was gone almost as soon as he had arrived. For a while there was also 'Mike Murphy', an Irish labourer, who was also played by more than one actor. Mr Murphy dreams a lot – of being in the jungle and saving a girl's life; of being a duke and saving a girl from ruffians; of being a tramp and rescuing a girl from Red Indians. He also dreams of capturing the Kaiser and winning the Victoria Cross.

On the first Christmas Eve of the war, a letter appeared in the *Bioscope* whose aim, its author admitted, was to quash a rumour that had been doing the rounds. The rumour concerned Winky, now Bamforth's biggest star, and it had to do with his origins, once again. This was an uncomfortable subject for the company, given the proclamations it had made, and repeated, and gone on repeating at every opportunity. The Warwick Picturedrome in Liverpool was one place where Winky films could be found on special 'all-English' bills. The Picture House on Westgate Road in Newcastle had promised that they would be accompanied only by British musicians. And the first film had, after all, been about honesty.

The author of the letter was the man responsible for the films. 'Winky is an Englishman,' he exclaimed, 'and the son of an Englishman!' But there was much he didn't say. Winky's mother was the daughter of an Irishman, for one thing. And when it came to his father's family, the position was even less comfortable.

Reggie's real name wasn't Switz. His father was Alfred Schwitzguebel, and though the two of them had been born in London, the grandfather was indisputably Swiss. His forebears had lived their lives on the shores of Lake Geneva, in a pretty village that was the summer retreat of the House of Savoy. Reggie's grandfather had taken to calling himself Jean Christ, and he had been the first Schwitzguebel to come to Britain. He settled in London and found work as a waiter, and before long, he was proprietor of the Hotel Giraudier in Haymarket. This place was only a short stroll from His Majesty's Theatre, where Beerbohm Tree's *Henry VIII* so entranced Will Barker, and in earlier times it had been famed for its coffee house, and for the *haut monde* that could be encountered there. But the prestige of those times had leached away by now, and the hotel had become little more than a common lodging house, its customers itinerant workmen and pedlars from abroad.

It wasn't long into his tenure that Jean Christ Schwitzguebel found himself appearing before the Marlborough Street police court, accused of having served alcohol on a Sunday. A constable who visited the Hotel Giraudier at two in the morning said he had seen several men nursing glasses of brandy. But when he was pressed, he conceded he couldn't say precisely when the drinks had been sold. It might have been on Sunday, he said, but he couldn't swear that it hadn't been before midnight on Saturday. The summons against Jean Christ was duly dismissed.

19

The undisputed king of the serials, however, was 'Pimple'. He was the creation of Fred Evans, another stage comedian who would become famous for his exploits on the screen. There were scores and scores of Pimple films, all produced from that studio on Eel Pie Island, upriver in West London. Fred had made his home there in the middle of the Thames, among summer houses, awnings, boatyards and bungalows, willow trees, walnut trees, and well-laid lawns.

The family into which he was born had its roots deep in the circus and the music hall. His grandfather had put on harlequinades, and his father had been a clown. Will Evans, last seen winning the 4.30 race, was his uncle, and Joe 'Piecan' Evans his older brother. Fred and Joe started out as clowns themselves. They performed with their mother and father, appeared in pantomime, and were taken on by Lord George Sanger. Then, they went into films. The Evans brothers worked for companies in Croydon and Whipps Cross, and at the studio of another uncle in Teddington, but after one too many rows over money, they decided to strike out on their own. That was when Fred came up with his great creation.

Pimple is light on his feet and ever so versatile. He can be seen as a constable, an inspector, a detective, and a judge; but also as a burglar, a thief, a master crook, and a stealer of children. And he is an anarchist, ballerina, boxer, busker, counter jumper, explorer, film actor, footballer, gunrunner, jockey, rent collector, schoolboy, screenwriter, sexton, spiritualist, sportsman, and stand-in toreador. 'There seems to be no end to Mr Evans's fertility of invention,' the *Bioscope* wrote, 'no shadow on the brightness of his humour.'

Whatever his trade, and whatever the situation in which he finds himself, Pimple always looks much the same. His jacket is too short and too tight, his pants are loose, and his hat doesn't fit. He has a gormless grin and, a vestige of those circus days, a muzzle of pan-stick white, made disconcerting by the dark lines around the edge. His hair is lank and he has to keep pushing it back. His nose looks turned up. And some of his teeth are blacked out.

Pimple is hapless, maladroit, and a buffoon, but he's ever so eager to please. He is Pierrot, from those harlequinades, but he is also an aristocrat, an MP, and a doppelgänger, a musketeer, a bad girl, and a mademoiselle. He is a thin man teaching a fat man to ride a bicycle, and crashing into a costermonger and getting pelted with fruit. He does the Turkey Trot and tries to play the flute, and when he is a billposter he gets stuck to a wall. He is an actor waving a pistol about, firing here, there and everywhere, hither and yon, and only he who knows it's a fake. And when he runs out of bullets, he puts his hand in his waistcoat and pretends he's Napoleon.

The eyot upon which these shenanigans took place lies a short distance from either bank of the Thames, at a point where patient fishermen might expect to be rewarded with roach and dace, barbel and bream. It had been a place of recreation since Tudor times, known to Thackeray, Dickens and Turner; the resort of ambassadors, dukes and princes. Access to it could be gained only by water, and skiffs, punts, rowboats, and houseboats could be seen thronging the foreshore, knocking into each other on the swell. The place was a blaze of flowers in the day, and of orange lanterns after dark.

'Phoenix' was the name Fred Evans gave to his studio there. He worked out in the open, making use of whatever was around him – a thicket, a field, a row of houses, the river itself. The esplanade at Twickenham can be glimpsed in more than one of his films, thronged with curious, cheering locals – or at least with locals who haven't already been pressed into service in Pimple's navy, police force, fire brigade, or Red Indian tribe.

And cheer they did, not only along the river, but also in halls where the films were shown, and in towns across the Home Counties when Pimple came to call.

Here he is touring Sussex, being collected at the railway station in Seaford, and driving through crowded streets in an open car. At the Empire, which is new, he is received by the manager, Mr Bravery, and he performs a brief bit of comedy business and utters some gracious words of thanks. Later, he's up the coast at Newhaven, standing in the bare entrance of the Cinema de Luxe. He is wearing a light suit, which fits him perfectly and is ever so smart, and he has a bowler hat on his head. A festival seems to be taking place there, because posters for *Lieutenant Pimple's Sealed Orders* and *What Happened to Pimple – The Suicide* can be seen on walls and noticeboards. Striped bunting hangs down from the top of the building, and a banner over the door reads, 'Welcome to Pimple'. There is a crowd present, too, made up of women as well as men, old folk as well as children. And with the exception of a single slick-haired young man, who seems to have something to do with the hall, not one of them is bare-headed.

When things were at their best, Fred Evans was as popular as Charlie Chaplin, his childhood friend. He had more of the burlesque about him, though; more of the truly absurd. He escapes from a whale, and duels with a dwarf, and pretends to be a gorilla, and gets put in a zoo. He steals a bicycle and gets arrested in 1962. He puts his money into a wife-machine and gets more than he bargained for. He turns his shed into a massive gramophone and hides away inside it. He wins the Derby on a pantomime horse and has six girls pretend to be furniture. He plays a man who fools everyone by pretending to be Pimple.

And yet, life on Eel Pie Island could sometimes be less than

Arcadian. People fell in the river and were drowned. Stealing, fighting and drunkenness were common. And in what was already a shaded place, a shadow even fell across the door of the Phoenix studio.

One spring day, not even a fortnight after the day of his wedding, Joe Evans found himself rising to his feet in the local police court. He had been accused of assaulting a woman named Emma Maude, an actress, who alleged that Pimple owed her a guinea. Ms Maude had gone to the studio intending to collect the debt, only to be confronted by Joe. 'If you don't get off the island I shall put you off,' he said, and when Emma stood her ground, he seized her by the arms and dragged her back to the boat on which she had arrived. Joe alleged that Emma struck him, which she denied, and he for his part denied striking her. A witness was called who claimed to have seen what happened, and said that Joe was telling the truth. Emma pointed out that the witness worked at the Phoenix studio and was dependent on Pimple for his living, but it was his evidence the court preferred. 'Mr Evans,' Joe was told, 'you are free to go.'

The Pimple films often reflected recent events. Their star was shown escaping a firing squad during the Mexican Revolution, and enlisting in the British Army at the very beginning of the Great War. And *Lieutenant Pimple's Dash for the Pole* is about the doomed rivalry between Amundsen and Scott – although the pole here is the North one, and the *North Pole* is just a pub. But what really made Pimple famous, and set him apart from Winky and the other serial stars, were his lampoons of other films. He could be seen as Ivanhoe and Hamlet, and in *Broncho Pimple* and *The Merry Wives of Pimple*. *Pimple and Galatea* owed something to the French director Georges Méliès, and *Pimple's Inferno* was his take on Dante. In *Pimple's Charge of the Light Brigade*, the source is not Tennyson's poem but an American film version of it, and the destination is simply another London pub:

Theirs not to reason why,
Theirs but to do or die.
And as their throats were very dry,
Into the *Valley of Death* flew the six hundred.

The American film was a recent one, and that was another reason for Fred's success: he could work at astonishing speed. *The Battle of Gettysownback* was on the screen within weeks of *The Battle of Gettysburg*, and *Pimple's Indian Massacre*, a pastiche of DW Griffith, came out even quicker. Nor was Barker safe from the treatment, for *What Happened to Pimple – In the Hands of the London Crooks* was separated from the company's *In the Hands of London Crooks* only by Christmas.

But it is *Pimple's Battle of Waterloo* that really takes the cake. The film it followed, *The Battle of Waterloo*, was long and lavish and again the work of Will Barker. The skit couldn't claim to be any of those things. It stars Fred as Napoleon to his brother's Wellington, all nose in the air and chin stuck out, with the bicorn hat and the hand inside his waistcoat again. But Pimple's horse is a pantomime one, with a man inside, and the mountains he crosses are obviously made out of cardboard. And victory is gained not with the rout of the Old Guard, but by a band of Boy Scouts. The film in fact makes a virtue of its tiny budget, choosing to stage the famous battle not in Belgium, but in the famous London railway station. Most importantly, it was ready to be shown in picture houses only days after the original.

In Folkestone, 'the whole house roared with laughter when Wellington and Napoleon met and tossed a coin for the first shot in the battle.' There were 'roars of laughter' in Todmorden as well, while the response in Pimple's own familiar Sussex was equally gratifying. In Lewes, where the picture house was half-timbered, 'people roared with laughter and it did one good to hear the hilarity of others.' And a reviewer in Bexhill-on-Sea noted that the film 'has served to keep cinema patrons in the best of good humour since Thursday.' It would be the benchmark against which future Pimples were judged, not least by the great man himself.

But when the roars subsided, something else done on Eel Pie Island would land Fred Evans himself in court.

20

Hot-air balloons were often a feature of those early films.

After Sybil de Bray's ascent, they were shown going up over West London or falling to earth in a lightning storm. A husband and wife could be seen travelling to their South Seas honeymoon in one, an inmate of Broadmoor hospital using one to make an audacious escape, and a sleuth named Paul Sleuth jumping into one from an aeroplane, to save an heiress from desperadoes.

The newsreel showed a military balloon being manoeuvred into place somewhere in France, its sandbags depending from it like carved horses from a carousel. Pimple used one to capture the Kaiser, in *Pimple Captures the Kaiser*. And in *Through the Clouds*, a girl rescued her father in mid-air by climbing into the basket of one from an aeroplane. That film was actually shot at 3,000 feet, and it drew large crowds to the Walpole Picture Theatre in Ealing, which was only a short walk from the studios of the Barker company. The place still had the corrugated roof and metal beams of the rink it had once been, but the proscenium, with its columns, capitals and twirling pediment, might easily have been made out of icing sugar.

Aviation of all kinds was popular in those days. Miss Gertrude Bacon employed moving films alongside lantern slides when she lectured on 'Flying Machines, Balloons and Airships.' *The Girl from the Sky* has an aeroplane being landed in a suburban garden. And in *The Flight of Death*, a monoplane crashes into a biplane to spectacular effect. Dirigibles were especially popular. They are shown again and again, being cajoled out of massive hangars, floating serenely about, and then turning around oh-so-slowly and being cajoled back in again.

A dirigible was used by a man and woman to make good their elopement. Another was shown in flight over Vienna. And the great dirigible *Schwaben* could be seen travelling from Gotha to Düsseldorf. There was *The Mysterious Airship* and *The Stolen Airship*, a balloon chasing an airship, and a fight between two airships. And audiences were treated to *The Mysterious Airship* and *The Airship in the Night*, and to film of the German airship *Schwaben*, which had recently been destroyed by fire at Düsseldorf.

And yet the Zeppelins came as a hell of a shock when they sailed in off the North Sea during the first, sodden, New Year of the war, and struck at Norfolk after the wind stopped them going any further. They seemed like bright stars over the sea, a schoolboy said, who had watched them for a while, and they separated only when they were in sight of the coast. Though the street lamps had been switched off in Great Yarmouth, nothing else had been offered by way of defence. The noise was eerie in the darkness, growing louder and nearer. There was a 'nasty drone, drone, drone', according to one witness, a 'zoom-zooming', according to another, or the sound of a dozen traction engines at work.

Flares were dropped, so as to bewilder people on the ground, and targets were picked out in the narrow streets and along the docks. William Gedge was in his father's pub when he felt the whole building shake. 'Open the door, boy', the father said, 'there's someone trying to get into the bar', and William heard the bombs falling all the way down to Fish Wharf. One of the bombs damaged Norwood Suffling's office, another landed right behind his house, and the *Piscatorial* was all but sunk on the Yare. Targets were picked out in Sheringham, Thornham and Heacham, and in Brancaster, someone said the wretched thing might have been coloured blue.

In King's Lynn, the manager of the Electric Theatre said it was 'business as usual', and the Chief Constable praised 'the general good behaviour of the populace.' 'There was no panic,' he told the press, 'and everything was taken in an utterly quiet, matter-of-fact way.' There had, though, been talk of espionage and secret agents, and of lights shone on Snettisham church to guide the attackers in. A motor car had been seen bowling along the coast road. And though some people took refuge in cellars, many more came out onto the streets.

These sorties had been specially approved by the Kaiser, his capture by Pimple notwithstanding, and they claimed the life of Alice Gazley, whose husband had lately been lost at the Front; of Sam Smith, a shoemaker; and of young Percy Goate. 'I saw a bomb drop through the skylight and strike the pillow where Percy was lying,' his mother told an inquest. 'I tried to wake him, but he was dead. Then, the house fell in.' A coroner's jury found that he had died 'from the effects of the acts of the King's enemies.'

But the Zeppelins didn't have it all their own way. Their home bases might be commodious – in Düsseldorf and Cologne, beside Lake Constance, at Cuxhaven on the North Sea – but the trip to England and back could be an uncomfortable experience.

They were insubstantial, inflexible and unstable things. The gondolas which held the crews were little wider than a man was tall, and full of the noise and fumes of the engines. And while the open sides made it easy to drop flares and bombs, they left men hopelessly exposed. There might be a score of them on board, all trying to go about their aeronautical business – men to scrutinise instruments, or repair the frame of aluminium or wood; men to pore over charts, take hold of the rudder, keep tapping away at the radio in the hope that all contact had not been lost. One man's job was to command the rest, but all of them were assured and physically fit.

The balloon from which the gondolas depended was as large as they were small, and that was unavoidable, for it had to hold a million cubic feet of hydrogen. So combustible is that gas that the men on board also included a sailmaker, whose job it was to make good any tear the moment it appeared. The Zeppelins were also tricked out with guns and bombs, with fuel tanks, and with ballast tanks full of water. That made them punishingly heavy, which in turn made them ponderous and slow, and terribly vulnerable. They would be buffeted this way and that in any high wind over the sea. And they were soon being assailed not just from on land, but also from the air, by pilots and aeroplanes hastily brought back from France.

It was tempting to seek safety higher up, but that only increased the discomfort for the men on board. Nausea and breathlessness, dizziness and unconsciousness had to be contended with, even once the apprehension of a night flight over hostile territory had been subdued. And there was the ever-present need for protection against the cold. Stout uniforms were therefore supplied, with thick woollen underwear to go beneath; felt overshoes; fortifying sausage, stew, chocolate, and *schwarzbrot*.

The commander often served as a figurehead. People on the ground claimed to have seen him in the gondola, perhaps wearing a moustache or beard, certainly wearing a cap with an elaborate badge, his greatcoat done up to the throat, a pair of binoculars depending from his neck, as he prowled around, shouting orders, taking bearings. Sometimes, they said they had seen him lean out and let something fall.

The Zeppelins came again with the snowdrops, sweeping over Suffolk and Essex this time. One bomb, left unexploded in a garden in Southend, had a handwritten label attached:

You English.
We have come + we'll come again soon.
Kill or cure.
German.

That promise was made good a short time later, in an attack on

Ramsgate whose consequences, at least at the Bull and George Hotel, can be seen on the newsreel. (*The broken clock gives actual time of raid.*) Trade in the town was crippled by talk of a repeat performance, and when the wretched things did come again, the Star picture house was struck.

There were two score of dead by now, and long, narrow shadows across the capital, where the Lord Mayor had offered £500 to anyone who could bring a Zeppelin down. A 'funk-hole' was created from the cellars beneath one picture house, while the people selling another one made sure to mention that it was situated 'well outside the Zeppelin danger area.' The government said that imminent attacks might now be announced to audiences – by buzzer, perhaps, or by a notice thrown up on the screen – but that whatever happened, the film must not be interrupted. And back in Ealing, where the Walpole was topped off with tin, the manager of the rival Kinema put it about that his place had an especially thick roof.

As a lattice of searchlights went up over eastern England, film-goers were being treated to *Menace of the Air* and *Beware of Zeppelins!* And those familiar with Mr Murphy's dreams could see *Mike and the Zeppelin Raid*. 'Much fun is poked at the Kaiser's pirate airships,' a newspaper noted, of a film that was said to have produced 'abundant mirth' in Bristol, to the west, and 'loud and hearty laughter' in Rochdale, in the North.

21

When Barker produced its expensive film about Queen Victoria, the company's rivals were turning out epics of their own. Sir Francis Drake and Guy Fawkes were their subjects; Robin Hood, Good King Charles, and Dick Turpin's improbable ride to York. After *Henry VIII*, there were other films filleting the works of Shakespeare, or telling the story of his life, and biographies too of Florence Nightingale, Buffalo Bill, and Joey Grimaldi, the most lauded of the white-faced clowns. There were brief lives of other notable authors, and versions of *The Prisoner of Zenda*, *The Vicar of Wakefield*, and *Little Lord Fauntleroy*. There was Charles Dickens by the shelf-load, and *A Study in Scarlet*, Conan Doyle's tale of early Mormons in the dusty American West, which gave the world Sherlock Holmes and portrayed the Latter-day Saints as procurers, enslavers and worse.

Classics such as these were a staple for Eric Williams, but he still found a way to turn them into something new. He had given his Bard in theatres and music halls across the land, often doing so with the aid of a magic lantern, but his masterstroke was to swap the glass slides for film and to have the films specially made. *Eric Williams' Speaking Pictures* is what he called them, and the point was they really could be heard. He produced *The Charge of the Light Brigade*, *Three Men in a Boat*, and *Julius Caesar* – an echo of earlier days – taking the lead in each film and then following it from hall to hall. And when there was dialogue, the audience would hear Eric himself reciting it from the side of the stage, in time with the character on the screen. He called himself an 'elocutionist', and as his fortunes improved and his audiences grew larger, there was a pianist to accompany him, and eventually an entire band.

If many films were content to cast a backwards glance, others reflected nothing so much as the preoccupations of the day. They were tricked out with motor cars and motor cycles, radium, vanishing rays, houses wired for electricity, and a machine that could see through walls. Some films, however, were preoccupied with nothing so much as the medium itself. In *Film Favourites*, a woman dreams she is Mable Normand and Broncho Billy, while *The Kinema Girl* sees a man who is infatuated with an actress cause chaos when he comes onto the set. And, as it had been for Charlie Chaplin, the deception of the cinema was a common theme: a man who takes another actress to see her own film then attempts to fight with her on-screen adversary; and an actor playing a cowboy mistakenly uses real bullets and shoots his female co-star dead.

In a medium that was all too often stationary, there was also lots of dancing. Ragtime was still popular, in films such as *Dreams of Ragtime*, *A Ragtime Romance* and, inevitably, *Ragtime Cowboy Pimple*. The Apache Dance, the Bunny Hug, and the Cowboy Twist were also popular. But most popular of all was the Tango – the Society Tango, the Brooklyn Tango, the Argentine Tango, the Oriental Tango, the Pearl Girl Tango, the Russian Tango, the Boston Tango, and the Tea Time Tango.

Tango Mad was the title of not one, but two films. And audiences could also see *Tangled Tangoists*, *Tango, Tango* and *Tonto Learns the Tango* (in which, the *Bioscope* helpfully noted, the eponymous hero is 'tangoing, tangling and tumbling everyone'). A man is converted from his rabid anti-Tangoism in *A Tango Spree*, *A Tango Tangle* ends in a mass brawl, and the hero of *Dick and the Tango* gets eaten by a cannibal. Audiences who had been informed that *Suzanne Wishes to Tango* could also see *The Tango in Tuckerville* and *Tango Troubles*, *Tango of Hate*, *The Tango of Death*, *A Tango Tragedy*, and *The Tango Dancer's*

Revenge. And they could see the dance being performed on ice in Switzerland, in a large new studio in the centre of Copenhagen, and by Jack Johnson, the champion boxer, during a sojourn in Europe.

And with the Tango, Tango teas became popular, in picture houses from Newcastle to Canterbury, Norwich to Guernsey. In Cardiff, they were so popular that they were held not just at four o'clock, but at seven o'clock as well. One such event was the setting for *Archibald in a Tangle,* in which the broad and clumsy character created by Joe Evans is last seen disappearing through a window. Doctors everywhere warned of the dangers. The Tango was reported to be the cause of broken limbs and bruised heads, of sudden collapse, especially in the old, and of a fatal stabbing at a ball on a plantation in the Deep South. It was banned by the Kaiser and King Victor Emmanuel, and the Pope was said to have instructed his priests to suppress it wherever it could be found. But it was first danced in Preston at the policeman's Christmas ball, in the presence of the Chief Constable and his charming lady wife.

These were known, not unreasonably, as 'dancing films', and Selsior was the busiest of the companies making them in Britain. The company's first film, *The Turkey Trot,* featured Ragtime music, as did *Ragtime Texas Tommy* and *Ragtime à la Carte,* which sent the audience 'frantic with delight' at the Majestic on Tottenham Court Road. *By the Sea* was pronounced 'a tasty little dish just in time for the summer season,' while *Tango Waltz* featured specially written music. The *Bioscope* pronounced that film the perfect accompaniment to a Tango tea, and those who saw it demanded that it be shown again and again. *Everybody's Doing It* and *The Tramp's Dream* were also Selsior films, while *Way Down the Mississippi* was the first to be filmed out of doors, and to have a story of its own to go with all the dancing. When *The Society Tango* came out, the company took to the press to deny a harmful rumour. Customers were assured that the Tango featured in the film 'is distinctly a ballroom dance, and has been danced at private and public balls in the highest circles, and before Royalty.'

The tune did not, of course, come from the film itself – more than a decade would have to elapse before that became possible. It was produced by a gramophone playing in the hall, or by a pianist or the members of a band. Selsior films even showed a conductor at the bottom of the screen, so that everyone could follow his baton and know exactly where they were.

This simple innovation was the idea of a gentleman named Oszkár Rausch, who had been the founder of the company and was still its leading light. Mr Rausch had come from Hapsburg Europe, via Egypt, Switzerland, and Jersey City. He had worked as an engineer and inventor before moving into films, and he made sure that the conductor was filmed at the same time as the dancers. For its part, the company made sure that the sheet music was provided free of charge, and it offered a full orchestral score could be had for only one and six.

But the films stopped dancing when Oszkár Rausch was taken into custody. He was already facing bankruptcy by then, with debts close to £400 and a host of creditors whose patience had worn thin. Now, this man who had been born in Budapest and brought up in Vienna was deemed an enemy alien and sent off to the Isle of Man. There, he was interned in the Knockaloe camp – an exposed and permeable place, whose whist drives and skittle alleys could not ameliorate the effects of the wind and damp, nor hide the fact that Oszkár had been prevented from seeing a doctor for far too long.

Music was important in those early days, not least because they were anything but silent. Many halls were separated from the cacophony of the street by only a single door, and no matter how deep the plush, the noise of the projector was often exceeded by the clamour of the audience. They had paid their money, hadn't they – these people who lived round about, saw each other every day, and might well have grown up together – and they simply refused to be excluded from the great liberty of chattering, cheering, sobbing, howling, peanut-shell-crunching, whistling, booing, catcalling, clapping, reading aloud the title-cards, seat-back-kicking, laughing, belching, sweet-wrapper-rustling, snoring maybe, shouting 'Siddown!' and saying exactly what they thought.

In one place, there was a piano but no pianist, and a notice on the wall invited customers to have a go themselves. Usually, though, any musical duties were discharged by professionals. Some of the tunes were improvised, the accompanist drawing upon her own expertise, and on whatever fund of light classics and popular favourites she had under her command.

Only rarely were musicians able to watch a film before it was shown to the public, but a skilled performer could vamp with the best of them, and come up with motifs for particular characters or emotions. A shanty might be used to represent life on board ship, some Mussorgsky for Russia. In one place, during a chariot race, *Thanks for the Buggy Ride* rang out. And Will Barker would be heard to complain that, in Birmingham, during the celebrated scene in *Henry VIII* in which Cardinal Wolsey laments his awful fate, the pianist struck up *Come Where the Booze is Cheaper*.

Jean Michaud knew exactly what it took. 'It ranges from cake-walks to symphonies,' he told the *Bioscope*, 'common street ditties to grand opera, and from two-steps to oratorios. Music of all ages and all climes is required at different times.'

Less confident musicians might have to fall back on cue-sheets, which came with the film and suggested tunes that might fit particular sorts of action. And if all else failed, there were hefty compendiums that did the same thing. All the beleaguered accompanist had to do – in the flickering near-dark, with the film racing erratically ahead and everyone hooting and jeering and maybe throwing things – was turn up the correct tab. 'Children' might yield *Babes in Toyland* or *Parade of the Dolls*, or 'Sea Music' produce *Fingal's Cave*, *The Flying Dutchman* and *Peer Gynt*.

Other options might be:

Aeroplane, Aesop, African (see Cannibal), Alpine, American, American Indian, American Negro, American Southern, Battle Music, Beaten Army, Bees, Birds (also see Butterflies), Bridal, British (see English), Bull Fights, Burlesque, Carnival, Cats (also see Trombone), Chinese – *Danse Chinoise, In an Opium Den, Ching Ling Foo, Chu-Chu-San, Kai-Fang-Foo, Chinoiserie, Hop Sing, Hop Loo, Hop Long Sing, Sing Song Girl, In a Chinese Tea Room* – Clowns, Comic, Coronation, Cowboy, Diabolical (see Gruesome), Dramatic, Drinking, Duel, Dwarfs (also see Gnomes), Eccentric, Egyptian, Emotional, Eskimo, Fire Music, French, Frozen, Ghosts, Gipsy Music, Goblins (see Gnomes), Gossip, Happy, Harlequin, Hawaiian, Hebrew, Horror, Hunting, Hurry, Joyous, Jungle, Love, Mad House, Marionettes, Massacre, Minor Hurries, Minstrel Music, Monotony, Passionate, Persian, Pigs, Pirates, Quick Action, Railroad, Reptiles, Robbery (Light), Robbery (Serious), Sinister, Skating, Skeleton, Storm, Sympathy, Telephones, Tension, Tin Soldiers, Toreador, Tragic, Tramp, Weird, Western, Witches, Yodel, Zanzibar.

And yet, no matter how plentiful or ingenious the suggestions, the experience could still be an unhappy one, for audience as well as performer. There were too many days, a correspondent signing himself 'EN' told a magazine, when 'some poor wretch of a girl strummed away for hours at a time on a derelict piano, with the most free-and-easy notions of harmony and rhythm.' 'Any sort of tune, played anyhow by anybody, was good enough,' a famous writer lamented:

> One small piano, as a rule, was the main support of most picture theatres, and it did not add any beauty to the afternoon's entertainment.

As ever, the press could be relied upon to notice such things. 'Even now,' the reporter from the *Bioscope* noted, 'there are still very few really capable picture pianists.'

> How some proprietors or audiences can stand the monotonous strum of waltzes and two-steps inflicted on them by some picture theatre pianists I have heard… I cannot understand.

And EN was left wincing at the memory:

> Until the cinema pianist came along, one never realised how badly music could *hurt*.

22

There were also films about tramps and gypsies and burgomasters. Martians and vampires made an appearance; navvies, Navy deserters, gay deceivers.

In a restive time – when the docks and railways could come to a halt, schoolchildren walk out of their lessons, policemen threaten mutiny, and gunboats train their sights on Liverpool and Belfast – the films reflected that as well. There are many, many strikers here, and they are doing much more than merely withdrawing their labour. They can be seen urging one another into acts of ever greater disobedience, attempting to blow up or burn down mills, mines and steelworks. They can even be seen stealing jewels, conspiring to rob millionaires, kidnapping babies.

Since the Siege of Sidney Street in the East End of London, and the newsreel images it produced of Winston Churchill, the Home Secretary, scowling in a top hat, there had been films about malcontents and dissentients of all kinds. Recent years had seen the assassination of a Tsar of Russia, the Presidents of France and the USA, and Kings of Italy, Portugal and Greece. In Tottenham, a constable and a young boy had been gunned down by anarchists. And the broad comedy of *The Anarchist and His Dog* soon gave way to the bile of *The Enemy Within*. The Barker company produced *The Anarchist's Doom*. *George Robey Turns Anarchist* saw the music-hall star make a dramatic, if uncharacteristic, attack upon the Houses of Parliament. And *Pimple, Anarchist* showed our hero embarking on an assassination mission of his own, only to discover that the King of Whitechapel was yet another pub.

Redemption too was in plentiful supply. Barker was also

responsible for *The Reclamation of Jim the Loafer*, while *Spud Murphy's Redemption* took place in China, after an unfortunate disagreement with a mob of locals. *The Bugle Boy of Lancashire* follows a man to the Western Front after he has been blamed for a robbery. And in *His Reformation* and *So Much Good in the Worst of Us*, thieves are turned around by the love of a good woman or the sight of a dying child. Immediately before *Five Nights* there was *In the Blood*, which sees a drunkard mend his ways when he discovers that his wife has not eloped with her lover after all.

And then there was all the boxing.

The noble art had been appearing in films ever since the people of Preston watched that woman undress. Thomas Edison was the first to show it, in a contest between two monkeys, and then one between two men. 'Gentleman' Jim Corbett was the first champion to be filmed. His bout with a man named Courtney took place inside Edison's studio, the 'Black Maria', which was lined with tarpaper so as to banish all light. The bout lasted six rounds, each of which was released as a discrete film, in a scheme that made Corbett and Edison, if not Courtney, a tidy sum.

Corbett had become the heavyweight world champion two years before, in a fight against John L Sullivan, the first man to hold the title. And when Gentleman Jim succumbed to the Cornishman Bob Fitzsimmons, that fight too was recorded. It went on so long, in fact, that the film became a feature, and possibly the first one ever shown. When the new champion was bested by Jim Jeffries, that too was put up on the screen.

Jeffries had immense strength and stamina, and for many people he was 'The Great White Hope'. But in Reno, on Independence Day, Jack Johnson knocked him down for the first time in his career, and then knocked him down twice more. This had been billed 'The Fight of the Century', but as Jeffries was led back to his corner for the last time, he told his seconds, 'I couldn't come back, boys. I couldn't come back.' His agony was witnessed by a crowd of 20,000, and by nine film cameras set up all around the ring.

It was the manner of the beating, as much as the result, which shocked the world, and which horrified portions of white America. There were serious disturbances all over the country, apocalyptic headlines, and more than twenty people reported killed. And though the film the nine cameras took was banned right across the South, it was also banned in Boston, Buffalo, Cincinnati, Detroit, Iowa, Maine, Massachusetts, Milwaukee, Minneapolis, Montana, Saginaw, Topeka, Wichita. In Baltimore and Washington DC, the ban was brought in at the behest of the Chief of Police, although the Chicago chief, who was himself the city's censor, declined to intervene. And authorities in New York, Seattle, Pittsburgh, and Portland also held firm. In Omaha, the Mayor said:

> I have seen innumerable views at moving picture shows which tend more to moral decadence than views of this fight would.

There were also fictional films about boxing, with many of them featuring a man taking on a champion in the hope of impressing a girl. That was what happened in *The Third String*, and also in *The Knockout*, in which Roscoe 'Fatty' Arbuckle plays the man and ends up chasing the champion from the ring with a revolver in his hand. Charlie Chaplin played a referee in that film, but when, in *The Champion*, he took the lead, he could be seen putting a horseshoe in his boxing glove.

Jack Johnson wasn't just the first black heavyweight champion; he was the first black boxer even to be granted a tilt at the crown. And he was as popular as he was provocative. Large crowds turned up when film of his fights was shown in picture houses, and the crowds were as large outside as inside the United States. The beating of Jim Jeffries did excellent business in Paris, Brussels and Dublin, while in Britain, the film enjoyed a good run at the National Sporting Club in Covent Garden. It was also shown in Longton, in the Potteries, just as soon as the Panopticon there could be converted from a rink. And there was even interest in the curious contest in which, as its title announced, *Pimple Beats Jack Johnson*. That interest was maintained, even though a match-up with the home favourite had to be called off at the last minute.

Eight thousand pounds had been promised to Johnson if he would fight 'Bombardier' Billy Wells, the new British champion. Earl's Court had been chosen as the venue, and Will Barker had begun advertising the film he hoped to make of the event. But Winston Churchill received a protest from the Archbishop of Canterbury, the bishops of London and Durham, and a bevy of senior Baptists. When he also received protests from Baden Powell and Ramsay MacDonald, it was plain in Westminster that something must be done.

Churchill in fact received many letters of protest from religious folk. They worried about the essential brutality of boxing and the fact that money was at stake. But they also worried about the spectacle of a white man fighting a black man. It might end up 'revolutionising our Empire,' someone from the Calvary Welsh Baptists wrote, 'and justly bringing down the wrath of Heaven.' And there was concern about the emotions film of the event might stir up inside picture houses.

The crowd was again large, outside the police court in Bow Street, when Jack Johnson turned up to plead his case. But though he would prove as formidable in the witness box as in the boxing ring, he would not prevail. He and Wells were bound over to keep the peace, and a promise was extracted from the Englishman never to fight the American anywhere in the land. When Johnson looked back on the whole business later, it was with resignation rather than surprise. 'That's you English all over,' he said:

You call the black man your brother.
You say he is equal with you; that we're all one family.
I must say you've got a queer way of showing your brotherly feelings.

Ahead of the big fight, with an eye to drumming up trade, Jack Johnson had arranged a tour of the country. He would turn up in music halls, town halls, and public halls; photographs would be given out and autographs signed; and hopefuls of all sizes would be given the chance to say they had laid a glove on the champ. All of that still happened, even after the bout was cancelled, and it too featured on the newsreels. Here is Johnson, being driven through Charing Cross in something like triumph. He is sitting in the back of an open car, which is all headlamps, big wheels, and buttoned leather. His supporters are teetering on the running boards, holding on and then letting go, running alongside and lifting up hands and boaters, trying to keep up but falling back, and finally trailing out behind, far, far into the distance.

And here is a film of Jack Johnson on board ship at the Manchester docks. He is carrying a cane, which he prods into the gloom over the Ship Canal, as if he has spied something of interest on the distant bank. He towers over his retinue of white men in their fine hats, unique also in that he is wearing a bow tie. Johnson shakes the hand of the only white man without a hat, who is crumpled and furtive and seems to have something to do with the ship. The man avoids Johnson's eye as the deed is done, and then he can be seen wiping his palm on his lapel – and then wiping it again, just to be sure.

23

When Jean Michaud spoke to the *Bioscope* it was as leader of the band at the Electric Pavilion in Brixton. There were cherubs' heads and plasterwork fruits around that auditorium, the ceiling ribs were garlanded, and 'Perfection in Pictures' was written over the door.

Born in Amsterdam of parents who had come from France, Mr Michaud had been part of the symphony orchestra in Utrecht. In England, he and his violin had featured in hotels along the South Coast, and in the popular cafés of the J Lyons company. In London, in ever more elegant picture houses, he had played in orchestras under Mr Vereyken and Mr Ferisescu.

These ensembles had become extremely popular, and not just in the capital. The lone piano, derided by many and decried in the press, was often now supplemented by a violin, a flute and a clarinet, possibly by a cello, a trumpet or a double bass, and even by a set of drums. In Gloucester, one musician had become accustomed to discharging his duties alone. 'George Ellis is an orchestra in himself,' a local newspaper wrote, but it was soon reporting a cheery ceremony at the City Cinema. Members of staff there had presented Mr Ellis with a silver-topped baton, to mark his appointment as conductor of the first musical band.

Nor was Jean Michaud's story uncommon. There were many foreign musicians working in Britain's picture houses, and a large proportion of them had come from the Low Countries in the last year or two. One ensemble, led by a Miss Caicedo, was a popular feature on Tottenham Court Road, and then at the Strand in the West End. And when it arrived in Cardiff, it was proclaimed 'a first-class orchestra, comprising, among others, Belgian and French refugees'. In Redhill, the Picture Playhouse boasted of its 'Belgian orchestra, under the direction of Monsieur Louis Pingen', while at the Cinema de Luxe in Walsall, violin duties were discharged by Max Seener one week and Mademoiselle Rose Sieveking the next. His proficiency on that instrument had delighted audiences and earned him encores galore, while she was Dutch and 'a first-prize winner at the National Conservatoire, Paris'.

The picture houses and press were full of debate about whether such people had a place in the country – as replacements, after all, for men who had gone to war. The controversy was so great that orchestras sometimes thought it prudent to bill themselves 'all-British', and conductors swore they wouldn't dream of employing anyone from abroad. But when Will Barker's *Sixty Years A Queen* was shown at the Premier Cinema Theatre in Bristol, it was given 'Special Music by Herr Anton Blazer's Premier Cinema Orchestra'.

Mr Blazer was by now settled in the Clifton area of the city, where he also gave music lessons and shared a home with the woman who would one day become his wife. He had been born in Rotterdam – despite what some people said – had gained a favourable reputation, and had even completed a successful European tour.

It was, however, at the Coliseum in Bristol that Anton Blazer made his greatest impression. This, the city's first picture house, had been converted from a rink. It had arches and balustrades, and doors the height of houses. Trams and carriages rattled past, a commissionaire paraded up and down outside, and men were content to leave their bicycles resting against the wall.

There, in intervals between the films, Anton played his own arrangements of Bizet and Liszt – *Carmen* and the *Hungarian Rhapsodies* – and the intervals grew longer and longer. 'The music at the Coliseum has always been a special feature,' a newspaper wrote, 'and under the direction of Herr Blazer it has been brought to a particularly high standard':

He presides at the piano each afternoon from three to five, also introducing the organ and the dulcitone at intervals.

This was a charming instrument: a small, simple keyboard, first created for missionaries in distant places, to be hauled over saw-backed mountains, across dark, yielding soil, through tall grasses, up to dun-coloured walls. And in Anton's case, it had been transported along the broad river, under the great bridge, and into the ashlar heart of maybe the Second City of England. Behind the Italianate façade of the Coliseum, its forks and felt-covered hammers will have responded to the touch with a sound as mellow as it was perfectly measured.

But then, everything changed. The problem was a letter someone claimed to have found lying in the street in the first days of the war. The letter carried Anton Blazer's name and what might have been his signature, and it spoke of an imminent attack on the barracks that stood near to his home. The police were alerted, and a rumour went around that Anton was really German and merely passing himself off as Dutch.

He was quickly arrested, and put in gaol while enquiries were made, and then he was charged with an offence connected to the letter and the foul plan it described. Under laws hurriedly introduced only days before, he was also charged with failing to register as an alien.

Only sometime later did the truth emerge, after he had spent an age behind bars, his brother had travelled to Bristol at great risk to himself, and evidence supplied by the Rotterdam police was finally taken into account. The prosecutor conceded that Anton was Dutch, not German; that the Netherlands was not an enemy and there had therefore been no need for him to register; and that the letter which had seemed to implicate him was nothing more than a hoax.

'This was a dastardly thing to do at such a time as the present,' Anton's lawyer told the police court, and he asked that no effort be spared to bring the real culprit to book. The magistrate was unmoved. There was no evidence against the prisoner, he said, and he would have to be discharged. But it had been perfectly proper for the police to lock him up.

Anton Blazer was gone from the city almost as soon as he was gone from the court, headed back to Holland, his dulcitone doubtless tucked under his arm.

24

In the year of *Five Nights* there was also *Heart of a Coster*, whose story – two young men falling in love with the same young woman – picture house audiences will have found familiar.

The men are brothers and also, as it happens, costermongers. And even though one of them has promised his dying mother he will care for the other, they fall out terribly and even come to blows. (*'Ands orf, she's my donah*, a title-card has one brother demanding, *We're goin' t' be married Easter Monday*.) They are very different men: Joe Moody, the maker of the promise, upright, solicitous, and kind to his donkey; Seth Moody a swaggering, drunken bully, hunched over, with unruly locks and his cap pulled down low over one eye.

The actress who played the 'donah' had also played Jane Shore, and for that reason, and because some of the action takes place on the pavement outside the Queen Victoria Hotel, the film must have been made by the Barker company. The hotel stood on Ealing Green, opposite the company's studio, and for a while, before he began touring the world, its licensee had been Will Barker himself.

Costermongers were tough, independent street vendors, and they too will have been familiar to filmgoers, for they were still plying their trade all over the capital. They were known from ancient ballads and the plays of Shakespeare and his coevals, from the pages of three-volume novels, and from the vivid paintings and engravings known as *The Cries of London*. They would yield, it was said, neither to authority nor to dreary social reform, and music-hall songs such as *The Coster's Pony*,

The Costermonger's Wedding and *The Coster's Serenade* carried their fame across the land.

The common people were their customers, cheap food and flowers their wares – violets, lavender, watercress, walnuts, chestnuts, gingerbread, Banbury cakes, loaves, muffins, crumpets, new potatoes, russets, turnips, hastens, apples, pears, oranges, cherries, plums, strawberries sold in their pottles, greengages, rhubarb, rabbits, Yarmouth bloaters, mackerel, oysters, sprats.

They were also difficult to miss. But while their lively patter and sing-song chants, their decorated clothes and sheer bloody-mindedness earned admiration in some quarters, it also won them plenty of scorn. Costermongers might stick together and cherish their animals, but outsiders couldn't be shaken from the belief that they were ignorant and insanitary, improvident, feckless, morally lax.

All of this found its way onto the screen. One of the earliest feature films made by the Barker company was *Nan, The Romance of a Coster Girl*, which tells of a young orphan, a singer who becomes 'the rage of the season,' only to lose her lovely voice fighting off a seducer. Ultimately, she is saved from a fire by her sweetheart and comes to realise 'that love is better than wealth.'

But if public opinion was divided, so were the films. Were costermongers the sort of people to rescue abducted children, make a fraudulent inheritance claim, or frame a young girl for the theft of a purse?

A claim of that kind was the centrepiece of *The Coster's Phantom Fortune*, which sees a man spend wildly in anticipation of a great bequest, only to lose everything when his fraud is revealed. He manages, however, to retain the respect of his comrades, and the film ends with him being presented with a new cart and donkey, and returning at least to the life he used to have. After that film was shown in Bedford, the audience inside the Picturedrome reconvened outside, so that the result of Jack Johnson's fight with Jim Jeffries could be vouchsafed to them by means of a green light shone from the roof.

Were costermongers more likely to save a toff from tramps and robbers, or to throw him into a pond and put a dead donkey in his car? That, too, the films found it difficult to decide.

In *Fog*, the saviour is a 'coster-girl', and the saved a toff who has received a blow to the head. She falls in love with him, only to step aside when his toff sweetheart arrives on the scene during a 'slumming party' in the East End. The film was 'most enthusiastically received' at the Electric Theatre in Folkestone, a former rink (and the home, during its one and only Christmas, to what was proclaimed 'the largest bough of mistletoe in Kent!')

But just as costermongers are also shown saving the lives of Army officers, and diving into the Thames to save a young girl's sight, so they are shown getting into fights on Hampstead Heath, helping embezzlers, and using a lamp to summon up Mephistopheles. One of them is even shown mistreating his donkey, threatening a nurse who intervenes on the donkey's behalf, assaulting a doctor who intervenes on behalf of the nurse, and then stealing the doctor's child.

Costermongers are generally portrayed as something it is undesirable to be. In *The Hon. William's Donah*, a woman, whom everyone expects to marry a nobleman, shocks him, and them, by pretending to have been born a coster. (She 'was loudly applauded' for her masquerade at the Prince's Hall in Hull.) And coster-girls who have somehow gained entry into high society are shown having to return to the life from which they came. The heroine of *Sunshine and Clouds of Paradise Alley* has married her toff, but she gives him up to go back to the slums, doing that so readily that some newspapers took umbrage. 'For some reason which does not appear clear,' the *Banbury Advertiser* wrote, 'she forgets what is due to her husband's position.' And the *Bioscope* concluded that this film proved nothing so much as 'the insuperability of social barriers.'

Where costermongers were concerned, there was plenty of anthropology to go with all the melodrama.

Here is one of them, in a newsreel film showing a presentation being made by a peer –

Hordes of people fill the screen, teetering on the very edge of the pavement, keen to see what's going on. They are dressed for winter, and standing right in the middle of them is a chubby, bored child.

A tall man strides out of the crowd, wearing a light overcoat, and some of the people seem to want to make his acquaintance.

This is Hugh Cecil Lowther, the peer in question. He was known even then as the 'Yellow Earl', because he favoured that colour in the gardenias he put in his buttonhole, in his dogs, in his many carriages and motorcars, and in the livery worn by his many, many servants.

He is wearing a flower now, as he is introduced to a man whose own coat is covered in pearly buttons. The man shakes the Earl by the hand, which is quickly returned to his pocket.

Hugh Lowther left Eton to join a circus. He said he could walk twice as fast as anyone else, and that he had knocked out John L Sullivan when he was still the champion of the world. He lost a fortune ranching in the American West and was the inspiration for a colossal cigar. A keen boxing fan, he gave his name to the sport's first championship belt, and he was president of the National Sporting Club, at which Jack Johnson's fight with Jim Jeffries was profitably shown. He was, however, another man who simply could not countenance the fight Johnson tried to have with Bombardier Billy Wells.

He was already Lord Lonsdale by then.

A third man, smaller and older than the others, is standing close by. He has a curious beard and is wringing his hands, and he lifts his hat, apparently for want of something better to do. The hat is a bowler.

The Earl gave a party for the Kaiser and was decorated in return. He brawled with a knight of the realm for the affections of Lillie Langtry, and the future King Edward announced that he was, 'almost an Emperor, not quite a gentleman.'

There are policemen in the crowd, and a few men in top hats, who crane their necks for a better view. There is also an elderly little woman, and the Earl talks to her.

There is a cart and donkey, being held by the pearly man, and then the old man and woman are sitting proudly in the cart with the Earl nowhere to be seen. The man is puffing contentedly on a fat cigar he didn't have before.

The owner of a handsome yacht, Lonsdale fled the country on the advice of Queen Victoria, and he very nearly came to grief while travelling in Alaska.

25

Once shooting on *Five Nights* was complete, six copies of the film were sent to Walter Stott and Fred White in Manchester. Those men had done their own deal with the executives of International Exclusives Limited, and they were now the proud owners of distribution rights across Lancashire and Yorkshire, Cheshire and Derbyshire. Any picture house proprietor wishing to show the film there would have to rent it from them. But the privilege hadn't come cheap. Fred claimed that it cost fully three thousand pounds – the most anyone had ever paid anywhere in the North.

For the copy of *Five Nights* that he rented from Walter and Fred, William Broadhead was charged a fee of £40 a week. He would lose money while ever it couldn't be shown to a paying audience. But at the King's Palace, after the unfortunate events of Monday afternoon, Mr Broadhead's copy had immediately been wound back onto its spool, put back in its cannister, and sent on to the next hall in his chain.

Those unfortunate events weren't quickly forgotten. At the beginning of the following week, the *Preston Herald* thought it necessary to assure its readers that the film now showing at the King's Palace was a 'wholesome drama' to which, 'even the most carping critic cannot object.' Across town at the Hippodrome, meanwhile, Mr Broadhead was said to be presenting a musical comedy that was 'beyond cavil or criticism.'

The next place in which his copy of *Five Nights* was shown was Eccles, whose people thankfully proved less excitable than their counterparts in Preston. Showings at the Crown theatre in the town proceeded without incident, and the film was then sent to the Broadhead hall in Ashton-under-Lyne, and from there to the Empress Electric Theatre in Miles Platting.

That place stood out on the road towards Oldham, close to the Royal Osborne theatre, just in front of the railway line, with an old pub called the Ram pressed up nice and close. It had a red brick façade and a stout gable, and more than enough crenellation to withstand the most determined threepenny rush. Inside, it was cream and bronze and green, tall and airy, and fervid with swags, cartouches and medallions.

The road, and the canal beyond, were all that separated the Empress from the cluster of streets and buildings known as the Tripe Colony. And it was there that many of the cinema's customers lived, in small, simple houses for which they will have felt privileged to be chosen. Those people were an essential part of the trade for which the place was named, even if they were prohibited from keeping pigeons or whitewashing their yards. They worked as strippers, bleachers, boilers and dressers; retrieving rumen and reticulum, manyplies and psalterium; transforming it into the seam, honeycomb and thin leaf tripe that could be offered for sale alongside cowheel, neat's foot, weasand, brawn and elder.

There were more than 200 tripe shops in Manchester, and seventy more down the road in Bolton. The stuff was available everywhere in Lancashire, often on different corners of the same street. It could be had right across the North, in fact – from Gothard's in Huddersfield and Greatorex's in Sheffield; from Charles Schluchterer's places on Derwent Street and Pow Street in Workington; and from any one of the fifteen places on Wearside that belonged to Harry Turley. It could be had in Derby, Mansfield and Boston as well; at Woolley's, Sid Widdison's and Fleet's. But it could also be had in the South of England: in Aylesbury, Chesham, Hendon, High Wycombe, Hounslow, Folkestone and Eastbourne. It could be had at Meads' and

Tillion's; at Mrs Mold's shop on Castle Street in Banbury; and at Pascoe's in Torquay. In the markets of Penzance and Redruth, it could be had for fourpence a pound. And across the Irish Sea, it could be had from Dwyer's in the Bull Ring in Drogheda; O'Regan's in Waterford; Hoy's in Portadown.

William the Conqueror was said to have eaten his with apple juice, Samuel Pepys to have slathered it in mustard. But many people preferred their tripe ready-cooked. That was how it could be had in Lancashire and Yorkshire, and in Burslem and Hanley, Methil and Barrhead. It could be had like that from the premises of J Netten opposite King's Cross station, where stewed eels and native oysters were also a staple. And as the dish became more popular, and even fashionable, special 'tripe suppers' could suddenly be had in all manner of places, from Fossett's in Reading and the Sydney Arms Hotel in Cheltenham to the Lorne Dining Rooms in Broughty Ferry, which stood near to the great, grey River Tay.

As the year of *Five Nights* dawned, restaurants were starting to appear that had dedicated themselves to tripe. There was a modest one in Fleetwood, just down from the docks. The one in Plymouth was owned by a man proclaiming himself 'The Tripe King'. While in Sheffield, the tripe restaurant on Upwell Street made a point of saying that it was close to the Picturedrome. In Coventry, at the Hayes's place, 'All tripe cooked Lancashire-style' was the proud boast. And in Rochdale, at Irlam's on Toad Lane, the speciality was a 'mixed plate', consisting of tripe, onion, sauce, peas, mashed potatoes and sausage. That could be had for sevenpence, with bread and butter tuppence extra and another penny for a serviette.

Perhaps the most audacious move was made by members of the Vose family. Already the proprietors of many of those tripe shops in Bolton, they now turned their attention to Wigan, and to a new establishment they named the 'Tripe de Luxe Restaurant and Tea Room'. This place would be a cut above the others. It had palm trees and wood panelling, white tablecloths and pink wallpaper. There was a three-piece 'Ladies' Orchestra' playing light classical music upstairs. And the menu went well beyond traditional fare. Special luncheons could be had. A 'ladies' afternoon tea' was served between 3.00pm and 5.30pm. And Bill and Cissie Stoker were provided with a wedding breakfast of tripe before they set off for their honeymoon in Blackpool.

There was a 'Tripe de Luxe' in that town as well, next door to the Grand Theatre, just up from the beach. It was in East Lancashire that the owner of that place had been purveying tripe – in Burnley and Brierfield, Padiham, Nelson and Colne – and this, his seaside venture, was endowed with tables of oak and windows of stained glass. It proved so popular that, before long, someone else in the town had opened not just another tripe restaurant, but another one with the name 'Tripe de Luxe'.

In Preston, meanwhile, the Cheapside Tripe Restaurant stood only yards from the King's Palace and its little archipelago of entertainment halls. The proprietor there had been a tripe-dresser for years, and he was always looking for new ways to attract new custom, even going so far as to place an advertisement in the *Lancashire Evening Post*. 'After leaving the theatre or picture palace,' the advertisement read, 'bring your wife or sweetheart and have a hot supper, ready prepared.'

26

Five Nights could also be seen in Manchester halls that weren't owned by William Broadhead. In Broughton, it was showing at the Tower Picturedrome, and in Higher Broughton at the Empire. It was also showing at the Empire in Blackley, which had an orchestra of its own and might have been the first place in the county able to make that claim. In Salford, a councillor who had seen it at a private showing said it was 'a beautiful film with high moral teaching.'

Across the country, things were much the same. *Five Nights* was booked solid and playing to large houses in Glasgow, Derby and Sheffield. In Birmingham, where magistrates saw the film at a trade show, they had no concerns. It could be seen in Liverpool, even though, as someone put it, 'they have some quaint unofficial censors there.' At the Picturedrome in Aberdeen, the Victoria in Dundee, and the Motherwell Theatre, it was accompanied by Miss Hall on piano, Mr Hartley's trio, and Madame Firth's Orchestra, respectively. It was showing at the Walpole in Ealing again, and at the King's Picture Playhouse on the King's Road, which claimed to be 'a British theatre run with British capital.'

In Wood Green, the film was the special attraction when the Picture Palladium reopened after a fire. This place had only recently been fined for showing films on a Sunday, and the flames came as yet another blow. The roof had fallen in first, not long after midnight, and by dawn the place was almost completely destroyed. The cause was thought to be a cigarette carelessly discarded near the screen, and the cost was estimated at £20,000. Faced with that prospect, the management decided not merely to repair, but actually to improve. A balcony was installed, a pipe organ too, and what had been the band suddenly became a special 'Ladies' Orchestra'.

Five Nights could also be seen in Bristol, while in Cardiff, it found favour not only with councillors, but also with the Chief Constable and the Lord Mayor. 'Its wonderful scenes have never been equalled in the history of cinematography,' wrote the *Western Mail*. 'In spite of all that has been said to the contrary, it is not marred by any objectionable scenes.' The film had been kept on for a further week in the city, where it could now be enjoyed alongside *The Kaiser Catches Pimple*. In some places, it was shown with *The Squashed Kaiser*, an ingenious cartoon, or with *Fatty's Jonah Day* or *Podgy Porkin's Plot*.

And *Five Nights* was also sometimes shown with *Gussle's Wayward Path*, a brisk comedy about a philandering husband who tries to hide a dog down his trousers and gets hung from a hook by his own belt. Gussle is an anxious-looking man, who wears a too-tight jacket and baggy pants. He carries a cane and has a curious moustache. But though he too was played by a Chaplin, he certainly wasn't Charlie. He was the great man's half-brother Syd, who, if only for the moment, was something of a draw in his own right.

Here is another film from those days; one that bears the singular name Will Onda, and that declares itself part of his 'Roll of Honour' series.

He is the man who opened Preston's first proper picture house, inside the one-time Temperance Hall, and who went on to own several picture houses that weren't owned by William Broadhead. But 'Will Onda' was merely a stage name; a vestige of years spent on the trapeze, the high wire, and the horizontal bars. This man, who had bestowed *Saved from Cannibals* upon the people of the town, and later got into so much trouble over *She*, in fact bore the equally singular name Hugh Rain.

He too made films as well as showing them. They feature the

people of Preston and things that occupied them – Empire Day and the Catholic Guild procession, the making of longcloths and flannelette, a local favourite taking on Bombardier Billy Wells – and they were intended to be seen in his picture houses before the week, or even the day, was out. That is what brought him to the railway station on a sunny afternoon in the middle of the week.

There are soldiers on the platform in this film – scores of them, all arriving and mustering and getting ready to go off to France. They have been in training down South, and a local paper will praise their 'soldierly bearing and obvious fitness,' their 'bronzed faces and improved physique.' There is little of that to be seen here, though, as the soldiers strike awkward poses and stare self-consciously at the camera. They are wearing buttoned-up uniforms and greatcoats, even though it is the height of summer. A schoolboy stands proudly in front of them, his hands in his pockets, a satchel over his shoulder, dark rings beneath his eyes.

Hugh Rain was the father of five children. The middle one, a son he called 'Carnie', had worked at the Temperance, and also at the Prince's and the Picturedrome, selling tickets, winding films back onto their spools, even operating the projector. He was one of the first men of the town to enlist, and the soldiers on the platform are from his company. They are clerks and young men of business, undergraduates, and old boys of minor public schools, and they were even now being called the 'Preston Pals'. Carnie is surely among them.

One soldier is especially noticeable. He has his greatcoat open and his cap pulled down low over his eyes. He is taller and younger than others, his face lean, his cheekbones prominent, and if he seems at all gauche, there is also a certain swagger. He is in the front rank, the last in a row of four. His comrades are tense, their smiles fixed, but this soldier is lolling slightly, and he uses his moment on the screen for a little bit of stage business.

124

He puts a cigarette into his mouth and twirls it between his lips. Seeing someone he knows, he cracks a joke and makes himself smile. He reaches into his pocket for a box of matches, and as the cigarette lights up, his face dissolves in a cloud of smoke.

Carnie Rain was hit by shrapnel on the Western Front, finally succumbing to his wounds barely two months after this film was produced, while his father was making a frantic, anguished journey across the Channel to be by his side.

There are parents here too, and sisters, brothers, sweethearts, wives. There are watchchains and best bonnets, eyes being dabbed and cap badges catching the light. There is hustle and bustle, to-ing and fro-ing. One soldier is wearing a comedy nose and eyebrows, while another is staring back down the platform but seeing no one he expected, or hoped, to see. People crane their necks and someone waves a rolled-up newspaper. The picture remains perfectly composed and just about everyone manages some kind of smile.

Martial music had resounded through the station that afternoon, courtesy of the brass band from the St Vincent's home. And as the moment of departure drew near, the Mayor and Mayoress went from carriage to carriage, shaking hands and giving out more cigarettes.

An elderly woman can be seen blowing a kiss at the carriages as they move off, and then biting her lip as the carriages gather speed.

The soldiers wave their caps through the doors in Third Class, and their farewells are returned by a sea of white handkerchiefs, seen only as reflections in the blind windows of the disappearing train.

27

There were, however, places where the mood quickly changed.

In Birmingham, the fact that magistrates had expressed no concerns about *Five Nights* did not prevent a petition being drawn up by sixty ministers of religion, demanding that the film be banned. It was 'immoral and depraving in its tendency all the way through,' one of the ministers wrote, while another announced that his wish was 'to purify the civic life of the city.' The petition received publicity and provoked debate, but ultimately, it benefitted no one save exhibitors, who could now say on their advertisements that the film was being shown 'despite strong protests from a number of clergymen.'

Elsewhere, though, opposition would prove more effective. In Weston-super-Mare, when HM Murdoch came stepping through the curtains at the Regent Street Picture House, he had an expectant crowd in front of him and a goddess holding a torch on the roof above his head. Mr Murdoch was apologetic from the outset. 'Under the circumstances,' he said, 'I am afraid we cannot run the film this afternoon.'

> Therefore, you are entitled to have your money refunded at the doors. Or, if you prefer to keep your seats, an attractive programme of subjects has been arranged. I need scarcely say I am sorry this has happened.

This was the result of a sudden and very recent change of circumstance:

We have advertised this photo-play since Friday last –

six days ago – and up until twelve o'clock today we had heard nothing from the magistrates as to there being any doubt in reference to our showing it. We arranged a special view for them at one o'clock, and at the close, they gave their decision.

He couldn't for the life of him see why a ban had been introduced:

I saw this film, as also did my wife, and I am quite sure that no ordinary educated person could take the slightest exception to it.

Some while ago, we showed *Three Weeks* – probably many of you present today saw it – and if any exception can be taken to *Five Nights* then *Three Weeks* must be absolutely disgusting, whereas we know it to have been one of the prettiest and most interesting things we have produced.

We shall be hearing about *Three Weeks* again before long.

As Mr Murdoch bowed his head and backed towards the curtains with as much dignity as he could muster, another man got up from his seat in the stalls. 'I am sure,' the man said, 'that everyone here today is possessed of a good sporting spirit, and that you will sympathise with the unfortunate position in which the management has been placed.' He paused, if only for emphasis, and then continued: 'I urge you to support them by retaining your seats, witnessing the programme arranged and declining to have your money refunded.' There was hearty applause and not a soul departed.

The following day, Mr Murdoch received a letter its author had left unsigned:

This shameless entertainment is not only a disgrace

to the person who produces it, but a scandal to every town who permits such a scandalous display. You will be judged for this sin!

But Mr Murdoch wasn't so easily deterred. Seeking to muster courage this time, he set up a special screening of the film, just for members of the press. And when that too was banned by the magistrates, he went in front of them to plead his case. 'It was a very expensive film,' he said, 'and I desired to show it before the visitors left town.' The chairman of the bench, however, proved impervious to these pleas. *Five Nights* claimed to be 'the most voluptuous love story ever filmed,' he said, but people who had seen it had told him that it was based 'upon a low, exaggerated sensuality throughout':

The whole interest of the plot is sexual from beginning to end.

Rejected though it might have been on the north coast of Somerset, *Five Nights* could still be seen in Edinburgh, Oldham and Dundee as the nights grew chillier. It could be seen in Newcastle, even though the Chief Constable had walked the streets of that city, demanding to be told where it was going to appear. And it could be seen in Barrow, whose streets James Watson had himself once walked, even though posters advertising the film in the town had been torn down on the orders of the local bench.

When *Five Nights* arrived in Lincoln, it was proclaimed 'the greatest and most daring moving picture play ever made.' It was showing there at the Picture House, where it could be seen not only from the pit and the stalls, but also from a lovely 'café lounge' on the first floor. 'Probably no film yet produced has been more talked of than this,' the *Lincolnshire Echo* said:

The photography of the work leaves absolutely nothing to be desired. It is almost gorgeous in some of its arrangement, and the acting is certainly superb, giving a series of pictures which stamps the work as a masterpiece.

Back in Birmingham, with memories of the clergymen's petition growing dim, the film was on show at the Ashted Row Picture House, whose owner was one of several brothers who had played for Aston Villa. It could be seen in Blackpool, in a place right next to the mighty Tower, in York and Mansfield, and in Derby, at the Cosy.

In Stoke-on-Trent, meanwhile, *Five Nights* was the star feature at the Majestic Picturehouse, where 'Exclusive rights for the Potteries secured at enormous expense' was the proud boast. This place was Wedgwood blue inside, and its band had not only a piano and a violin, but a cello, a clarinet, and a double bass as well. 'The men are very capable players,' the *Sentinel* reported, 'and have good instruments and provide music which synchronises with the picture subjects.'

The film was also a feature in Sheffield, at the Cinema House, which was a mass of white faience tiles, even on the tower above the entrance. The auditorium here was panelled in oak and hung with tapestries. The carpets, seats and curtains were different shades of blue, and there was an Elizabethan seascape filling the proscenium arch. In Manchester, the film could now be seen at the Grosvenor Picture Palace, where the faience tiles were cream in colour, with green ones running up and over the doors and forming bays all down the side. This cinema had opened only recently, with a gala performance of Will Barker's *Jane Shore*, and it claimed to be the largest one outside London.

And if the welcome *Five Nights* received in Darlington was particularly warm, that was only to be expected, given what had already happened there.

28

The man who opened the Alhambra Palace had worked for Buffalo Bill, ushering his Wild West show around Europe, looking after the broncos and steers, the sharpshooters and rough riders, the First Scalp for Custer, and the Indian Attack on a Burning Cabin. He struck out on his own after that, putting on films wherever anyone would pay to see them, but it was the tents and booths of Darlington he found himself coming back to most readily. The Cherokee he brought with him had been part of the show, and he could haul up a king-pole and work a projector with the best of them.

He chose for his place a name that spoke of the trellised and courtly; of roses, oranges and myrtles, running water and the nightingale's song. And even if it was built too close to the Durham road, and there was a court case about that, everything inside was emerald, apple, jade. Then, *Sapho* arrived, and nothing was tranquil again.

The film was an American one, based on an old French novel, and its heroine was altogether too much for many. One critic called her 'a trifler to whom trifling becomes the all-in-all,' while another complained that she had 'drunk deep of the dregs of life in the underworld of vice.' She had been all sorts of woman to many different men, and some of those men were now shown talking frankly about what she had done. And though her seduction of a much younger man was controversial, what was most controversial was the enormous fun she seemed to be having. The actress who played her had turned down a fee for a cut of the takings.

Sapho was a sensation, and it seemed to be showing

everywhere – from the Electric Theatre to the Pavilion, the Panopticon to the Cinema de Luxe; at the Andrews' place and Black's, Cadogan's and Ruffell's; in Wealdstone, at The Wealdstone, and at the place in Sydenham that wouldn't let anyone forget it had once been a rink. The film was an 'extraordinary success' at the Electric Coliseum in Harringay, even though the doors of that place had to remain closed on a Sunday, while in Forfar, it 'won the warm appreciation of those who saw it.' A singing soldier and a Gypsy soprano accompanied it in Todmorden. And in Hartlepool, there was scarcely enough room to stand. When the film was shown in Bexhill-on-Sea, at the small but glittering Bijou, a large crowd stayed behind past midnight for news of the Bombardier's latest fight to be telephoned through. At the Bijou in Cheetham Hill, meanwhile, the owner put the film's popularity down to his customers' 'continental' tastes.

If the prosecution, when it came, was the first of its kind, it can't have been much of a surprise. A stage version of *Sapho* had been halted on Broadway and its leading actors arrested, and there were places in England where the story had received a cool response. Birkenhead rejected it out of hand, and the film was banned in Leeds without a single councillor having seen it. The owner of the city's Savoy cinema was beside himself. 'Compared with another film which has been going round lately,' he said, 'and which deals quite frankly with the white slave traffic, it is quite innocuous.' Posters advertising that other film were themselves controversial, as 'Observer' wrote in a letter to the local paper:

> For some years now drama producers, in the desire to call attention to their wares, have almost reached the limit of human endurance in the matter of sensational pictorial display. But this picture and the letterpress accompanying it are surely as suggestive as any *Sapho* film could possibly be.

And yet, *Sapho* was shown in next-door Bradford without incident. 'The thing is not worth making a fuss about,' a columnist there wrote, 'either to praise or blame.' 'But supposing it had been otherwise,' he went on:

Supposing it had been something fine, something one really ought to see? Then, you say, it would never have been condemned at all. But wouldn't it? Are you sure? I'm not. The point is, of course, as to whether these gentlemen, worthy citizens though they be, are really qualified to judge matters of taste. No doubt they do represent fairly well the average point of view, but is there not some danger in vesting such arbitrary power in such hands? As far as Bradford is concerned, I readily agree that we have not much to grumble about, but is it not inconceivable that what is reported of Leeds might occur with us?

It was the height of summer when William Lancaster rose to his feet inside the police court in Darlington. He was the manager of the Alhambra Palace, and the allegation he faced was that he had exhibited an objectionable film and thereby broken a condition of his licence.

Mr Lancaster denied the charge. There was nothing objectionable to be seen in *Sapho*, he said. For the prosecutor, it wasn't so much what could be seen as what it might make people think. A constable said the film was suggestive of immorality from beginning to end, and an alderman who had watched a good part of it said it would certainly be demoralising to innocent and pure minds. The poster had proclaimed it 'the most talked-of photo play ever produced,' and William had been observed walking up and down outside the hall just before the lights went down, shouting, 'Hurry up! Hurry up! This will be the last time *Sapho* is shown.'

The bench that heard the case was seven magistrates strong – rather more than the usual complement – and they were able to watch the film for themselves, at a private showing that certainly wouldn't be the last of its kind. Once the evidence had been concluded and the magistrates had filed out of the picture house, they took only a few minutes to come to their decision – Mr Lancaster had been right: *Sapho* was not objectionable. The case would be dismissed.

This came as a relief to the *Bioscope*. 'It is far better for all concerned that police interference in entertainments is reduced to a minimum,' the magazine said:

> After all, public opinion is the surest safeguard, and the showman flying in the face of an obviously expressed desire on the part of his patrons would soon find himself in difficulties.
>
> This action on the part of the police to establish themselves as guardians of the public morals has failed, and we trust that no more may be heard of this and similar unnecessary interference.

In the press, in the wake of all this, some new advertisements began to appear. '*Sapho* Spells Money,' they said. '*Sapho* will test the full holding capacity of the largest halls in the country.'

> Smart managers and proprietors who are desirous of being introduced to *Sapho* must send in their cards now, at once, because the wires are burning up with applications to make her acquaintance from all over the country and hitting this office to beat the band.
>
> Now is your time to get busy.
>
> It's a sure thing!

The advertisements had been placed by Walter Stott and

Fred White. In much of the country, and especially in the North, they were the men who had been hawking *Sapho* around. Once the court case was over, they redoubled their efforts, and they were amply rewarded, as demand for the film continued to grow.

That was certainly the case in Dublin, where both the novel and the play were already well known. *Sapho* was showing there when *Five Nights* should have been showing in Preston, and as a result, large crowds were to be found in the Phibsborough district, where James Joyce had lived as a young man.

The Bohemian Picture Theatre there stood only a street or two away from the house where he had known little but grief, poverty and frustration. The management proclaimed it the most luxurious cinema in the city, and not without good reason. Ornate finials and chiselled limestone dressings enlivened the red-brick façade. The seats and carpets were deep blue, and fibrous plasterwork ran across the ceiling and down the walls. There was an orchestra, led by Mr Percy Carver, and the projector was in the hands of twenty-year-old Harry Mitchelson, who was counting down the days until he could join the West Yorkshire Regiment.

And patrons of the 'Boh' will have been distracted only slightly by the protests of concerned townsfolk, assembled on a corner close by, or by the brass band the townsfolk had hired to parade up and down outside the hall, parping and tooting away.

29

There might have been brief consternation in Birmingham, and something more significant in Weston-super-Mare, but as far as *Five Nights* was concerned, the first sustained trouble came on the Wirral, in what had once been a Presbyterian church.

The pews had been removed from the Lyceum Electric Palace in Wallasey by now, so customers no longer had to crane their necks to get a proper view. And while there were still stout columns across the front, supporting a triangular pediment and the customary tympanum, the auditorium had a deep red carpet and pink lightshades, and the manager, who was also the conductor of the band, would happily sing a song or two while the reels were being changed.

Councillors in the town were shown *Five Nights* on the day James Watson went to see it in Preston, and their response was delivered with equal speed. Disregarding, or perhaps acknowledging, the municipal motto – 'We are bold whilst we are cautious' – they announced that they had banned the film, even though what they had really done was neither so direct nor its effect so immediate as they implied. 'The councillors could not enforce their prohibition of the exhibition of the film,' the *Liverpool Echo* explained, and yet:

> … they hold the whip hand in that there is no obligation upon them, as the picture house licensing authority, to grant the renewal of any licence when the present term expires.

So, while the Wallasey 'ban' might be questionable from a legal point of view, anyone disobeying it would run the risk of losing his livelihood. That was precisely the conundrum that had been presented to William Broadhead in Preston, and readers of the *Echo* will not have been surprised to read that, 'discretion being the better part of valour, the managers of the cinema have yielded to the ban.' But then, with a helpful glance across the Mersey, the newspaper added, 'the film showing in Liverpool is on at all performances.' Upriver in Birkenhead, meanwhile, it was magistrates, not councillors, who were given a private viewing, and, having once come down against *Sapho*, they now came down against *Five Nights*. They did so, indeed, without leaving the picture house, the chairman of the bench declaring from his seat in the stalls that it was 'not fitting to the preservation of order and decency' that the film be shown.

In Dublin, there would be no need for a concerned committee, nor for any marching around or parping and tooting, because the showing of the film would be prohibited by the Lord Mayor himself. Prohibitions were also introduced in Nottingham and Leicester, while in Coventry, all eyes turned to Charles C Charsley.

He was an accomplished footballer, who had been appointed Chief Constable not long after he played in goal for England. And once he heard that *Five Nights* was showing in the town, he decided he must make inquiries. That was only two days after James Watson had done something similar in Preston, in the middle of what was proving a busy week. Mr Charsley had already presented a marble clock to a constable who was retiring after three decades' service; he had appeared in court to oppose bail for a young soldier charged with murder; and he had led the police cricket team to defeat against a team of ladies. (Opening the batting, Charles had been dismissed for just two runs, caught by Miss Hyslop off the bowling of Miss Hallam.)

Now, Mr Charsley found himself walking under the ornate metal and glass canopy of the Globe Picture Theatre, and up the steep stone steps. He managed to find a seat in what was a very crowded house, and he watched the whole thing through, from beginning to end. Then, he sent word to the manager that the film must not be shown again.

There were also bans in Bridgwater and Clitheroe. And though in Bath the ban came very late in the day, there was still time to arrange for *At the Mercy of Tiberius* and *The Avenging Conscience* to be shown instead. In St Helens, meanwhile, magistrates saw the film at the Hippodrome, before the doors had even opened to the general public, and having done so, they imposed a ban of their own. The following day, in a letter to the *St Helens Reporter*, Owen H Thomas wrote:

The bolt has fallen.

We in St Helens are not to see the film *Five Nights*. Our grandmothers – pardon, justices – have sat in solemn conference and, after an hour's free entertainment, decreed that no one else must go through it.

No doubt their own sufferings were so acute that they felt sorry for the misguided St Helens public.

The maiden aunts – again, pardon, the justices – probably fresh from a Sunday prayer meeting, are now free to go and see Great Men with Normal Minds at the Dottydrome.

Within days, though, the St Helens decision would be the subject of a legal challenge.

In Accrington, *Five Nights* was viewed by the Chief Constable, and he produced his own list of cuts that would have to be made. Those cuts proved insufficient, however, even though they accounted for a hundred feet or more, and after the town's magistrates had seen the film, alongside a claque of clergymen, they decreed that it must not be shown. Their counterparts in Halifax went so far as to describe it as 'offensive, objectionable, and an exhibition of suggested immorality from beginning to end.'

And just before Halloween, the challenge to the St Helens decision was dismissed in the High Court. In words that will have disappointed the men who brought the challenge, the judge told them that as they did not themselves own the Hippodrome, any interest they had in the showing of *Five Nights* was too remote to count.

Walter Stott and Fred White were the men in question, and their disappointment will doubtless have been intensified by the thought of the £3,000 they had laid out and the rental fees they would lose. The judge also ruled that even though the Censor had given the film a certificate, that was not binding on the bench. In the weeks to come, the press would declare that every council was now its own censor of films. But no matter how disappointed Walter and Fred might have been, they were not yet finished with the justices of St Helens – or, for that matter, with the High Court.

Before long, another Hippodrome – the one in Bradford – was also the subject of a ban. 'The world before your eyes,' its advertisements promised, and 'If anything happens, we've got it.' The manager there was George Mozley, whom everyone knew as 'Charlie' on account of his impersonations of Mr Chaplin. George had known the young Charlie Chaplin well, and when (as it often did) the projector broke down, he too would step out in front of the screen and do a turn.

The private viewing at this place went on longer than had been expected, and after the ban was announced, a columnist for the *Shipley Times and Express* observed that:

Members of the city council who were deputed to say whether or not the cinema picture *Five Nights* is a fit and proper one for public exhibition were reported to have gone twice to see it!

As *Five Nights* – and *Sapho* – continued to create a stir, a new American film was shown to the trade in a hall in Salford. *The Rosary* tells the story of a kindly priest, who has given up his sweetheart for the Church. It deals with jealousy and betrayal, emigration and loss. And it ends with redemption all round and the happy reuniting of man and wife. The hall was owned by a man who claimed to enjoy the patronage of Queen Alexandra, but it was hemmed in by the tramway and the railway line, by a cattle yard, and by the Red Cow – a beer house named for a Sioux abandoned when Buffalo Bill left town.

The film would do excellent business. There would be a sumptuous promotional brochure, crowds queueing to get in, and dozens turned away. In place after place, local artistes would be hired to sing the sentimental song upon which the film was based, and audiences wouldn't be able to stop themselves from singing along. And all of that would come as a blessed relief to Fred White. He was the man hawking *The Rosary* around, and he was doing that now without any assistance from Walter Stott.

There was, however, one thing left for the two men to do together.

30

Bury was another place where neither magistrates nor councillors had seen any reason to object to *Five Nights*, and the film was shown there with little or no dissent.

Then, a letter appeared in the *Bury Times*, its author the Reverend EA Glenday, vicar of Holy Trinity Church:

> Will you kindly allow me space in your columns to protest against the decision to allow a notoriously suggestive and indecent film to be exhibited in one of the picture halls of the town?
>
> That this film is at all events of doubtful propriety is proved by the fact that it has been banned at Preston, St Helens, Nottingham, and other places.
>
> Of course, no one could deny the right of the councillors of Bury to use their own judgement in a matter of this sort, or their claim to sanction an entertainment even though it had been banned in every town in the kingdom. But even they cannot claim to set up their own judgement against that of the ratepayers of the borough, to whom, ultimately, they owe their authority to exercise the function of censor of public entertainments.
>
> I have no hesitation in asserting that by their present action they have outraged the sense of decency of every sober-minded citizen of this town.
>
> One such called upon me the other day to draw my attention to the presentation of this debasing film, and he commented, 'I think this is simply abominable.'

Another gentleman, a well-known public man in the town, expressed himself to me in similar terms, adding, 'The only book I have ever regretted reading was that by the author of the book which is illustrated by this film. It is absolutely putrid.' And this is the kind of garbage that has been offered with the sanction of authority during the present week for the entertainment of the people of Bury, young and old. In the factories, decent-minded people expressed the opinion that the film would be withdrawn before the week was out. But they only showed how little they understood the councillors...

A play answering to that description ought not to have been passed for presentation in any shape or form, pandering as it does to the lower appetites of human nature.

The object of this letter is to make it known to those in authority that there is at any rate a section of the ratepayers – I think they constitute a majority of those who take a genuine interest in the borough – who will not tolerate a repetition of this kind of thing. We can prevent it at the hustings and the polling booth if we fail by other means.

I have written strongly because I feel that public decency has been cynically outraged. It is no time for mincing one's words.

The town was another of those in which Walter Stott and Fred White's £3,000 had secured them the exclusive right to rent out the film, and this letter annoyed them greatly. It annoyed them so much, in fact, that they decided they must once more go to law. Reverend Glenday would soon be hearing the words 'a notoriously suggestive and indecent film' again.

31

As well as the debate concerning the employment of foreigners, there were several others in the early days of picture house orchestras.

One debate was about music: should it be played at all, and if it was played, should that be during films or only between them? Might music even be played continuously? And need any attempt be made to tailor it to events on the screen?

On a tour of halls in Edinburgh, a correspondent from the *Bioscope* said he had encountered 'pictures *and* music, not pictures *with* music.'

> You get eight or twelve bars of something well-known and pleasing to the ear, when, for no reason whatever, the scene or situation not demanding it, you are suddenly switched on to another eight bars of something totally different in character, and so on to the end of the part.
>
> It is inartistic, gives one the idea of a horrible jumble and jangle, and causes uncomplimentary remarks from the audience on the scratchy and disjointed performance.

The treatment of *Five Nights* provides a suitable illustration. At a picture house in East London, selections were played from *The Geisha* and *San Toy* – two musical comedies that were undoubtedly popular, but only one of which had anything to do with China. And at the point at which Hop Lee discovers Lonsdale and Suzee in their embrace, the pianist struck up 'The Interfering Parrot'.

In many picture houses, however, an accommodation

of sorts had been reached. 'The accompaniment throughout was distinctly good,' one newspaper reported, while others spoke of 'appropriate music' and 'a suitable and sympathetic accompaniment,' and of the orchestra having 'entered thoroughly into the spirit of the film.'

The critic who visited Cupid's Cinema in Leicester Square will have found the few seats hard and the light bulbs as bare as the walls. But he was pleased with what he heard, nonetheless. 'Under the direction of Miss Caicedo,' he wrote, of an ensemble with a familiar leader, 'the band has everywhere made a great success, admirably adapting the music to the film, and the appreciation of audiences at every performance must be very gratifying to the conductress.' Elsewhere, it was reported that her music 'has been much admired for its intrinsic excellence, and also for its tactical appropriateness to the films. She is a daughter of the world-famous King-of-the-Wire.'

In Bexhill-on-Sea, meanwhile:

There was a general wish to see the concluding chapter of the story of the Cannibals, which was announced for the beginning of the week.

These unique pictures of a little-known spot of the earth recently explored by a white man and his wife, equipped with cameras, have been a feature at the St George's for several weeks, and their success has been not a little enhanced by the appropriately weird and savage music supplied by the theatre orchestra, which is very clever in some of its accomplishments.

This place had only recently changed its name to the St George's, doing so simply on account of the war. It was the place that had previously been known as the Bijou, but it was no less glittering, and no less small, now.

In Bedford, a correspondent who signed himself 'A Sapper'

wished to praise the band at the Picturedrome (from where news of Jack Johnson's victory over Jim Jeffries had been so dextrously communicated). 'They really play *to*, and not *in spite of*, the pictures,' he wrote. In one recent show:

> … they worked up a gradual crescendo towards the climax of the play – the point where the criminal is accused of his crime.
>
> At the critical moment there was a death-like pause.
>
> A gripping title-card then flashed on the screen, followed by a resumption of the melody, which seemed, after all, not to have been interrupted on account of the picture, but almost accidental.

This was a decorous place, with round windows on the front and a roofline that twirled as it rose. It had opened with film of the funeral of King Edward and a short speech from a local man with whom the monarch had once shared a few words. The place stood beside the Old Stone Bridge, so close to the river that swans could be fed from the front steps. And 'A Sapper' was impressed by what he found there. 'To make the lilt of a tune fit the action of a picture exactly must take some doing,' he wrote:

> I may mention, too, that the Picturedrome orchestra accompanies comedies as well as dramas, and does not play all Ragtime for the humorous films. It is so often left to the poor pianist to grind out old favourites while Charles Chaplin is convulsing the house.

Another debate concerned not the music, but the musicians, and precisely where in a hall they should be located.

Early pianists often found themselves pushed to one side, maybe against a wall, and not all of them could see what was going on. A handbook said it was 'advisable to sink the piano in

144

a well close to the picture,' while in Wymondham, a lady named Winne played her ancient instrument from behind a curtain, so as not to distract the customers. This proved nothing but an incitement, however, and schoolboys were forever throwing balls of paper over the curtain, in the hope that Winne would be struck and the music would stop.

The problem only got worse as more and more musicians began to appear. Special arrangements had been made in the days of the rinks, not least in Ballsbridge, where it was felt the music should be seen as well as heard. And those arrangements were now repeated for the films. At a hall in Glasgow, the orchestra was placed in front of the screen but below the level of the audience. Elsewhere, a manager insisted that it be placed at the back of the hall, or even in the balcony, leading the *Bioscope* to offer the example of a tune that had been composed to be played softly:

> What chance is there of that beautiful number being heard by the 'intelligent' audience, or by the highest-priced seats, if between them and the music there are a dozen or couple of dozen rows filled with noisy children and young men and women to whom no music appeals unless it is 'Are You From Dixie?' or some similar commonplace Ragtime?

In Liverpool, at the Belmont Road Picture House, the orchestra was located 'in a special balcony near the screen,' at least when the man from the *Bioscope* came to call. He pronounced it 'a splendid combination under the direction of Mr Henry S Feiler, himself a noted solo violinist.'

Important changes had come into the life of this gentleman of late. Across the River Mersey in New Brighton, just before the invasion of Belgium, he had been billed as 'Herr Heinrich Feiler'. That was the name under which he performed at the Tivoli, and at the Gaiety, where he was a member of Herr Blattner's Orchestra. In even earlier days, he had performed under that name at the Southport Opera House. But after the declaration of war, something more English was plainly required. Henry used his new name in connection with his duties at the Belmont, and he also used it when he married Gertrude, a young woman he had met in Bootle.

Recently, to accompany the showing of *Jane Shore*, Henry Feiler had combined pieces of music by Sir Arthur Sullivan and Sir Edward Elgar with the sixteen bars Edward German composed for *Henry VIII*. 'A special, all-British arrangement' is what he decided it should be called.

32

Two women are standing in a clearing in a wood. They are wearing long skirts, shawls, and flowery bonnets.

The women are talking excitedly in front of a makeshift fence, one in a light dress, the other in a dark dress, each holding an umbrella aloft.

This is a film made by the Bamforth company when Victoria was sixty-two years a queen.

The women wave their hands around and jab their fingers, each leaning towards the other in turn, determined to make her point.

Their heads go nodding and dipping, the blooms on their bonnets wagging, and sometimes they nearly knock together. One woman pats the ample bosom of the other.

Then, the women are seen as if from behind the fence.

Two men creep into view, wearing aprons, braces, and flat caps. They are on the nearside of the fence, plainly up to no good.

One of the men crouches down and cups his hand to his ear, listening intently. Then, he beckons to his mate and tells him what to do.

The men take hold of the women's skirts, pull them through a gap in the fence and nail them to one of the timbers.

The women are horrified when they realise what has been done. They are open-mouthed and wide-eyed, and one of them throws her hands up and her umbrella into the air.

They flap their arms as if they were wings and manage to repel the men. Then, seen from the front again, they struggle and struggle, and finally get themselves free.

The film goes by the name *Women's Rights*. It is a rough-and-ready affair, and irregular, too – each woman remains on the same side of the screen, whether she is seen from the front or from behind. The fence is only a single plank in length and offers no sort of impediment. And when the fence breaks, and there's no more struggling to be done, one of the women looks right into the camera and laughs.

Also, and this is impossible to miss, the women are really men. The laughing one, indeed, is Fred Bullock, taking a break from his duties as the Holmfirth blacksmith.

This wasn't the first time James Bamforth had addressed the subject. A decade before, he had produced a set of lantern slides with the same title he would give to the film. And those slides, painted crimson and deep blue, pink and taupe and gold, depict precisely the same events. *In earnest discussion, An attentive listener* and *Companions in mischief* are their titles; *They hatch a plot, They nail the ladies, The ladies in disarray*.

Nor was the film the first of its kind. The year before it was made, as Parliament dallied over a bill that would have given at least some women the vote, another company produced *The Lady Barber*, whose subject is a suffragist shown frenziedly hacking at the hair of some bewildered men. Then, Emmeline Pankhurst demanded 'deeds, not words' and her daughter was fined for causing a disturbance in Manchester. When Christabel Pankhurst refused to pay her fine, she was sent to Strangeways prison, next to the Assize Court, and the word 'suffragette' entered the English language. That was also when *The New Woman* arrived in cinemas. It has a wife forcing her husband to do the housework while she takes over his job, and it received a sort of response in *Sweet Suffragettes*, which shows a young woman in uncomfortable close-up, her face being pelted with eggs as she tries in vain to make herself heard.

Not content with addressing the subject on glass slides and film, the Bamforth company also did so on its tinted cards.

One of them shows two men standing outside a pub, looking at a woman in a big hat who has a sign around her neck. Her jacket is purple and her skirt green, and the sign reads 'Votes for Women.' The woman is slender and her features perhaps masculine. 'There ain't much 'am in that sandwich, 'Arry,' one of the men says. 'No,' replies the other, 'but there's plenty of mustard.'

There was a huge demonstration after Christabel was sent to prison, and a rally in Hyde Park drew nearly half a million people. In one film of that time, a man disguises himself as a woman to infiltrate a meeting, while in another, suffragettes discover that one of their number is a man in drag. *When Women Rule* sees men actually forced to wear skirts. *If Women Were Policemen* contemplates that very possibility. And *Suffering Suffragettes* was said to be 'screamingly funny throughout.' As one Parliamentary bill followed another, and all of them failed, suffragettes began chaining themselves to railings, smashing windows (not least in Westminster) and throwing stones with messages tied to them (not least at Mr Lloyd George). And then the hunger-strikes and the force-feeding began.

Here is a plump, elderly woman being apprehended by a policeman. This too is a Bamforth card. The woman is lying back in the policeman's arms, her feet off the ground. She is gazing into his eyes and waving a pennant with 'Votes for Women' written on it. 'Slow march, constable,' the woman says. 'I'm having the time of my life!'

In the summer between two general elections, thousands of suffragettes took part in a 'Prison to Citizenship' march through London. They did that in support of yet another bill, and many of them can be seen on the newsreels, holding aloft the broad-arrow symbol that showed they had spent time behind bars. But when that bill, too, failed, and a delegation was turned back from Parliament, something close to a riot ensued, and many women would say they had been molested by policemen and bystanders. *The Suffragette's Downfall* was on the screen within days. Its subject leaves her husband in charge of the house while she goes off to play golf, but when she comes back, he serves her a rat for dinner. And though she shouts at him, and even punches him, she ends the film promising to pay more attention to her domestic duties.

When it became clear that the franchise wouldn't soon be enlarged, there was a fresh wave of attacks, with windows this time the principal target. 'The argument of the broken pane of glass is the most valuable argument in modern politics,' Mrs Pankhurst said. It was one that would be played out at banks, department stores, restaurants and post offices across the land. Golf courses and cricket pitches were dug up as well, telegraph wires cut, post boxes set alight. And there were impassioned gatherings in rink after rink. Five hundred suffragettes flocked to the one in Aldwych on the night of the great Census. 'Until women are recognised as people,' Emmeline told them, 'they will refuse to be numbered as people.' Then, at a gathering in the Albert Hall, she went further. 'I incite this meeting to rebellion,' she said.

Christabel had fled to France by then, fearing that she would be locked up once again, and a film entitled *The Elusive Miss Pinkhurst* was all the rage. A toy named *Elusive Christabel* was all the rage as well. It alternated images of Ms Pankhurst and her hapless pursuers, and contained a satirical verse:

They seek her here, they seek her there;
    Detectives prowling everywhere.
Their heads with big importance swell –
    She's Gone! Elusive Christabel.

This time, the response in picture houses was *Milling the Militants*, in which the husband of another suffragette is left at home while his wife goes off on a demonstration. She has a hammer in her hand and is wearing an apron with a slogan on the front, and she and her acolytes are shown breaking a window and setting a fire, and then dancing around the flames as if taking part in some strange, arcane rite.

In his wife's absence, the man dreams he has been made prime minister and has brought in laws punishing suffragettes for their deeds. They are shown being forced to shovel horse droppings, dig the road, and smoke pipes. They are put in the stocks, and paraded down the street wearing trousers, to their evident distress. And one of them is fastened to a stool and ducked in the river in time-honoured fashion. But the husband wakes with a shock when his wife tips a bucket of water over his head, and he is last seen down on his knees, his hands clasped in front of him, begging for mercy. In Halifax, when the film was shown at the Electric Theatre, the town's *Evening Courier* newspaper described it as 'a dream of the day, seemingly far off, when suffragettes will be completely subdued.'

There is another kneeling man on one of the Bamforth company's cards. He has a woman standing over him, and he is wearing a pinafore on top of his clothes. His cheeks are red and he looks ever so bashful, as the woman grips his ear between her thumb and forefinger. 'My wife has joined the Suffrage Movement,' the caption reads. 'I've suffered ever since.'

Jack Johnson, however, offered a more pugnacious response. At a time when he still expected to fight Bombardier Billy Wells, as he drove around Britain trying to drum up trade, the great champion's stately progress was impeded by a group of placard-wielding suffragists. And when he was asked about them, he did not hold back. 'They are a nuisance,' he told a reporter:

> If they want votes, let 'em put on pants and go out and make a living. After they'd been in power a month every woman would be fighting every other woman she met on the street. Why? Simply because they yarn too much.

They're all jealous of one another. If you'll show me one smart woman in the combination, I'll swing back to America. Has there ever been a worthy woman leader?

Alongside its decorous postcards, the Bamforth company also offered audiences *Winky as a Suffragette*, in which the eponymous star assumes a new identity in order to get his hands on campaign funds and only reveals his true one at the end, from the window of a train, as it steams out of Holmfirth station.

The making of this film caused great excitement in the town. The cast was the largest ever assembled there, and women who agreed to play the part of suffragettes were promised as much as a shilling a day. At the end of shooting, the women were marched back from the station in a group and led down Station Road. As they approached the Bamforth studio, they were met by the company's employees, augmented by members of the local fire brigade. Then, at a given signal, the firemen opened up their hoses and the women were given a frightful drenching, with the Bamforth cameras still rolling, so that not a moment of their discomfiture would be lost.

Nor was Fred Evans to be left behind. If *Miss Pimple, Suffragette* saw him pose as one in order to blow up a boat race, that was merely him at his most brazen. Suffragettes are encountered in several of his films. *Pimple's Battle of Waterloo* sees his Napoleon nearly being assassinated by them, while the Hell in *Pimple's Inferno* is peopled with them – and peopled with popular film comedians as well.

Amid all the antipathy – the ducking-stools, the drenching, and the pelting with eggs – the occasional glimmer of acknowledgement can also be seen. It is present in *Did'ums Diddles the P'liceman*, which was doing the rounds as Christabel Pankhurst made her fugitive journey across the Channel. The star of the film is a small child in ringlets and bows, who is shown tormenting a constable wearing a fine moustache. 'I'm not a suffragette,' the child says, 'but I'll see what I can do for you,' and over the course of the next few minutes, she rolls a hoop at him and knocks him down, gets him run over by a brougham, falls on him from a height and pins him to the ground, kicks him, runs away from him, trips him up, strikes him with a horsewhip, escapes from him in another brougham, wrestles him to the ground, traps him in a manhole, steals his helmet, swaps the helmet for her own bonnet, punches him in the head, daubs his face with paint, sends him flying into a pond, and humiliates him in front of his comrades.

And throughout all of this, the child repeatedly thumbs her nose at the constable, shakes her fist at him, laughs the broadest of laughs, and slaps her thigh over and over again. She too is having the time of her life (even if 'she' is another one who might actually be he).

33

Matters were expected to come to a head when suffragettes, dismayed at yet another Parliamentary reverse, took to the streets of Westminster. There were 2,000 policemen on duty that day, but what the newsreels showed was platoons of women with placards around their necks, trudging disconsolately through the rain. Before long, though, Lloyd George's lovely new house was in flames and Christabel Pankhurst was telling a reporter, 'We are fighting a revolution.'

The spring brought images of the 'St Leonards Outrage', which devastated another lovely house, and for which a stage performer named Kitty Marion claimed responsibility. Ms Marion billed herself as 'a refined vocal comedienne', but she was apprehended several weeks later after starting a fire at a racecourse next to the River Thames. At trial, Kitty was prosecuted by Archibald Bodkin, who had once made the case for the Sunday opening of cinemas. In prison, following her conviction, though she was force-fed repeatedly, she said she regretted nothing of what she had done, save that no film camera had been present 'to immortalise the comedy of it.'

The comedy of it was something that, as the flames grew higher, films found it difficult to reflect. One of them shows a suffragette destroying a pillar-box and with it the letter that would have saved a child's life. Another takes an allegorical turn, with Pity, refused the vote by John Bull, abducting a child. And the subject of *The Child of a Suffragette* is seen trailing her mother, and foiling her by extinguishing a bomb she had planned to explode.

Then came the Derby and the trampling of Emily Davison in

the run-up to the home straight. She was one of the women who had thrown stones at Lloyd George. She too had been force-fed. And her hands had been among the many that carried a convict arrow in the great suffragette march. 'A Serious Accident,' the newsreel said. 'A Woman's Attempt to Seize the King's Horse.' The precise moment was captured in another of the front-page photographs for which the *Daily Sketch* was famous. And Ms Davison's obsequies, in Bloomsbury and Morpeth, were depicted at length, not only in newspapers, but also on the screen.

In the middle of summer, some 'Law-abiding Suffragists' converged on Hyde Park. (The term, and the inverted commas, were the newsreels' own.) But from then on, films seemed to lose their appetite for antagonism. Even as Trafalgar Square dissolved into tumult and Emmeline Pankhurst was frogmarched away from Buckingham Palace, there was a discernible return to the comedy of it. Films now chose to show a maid using a magic lamp to save a suffragette from a sultan, and a drunken man waking up without his trousers in the middle of a suffrage meeting.

Here is a last Bamforth card. It depicts the view from the stage of a theatre, where another meeting is taking place in the stalls. A forest of hands has been raised by the women, and men, present, and the caption on the card reads, 'Will those in favour of women's suffrage please hold up their hands?' One of the men, who is sitting next to a much larger woman, has had his hand raised by her.

Throughout the tumult, some films were unafraid to show women acting determinedly, rationally, resourcefully, and even selfishly. In *Finding his Counterpart*, a hapless young man is repelled by a young woman into whose house he has intruded, and then by four women at a tea party on the lawn. He is crushed underneath a cabinet, defenestrated, and thrown into a lake. And when he ventures onto the platform during a suffragist rally, he has a bomb set off beneath him.

This film, too, was made in Holmfirth, nearly two decades after that fence and those questionable ladies in their long skirts. And even if every woman but the first is in fact a man, none of them this time is shown in disarray.

The *Tilly* series of films takes things further, not least by having a young woman – Alma Taylor – in the leading role. Alongside her friend, played by Chrissie White, Tilly is shown helping smugglers only to have them arrested, confounding an election candidate, locking a nurse in a wardrobe, and tricking her uncle as he tries to flirt with the maid. Ms Taylor said she had first been filmed at a children's party when she was twelve years old, and she quickly proved to be a natural in the business. The readers of *Pictures and the Picturegoer* magazine chose her as their favourite film performer, thousands of votes ahead of Charlie Chaplin, and even more votes ahead of Pimple.

In *Tilly and the Fire Engines*, she and Chrissie steal a fire engine and make off with it, pursued not just by firemen, but by ordinary men and women in boaters, caps, and straw hats. The great engine tears off down the road, its huge wheels lifting into the air, dust billowing around in huge clouds. And Tilly can be seen up on her feet at the back, her long hair streaming backwards on the wind, as she swings a huge stick from behind her head and urges the horses on.

When the girls eventually come to a halt, they unspool the firehose and give their pursuers a frightful drenching. The firemen are pinned against a fence by the force of the jet. And the film ends with Alma and Chrissie presenting each other with medals for their bravery, and pulling face after face. Alma is wearing a great brass helmet she must have stolen. She raises her right hand in a mock salute, and laughs, and laughs again. Then, she opens her eyes wide, looks straight into the camera and smiles a smile that goes beyond Tilly and Chrissie and the film – beyond films in fact, and probably beyond make-believe of any kind.

34

The number of places showing *Five Nights* continued to grow. Hounslow and Whitstable were among them: the Coliseum and the Palais de Luxe. In Hawick, a clergyman had called picture houses 'one of the Devil's most blatant instruments for the destruction of all that is pure and holy,' but the film could be seen at the Pavilion, nonetheless. That place squatted between square, bare towers, but the lights inside cast a warm pink glow, and the pink curtains were satin and soft to the touch. The film could also be seen at the Palace theatre in Hartlepool, where an advertisement proclaimed it a 'Phenomenal attraction. The world's greatest pictorial masterpiece,' and customers were promised a 'special lecture by TV Padden esquire.'

The role of film lecturer was a familiar one then, when storytelling techniques hadn't yet been established, title-cards were few and brief, and the whole thing could be terribly confusing. Many people, from the threepenny seats to the curtained boxes, will have welcomed a word or two of explication, whether they were willing to admit the fact or not. And if the role owed something to elocutionists such as Eric Williams, it also carried an echo of even earlier days; of the sun-filled room in Holmfirth, *Abide With Me* and *What Should England Fear?* It will have been especially familiar to audiences in Hartlepool, for the Palace was still hosting lantern shows long after it had begun showing films.

TV – Thomas Vincent – Padden had been neither a lanternist nor an elocutionist. He was an engineer before he went into the pictures, in shipyards up and down the Tyne, and when he left that trade it was so that he could become manager of the Palace in Jarrow. He stayed there until the place burned down, and he moved to the Savoy Electric Theatre in Sunderland after that.

This was for him a very different life. Wearing his best bib and tucker, rehearsing under his breath a few familiar words of welcome, he will have positioned himself to one side of the screen and waited for the darkness to come in. In Hartlepool, he might have positioned himself *below* the screen, for the Palace possessed a broad, deep orchestra pit.

Standing there in the half-light, TV Padden will have tried to make sense of it all. He will have spoken about the setting and the characters, introduced the actors and actresses, and suggested where his audience might have seen them all before. Taking care not to fall behind the pace of the film, he will have explained the comings and goings and the jokes, and even tried to fill in the gaps. He might have done that in different voices – this one a toff, that one a cockney costermonger or a comic Chinaman – and he will often have had to do it over the noise of the projector, the piano, or even the band.

Where *Five Nights* was concerned, Mr Padden will have begun as he meant to go on:

This Lonsdale is quite the man, don't you think?
He's a successful artist, well-fortified with private means, travelling in search of inspiration, and sipping joyously at all the world provides to gratify the needs of an impulsive and artistic temperament.
And what about the blazer? And that handkerchief?

Thomas Padden was by no means the only film lecturer. There were many people speaking from the half-light in those days, and they often did so in a language that wasn't English.

The role was a familiar one right across Europe, recalling as it did the minstrels of old, who wandered from place to place, exchanging tavern for hiring fair, singing songs and playing instruments, embellishing as often as creating, and spreading news, gossip, disease, dissent.

The *kinoerzähler* were a feature of picture houses in Germany, the *imbonitore* in Italy, the *bonimenteur* in France. The *explicador* in Spain would take questions from the audience while brandishing a bamboo stick. And if the role was one of explication, it was one of impersonation too, with the voice of the lecturer frequently being leant to the actors on the screen. The role might even be one of interpretation, especially if the film was American or English and the picture house was in Augsburg or Zaragoza, in Quebec or among Yiddish speakers on the Lower East Side.

The role perhaps reached its apogee in Japan, where it became the province of the *benshi*.

These stylised performers emerged during the war with Russia, when the fierce patriotism they were able to summon up struck a chord in picture houses. They had as their influences *Noh* theatre and *kabuki*, *bunraku* puppet shows, the musical *joruri* and scholarly *kodan*. And they evoked memories of Japan's own wandering minstrels, the blind monks who delivered epic ballads to the accompaniment of the lute; and of the lanternists of more recent days, who told of love and hate, poisoned sake, and cherry blossom bursting suddenly into flower.

As their counterparts did elsewhere in the world, the *benshi* explained what was happening and gave the characters voice. And when a film came from the West, they would try to provide guidance. 'Here is Napoleon,' one of them was heard to announce to his perplexed audience. 'Napoleon is... Napoleon.' They might also provide commentary, and even some conclusions of their own. And if they were criticised for doing so – accused of misrepresenting a film, of distorting its message – that was nothing they couldn't handle.

The *benshi* had trained in special academies, under acknowledged masters of the art, and they possessed huge reserves of character and stamina. All of that served them well, for alongside the critics and historical foreigners, there might be five shows a day to contend with, every day of the week, with a change of film every seven days. The huge cinemas of Osaka, Tokyo and Yokohama were often filled beyond capacity and offered little in the way of amplification. Yet the *benshi* conducted themselves with great panache. Attentive always to rhythm and intonation, they could be grave and terribly grand, passionate, dramatic, understated and intellectual. They might have the accompaniment of traditional instruments, and they often brought in material that was entirely their own.

Standing next to the screen, dressed in traditional kimonos, or tails and striped trousers, the *benshi* were magisterial. They alone possessed both the power and the will to control a performance – to quieten the musicians, or command a hasty projectionist to take more time. It was even said they influenced the way Japanese films were made, by giving directors confidence that any rough edges would be smoothed out, any infelicities explained away. The role and what the *benshi* brought to it made some of them famous and earned them huge rewards. They, not the actors in a film, were said to be the ones responsible for filling the picture houses, and theirs were often the names given top billing on the posters outside. *Banzuke* were published, ranking them as if they were *sumo* wrestlers, and ardent fans would leave lavish gifts for them at the edge of the stage.

For others, though, the jingoism of the early years had given way to something more radical, and what they brought in was satirical in nature, even downright subversive. These *benshi* spoke about being poor and exploited, about heartless landlords and employers. They sometimes went out on strike themselves, and they could expect to have their words scrutinised by police officers in the stalls. And the barbs they gave were returned with equivalent force. The authorities condemned them as uneducated or, worse, pretentious. Their trade was proclaimed the last resort of libertines and peculators. They were called drunks and philanderers, whose performances were indecent when they weren't downright incoherent. And the men among them were said to be the sort to cheat a woman out of her savings.

35

In South Shields, come the New Year, *Five Nights* was showing at the Crown Electric Theatre. ('Adjoining Tyne Dock Station,' the newspaper advertisements helpfully stated. 'You can get there by tram or train!')

That town, where Will Barker's *Henry VIII* proved so popular, had received a visit from a Zeppelin the previous summer. A bomb was dropped on a fairground down by the river, shaking the carousel horses to bits and making the water ripple across the dock itself. But the attacker proved elusive. A 'pom-pom' gun failed to hit it, despite loosing off twenty shells, and two pilots sent up from Whitley Bay got lost in the dark skies over the North Sea. While this might have been the first raid to go beyond East Anglia or the Garden of England, the ones that followed would target Sussex and Hertfordshire as well.

In some places, the showing of *Five Nights* was merely the prelude to its being banned. That was the case in Brighton, where 30,000 people had seen the film at the Palladium in just one week. It was also the case in Southport and Runcorn. And it was certainly the case in London, where the film had been doing the rounds for fully two months before it fell afoul of the County Council. Business was particularly good in Chelsea, at the King's Picture Playhouse on the King's Road, which had once boasted of its Britishness, and where a sign over the door had promised 'The World and its Wonders Daily.' The King's claimed to have *Five Nights* exclusively, even though it could be seen in next-door Fulham as well. Nine cinemas were soon showing the film in the West End, in fact, a quarter of a million people had seen it and a similar number been turned away.

At the Imperial Picture House in Walsall, *Five Nights* had been a 'stupendous attraction' before it was banned. This great edifice had been the Agricultural Hall, the St George's Hall, and the Imperial Hall. It had hosted concerts and exhibitions, boxing matches and a meat-dressing competition, a dinner for old people, and a breakfast for 3,000 children. And if censorship had arrived in this town much earlier than in others, that was the result of a tragedy that had been only narrowly averted.

The very first films were exhibited at the Brine Baths, under the auspices of the Literary Institute (which normally met in the Temperance Hall). They were also shown at Her Majesty's Theatre and the Town Hall, but it was at the Imperial that the broadest selection could be found. *From the Cape to Cairo*, Will Barker's *entrée* into the business, was an early favourite, while *The Brigands of Calabria*, *The Redskins* and *The Pirates* were popular, too. *The Wilbur Wright Aeroplane* and *The Electric Hotel* had been displayed in all their glory, together with *Streets of Paris*, *Moscow Under Water* and *The Destruction of Hyderabad*. But when a fire was discovered in the gallery of the Imperial, it came as a terrible shock, even though *The Smell of Smoke* had been shown recently and *The Incendiary* was the evening's main feature. The cause of the fire was a carelessly discarded cigarette, its result a strict new prohibition: picture houses would no longer be permitted show any film 'of which the Council, acting by the Chief Constable, may disapprove.'

Across the Midlands, meanwhile, *Five Nights* opened at the Silver Street picture house in Leicester on a Monday evening. It played to large audiences and earned the praise of local clergymen, but it had been banned before the weekend arrived. The town's *Evening Mail* expressed its surprise:

> The scenes in the artist's studio which aroused opposition in other towns do not strike the writer as being objectionable. Judged from the standpoint of art,

they are well conceived, cleverly carried out, and in good taste.

This was too much for the councillor responsible for the ban. 'The use of the word "Art" covers a multitude of sins,' he said, 'and to talk of this film being artistic is piffle.' It was probably all the fault of the cinema anyway, for its proprietor had advertised that *Five Nights* would be shown 'positively for six days only.'

In other places, however, *Five Nights* was shown only after it had already been banned.

One such place was Hull, where there were two dozen picture houses and a couple of picture house seats for every score of citizens. The city had suffered the costliest Zeppelin raid so far, with more than twenty people killed and £50,000-worth of damage done. When councillors there were invited to a second private viewing of the film, they displayed what the city's *Daily Mail* newspaper described as 'calm phlegm' and 'sat it out with exemplary zeal and patience, between contented puffs of tobacco.'

> 'Censored in Preston? Well, what of it?' was the general view. 'Someone has been carried away by his zeal, that is all. Some new broom has swept too clean.'

The lifting of the ban prompted the newspaper to call for calm:

> We don't break butterflies on the wheel. Nor do we fancy that people are so crassly and slavishly imitative as to be swayed this way or that by the kind of 'stagey' abandon and dashing bohemianism they see on the stage.
>
> The solid burgher, instead, sits tight on his plush chair puffing vigorously, and his wife or fiancée makes short work meanwhile of the chocolates. But it would be

almost a joke to think of this sensible typical pair being influenced by the vehement lovemaking of the mimes on the screen. It would end in real life in a stunning box on the ears.

In future weeks, *Five Nights* would be seen at the Théatre de Luxe in Hull, and at the National cinema, which had an oculus to go with its splendid orchestra. It would also be seen at the Central Picture Theatre – 'The Rendezvous of the Elite' – and at the Picture Playhouse, where there would be four showings a day. 'Judging by the enormous advance bookings,' the *Daily Mail* warned, 'the house will be filled to its utmost capacity at each performance, and it is advisable that seats should be booked early.'

On the same page, the newspaper carried an advertisement for the London Guarantee & Accident Company Limited. Headed 'Zeppelins!' the advertisement promised that the company:

Will grant a policy to any British Subject of either sex between the ages of 12 and 70 whilst resident in the United Kingdom of Great Britain and Ireland against Death or Injury directly caused by Aircraft (hostile or otherwise), including bombs, shells and/or missiles dropped or thrown therefrom or fired thereat, on the following terms –

A Premium Of 5/- For Six Months, Or 7/6 For Twelve Months, or 10/- for the Duration of the War, Will secure the following benefits –

£500 payable in the event of Death. £500 payable in the event of the Loss of Two Limbs or Two Eyes, or One Limb and One Eye. £250 payable in the event of the Loss of One Limb or One Eye. £2 per Week payable during Temporary Total Disablement, for a period not exceeding 13 weeks.

36

There were many film lecturers in those days, and they all had their own reasons for taking on the role. Some were attached to a particular film and followed it around the country, providing elucidation in Lincolnshire one week, Lanarkshire the next. Some were in business on their own account and had to accept work wherever they could find it. And some lecturers had alighted upon a particular picture house and pretty much taken up residence there.

Charles Hand could be found speaking to the pictures in the West Country, and Percival Craig in West Yorkshire. Jack Carlton Baker had enhanced the enjoyment of *East Lynne* in Glasgow, and Frank Allen displayed his 'fine elocutionary powers' in Whitstable. Roger Temperly, who covered much of Scotland, also crossed into northern England once in a while. And at the Blue Halls in London, Caron James was 'listened to with rapt attention by vast audiences daily.' In Manchester, AJ Daniels had built his reputation going from hall to hall, and by the time he arrived at the Ceylon Picture Palace, he was calling himself 'Professor'. That place was in Rochdale, next to the Yorkshire road, and save for the odd patch of pine panelling, it was as bare as could be.

However modest the auditoriums in which they appeared, and whatever the motivations which carried them from one town to another, there was one thing all these people had in common. Whether it found expression on posters and advertisements, in interviews with the trade press, or only within the confines of a darkened, expectant hall, they all possessed great confidence in their own abilities. And that confidence served them well, in good times and in bad. James Morris claimed to be able to provide not only a lecture, but also lessons in logic, elocution and psychology. Leslie Paget, who could impersonate characters from Dickens, could also talk about the wonders of the deep. And Fred J Hudson promised nothing less than a trip around the world, starting out at the Picturedrome on Lord Street in Southport, and ending up there as well, fully two hours later.

In Hartlepool, Harold Mitschke dubbed himself 'the versatile exponent of mirth, mimicry, pathos, tragedy.' He too was accustomed to public speaking, and at the Northern Pictures – the 'Northerns' – he explained *David Copperfield* and *Silas Marner*. Mr Mitschke was also a jeweller, a writer and a photographer, and his versatility as a lecturer knew no limit. 'From grave to gay,' a newspaper wrote, 'from comedy to tragedy, Harold Mitschke runs through the whole elocutionary gamut without a jarring chord.' He shared the stage with instrumentalists, singers, lanternists and musical waxworks. He took part in a debate on phrenology and produced a treatise on picture house management. He lectured on Mormons and Mormonism, which Conan Doyle had turned into a topical issue. And sometimes, he would even deliver himself of a poem of his own composing, on the subject of the bringing down of a Zeppelin.

Competition was especially strong in the North East, among the likes of Bert Alberto and Will Power, John Hurley and James Burley. Some men even appeared in places known to TV Padden. One such place was North Shields, where Syd Codner was said to be 'acknowledged the finest lecturer at moving pictures.' In earlier days, Mr Codner had been in charge of the Kilburn Empire, before managing picture houses in Airdrie, Glasgow, Dunbar and Kilbirnie. Such was his popularity that he was given a bag of gold when he left Kilburn and a bag of sovereigns when he left Kilbirnie.

In the pit villages of Sacriston and Horden, lecturing duties were discharged by Bert and Ivy Velma, a married couple. He was a ventriloquist, often lauded for his courtesy and hard work, while she had begun as his substitute when he was indisposed, and together, they surrounded their films with dancers, duettists and patterers. They raised £5 for the Belgian Relief Fund and twice that on French Flag Day.

There were two couples lecturing in Aberdeen, and sometimes there were three couples, and maybe even four. The people of that city had been watching films since the Lumière brothers first ventured beyond their native land. And the showmen of the region hadn't confined their visits to the grand old Music Hall on Union Street. They also toured the towns and villages roundabout, setting up in Stonehaven, Inverurie, Peterhead and Keith, Monymusk, Fetterangus, Banchory, Tough; captivating audiences in school halls, church halls, sundry YMCA Halls, the Dalrymple Hall and the Fordyce Street Hall. They might show a score of films in an evening and have the bailie or provost as a guest, but they never forgot to mention that everything had come straight from Paris.

William Dove Paterson was one of those men. He too had been a lantern lecturer, made films of local people and visited the Music Hall, but his business had taken him to the USA and Canada as well, and to Balmoral on more than one occasion. He opened the Gaiety picture house with the aim, he said, of providing 'an intelligent dialogue for every picture I show.' He painted the walls there vermilion and the pilasters cream, and the sign he hung over the door had 200 lights in a host of colours. When the *Bioscope* came to call, it was struck by 'the dramatic, picturesque, and illuminative comments and descriptions' Mr Paterson supplied.

He was an innovator, and that was as true in his lecturing as in any other aspect of his business life. The Gaiety had been Aberdeen's first permanent picture house, although its proprietor was also happy to show films on the beach or in the poorhouse, and he changed them more frequently than his rivals did. And as the years went by, and Dove developed a style of presentation that was all his own, he decided to take on a collaborator.

Marie Pascoe was the person he chose for the role. She was more than ten years his junior, the daughter of a silk merchant, and a descendant of the man who made the flags say 'England Expects...' for Lord Nelson. She was a descendant of actors as well, and had been on the stage since she was fifteen, appearing in pantomimes, burlesques and musical comedy. Most recently, she had sung songs between films at the Electric Theatre in Leamington Spa. Dove gave her a four-week trial, and then a short-term contract. And then he made Marie his wife.

The style they developed together was even more innovative. It involved what the *Bioscope* called 'dialoguing to pictures,' which meant standing next to the screen and speaking the words mouthed by the actors in the film. Or speaking words the actors seemed to mouth. Or trying to imagine what the characters the actors were playing might really want to say. It required panache and concentration, and a good deal of preparation, and in the days before a new film was shown at the Gaiety, Dove and Marie would convene over the dining table, work out a suitable script, and then divide up the lines between themselves. On the Monday the week's performances were to begin, they would spend the afternoon in rehearsal, and then, in the evening, they would, as the *Bioscope* put it, 'deliver their parts "letter-perfect" to the public.' They did this at the Gaiety and then across the city at the Coliseum, and they received an enthusiastic response. 'Without doubt the people were waiting for this,' the *Bioscope* said, adding that it was 'often hard to say which attracts the crowds: the elocutionary efforts of Mr and Mrs Paterson, or the pictures.'

Such was Dove and Marie's devotion to their craft that if they could not speak to the pictures themselves, they engaged others to do so on their behalf. Mr and Mrs Len Delmar sometimes did the honours at the Gaiety, Miss Hilda Merrilees and Mr Philip Durham at the Coliseum. Elsewhere in Aberdeen, meanwhile, another couple was firmly ensconced.

Bert and Nellie Gates presided both at the Globe Picture Palace on Nelson Street and at the Star on nearby Park Street. This place, known to everyone as 'The Starrie', took its name from the large red glass sign that had hung over the door since it was the East End Mission Hall. There was a piano inside and a phonograph, and Bert and Nellie would go among the audience, spraying them with disinfectant every once in a while, and then they would go among them again just to be sure.

Like Dove and Marie, Mr and Mrs Gates loaned their own voices to the characters on the screen. And, standing in the half-light, they also added sound effects they had bought as a job lot for £5. 'You will actually hear the lions roar,' audiences were promised, when *Neath the Lion's Paw* was being shown at the Star. And that wasn't their only innovation. To go with the bird-whistles, the rumble of thunder and the footsteps on a gravel path, they added a peculiarly local seasoning to their performances, often delivering them in the Doric dialect of the region and peppering them with references to local people and events. That approach was audacious and unique, and it brought Bert and Nellie closer to the formidable, indefatigable *benshi* than anyone else in Britain would ever dare venture.

W Peet Leslie was also well known in Scotland, where he was a frequent visitor to Glasgow and Edinburgh. He was known in many other places as well, though, from Newcastle and Sunderland to Liverpool and Leeds, Hounslow, Portsmouth, Bath; at the Broadway, the Pump Room, the Synod Hall, and the Philharmonic Hall. War films were his speciality, but then he too started talking about the wonders of the deep, and he got a severe shaking when he tumbled off the stage. 'He will not want to repeat that acrobatic stunt at every performance,' the *Bioscope* deadpanned. Peet had found a hall of his own within weeks. The

Bohemia in Finchley had an orchestra, of course, and it offered whist drives on the one night of the week when the Ragtime banjo dancing came to a halt.

This was hard work, and Leslie Paget knew first-hand what demands it made. He too had travelled the highways and byways of Britain, as well as taking his Fagin and Micawber around South Africa. Discipline and self-denial were the thing. 'Talking continuously for two hours, twice daily for weeks at a time, is no mean undertaking,' he wrote. The lecturer should take care of himself and resist temptation. There must be 'no late nights, no over-eating and no over-smoking.' Dove Paterson, meanwhile, put it rather more succinctly. 'I have been a lifelong abstainer,' he said, 'and Lady Nicotine claims none of my affections.'

In some places, though, the warnings went unheeded.

When the *Bioscope* visited Oldham, it spoke favourably of Frank H Vernon, the incumbent at the Empire. 'Mr Vernon is a gentleman of commanding personality,' the journal said. But even though he had been there for only a few days, he would remain there for only a few days more. That was because of £11 that had gone missing from the pay box, and because Frank had been hauled up before the police court as a result. He blamed it all on alcohol, and before long, he had fetched up in Northampton, at a picture house that had the word 'Temperance' in its name.

It was £90 that had gone missing in Richard Lloyd Horner's case, and he could see no point contesting the charge. He had been the lecturer at the Lyceum in Leeds, and when he disappeared, he left behind a note saying, 'I have proved utterly unworthy of all the trust and confidence you placed in me.' Richard blamed it all on gambling, saying that he had lost £800 on the Derby alone. 'A respectable-looking man,' according to the *Yorkshire Evening Post*, he was sent to prison for three months.

He too had once been praised. 'To hear the story so succinctly explained as Mr Lloyd Horner can do it is indeed very helpful,' the *Bioscope* wrote, of his efforts at the Hippodrome in

Wakefield. That place was small and fragile, known to many as the 'Tin Tabernacle', but Richard had purchased it with borrowed money and his liabilities were soon twenty times his assets. He had experienced heart problems as well, and been forced to give up his talks, and he offered that as the reason the takings had fallen away. 'It rather implies that *you* were the attraction, and not the films,' the lawyer in the bankruptcy court said.

'Yes,' Richard replied. 'I believe I was.'

37

It wasn't just in Liverpool that *Jane Shore* received a special accompaniment. When that Barker epic was shown in North Shields, at the Albion cinema, there was some Schubert and Saint-Saëns to go with the Percy Fletcher. This dependable place had a façade that was as much bright white tiles as red brick, and its conductor now had an 'augmented' orchestra under his baton.

There had been an increase of late in the number of musicians clustering together at the front of picture houses – or at the back, up in the balcony, or behind a curtain, under a hail of paper balls – and that was something managers were keen to boast about.

In Cardiff, patrons of the Castle cinema were informed that 'our renowned orchestra has been largely augmented under the directorship of Monsieur Samentini, the famous cellist, known to every music lover in South Wales.' And up the road at the Cinematograph Theatre, posters announced that *The Battle of the Somme* would be shown with a 'grand augmented orchestra and effects' (and also with 'exclusive pictures of the Zeppelin disaster').

In the capital of England, meanwhile, the Italian film *Parsifal* was accompanied by a 'full Wagner orchestra' at the West End Cinema. There was ripe plasterwork inside this hall, which was tall and narrow and had the very first neon sign. 'West End', the sign thrummed, in letters glowing red and huge. In Brighton, the municipal orchestra had been engaged, with all its eighty members. And in Glasgow, a change was coming that warranted an announcement in the *Belfast Telegraph*:

In recognition of the wonderful growth of musical sentiment and the demand for better music, a new experiment, bold in conception and of far reaching importance, will be inaugurated at the Picture House on Monday, from 3 to 5pm and again in the evening – A grand symphony orchestra of 40 Performers, under the conductorship of Signor Enrico Cingarelli, will give a series of orchestral selections chosen from the works of the best-known composers.

The new maestro was a violinist, who the newspaper said performed with a 'sense of style and clear-cut cameo-like brilliance of detail.' 'The augmented orchestra will also play incidental music to the pictures,' it added, incidentally.

Fresh from *Parsifal*, the West End Cinema again employed an augmented orchestra for the showing of *Cabiria*, which was also Italian, and which some consider the very first film epic. The correspondent from the *Bioscope* reported that this ensemble 'played the specially arranged music in a most finished and artistic manner.' He was less happy about a showing elsewhere in London, which he said was 'accompanied by a lady who knew as much about the instrument she was presiding at as I know about manipulating a Zeppelin.' And he also took a dislike to the sound effects. 'When it came to a horse walking over some grass,' he wrote, 'there was enough clatter for five hundred millworkers going along a paved street in Lancashire with their clogs on.'

The orchestra led by Monsieur Louis Pingen in Redhill, which had once been described as 'Belgian', was now said to be 'augmented'. In Coatbridge, a pipe band had been added to the regular band. And at the Broadway Cinema in Hammersmith, the number of players had been increased to more than thirty, 'exclusive of the usual piano.' The desire for ever more augmentation had its limits, however, and in Wolverhampton, one manager was left frustrated by the attitude of the authorities. He had asked for permission to employ a full symphony orchestra, only to be informed that 'no brass instrument could be allowed in any picture theatre orchestra in that town.' So what, he asked, should he do? 'Why not send the symphony without the brass?' came the reply.

Given these developments, picture house managers, never bashful in their use of language, now became even less so. The Strand in Grimsby claimed to have 'the largest cinema orchestra in the district.' La Scala Photo Playhouse said it had the largest one in Aberdeen, to go with its crystal lamps, chintz, and piano that played itself. And, with the sound of *Parsifal* and *Cabiria* still ringing in its ripe plasterwork, the West End Cinema took to describing itself as 'The Acme of Comfort. The Best of Films Shown. The Finest Orchestra in London.' (It also described itself as 'Entirely British – in ownership and management,' after its proprietors were revealed to be German and the *Evening News* started calling for a boycott.)

There was a particularly fierce battle back in Cardiff, with the claims of rival picture houses seemingly impossible to reconcile. The Park Hall might have laid claim to the largest orchestra in the city, but the Cinematograph Theatre now said it had the largest one in Wales. And the Bohemian in Phibsborough acclaimed itself the acme in Ireland. There, where posters promised 'Good Music' as well as 'Refinement' and 'Clear, Steady Pictures', the orchestra led by Percy Carver might have as many as sixteen members, and could be relied upon to play right through every performance.

If the picture houses of north Dublin weren't always harmonious places, the Bohemian was perhaps the least harmonious of all. It had barely recovered from all the parping and tooting raised against *Sapho* when a man named Larkin rose to his feet during *A Modern Magdalen*. This was an American film starring Lionel Barrymore, in which a woman rejects her lover for someone wealthier, she dances a provocative dance and ends up seducing the man who tries to stop her, and a factory is burned to the ground by striking workers.

William Larkin was an inveterate protester, and a member of something calling itself the Dublin Vigilance Committee, which wished to have picture houses purified and films more rigorously censored. Campaigning to that end had gathered pace in recent weeks, with leading churchmen writing letters to newspapers and sending deputations to local councils. There had been demonstrations against Sunday performances and salacious posters. Actors had been chased from the stage in Limerick when they attempted to perform a revue at the Rink Palace theatre. And in Dublin, Mr Larkin himself had addressed a crowd of 20,000 outside the Mansion House.

It was the provocative dance that he took as his cue. After hissing through his teeth for a while, he shouted, 'Dirty Catholic Ireland!' at the top of his voice. The result was panic, a lot of girls screaming, and a stampede out of the sixpenny seats. As William was dragged from the auditorium by the manager, he attempted to address his supporters in the foyer. 'There is a woman prostituting herself on the screen in there,' he cried, and peace was only restored when the police arrived. In his defence, Larkin argued that what he did was lawful, because the woman's breasts had been bared, but the magistrate, who took the precaution of viewing the film for himself, disagreed. William was convicted, fined six shillings, and ordered to pay £5 in costs. 'I shall not pay,' he said, 'nor shall any of my friends.'

Discord, as we shall see, was general all over the kingdom once the lights had gone down and the projector started up.

In Ealing, the thick roof wasn't the only thing the Kinema boasted about. 'Our orchestra is making for itself an enviable reputation,' it said, 'and is attracting music lovers from all parts.'

A qualitative standard was often applied when it came to music. The Cinema de Luxe in Walsall claimed to have the 'finest orchestra in the Midlands,' while in Lincoln, there was another irreconcilable dispute. The Cinematograph Hall had the Lindum Orchestra – 'the city's finest pictures and orchestra!' – but the Grand claimed, 'the world's greatest pictures and the city's premier orchestra.' The conductor there made a point of saying that he would present the works of Eric Coates alongside those of Félicien David and Franz Lehár.

The Winter Gardens boasted it had 'the finest orchestra in Cheltenham,' and that honour was claimed in Coventry by the Globe, where Chief Constable Charsley made his presence known. The attraction there was 'Signor Avanzi, the wonderful Italian violinist, and his band of talented musicians.' 'We have the finest string band in Coventry,' the management announced. Before long, this was 'the full Globe Symphony Orchestra' and, notwithstanding what was said in Walsall, 'the finest orchestra in the Midlands.' And some managers went beyond the local, or even the regional. That was so in Cardiff and Dublin. In Newcastle, the Queen's Hall announced that it had 'undoubtedly the best cinema orchestra in England.' And in Liverpool, the Scala claimed for itself 'the finest cinema orchestra in the United Kingdom.'

38

Black

A night of storm

It's the Chinese girl: the same one as before –
Suzee bored.
She is in the same house: the one with the tracery.
She is holding a letter, which then appears on the screen –
'Under the circumstances, I shall be unable to turn up for at least a week. Hop Lee.'
He is her husband, from the tea house, and he seems to have left her to her own devices.
Suzee walks over to a cabinet standing nearby and opens a drawer.
She pulls out necklaces and money, and pushes it all down the front of her dress.

*

Here is the woman who posed in the flimsy gown, and she is sitting next to the man who was with her at the piano –
Viola and Lawton attend a rehearsal.
They are in a private box, during a performance of some kind, and they are facing each other across a table.
On the edge of the box there is a top hat, squashed flat.
And on stage, the backdrop is a night sky filled with stars.
The moon, done in cloth, is full and glorious, and it seems to light up the wispy clouds beneath.

There is also a riverbank and some palm trees, and two pyramids around which a crowd of people has gathered.

Many of the people are wearing fancy hats, and two of them are wafting large, leaf-shaped fans.

Viola and Lawton are looking at one another, not down towards the actors.

Their hands are so close they could touch, but there is the width of the stage between their eyes –

Viola discourages Lawton's advances.

On stage now, where the performance has come to an end and Viola and Lawton are standing among the actors.

She is wearing another flimsy gown, drawn in beneath the bust, with a thin shawl draped across her shoulders.

One arm is by her side, the other held out in front, its fingers only loosely curled – as if Viola has paused between beckoning and making a fist.

And when Lawson attempts to take hold of her arm, she pulls away and quickly leaves him trailing far behind.

*

Inside Lonsdale's studio, a great deal is familiar.

There are the old heads and bare bodies, the palette and brushes – and Lonsdale, standing at his easel, is wearing a loose velvet jacket over a shirt with a soft collar.

He has a dark cravat around his neck and tucked into his shirt, and there is the same white handkerchief in his cuff.

A young woman comes in –

Veronica poses for Lonsdale.

This woman is new.

Lonsdale takes her cloak, and it is plain that all she is wearing beneath is a leopard-skin.

Her arms are left bare, and much of her shoulders, too.

There are vines running around her body and legs, and

through her dark, tousled hair.

And the leopard-skin rides up on her thighs.

Lonsdale seats Veronica on a barrel and then begins to pose her.

He has her raise some grapes in her hand, and then he grasps the hand in his own.

Suddenly, Viola is standing in the doorway – and as she walks towards Lonsdale, he pulls away from Veronica.

She, however, seems utterly unconcerned, as she leans back on her right hand, her left hand on her hip.

The leopard-skin seems to have ridden even higher on her thighs, and the leaves of the vine cast a very curious shadow.

Her head is tilted back, her eyes half-closed, and her lips have formed a mocking smile.

Behind her is the cloak she was wearing, which either she or Lonsdale let fall to the floor.

Viola turns to Lonsdale –

'Darling, I don't like Veronica.'

*

Here is Suzee again, among several other Chinese girls in traditional costume.

There is an old woman there, too, with large hips, a headscarf, and a long chain across her huge bosom.

Suzee and the girls are reclining on wooden benches, and the old woman seems to be in charge of them.

She is talking to an elderly Chinese man –

Li Wung desires a wife.

He is wearing a small cap with an elaborate pattern.

The old woman goes up to the girls and beckons Suzee, and then she pulls her out of the room by the wrist.

Suzee is pushed towards Li Wung, and she sits down in front of him.

He holds out some banknotes, but Suzee seizes his hand and thrusts the notes back at him.

She takes some banknotes of her own from down the front of her dress and gives them to the old woman.

Then, she quickly leaves the room.

*

Veronica is posing for Lonsdale again.

He is standing at his easel, painting – but suddenly, he puts down his palette and brushes and goes over to her.

She is sitting on the barrel again, dressed in the same way, with the leopard-skin and the vines, and there is that same dark shadow at the top of her legs.

Veronica rises from the barrel and puts her arms around Lonsdale's neck.

Then, with his arm around her waist, he leads her out of the studio.

In another room, they are kissing passionately.

Viola appears in the studio, and, finding no trace of Lonsdale, goes up to the door through which he and Veronica passed.

Pulling aside the curtain, Viola sees the two of them, still kissing passionately.

In the studio again, Lonsdale and Viola are alone. She is angry and they are plainly quarrelling.

Veronica comes in, wearing outdoor clothes now.

As she leaves the studio, she tosses her head at Viola and sneers.

*

Viola is writing a letter.

And then a sitting-room appears that hasn't been shown before –

Viola visits Lawton's rooms.

She comes in.

There is a large table in the middle of the room.

On the table there is a revolver – just lying there – and Viola picks the revolver up, looks at it, weighs it in her hand, and twirls it about.

*

Now, it is Suzee who is writing a letter.

She brings the pen to her lips every now and again, as she tries to marshal her thoughts.

The letter done, she puts it in an envelope and writes out the address.

She is in a corridor now, holding the letter and hurrying towards a closed door.

There is an old man sitting nearby, and he starts to shake his head, but when Suzee pulls out some more money, the old man lets her through.

She is out on the street, looking around to make sure no one is watching, her dark eyes flicking from side to side.

Suzee is running down the street, and when she comes to a post box, she puts the letter inside.

*

When Viola appears again, it is in the same sitting-room as before.

She seems upset, but the gun is back on the table.

Lawton arrives, and, hearing him, Viola tries to find somewhere to hide.

She is right behind the door when he opens it – and as he comes in, she tries to rush past him.

He stands in her way, though, and pushes her back into the sitting-room.

Lawton shuts the door, then locks it, and he puts the key into his pocket.

He takes hold of Viola, his arms around hers.

Then, his arms are around her waist, and he pulls her towards him and tries to kiss her on the mouth.

There is a terrible tussle and the table is overturned.

The revolver drops onto the floor and Viola seizes it – and as Lawton lunges at her again, she puts the gun to her head and shouts –

'Don't touch me! Open that door or I will shoot myself!'

What can he do?

The door is opened. Lawton steps aside, and Viola passes through.

When she arrives at the studio, Lonsdale is inside, again looking sad, the clock showing three.

He sees her and they come together in a fierce embrace –

'Thank God you have come back.'

The hideous Black Night ends.

39

'Are you learned in mythology?'

'No, I am not.'

Walter Stott could see no point in lying. The Chief Constable's barrister had asked him what he thought Veronica, posing with the barrel and the grapes, was supposed to represent. 'Bacchus,' he had replied, 'or something of that sort.'

And now for the tights. 'Can you see they are tights on the film?'

'Yes.'

'That is, one hopes they are?'

'They are.' Mr Stott was adamant this time. 'You can see them.' He was willing to accept that Veronica made Viola jealous, and that she was kissed and embraced by Lonsdale. But beyond that, he simply would not go.

Hadn't someone complained about the leopard-skin and the vines, and said, 'It looks very black between the legs'?

'No.'

'Nothing of that kind?'

'No.'

'It would be a rather strong observation to make, would it not?'

'Yes.'

'It is a strong thing to say?'

'Yes.'

But back in Preston, Margaret Buck and Frederick Daggers had certainly made their views known on the subject of the leopard-skin and the vines and the curious shadow they cast. 'He poses her in what I consider to be a very disgusting position,' she said, 'with her bare legs wide apart.' 'She was sat in a high position and looks very indecent,' he said.

In Coventry, meanwhile, Chief Constable Charsley had been particularly exercised by the scene. 'It portrays the licentiousness of Lonsdale,' he said, 'and the ease with which he can turn from a woman he has wronged to toy with a woman of the Bacchante type.' (While Mr Charsley might have been learned in mythology, or more learned than Mr Stott at least, his cosmopolitanism had its limits: he referred to Suzee as 'the Japanese girl.')

Now, the barrister was pressing the point.

'Do not you think other people might object to it, if it were so? Just think. Here is a representation of a woman whom apparently this hero – who kisses everybody he meets – kisses and embraces. She is brought upon the film with her legs looking very black between them, and he cannot see the object of it. Now I want to ask you, is not that a thing which other people besides funny people might object to and properly object?'

'No one with a clean mind could object to it. A clean, healthy mind would never think of anything wrong with it.'

'Why not? There it is shown straight before you?'

He had produced a photograph from somewhere.

'Unpleasant, is it not?'

'No.'

'Suggestive?'

'No. It is a representation of a picture that is hung in the public art gallery for anyone to see.'

If not her clothing, might the woman's behaviour cause offence? 'I suppose there is no doubt that Veronica was a wanton, or intended to be displayed as a wanton?'

'Not necessarily.'

'What do you understand by a wanton?'

This was taking a worrying turn. 'Well, shall we say a loose woman? Is that what you mean?'

'I am asking you what you understand by it. Is Veronica there represented at all as a loose woman?'

'No.'

'You do not think so?'

'No.'

'Did she behave, in your mind, as a wanton might?'

'No.'

'Do you think a clean-minded man could regard the behaviour of Veronica in that studio as the behaviour of a wanton or loose woman to a decent man?'

'Just repeat that.'

'Do you think a clean-minded man could regard the behaviour of Veronica in that studio as the behaviour of a wanton or loose woman to a decent man?'

'That's rather a long sentence, is it not?'

40

Mary will have found the journey to Sitka much more congenial than her crossing of the Pacific. With her new husband by her side, she will have left the port of Victoria aboard a comfortable steamer, heading northwards through the famed Inside Passage. This long string of channels, sounds, reaches and straits will have taken them all the way to their destination, while keeping them close to shore and sheltered by an archipelago of 1,000 islands. Over the several days of the voyage, they will have had revealed to them humpback whales and dolphins, fin whales, porpoises, salmon sharks, and the sea otters whose fur was what first brought Russians here. While some among their fellow passengers might have been merchants, teachers or bureaucrats, others will have been adventurers attracted by the prospect of Klondike gold.

The great dark birds will have been the first intimation of the harbour, as they swooped in, only to wheel away at the last moment. The huge, flat mountain will have come into view, and other mountains with backs sharp as saws. She might have thought the boats were coming out to greet her, as she stood expectantly in the prow – the cedar canoes and sealers; the vessels much like her own trailing smoke; the 'trollers' and 'seiners' that went in search of fish. The long docks might have seemed to totter on their tree trunk legs, as the sawmills and pulp mills lurked beyond. She will have spied the Orthodox cathedral and the Imperial Redoubt, the mission school, and the Tlingit village. And she will not have been able to ignore the rows and rows of herring eggs strung out on hemlock branches to dry.

The old pier will have been teeming as Mary and Ah Bong disembarked. The arrival of a steamer was a festive occasion, and countless people will have come out from their houses made of planks. Bonnets and caps and parasols will have bobbed up and down in the throng, perhaps seeming to keep time with the mission school cornet band as it went parping and tooting along.

She will have made her way through this, up the hill between buildings with steep roofs and rough dormers, along walkways that were just boards suspended over the dark, damp earth. The town will have presented to her its post office and cable office, its firehouse and jail, its higgledy-piggledy piles of lumber. And like many a visitor, she might have paused outside the old Russian trading house, with its log walls and its roof all lolling and wry.

The streets of the place had illustrious names – Lincoln and Seward, Maksoutoff, Peschouroff, Kostrometinoff – and they too will have been thronged. Mary will have seen malamutes stepping nimbly in and out; berry-sellers crouching in doorways, their faces lost inside patterned shawls; sellers of all kinds, in fact, their wares laid out before them: furs and carved things, silver things, baskets, moccasins. She will have walked past the Millmore Hotel and the Baranoff Hotel as she made her way towards her new home; past a photographer's shop and a reading room, a billiard hall, and a bowling alley.

Once they were settled in Alaska, Mary bore Ah Bong two daughters, whom she named Katherine and Annie. She looked after them, and him, and helped run the bakery and restaurant as well. She also worked in the Sitka Steam Laundry, which was another of his businesses. It stood between Peschouroff and the old flume, belching away on a rough track near a bend in the river.

Mary made friends with fishermen, loggers and miners, and with the Tlingit who came in for sourdough bread and custard tart. She picked up the Indians' complex, guttural language and was soon speaking it as freely as she spoke English. She was patient and steady, and – there being no doctor around – the women often asked her to deliver their babies, teaching her how to make jewellery in return.

Mary lost the bakery and the laundry when Ah Bong died, and her fortunes shifted this way and that. She went back to working as a maid, and earned enough to pay off her debts, but then Katherine too died, back in Victoria, after a last anguished visit from her mother. Mary was married to a merchant for a little while, but she divorced him so she could wed his friend, a much less wealthy man named Fred Johnson. He was a Finn, or maybe a Swede; almost certainly a relic of those Lutherans. He and Mary would stay together for more than thirty years.

Here is another photograph. It shows Mary standing in front of some trees, one arm by her side, the other bent behind her back. She is older now, nearing thirty maybe, and fuller in the face. Her hair, still dark, has been gathered up into a pompadour, though a few wayward strands still play around her cheek. She is in a copse, or at the edge of a farmer's field, where some attempt has been made to clear the ground. The photograph is different from the earlier one: not formal or stylised, not official in any way.

The dress Mary is wearing this time is Western and modern, and so long that it sweeps the stubble under her feet. The white bodice has a frill around the edge, and a high collar that touches her jaw. The waist is cinched, with a little bow in front, and the skirts are dark. The arms are tight-fitting, also dark, and ruched at the elbows. But there is another white frill at Mary's wrist, with the hand beneath unclenched and the fingers quite relaxed.

She is not wearing a topcoat, nor a hat or scarf, so the weather must be fine. The trees are full of life. Most are saplings, their leaves made pale by the sunlight, but one of them is taller and more rounded than the rest. Neither has Mary felt the need to be shown doing something that might hint at her usefulness.

She is simply looking out of the photograph, her head slightly inclined. She is looking *straight* out of the photograph, in fact, engaging the viewer directly. Her brows are evident now, and maybe they are drawn together. But her gaze remains level, her mouth straight. Although the dress is long, Mary can be seen to be standing with her feet well apart. She will always be steady.

41

The trial for which Walter Stott, Fred White and James Watson had been waiting since before Halloween began the day after Valentine's Day, the venue for it the old Assize Court in Strangeways, hard by the prison. Both buildings had been designed by the same hand, put up together as well, and each favoured the Venetian Gothic style sometimes named for John Ruskin, its boldest advocate.

The court stood taller than any other building in Manchester. It was made from granite, brick and terracotta, pale orange Derbyshire stone and the blue-green stone of the Forest of Dean. The roof was steep, with horizontal stripes, and the broad floors were laid with tiles the colour of chocolate and cream. Numberless steps ascended through a huge porch. The façade was busy with lancet arches, tracery and finials. And a rose window glowed red and blue from the massive gable, above the place where the carriages all pulled in.

Opinion about the edifice had been favourable. Gladstone called it beautiful. *The Times* said it made for the best law courts in the world. And Ruskin himself praised what he said was, 'a very noble building indeed, and much beyond anything yet done in England on my principles.'

The stones of the Assize Court were especially notable: carvings of acanthus leaves and vines, gargoyles and heraldic animals; the Judgment of Solomon and the Murder of the Innocents. There were statues of great lawgivers across the front, with a wild Moses ninety feet above the ground. And the theme was continued in the entrance hall, where punishments through the ages were depicted – the pillory, stocks and guillotine, the breaking wheel, and the laying on of weights – each in its time ordained by the very letter of the law. One carving was of a bound, recumbent figure being forced into a terrible act of swallowing. *Torture by Pouring Water Down Ye Throat*, the legend read.

There seemed no limit to the money spent or the care taken. Polished wood and gleaming brass were everywhere, noticeboards abounded with Latin words, and the fabrics were the plushest of the plush. Discrete entrances and chambers had been provided for judge, juror, barrister, witness, defendant, plaintiff. There were clerks' offices, dining rooms and a library, and discrete entrances, too, for members of the public, the more respectable of whom were diligently separated from the less. At the back of the building, the lofty, vaulted courtroom rose from a broad central well. It could hold 800 people and had ten doors, two of which led to a special gallery set aside for ladies.

If the picture houses that surrounded the Assize Court couldn't hope to compete with its grandeur, their sheer number, at least, made sure they stood out. They were everywhere in the city and neighbouring Salford; more numerous there than anywhere outside the capital. In Strangeways and Cheetham Hill, and just across the River Irwell, picturegoers would find the Shakespeare and the Globe, the Electric Theatre (a one-time rink) and the Empire Electric. They would find the Salford Cinema, which had been a Presbyterian church but now boasted swags, a balustrade, and its own name in tiles on the half-moon pediment. And they would find the Central Hall and the Market Street Picture House, the Cosy Corner, the Victoria, the Temple, the Tower.

The Hightown Picture Pavilion belonged in this group only because of its location, for it had until recently been the Pankhurst Memorial Hall and a very august place. Named for Richard Pankhurst, the free thinker and proponent of women's suffrage, it provided a home for the Independent Labour Party he had helped found. The hall was built with funds raised by Richard's widow, Emmeline, and decorated after the Arts and Crafts style by the couple's young daughter, Sylvia. She had studied at the Royal College of Art and, like Ruskin before her, been captivated by shimmering, ancient Venice. When she came back to Salford, Sylvia Pankhurst set about filling her father's hall with elegant murals of lilies, doves, bees, butterflies, corn, roses, sunflowers, apple trees, lunaria.

More typical of the cinemas of Manchester was the Premier Picture Hall on Cheetham Hill Road. It stood less than a mile from Hightown, right next to the Temperance Billiard Hall, and was the place where *Five Nights* had been shown before almost anywhere else.

The craze for Temperance Billiard Halls came in with the new century. It owed something to a desire for novelty, of course; but it owed just as much to an improving impulse that will have been very familiar. Men were felt to need somewhere to amuse themselves away from alcohol and other temptations of the street, and for a while, the cause and the pastime seemed ideally combined. The pubs might grumble and the police dissemble, but the halls were packed and their proprietors were announcing dividends galore.

They sprang up all over, from Heaton Park to Chorlton-cum-Hardy, Irlam to Ardwick Green. The one in Eccles was near to William Broadhead's Crown theatre, and there were also halls in Wigan, Bury, Altrincham, Sale. It was a shilling an hour, maybe sixpence before six, and the Lads' Mission in Harpurhey had had an anxious year. The picture houses might be everywhere and cheap, but it was the Temperance Billiard Hall that was drawing the older ones away.

The halls sprang up in Liverpool and Birkenhead as well, and in the main towns of Lancashire, Yorkshire and the

Midlands. And they sprang up in the capital, from Walthamstow westwards: Fulham, Hammersmith, Putney, Richmond, Twickenham, Kingston. The one in Chelsea, opposite the King's Picture Playhouse, was built by a Mr Barley.

But while the halls might have shared the proportions of many of the picture houses, they were less variegated in appearance. There was usually a hint of the Arts and Crafts here, in the form of rounded roofs and gables, and gently swelling bays. There were dormers, ox-eye windows, and cupolas like half a child's top. The tiles and stained glass were green and red, with motifs of birds, insects and flowers, and any walls that weren't tiled were invariably covered in terracotta or white stucco. Inside, there were gas lamps in rows, depending from metal trusses that held up the roof, glowing soberly through coloured shades, and bestowing discrete cones of light that illuminated little, in truth, but the tables beneath.

Men could be found perching over these pools of green baize, like drab kingfishers; raising their heads every so often to banter with comrades or sip from a glass of sarsaparilla or ginger beer. In the gloom along the walls there were scoreboards, racks for cues, and benches of worn leather. And if women were to be found, it was only early on. 'At night,' the *Manchester Evening News* reported, 'when the rooms are crowded with men, no woman apparently cares to venture into such unaccustomed scenes.' Each hall absorbed something of the place in which it stood. On a visit to one in Bolton, the correspondent from the *Yorkshire Evening Post* found it not only packed, but also clamorous. 'As everybody wore clogs,' he wrote, 'the noise around the tables was likely to upset the nerves of a professional player.'

Then, just like the one for rinking, the craze for Temperance billiards was over. The hall at Highbury Corner began showing films, as did the one in Openshaw. The one in Salford became the Temperance Picture Theatre, and then dropped the word

'Temperance' altogether. And when the Imperial wanted to become a picture house, the owner's lawyer found himself in front of the bench. 'In certain districts,' he explained, 'it has been found that working men do not care for billiards.' 'This is the first time I have heard of billiards going to pot,' the chairman replied.

42

In the months before the trial, between the dog days of summer and the first crocuses of spring, there had been more melodramas, and more films too on the subject of the war. *Somewhere in France* showed a soldier pretending to be a priest in order to rescue his own wife. *Remember Belgium* and *An English Girl's Honour* played upon familiar fears. And when it came to *A Belgian Girl's Honour*, readers of the *Bioscope* were advised that 'the actual Belgian shown in the film appears on the stage and sings a song.' *Nurse and Martyr* was about Edith Cavell, who had recently been put to death. *The Angels of Mons* retold a popular myth. And during showings of *You*, a note asking, 'What are you doing for your country?' was passed through the audience from hand to hand.

Ragtime and the Tango couldn't help but seem trivial against all this, and with Oskár Rausch bankrupt and interned, the dancing films came to an end. Audiences could still see adaptations of the classics, however, and more films about anarchists, costermongers, boxers, and tramps. There was *Charlie on the Brain*, 'a sparkling little comedy giving an example of the dire results of a too fervent worship of Charlie Chaplin.' But those who saw *Charlie Chaplin Special Constable* will have quickly discovered that it doesn't feature the great man at all, just another man merely masquerading as him.

This was the moment the Bamforth company chose to put out its first feature film. *Paula* has a beautiful heroine, who is learned in Latin and Greek, and accomplished as both a dancer and a playwright. She falls in love with a critic, only to leave him for a man who promises to produce her work on the stage.

Although the producer is a cruel man, who beats Paula savagely, he soon drops dead and she is free to return to the critic. He, it turns out, is seriously ill, but it is with Paula's death that the film ends, after she has followed her lover to Italy and donated the blood that will save his life. This film, too, was based upon a novel by Victoria Cross, even if its director was more used to working with Winky. He and the company would next collaborate on *Zeppelins of London*.

There had been a swift return to picture house screens for Eve Balfour. In *The Woman Who Did* – her only other film for Will Barker – she is a suffragette who rejects marriage to live openly with her lover, at least until he dies of typhus, again during a trip to Italy. The lover is played by Thomas H MacDonald, who had previously been Lonsdale to Ms Balfour's Viola, and when the film was shown in Stockton-on-Tees, a poster there billed her as 'Of *Five Nights* fame.'

Nor had the Chief Constable of Preston been idle during those months. He had taken part in the usual court business, of course, pitting himself against alleged prostitutes and deserters. He had prosecuted a ten-year-old boy, a man with no arms who played an organ in the street to make a living, and two men charged with attempting to commit suicide, who were discharged by the magistrates after they promised not to do it again. And, as he became familiar with everything his new role entailed, James Watson had found himself commending men who had hauled others from the chilly River Ribble. He had presided over the annual treat for the children of the poor, banned fireworks on Guy Fawkes Night, and issued a warning about women who pretended to tell fortunes. And he had been pleased to report a fall in both in larceny and the number of registered aliens.

Casting a weather eye to the south and east, Mr Watson had also asked that the chimes of the Town Hall clock be silenced after six o'clock. And it was in that direction that the thoughts of a famous author now strayed as well.

Victoria Cross had recently been quoted in the *Preston Herald* on the subject of the *Five Nights* film, and she returned the favour by sending the newspaper a poem of hers, entitled *Song of the Zeppelins* –

We come and go as we please,
    Free as the birds of the air;
We rain down death upon England,
    But what do the English care?
They don't seem to wish to hurt us,
    So why should we hurry away?
And the night is fast approaching
    When we come to England to stay.

Given the claim Walter Stott and Fred White had made, and the fact that they sought damages in respect of their loss, a jury would have to be impanelled to hear the case. Every member of the jury would have to be a man, in fact, and that would be impossible to miss, while the judge would be Mr Justice Shearman.

The son of a solicitor, and the recipient of a 'double-first' degree from Oxford University, Montague Shearman had practised as a barrister for many years. And though he became 'Sir Montague' when he was elevated to the High Court bench, his intimates never stopped calling him 'Tont'. He was a keen sportsman, who had run the 100 yards in barely ten seconds, gained a 'blue' at rugby, and helped found the Amateur Athletics Association. For a while, he was a member of the Wanderers, the club that won the inaugural FA Cup, and he would write the first proper history of the game of football. Tont Shearman was also a High Churchman and a stern moralist, who had been heard to complain that gentleman athletes from the South of England were being eclipsed by working class athletes from the North.

It was ten o'clock on a cold, wet morning when the judge

and jury took up their appointed places, on oak benches beneath a public gallery that was already well filled. *Five Nights* had become a true *cause célèbre*, its ins and outs tossed this way and that in picture houses, council chambers and Temperance Billiard Halls, and the many doors of the Assize Court will have been forever opening and closing.

The Mayor of Preston was there, of course, sitting in the gallery with the Town Clerk by his side. And Billy Boyle, the manager of the King's Palace, had come along as well, even if his employer, William Broadhead, was present only in the person of an emissary from his headquarters across Manchester. The city's Chief Constable, meanwhile, could also be seen on the oak benches, seated among sundry councillors and clergymen, and among what the *Preston Herald* described as 'numerous theatrical celebrities.'

43

There had also, in that period, been films about –

Kidnap, smugglers, borrowed babies, secret earls, silly old flirts, bull-fights, masques, dancers, masked dancers, bohemians, houseboats, duels, beggars, wastrels, asylums, mad-doctors, mad doctors, children's prayers, lustful landlords, wards, apprentices, lockets, garrets, blind fiddlers, fat schoolboys, ruffians, tiaras, donkeys, wooden horses, garden parties, adopted children, pinpricks, ice creams, barrels of beer, usurers, mystics, dummies, gamblers, rapist launderers, jail-breakers, hypnotists, governesses, secret drinkers, widows, sharpshooters, gallows, touts, ants, wizards, blind men, dumb men, dumb waiters, disguises, buskers, seducers, squires, bastards, bequests, crooked lawyers, rightful heirs, clandestine marriages.

Underground passages, mothers-in-law, mummified hands, munitions, parrots, gamekeepers, bosuns, outposts, magic charms, sprites, attachés, models, brigands, foundries, bankrupts, jockeys, simpletons, sleeping draughts, penitents, archaeologists, eyeglasses, beaus, housekeepers, rebels, nobles, opera stars, bailiffs, countesses, baby shows, violinists, mistresses, meerschaum pipes, striped stockings, milliners, majors, commissionaires, lecturers, looms, publicans, handprints, travelling players, cobblers, minions, mansions, racehorses, shepherdesses, shepherds, valets, sculptors, balls, fancy dress, escaped apes, merchants, poultrymen, grocers, bachelors, piebalds, reunions, Ottomans, henpecks, necklaces, kleptomaniacs, mobs, half-brothers, barmaids, clumsy maids, amnesiacs, card-games, cardsharps, real cards, cards, cads, charlatans.

Shrews, typists, musicians, modistes, playwrights, blacksmiths, woodsmen, villagers, village idiots, occultists, monks, wild oats, gorgonzola, errors, frogs, sharps, flats, singing dogs, ballet dancers, inventors, prehistoric monsters, bullies, bargees, poison gas, conjurers, boarders, clerics, rich uncles, ghosts, slaveys, blackened faces, blackface, clerks, counterfeiters, novelists, death beds, mechanical geese, doves of peace, gems, bluffs, barges, rivals, dilemmas, death stimulants, boarding houses, seducers, sweated labour, swindlers, burning barns, bonfires, chauffeurs, bus drivers, bookmakers, daytrips, poachers, acrobats, clowns, priests, shipwrecks, professors, butlers, extortionists, magic globes, triplets, bounties, cowboys, coquettes, persistent counts.

Bad eggs, tumblers, cabbies, fisher-girls, surgeons, inheritances, hags, coconuts, elopers, escaped lunatics, bank robbers, runs on banks, bankers, the depths of despair, childhood sweethearts, bloomers, jungles, nightmares, good turns, scapegraces, long-lost husbands, toadstools, rakes, amnesiacs, shopwalkers, poachers, night birds, socialites, socialists, seamstresses, motorists, cripples, viziers, warrior-kings, Shulamites, slips, slops, codfish, aloes, vultures, hansom cabs, vagabonds, wraiths, witches, tough nuts, phantoms, monocles, knuts, quicksand, scorpions, octopuses, wagers, ingrates, freaks, jokes, mokes, altars and Heba the Snake Woman.

44

'I choose to go down for five days.'

It was either that or pay a fine of ten shillings, not to mention costs, and the man in the dock was in no mood for compromise. 'I want to rouse the people of Preston to this matter,' he said: 'That the town should purify itself is my fervent wish.' A brief pause for reflection, then: 'When shall I require to be taken?'

'You won't be allowed to leave the court.'

'Ah, well! This is a quiet week. Perhaps I can afford the time better now than later on.

In front of magistrates of the town, with sundry aldermen, councillors, medics, and ministers of religion looking on, John Rigg had been found guilty of defacing posters put up on hoardings near his home. He would soon be making a trip to Manchester, to sit on the oak benches beneath the hammer beam roof. For now, though, he was himself at the centre of things. And neither that nor his considerable phlegm should come as a surprise: Dr Rigg did not shrink from attention, and this reverse was as nothing compared to others he had had to endure.

A devout Christian, as well as a physician, he had spent a decade as a medical missionary in China, ministering to both the souls and the bodies of the people of Kien-Ning, in the country's far south-east. He would later produce a memoir of that time, in which he described a place shut in by saw-backed mountains covered in forests of bamboo and pine, and in soil the colour of chocolate.

The place stood at the confluence of fast rivers, amid tea fields, rice fields, and vegetable gardens. It had ancient, dun-coloured walls thirty feet in height. Fleets of little boats crowded its gates, knocking into each other on the swell. And pigs and dogs were everywhere, sniffing cautiously at the earth and the air. The people of the place, in his rendering, were slight, swarthy, lithe and active, subtle-minded, suspicious and proud. They were courteous to guests but intolerant of settlers, and they could not be shaken from the belief that what the missionaries most wanted was to rob them of their eyes.

John Rigg nearly came to grief soon after he arrived in China, when a mob of locals hurled him into a pit of manure. But that wasn't the only baleful surprise the country had in store for him. His young daughter, Agnes, died there, and he would describe his final departure as 'forced'. He returned to England during the Boxer Rebellion, and a popular film of the time depicts something of the fear and confusion he will surely have known. Entitled *Attack on a China Mission*, it shows sailors coming to the rescue of a woman whose husband, another missionary, has been murdered by the rebels. The film has a large cast, at least by the standards of the day. It features gunfire and impressive explosions. But it was made in Hove, in the grounds of a large, old house, and its first public airing was in the Town Hall there one Saturday night. Four minutes was all it took for the film to be shown, and when it was over, the audience demanded that it be shown again.

The preoccupations of John Rigg were well known in Preston by now. He had written numerous letters to the local newspaper, complaining about all manner of things. He didn't think much of the town's trams, for a start: they had clanked past his house since the days when they were pulled by horses, and he argued that little had changed for the better in the decade since they were electrified. In one missive, Dr Rigg called the conductors of the trams 'a slow lot of ten-thumbed individuals' and said they were not of the right quality. In another, he called for Preston's streetlamps to be switched off at night, to guard against an attack from the air. And he also made a foray against the town's old soldiers.

When it became clear that the war would not be ending any time soon, those men had asked to be issued with uniforms and maybe a rifle or two. They had seen service across the Empire – at Klerksdorp, the siege of Kimberley, Magersfontein, Oliphant's Neck – and they were keen to do their duty once again. They were too old to actually fight, of course, and that was the point the doctor hammered home. The veterans should be realistic, he announced, during a meeting of the Preston council, and they certainly shouldn't deceive themselves 'that they are doing as well as if they went to the Front.' This was too much, and the *Preston Herald* decided that its own duty was to respond. 'May we remind Dr Rigg,' it wrote, 'that his hazy generalisation might easily be turned against himself.'

> We might argue that he, as a member of his profession who has seen foreign service, is not serving his country so well at home as he would be if caring for the stricken on the continent.

He had been going on about the war a lot, in truth, and he did so again at a large gathering of missionaries in the spring. 'We are met at a fateful time,' he told them:

> England's stout heart is not quite staggered, but we are depressed and anxious, and we know we must suffer...
>
> I believe, and quite honestly so, that the motive of the war is a motive of righteousness. The air has been cleared by war. Some of you have been apprehensive of the national life and you almost thank God for the war, which has come as a strong breeze to sweep these things away.
>
> And I hope that we will come out of the war a chastened, purified nation, better fitted to carry on the work that God has given to England to do in the world.

Most of all, though, John Rigg had complained about the posters he said he was forced to look at as he made his way up the hill into the middle of the town. There was a certain hypocrisy in this, of course, as the *Preston Herald* was again not slow to point out, for the council owned the hoardings on which the posters were displayed and Dr Rigg was one of its more venerable members. In this case, several particularly gaudy examples had been stuck up, one of them for a film whose contents had made it notorious.

'Practically the whole of the figure was torn out,' the witness said, still seeming surprised by what he had seen. The man was the council's billposter, and this wasn't the only damage that had been done. 'The upper part of the figure, the dress, was removed, but the leg was left.' In his opinion, something sharp – a 'clean instrument' – had been used, and it 'had gone right through four or five layers of bills to the bare boards.'

At first, John Rigg had taken an assertive line. He had even objected to the prosecutor, for George Oakey was not only an alderman of the town; he was also in charge of the committee responsible for the sticking-up of posters, and that surely made for a conflict of interest. Mr Oakey, however, said he was present today as an advocate 'pure and simple', and that proved sufficient for the bench. Invited to enter a plea, Dr Rigg replied, 'No one knows I did it but myself, and I admit the offence.' Then, he changed his mind. 'Not guilty,' he announced, before changing his mind again. 'Of course I damaged the pictures,' he said.

Mr Oakey said the defendant had a right to his opinion, but opinions differed, and while some people might consider a thing indecent, others might not.

These posters were put up all over the country, in cathedral cities and large towns… and up to the present, so far as I am aware, there has been no objection taken to them, and they have been allowed to be on the walls unmolested.

When the time came for him to speak, Dr Rigg did not offer an apology. If the damage was done by him, he said, he was entitled to do it, because of his service to the council. It was, in any case, the posters themselves that were to blame. They were 'provocative of disease, by illustrations calculated to create sensual desire,' and that would surely 'lead to disease in a way only a doctor can realise.' His theme, as he warmed to it, turned out once again to be an antiseptic one:

If a person sees a garment infected with scarlet fever, and destroys it by throwing it into the river, he cannot be held liable for damage. So, if a person sees anyone exposing himself, and in an attempt to cover up the indecent exhibition spoils any clothing, there will be no claim for damages.

I think the magistrates of Preston, as well as the town council and everyone connected with the government of the town, wants a pure, class town, free from disease, and, just in the same way as one is justified in destroying the garment containing infection, so there was justification for destroying these pictures, and the person who did destroy them does not deserve to be put into the dock as a criminal, but deserves the thanks of the community.

There was murmuring in court – 'Hear! Hear!' – and it quickly turned into a commotion. As John Rigg was about to be taken down the steps to the cells, his supporters closed around him. There were arms and legs, hands and feet everywhere, pushing and pulling and prodding and jostling.

'I will pay his fine!'

'You will do no such thing!'

Some coins were pushed across the desk of the magistrates' clerk.

'Dr Rigg, you are free to go.'

45

This time, the *Preston Herald* was on his side. 'Dr Rigg has made a spirited protest against what he considered to be objectionable posters on public hoardings,' it said:

> The doctor was obviously actuated by the best of motives: the purifying and cleansing of our public life. His action was to protest in the most explicit manner against what he deemed to be unseemly posters. No one will doubt his sincerity, and no one will accuse him of wanton destruction of other people's property out of mere caprice. He saw a poster which offended his taste, and he was anxious that the objectionable thing should not be infectious or offend other eyes.
>
> In doing this he took the law into his own hands, which no one is allowed to do. Out of the case, however, there is certain to arise questions as to the attitude of the council towards flaring, suggestive and indecent posters.
>
> One of the posters presented by the court, and which we can quite understand was provocative of moral resentment in men of Dr Rigg's temperament, represented a girl in the nude... It is cleverly drawn, but it is also a trifle suggestive, and it is regrettable that councillors should have sanctioned its publication on the hoardings.
>
> We must insist on the public hoardings being kept clean, and free from ugly, suggestive posters. In future, greater supervision is required. That is the moral to be derived from Dr Rigg's prosecution.

And the Church was on his side as well. Before long, the clergy of Preston issued a statement, protesting about his treatment. At a public meeting held on church premises, he was hailed 'the champion of cleanliness and purity in the town. (Applause.)' Then, the meeting passed another, similar resolution. The posters were 'an outrage to Christian decency,' the resolution said, and 'in the name of purity and morality,' the council should take a lot more care in its supervision of the hoardings.

When Dr Rigg took the floor himself, it was clear that he had been mellowed not one jot by his experience in court:

For months past there has been a number of placards which have been very undesirable from every point of view. (Hear, hear.)

When the statement was made in the court that these things had been put up in many cathedral cities, I was very sorry to hear it, and I wrote to the Bishop of Manchester, who replied – 'I am interested to know you have been interesting yourself in the matter of these abominable kinema shows. We have also been doing this work in Manchester, with the result that five of our clergy are summoned for libel. So, whatever is said of cathedral towns, it cannot be said that Manchester is indifferent.'

As a member of the health committee, I feel it is no use being an educationist and sanitarian unless one looks at the moral as well as the physical side. Whatever springs out of impure thought must be hurtful to the community.

I am perfectly surprised at the way women allow their sex to be degraded. There have been all sorts of pictures degrading and animalising the sex, and I think the women of England should have risen long ago against it. Women ought not to allow that sort of thing, which is all over England, and all over the world. They should tear them down and tear the hair of the men who put them up. (Applause.)

In the same week, Preston councillors were told that the controversy had proved all too much for the town's billposter – he had handed in his bucket, brush, and ladder after nearly forty years in the job. The councillors were dismayed by this news, and George Oakey's committee, and his stewardship of it, were soon called into question. 'An apology is due to the public for this,' the Mayor announced:

That objectionable posters should be posted all over the town is an affront to the general public which they have a right to resent and to be protected from, not only on their own account, but on behalf of their children.

Nor did Dr Rigg hold back. With memories of their recent tussle before the magistrates doubtless still fresh in his memory, he declared that Mr Oakey had neglected his duty. There was consternation in the room, before the Alderman struck back. 'If you are going to carry this thing to its logical conclusion,' he shouted – and here he was pointing out of the window, in the direction of the Free Library:

… you have only to go and look at the pediment there. The figure there might be considered indecent, and there are things inside that might be considered indecent. But they are exhibited there for anyone to go and look at. Why not take a ladder and knock that pediment down?

Mr Oakey did not, though, mention the King's Palace and the classical scene on the panel above the screen on which *Five Nights* had, however briefly, been shown.

On Christmas Eve, the *Preston Herald* reflected upon the whole business. John Rigg, it said:

> ... might fairly claim to have gained his point. His protest was not made in vain, and in his endeavour to keep our hoardings pure and free from offensive vulgarity he has gained more than in his more sanguine moments he could even have anticipated.

This was a reference to a new and surprising development.

Following the council meeting and his *contretemps* with the good doctor, responsibility for Preston's billboards had been taken away from Mr Oakey and his committee. It was not a comfortable responsibility, the newspaper acknowledged, because so much depended upon individual taste: 'A feature that will please one, and satisfy the most puritanical scruples, would seem tame, inartistic and possibly vulgar to another,' and yet, 'the happy medium, deemed to be the best possible policy, if designed to please everybody, might result in pleasing nobody.' It was 'a task well-nigh impossible,' in fact. And then, turning to the person to whom the task had now been entrusted:

> Mr Watson has an unenviable job.

46

The recent raids had been the most distressing so far. Although Zeppelins hadn't yet reached the streets for which Dr Rigg was so concerned, they were a familiar sight over East Anglia, the North East, and the Home Counties. Hatfield had been hit, Hertford too. Bombs had fallen on Tunbridge Wells. And the ones that landed on East Croydon killed three young brothers in Beech House Road.

This too was reflected in the Bamforth company's postcards. One of them shows a schoolboy with plump, red cheeks pointing to a high wall over which a long, long nose can be seen to protrude. 'By gum!' the boy exclaims. 'It gave me a start – I thought it was a Zeppelin.' And the films kept coming as well. *Britons Awake!* promised a 'stirring drama depicting love and war, showing Zeppelin raids,' while in *Too Much Sausage*, a man dreams that his evening meal has been transformed into an airship and sailed off into the sky. The man follows the airship from down on the ground, chasing it backwards and forwards, hither and yon, and he fires off a few shots in its general direction. But then a bomb drops and the man is blown to bits.

The natural response was to try to make the best of it all. 'England Undismayed by Terrorists of the Air,' said the *Daily Sketch*, while the manager of a picture house in Hull said the fuss was 'a blessing in disguise.' In North Shields, meanwhile, the Albion put itself forward as 'An Antidote for the Zeppelin Raid.' 'Who would stay at home when it is said by regular patrons of the BOS Cinema that the class of picture shown dispels all thoughts of Zeppelins?' they asked in Todmorden, of a hall that had been named for its proprietors – Messrs Batty, Ogden and Spencer

– but which stood in a town that had not yet experienced an attack. And the *Daily Sketch* was keen to demonstrate that it was itself undismayed. 'The Zep Raid Over England,' ran a headline on the front page. 'More Vivid Air Raid Pictures (See Pages 8, 9 & 16).'

Real damage had, however, been done at Cramlington and Wallsend, even though the culprit had come under fire from soldiers of the First Northern Cyclist Battalion. Haystacks had been burnt in fires started by Zeppelin bombs, new craters formed in the land, and a cottage left broken-backed. And all of it had been recorded by an enterprising cameraman, who then showed his film across the region, using a map and pointer to demonstrate the precise route the interloper had taken. (Blyth, Cambois, West Sleekburn, Choppington, Bedlington, Seaton Burn, Annitsford, Killingworth, Forest Hall, Longbenton, Hebburn.)

Pimple's Zeppelin Scare was the great man's own inevitable attempt to get in on the act. It features a man and a woman who, hearing music on the street, mistake it for an air-raid alert, take refuge in a basement, and remain there, hunkered down, until the war's end. The film was shown alongside *Five Nights* in Dorking, while across Surrey, in Redhill, it was part of the same bill as two Apache Dancers. Advertisements stressed the benefits that might accrue to cinema owners: 'Zepps! Zepps! Inflate Your Pay Box and Bomb Your Opposition!' And tasteless though this might have been, it seemed to do the trick. *Pimple's Zeppelin Scare* was booked everywhere from Folkestone to Barrow, and from Christchurch to Rochdale. In North Shields again, it formed part of a 'Grand Patriotic Programme' at the Gaiety and 'created no end of amusement.' And it was adjudged 'a screamingly absurd farce,' a 'screaming comedy film which will create roars of amusement' and, at the Zetland Picture House in Bristol:

A Scream! A Scream! A Scream!

Here is another card: a man in a dressing-gown is carrying a candle and peering into the gloom, where the silhouette of a canoodling couple can be seen. 'I say, you two, come out of that cellar,' the man exclaims. 'The airship's been gone ever so long!'

The raids on London became more and more intense, even if they were chiefly confined to the east of the city – the Isle of Dogs and Millwall Docks, Deptford, Woolwich, Greenwich, Bermondsey – so as not, it was said, to inconvenience the Kaiser's cousin further west. And consternation was widespread well beyond the country's fringe.

The breweries of Burton-upon-Trent soon proved a target. Rolls-Royce in Derby came under attack, together with the railway works, the gas works, and a lace factory. And on the last night of January, the lights at the Imperial picture house in Walsall suddenly went off. This was the first intimation that the Zeppelins had now reached the West Midlands, and it heralded a raid in which many people would lose their lives. The dead included the Lady Mayoress of the town, who was a passenger in a tram that received a direct hit, and a courting couple, who had been walking beside the canal. A coroner's jury found that they had been wilfully killed, and demanded that the Kaiser be had up for murder.

Nor did the raids go unnoticed further north. In Manchester, as a precaution, the city had been plunged into darkness. There was perfect composure in the entertainment halls, the newspapers noted. A meeting addressed by the Bishop of Manchester was illuminated by the light of a torch. And a public lecture went ahead by candlelight down the road at the University. A special conference of chief constables was held at the Town Hall, and afterwards, on the very eve of his trial, James Watson issued an edict to the people of Preston. They should keep off the streets, he said, and draw their blinds. And the managers of picture houses should make sure their outside lights were switched off.

47

But Pimple had more to worry about than German airships. As Preston's Chief Constable found himself doubling up as the censor of posters, Fred Evans was himself setting foot in the High Court. Writs had been issued and defences served, and now, he was caught up in a case brought by a famous author, who didn't appreciate what he had done with her most notorious book.

Elinor Glyn was of a similar age to Victoria Cross, and she too had spent her early years on the fringe of the British Empire. A child of families that were as French or Irish as English, and as Scottish as anything else, she lived in Canada for a while, in a lovely limestone house with a deep portico, mature trees and a vast lawn. She was attended by governesses and tutors, and though she might be required to sit in silence, in the cause of self-control and good manners, there were dinners to dress for and crates of finery, sent by relatives in Paris, to unpack.

After her family moved to Scotland, Elinor lived for a while in a castle in Galloway. She would be locked in her room at night, so that her nurse could go trysting with a local gamekeeper, but she was given the run of a vast library. Her tutor, she would remember, was a Frenchman with a curious moustache and the smell of stale tobacco about him. He enthralled her with tales of the Greek gods, and she would later remember languorous days spent devouring Pepys, *Don Quixote* and Voltaire, *The Decline and Fall of the Roman Empire* and *Idylls of the King.* When she raised her gaze to the world outside, eventually moved to London and had herself presented at court, Elinor discovered to her delight that her red hair and pale skin were not the disadvantages she had once supposed.

Her marriage, when it came, was to a spendthrift barrister whose habits she readily came to share. He hired a swimming baths for the sheer joy of watching her swim naked, her long, long hair streaming out behind, casting an auburn fan on the water. But as they fell deeper and deeper into debt, he lapsed into unreason, sitting up all night staring at a pear, so as to be sure then when he ate it, it would be at the very moment of its ripening. Elinor consoled herself in affairs with a string of aristocrats, some of whom were much younger than she, and some of whom lent her husband money she would have to repay. When she turned to writing novels, it was with that aim in mind.

On the day her own trial began, Elinor Glyn was the mistress of at least two Cabinet ministers, one of whom, Lord Curzon, had been Viceroy of India and would soon be Foreign Secretary. The loan he had made to her husband would today be worth almost £250,000, although she, perhaps not disinterestedly, declared that by accepting it, her husband had repudiated his wedding vows. Lord Curzon was a graceless, if hard-working and unquestionably learned, man. Possessed of an 'air of ineffable superiority' according to a Parliamentary sketch-writer, of 'enamelled self-assurance' according to the prime minister's wife, he was also possessed of a lifelong devotion to the British imperial cause. While that led him to oppose Home Rule and what he believed were the ambitions of the Czar, what he objected to most fiercely was the widening of the franchise.

In a pamphlet that came out in the same year as *If Women Were Policeman* and *When Women Rule*, Lord Curzon wrote: 'Women have not, as a sex or a class, the calmness of temperament or the balance of mind, nor have they the training, necessary to qualify them to exercise a weighty judgement in political affairs.' This was the fourth of fifteen reasons he gave in support of his view, and if it looked to the present, other reasons found him raising his gaze. 'The vote once given, it would be impossible to stop at this,' he wrote, giving his tenth reason. 'Women would then demand the right of becoming MPs, Cabinet Ministers, Judges, &c. Nor could the demand be logically refused.' It was no surprise at all when, in the year of *Did'ums Diddles the P'liceman* and *The Elusive Miss Pinkhurst*, Lord Curzon agreed to become president of something calling itself the National League for Opposing Woman Suffrage.

By the time of their first meeting, Elinor Glyn was already acknowledged an authority in matters of manners and breeding, fashion and beauty. And even if that position had been bestowed on the evidence of nothing more than a few magazine articles, she made the most of it when promoting her novels. They were *romans-à-clef* in the main, none too subtly chronicling their author's social and romantic adventuring, and while each one was scandalous enough, it was *Three Weeks* that made her truly infamous.

The hero of that tale is a young British aristocrat, who is sent abroad to save him from an unsuitable match. There, he is seduced by an older woman, known as 'The Lady', and he makes her a gift of the tiger-skin rug upon which they will consummate their relationship. She, it turns out, is Queen of a small country in the Balkans, and when she returns there to give birth to her lover's child, she is murdered in a fit of jealousy by her husband, the King.

Three Weeks took six weeks to write. It is overwrought and sentimental, and it was derided by critics. It has a glorious setting, though, taking readers from deepest England to Switzerland, Venice and the Dead Sea coast. And it is replete with what Ms Glyn herself described as 'fine buildings, splendid rooms, rich silks and blazing jewels adorning handsome, soigné men and lovely, carefree women.' The scenery and props helped make the book a massive success, but the shenanigans also played their part. They were said to recall ones Elinor had shared with a brother of the Duke of Roxburghe, and before long, everyone was reciting a lubricious rhyme:

> Would you like to sin
> >with Elinor Glyn
> >>on a tiger skin?
> Or would you prefer
> >to err with her
> >>on some other fur?

When *Three Weeks* came out, at the same time as Lord Curzon's pamphlet, Elinor dined with Mark Twain at a fashionable restaurant in New York where, she would later recall, she wore a green silk gown to go with her eyes. Then, she put out a pamphlet of her own, announcing that the great man had been lavish with his praise. 'I think you have written a very fine book,' she had him say. 'You are a very deep thinker.' His recollection, though, was altogether different. He called *Three Weeks* 'a very harmful book', and said he had told her it was a mistake. 'I am not well pleased with her conduct,' he added.

King Edward refused to have the book mentioned in his presence. It was banned in Canada, and banned at Eton, too, even though the school's headmaster conceded that he hadn't himself read so much as a word. There was, however, feverish bidding for the rights, which were eventually sold to an American company. And when the first film adaptation came across the Atlantic, Ms Glyn received a very special gift – a tiger-skin rug sent by Lord Curzon, made from a beast he had killed himself.

It wasn't that film, however, which annoyed her, but another one, made in England by a familiar, but much less respectful, hand. *Pimple's Three Weeks (Without the Option), with Apologies to Elinor Glyn* had in fact been made in the middle of the River Thames. It had been showing in picture houses at the time of that unpleasant business involving Fred Evans, his brother Joe and the woman who said she was owed a guinea. And while the film's creator was content to doff his cap to the celebrated lady author, he was also keen to capitalise upon his own reputation.

'Remember *Pimple's Battle of Waterloo*,' an advertisement advised, 'and don't miss this – which is better.'

The English film was a burlesque of the American one, though much shorter and cruder, and the two shared almost nothing in the way of plot or dialogue. The regal seductress portrayed by Fred Evans wasn't even The Lady, but 'Princess Pimpelian'. And yet, Elinor Glyn was not reassured. She alleged that her copyright had been breached, and she claimed damages and costs. She also claimed any profits Fred had made, and she demanded that his film be destroyed. Her case was about commerce, not taste and decency, at least at first, and at least in her mind.

The judge proved to be no fan of the Pimple film. 'Nothing but a vulgar intrigue,' he called it, at the end of a short trial. But he was no more a fan of Ms Glyn. Her novel was 'hackneyed and commonplace,' he said, and the episode on the tiger-skin 'nothing more or less than a sensual adulterous intrigue.' And then he brought up taste and decency. The book was, he said, 'a glittering record of adulterous sensuality masquerading as superior virtue.'

Elinor Glyn lost her claim for two reasons. The first was the great difference between her work and Fred Evans's, and the fact that he had, as the judge put it, 'bestowed such mental labour upon' the novel, and 'subjected it to such revision and alteration, as to produce an original result.' Vulgar she might have been, but Princess Pimpelian was Fred's own creation. It was the second reason, however, that will have caused Ms Glyn the greatest embarrassment. As the critics had done before him, the judge excoriated her book. It attempted to justify adultery, he said, and was 'of highly immoral tendency,' and it was therefore 'disentitled to the protection of the court.'

These were uncertain times for Elinor Glyn and Fred Evans. Her anguished husband had died only a short time before the case came to court, and though her lover, Lord Curzon, had commissioned a beautiful portrait of her, and put it on show all over London, he had also begun trysting with the woman who would take her place. As for Pimple, as he stepped into the daylight and strode off westwards towards Eel Pie Island: he wouldn't have known it, but his best days were already behind him.

48

It isn't clear how far Elinor Glyn shared Lord Curzon's opinions, but a clue as to her opinion about women's suffrage may be found in *The Career of Katherine Bush*, a novel Ms Glyn published in the very year she was rejected by her lover and found herself tangling with Pimple.

'You are not a suffragette?' the heroine of that book is asked.

'Oh, no!' she replies. 'I like women to advance in everything, but unless you could destroy their dramatic instinct, and hysteria, I think it would be a pity for a country if they had votes.'

'You despise women and respect men, then?'

'Not at all; it would be like despising bread and respecting water. I only despise weakness in either sex.'

Ms Glyn regarded the Countess of Warwick as one of her closest friends. It was, after all, she who introduced the young Elinor into society, and who proclaimed her 'the loveliest woman in England.'

Frances Greville was widely known as 'Daisy', and she probably inspired a popular music hall song. It was thought she might provide a stylish marriage for Queen Victoria's youngest son, but she caught the eye of the oldest son and quickly became his mistress. Her marriage to the Earl of Warwick proved no obstacle in that regard, nor did her position prevent the Countess from embracing socialism. She argued against the Great War and in favour of the October Revolution, and she stood for Parliament in the Labour cause. A gossip with a way with words, it was natural that Daisy would turn to writing. Her books include biographies of William Morris and Joseph Arch, the champion of agricultural workers; a history of Warwick

Castle and its occupants; and a frank memoir that would prove altogether too much for many. Her own opinion on the question of the suffragettes was made abundantly clear. She commended their 'courage and perseverance', but said that, as a socialist, she wished to see general adult suffrage, not just 'votes for rich women'.

In one of her books, a collection of essays published just after the *Five Nights* trial, Daisy wrote about the cinema. She hadn't expected much of it, she said, recalling the 'vulgar, fantastic or silly' posters she had seen on hoardings, which 'make the streets of even the small provincial towns more than necessarily offensive'. But she had been delighted by a film she had seen at the Scala theatre in Covent Garden. (The walls of that expensive place were bare stone, the bronze embellishments scarcely worthy of the name.)

Soon, Daisy was writing for the screen herself. *The Great Pearl Affair* might have been one of hers, and *The Eleventh Commandment*, though credited to someone else, almost certainly was. It features a young woman who is forced to contemplate desperate measures after her fortune is lost. When the film came out, Daisy told the *Bioscope* that she had been looking in the castle archives for material for future projects. She had recently threatened to publish intimate letters sent to her by the late sovereign when he was still Prince of Wales, and she said her next film might be about Piers Gaveston, the close confidant of an earlier King Edward.

Daisy Greville wasn't the first peeress to write for the screen. That distinction was claimed – frequently – by Gwladys, Marchioness Townshend, another woman who had once been called the most beautiful in the land. (She is also the famous writer whose unfavourable opinion of cinema pianists we have already heard.)

Gwladys wrote plays, poems and novels as well, and she sometimes shared a publisher with Victoria Cross. She said she became interested in the film business when she saw 'quite a bad picture' of waves breaking on the shore. She built a tiny theatre in her garden, to give her somewhere to work out the detail of her plots, and she filled it with cardboard buildings and photographs of people cut out of illustrated magazines. (When she was working on *The Convent Gate*, the cut-outs were of nuns.) She was paid £50 for each film she wrote, and one of the films, *A Strong Man's Love*, became the first to bear its author's name.

The Love of an Actress, *The House of Mystery* and *Wreck and Ruin* are among the other films Gwladys wrote. But if melodrama was her speciality, she was keen to stress that it was not 'that class of melodrama which merely consists in piling up of impossible situations.' And yet her final film, *When East Meets West*, features a fakir who mesmerises a young woman and uses an electric ray to explode gas bulbs on the other side of the world. The *Bioscope* would conclude that, in her work, 'plausibility has been sacrificed to the exigencies of melodrama.'

Elinor, Frances, and Gwladys were uncommon to the point of being exotic, but they were by no means unique: a number of women wrote for the films in those early, silent days. A fair proportion of them, indeed, did so at the studios of the Hepworth company, down by the river in Walton-on-Thames. The company's creator and guiding light was Cecil Hepworth, who – like James Bamforth in Holmfirth and Dove Paterson in Aberdeen – had made his start with magic lanterns. But Cecil's films of rough seas and heavy skies quickly became more popular than his slides.

The films Edith Banks, Gertrude Allen and Kate Murray wrote for the company were themselves often melodramas, with titles such as *Spies*, *Her Boy* and *Behind the Curtain*. Muriel Alleyne produced a score of stories, including *The Forsaken*, *The Dead Heart* and *Time and the Hour*. And Alice de Winton would prove a Hepworth stalwart.

Showbusiness ran in Miss de Winton's blood – her grandfather had been the 'Colossus of Equestrians', his father the 'Flemish Hercules' – and she gained plaudits in the West End and on Broadway before making the journey out to Walton-on-Thames. The sketches and short stories she wrote would form the basis for films such as *One Fair Daughter* and *A Throw of the Dice*. And Alice never entirely lost her love of performing. 'The society adventuress type' was what she most enjoyed playing, she told a newspaper, and she was always as likely to be the star as the creator of the Hepworth company's films.

Those films had been growing steadily more sophisticated. After some early experiments with sound, Cecil Hepworth had made a series of 'trick' films that appeared to show a man laying a large egg, a motor car exploding, and (as the title had it) *How it Feels to be Run Over*. He had also made films about costermongers, their titles echoing the music-hall songs to which they were related – *The Coster and His Donkey*, *The Coster's Wedding*. Some of these films were playful. One shows a donkey refusing to cross a puddle of water, before, in another trick, the film is reversed and the donkey appears to go backwards. But the costermonger who framed the flower-girl was also Cecil's creation, as was the costermonger who jealously assaulted the curate.

When Cecil Hepworth turned to something more substantial, it was with *Alice in Wonderland*, the first film version of that beguiling, unsettling story. It stars Cecil's wife, Margaret, as the White Rabbit. It has a Cheshire Cat that really does appear and disappear. And it ends with a procession of children dressed up as playing cards. *Rescued by Rover*, Cecil's next film, featured yet more technical innovation, and it too proved a success. Margaret Hepworth took the starring role again, and she was also credited as the film's writer. There was a part for Margaret and Cecil's young daughter, Barbara, while the family dog, Blair, took the title role. The film cost £14 to make, but 400 prints were sold, at a price of £8 each, and those prints circulated for years and years. So many prints were sold, in fact, that the negative wore out twice and the action had to be filmed again each time.

Alongside these films, Cecil Hepworth's catalogue included the familiar ones of Royal events, foreign expeditions, and military parades. But when it came to the noble art, he turned to fiction.

The White Hope came out in the year of *Five Nights*, and it may have been the first British film to have boxing as its subject. The film's titular hero is given a tilt at the world title under the patronage of a benevolent earl, and Cecil Hepworth has him falling for the earl's sister as well. 'A stirring story of love and boxing,' is how one newspaper described the film, adding, 'The fight scenes are of the very best.' Those scenes had been arranged by a man named George Gunther, who also played the part of the man bested by the White Hope, and who, as other newspapers wasted no time in telling their readers, was a noted 'negro pugilist'.

Mr Gunther was well known in England by now. He had fought in Birkenhead and Liverpool, Southwark, Holborn, Hackney; at the Drill Hall and the King's Hall; and at the National Sporting Club, with which Lord Lonsdale, sometimes a less-than-benevolent earl, was closely connected. On several occasions, George Gunther even fought at Wonderland, on the Whitechapel Road in East London, which was said never to be fuller than when he was on the card. In Paris, he fought Georges Carpentier with the European title at stake, and though he lost, it was only after twenty rounds, and only on points.

He fought in England only after he had fought in America, and he finished fighting there only after an unsavoury incident on the lower reaches of the St Louis River, in a place where patient fishermen might expect to be rewarded with walleyes, muskellunge and ruffe. In a scow that had been towed onto the boundary between the states of Minnesota and Wisconsin, he took part in a contest of dubious legality with a man named Walter Whitehead. The pilot of the scow had a struggle to keep it in place, as the skiffs and barges of the many spectators knocked into each other on the swell of a September afternoon.

And if no satisfactory conclusion was ever reached, that is because of what happened as evening fell, the pale peach of a sun began its decline, and lights came on along the opposing esplanades of Duluth and Superior. That is when the whole misbegotten contest was brought to a premature end, by the local sheriff, in faltering English, in the middle of the twelfth round. The sheriff had to raise his voice because of the uproar created by the spectators, but then George and Walter, who had been sent back to their respective corners, were seen to come together again and shake hands in the middle of the ring.

The sheriff's power to do what he did wasn't universally acknowledged, and boos and jeers greeted him as he returned uncertainly to his little steam launch. He was jostled from all sides, and someone even suggested that he be tipped into the river himself. But even though Gunther and Woodward were arrested the moment they returned to dry land, and then locked up in the county jail while everyone tried to work out what to do with them, they would never face a criminal trial. No evidence could be found that their fight had been for money, and not the friendly exhibition the two men claimed, and questions started to be asked about the conduct of the police. Several deputies had been seen on the vessels surrounding the scow, and the sheriff, who was present from the very beginning of the bout, had waited a very long time to intervene. There were even those who said everyone concerned had cooked up some sort of a deal.

Cecil Hepworth's other films featured Tango dancers, harlequinades, and soldiers setting off for the Boer War. He was responsible for the popular *Tilly the Tomboy* series, and he went

226

on finding roles for Alma Taylor and Chrissie White long after their years of youthful rebellion were done.

Alma can be seen in one film, confronting a policeman and waving a sign saying, 'Votes for Women.' She can also, however, be seen dancing behind an odd little man singing 'I Do Like to Be Where the Girls Are', and it is one of Chrissie's films that perhaps better captures the mood of the times. *Wife the Weaker Vessel* was also doing the rounds at the same time as *Five Nights*. It features Chrissie as a young woman who pretends to be shy in order to snare a wealthy man. When he displeases her, however, she reveals her true nature – as 'Physical Culture Phyllis' – and proceeds to give him a fearful thrashing. A table is overturned, a cigar is swept from the man's mouth, and his monocle is suddenly nowhere to be seen.

For a while, Blanche MacIntosh was the Hepworth company's senior writer. She had known Cecil since she was a child, having first met him when she was on holiday with her family in Kent. She worked as a clerk in the Civil Service before going into films. And her first piece of work was an adaptation of *The Vicar of Wakefield*, prepared while she was pregnant with her second child.

Blanche brought other classics to the screen as well, sometimes going to the library to select suitable books for herself. In her own original stories, meanwhile: a man discovers that his daughter is betrothed to his own adopted son; a blind girl identifies her father's killer by his broken finger; a doctor forces his secretary to become a morphine addict; and a deserted bride falls into a twenty-five-year trance. Cecil Hepworth was not slow to acknowledge his debt to her. 'The first small step in the right direction was asking Blanche MacIntosh to write a script for us,' he wrote, adding that he almost never altered the work she produced for him. After entering his employ, she never wrote for anyone else.

Perhaps the most successful Hepworth film to be written by

a woman was the work of a woman who considered herself an actress first and last. *Annie Laurie* took its cue from the popular Lowland Scots ballad of that name, which had once been a staple of James Bamforth's painted glass slides. And though it was produced and directed by Cecil Hepworth, much else in the film was the work of Alma Taylor. She elaborated upon the plot, adhering none too closely to the song, and she took on the title role, as a country schoolmistress – 'a wistful, wide-eyed lassie' – who marries an old laird and, though she is romanced by his nephew, remains true to him until the very end.

The film did excellent business, and critics praised the energy of the performances and the beauty of the rural locations. They also praised the music chosen to accompany the film, which often included the tune of the ballad itself. On occasions, however, the music was a problem, and not a boon, for once patrons detected the merest hint of a melody, they couldn't help but sing along:

> Her voice is low and sweet,
>   And she's a' the world to me;
> And for bonnie Annie Laurie,
>   I'd lay me doon and dee.

Conduct of this sort might be a breach of licence, especially in towns where a strict distinction was maintained between picture houses and music halls. During one performance, a constable was said to have risen from his seat in the stalls to remonstrate with the audience, while in Leeds, councillors announced that the singing must stop.

And while Alma Taylor received her share of the praise for *Annie Laurie*, it was largely confined to what she had done on screen. The writing of the film went largely unmentioned, and Ms Taylor herself would complain that it had proved a wholly unwelcome distraction.

49

Irene Miller might have been the most eminent woman writing silent films in Britain. She was certainly a significant part of the films Will Barker made, up on Ealing Green.

Born in the north of the capital, Ms Miller said she had been encouraged by her mother to develop entirely along her own lines. She always intended to be a writer, and she went into the theatre to 'find out at first hand exactly how plays are staged, and how they need to be written.' She studied art and worked as a designer, but in her spare time she wrote short stories she found it easy to sell. Her novel *Sekhet* is about a young woman in thrall to the ancient Egyptian goddess of love and cruelty. The woman is ruined by a much older man and cast aside, but she comes back to gain her revenge. The *Globe* praised 'the power and dramatic significance' of the tale, and though the villain was pronounced 'more suited to melodrama than to a novel with an apparently serious purpose,' the overall assessment was favourable. 'The book is one of many promises,' the magazine said, 'and its author should do better things.'

It was another of Irene's novels that provided her with her first film. *Mrs Cassell's Profession*, which had also been adapted by her, was produced by the Barker company in the year of *Five Nights*. Billed as 'A Story of Modern Society', it has as its heroine a young woman, the maid to a fashionable Lady, who takes the blame when pearls belonging to the Lady are stolen by thieves led by the young woman's own mother. The film was also known as *The Striped Stocking Gang*, and it was declared 'a sensational drama' in Dover. In Arbroath, it was 'a story that will linger in the memory long after the last foot of the last reel has passed from the screen.' And when it played in Dundee, advertisements made sure to mention the writer by name.

Irene Miller had a very clear idea of what her job required: 'a strong sense of the drama and a fertile imagination – inborn talents that cannot be acquired – and a knowledge of the "tricks of the trade," which anyone can learn very quickly.' And her time with Barker gave her an equally clear view of the position of women. They had not had to fight their way into films, she said, in a talk given at a dinner for producers and directors:

> They have been welcomed as a matter of course, they receive equal wages for equal work, and occupy positions of importance in every branch of the business.

Her mother had been an eminent suffragist, and Irene Miller pursued that cause with vigour. She had been shouted down when she attempted to speak in Hyde Park. She wore a sandwich board around London with 'Votes for Women' written on it. She was ejected from Parliament after unfurling a banner from the Ladies' Gallery. And she carried another banner in the great march of former suffragette prisoners. Shortly before *Sekhet* was published, she wrote on her Census form, 'I refuse to assist in any Census whilst women are unenfranchised,' before adding, 'The above statement was written with the pen with which I earn my living.'

Her dedication was unquestioned, for it had made her not only one of the first women imprisoned for the cause, but the very first suffragette to be arrested in the capital.

The arrest came after Irene had been part of a group of women that marched on Downing Street. There were around forty of them, hoping to impress the merits of their cause upon the prime minister, Sir Henry Campbell-Bannerman. He was preparing for a Cabinet meeting at the time and didn't welcome the intrusion, and the women were curtly refused admission.

This was not just his official residence, but also his home. (It would shortly, indeed, be the place in which he would end his days.) Things turned ugly when the door was slammed shut a second time. 'The irate ladies roused the echoes of sedate Whitehall by a determined tattoo with the First Lord's knocker,' a newspaper indignantly reported, and it seems it was Irene who was chiefly to blame. 'She is a tall, fine woman,' one of her comrades said, 'and I admit that she did knock very loudly.' Irene was taken around the corner to Scotland Yard and kept there while a constable went to speak to Sir Henry. Eventually, she was informed that she was free to go.

Her first period of imprisonment came a few months later, when the group of women of which she was now a part attempted to hold a meeting outside Parliament itself. The group included Sylvia Pankhurst and Annie Kenny, who had done as much as Christabel Pankhurst to coin the very word 'suffragette'. The meeting was broken up by police, and Irene, Sylvia and others were charged with offences to do with their language and behaviour. When the matter came before the police court in Westminster, the women refused to give assurances as to their future conduct and were therefore sent to prison. In Holloway, as the door clanged shut behind her, Irene sent out a message. 'We are glad to undergo the indignity of imprisonment,' the message read, 'because we know thereby we are helping to raise the status of the womanhood of the country.'

She and her comrades spent a month in custody, and when she was released, she told a reporter that 'their imprisonment had made them all feel that the women's suffrage cause was much dearer to them even than it was before. It had not in the least cooled their ardour.' 'Of course, we found it very galling to be constantly under supervision,' she said, 'but I could stand against much greater hardships.'

Some months after that first, fateful trip, Irene Miller was at the head of another deputation that made its way to the door of 10, Downing Street. The objective this time was an interview with Sir Henry's successor, but when she handed in a letter of petition, she was told that Mr Asquith had nothing to say on the matter that he had not said before. The result was commotion once again.

The crowd had become swollen not only by other suffragettes, but also by their antagonists, and by intrigued members of the general public. There were cries of 'Votes for Women!' Someone tried to chain herself to railings. And several women began addressing the others, only to be led away by constables. Climbing the steps of the prime minister's car, conveniently parked nearby, Irene said, 'My friends, we ask for your sympathy. Three women have been arrested…' 'You mean four women,' a voice cried out, as Irene too was led away.

She was wearing a summer costume when she entered the dock, the newspapers observed, and she gave the magistrate a pleasant smile. But when she was told she could be bound over or sent to prison, she was resolute. 'Of course I shall go to prison,' she said.

In a letter to her sister that found its way to the *Westminster Gazette*, Irene described the conditions she had experienced in Holloway Prison.

Upon arrival, she wrote, she was led to a white-washed 'cellule' whose dimensions were those of a coffin. There were scribblings on the walls, some of them uplifting, others less so: 'Martha Jones, barmaid. Six weeks for pinching.' In that grim place, Irene was given 'a sack-like gown of coarse green linen' to wear, 'the distinguishing arrow painted on here and there in a nasty, dirty sort of yellow.' She slept on a crude, hard pallet, covered with a mattress full of coconut fibre, and a pillow that was no use at all. And she spent her days in solitude and silence, with only a single book from the prison library once a week to relieve the monotony. 'Of course the book is a comfort,' she wrote, 'but one has to sternly limit one's day's allowance of reading, or there would be none at all left for the succeeding days.'

Yet, despite these hardships, Irene refused an offer of early release. It came with conditions, and she simply would not promise to make no more speeches in Downing Street.

She was hatless when she finally left prison, looking jubilant in a blue dress, and carrying that morning's ration of hard, dark bread. She was treated to a pleasant breakfast at a café on The Strand and had the prospect of a lavish dinner in Leicester Square to look forward to in the evening.

50

Here is an old film, entitled *The Kiss in the Tunnel* –

The entrance to the tunnel is slowly approaching, as a train emerges on the other line and comes past billowing steam. It has one, two, three, four, five carriages.

The screen goes dark, before the inside of a carriage appears. A man and woman are sitting there, in seats that face each other.

He is reading a newspaper, she a book. They seem quiet and content, even though everything is swaying from side to side.

They are dressed in their finery, both with hats. She is wearing gloves and he has a buttonhole.

He is smoking a cigar, and suddenly, he looks up from his newspaper, leans forward and chucks her under the chin. She smiles and laughs.

Then, he leans closer and chucks her again, first with his left hand and then, swapping the newspaper over, with his right.

He returns to his seat, before removing his cigar, putting down the newspaper, standing up, and taking off his hat.

He kisses her full on the lips.

She laughs again at that, then seems to come over all bashful and hides her face behind her book. Looking up, she leans towards him and shakes her head, laughing still.

He too is laughing. He takes off his hat again, and puts it on his seat. Then, getting back to his feet, he beckons her.

She leans towards him and he kisses her on either cheek, as she keeps hold of the book in her left hand, her arm outstretched.

When he returns to his seat, he sits on his top hat, so that it is squashed flat, and he has to punch it out several times with either hand. He is annoyed at that.

They go back to their reading, and at one point, she looks up, apparently about to say something to him.

The screen goes dark again, and the train comes out of the tunnel.

When Laura Bayley shared that kiss in the tunnel, she had been married to her co-star for more than a decade, and together, they had produced a series of truly audacious films. Her husband, George Albert Smith, was a photographer and stage mesmerist, whom most people called 'Bertie'. He was also the proprietor of St Ann's Well – six leafy acres in Hove laid out around an ancient chalybeate spring. Entrance was sixpence on Sundays, half that in the week, and there were balloon rides, a Gypsy fortune-teller, and a hermit in a cave. Bertie and Laura held parties there for 2,000 people, and while she kept the phonograph going, he would thrill everyone with the speed at which he could move from one painted glass slide to another.

Their films, made in the open air when daylight was at its strongest, were gentle affairs. They show Cinderella and Santa Claus, old maids receiving unexpected Valentines, and yet more stolen kisses. There are spiders in a web, waves breaking on the shore, and a miller tussling with a sweep, each covering the other with flour or soot.

For a while, Bertie Smith also worked with Georges Méliès, and their collaborations, including a 'pre-enactment' of King Edward's coronation, were shown in Paris. They were also shown in Brighton, at the Palladium, where *Five Nights* would briefly enjoy great acclaim. Bertie and Georges were among the first filmmakers to use reverse motion, 'dissolves' and 'wipes', and their work would prove highly influential. The Bamforth company made its own version of *The Kiss in the Tunnel* on the railway line running between Holmfirth and Huddersfield. The close-up was another of Bertie's innovations, and it was used by him in films of a man drinking a glass of beer, or grimacing as he gives himself a shave, and of a woman's eye seen through a reading glass, or her ankle through a telescope.

Laura Bayley was the star of many of her husband's films. She is Cinderella and the old maid, both the recipient and the donor of stolen kisses, and the eye and the ankle probably belonged to her. A veteran of pantomimes and seaside revues, she had a flair for slapstick, and she might have been the first film comedienne. She also had a talent for pulling faces, and some of the close-ups are likely to have been filmed by her. For that reason, she is often said to have been the first woman director.

Her skill can be seen to best effect in *Mary Jane's Mishap*, in which she plays a feckless maid, who yawns and stretches, and spits on the boots she is supposed to be cleaning. She gets blacking on her face, where it forms a moustache, then she squints down her nose and can't help going cross-eyed. She admires herself in a mirror and smiles a toothy smile. Then, looking right into the camera and winking once, twice, three times, she pours liquid into the stove. There is a great explosion, and she is blown up the chimney and out of the house. In the graveyard, a headstone reads, 'Here Lies Mary Jane, Who Lighted the Fire with Paraffin. Rest in Pieces.'

Only a street or two from St Ann's Well stood Hove Town Hall. Designed by the same hand as the Assize Court in Manchester, it too was made from brick and terracotta, its walls a lovely warm red, with stone this time from the Dorset town of Portland. And it too had a steep roof, coloured glass windows, and a real sense of municipal heft. It also had a tower whose bells played *Sussex by the Sea* and *God Bless the Prince of Wales!* The first film shown at the Town Hall was probably made by Bertie Smith. And it was there, not long afterwards, that a presentation was given by the woman some say was really the first to make a film. Only a week after *Attack on a China Mission* had been shown, the limelight fell on Mrs Aubrey Le Blond. She was a contemporary of Laura Bayley, and her house was itself only a few streets away from the studio Laura shared with her husband.

The daughter of a baronet, Mrs Le Blond was often known as 'Lizzie'. She had been brought up in Ireland and married a British soldier and adventurer. After his untimely death, in the doomed attempt to relieve General Gordon at Khartoum, she moved to Switzerland, where she scaled Mont Blanc by accident and then did it again on purpose. Sometimes, she set out in a skirt, so as not to offend local sensibilities, only to change into something more suitable once she had left the foothills behind. She climbed other peaks as well, in the Alps and much further north, and she took a camera with her wherever she went.

With another of her husbands, Lizzie Le Blond travelled widely – in North Africa and the Raj, China, Korea, Japan – and in Moscow, she found herself bearing witness to the last days of the Tsars. Those experiences provided rich inspiration, and when she came home, Lizzie gave magic lantern talks illustrated by her own photographs. She wrote books about mountaineering and travel, but also history books and novels. And she put together the films she would exhibit in Hove – *Figure Skating on the Kulm Rink, Bobsleigh Racing, Tobogganing on the Snow Run at Belvoir Restaurant, Hockey on the St Moritz Lake, Sleighing and Snowballing*.

A camera was also among the things Jessica Borthwick took with her on her travels – that and a revolver she never let out of her sight. Her father had been a general and her aunt a newspaper editor, and their influence, coupled with a sense of adventure she shared with Mrs Le Blond, took her all over the world.

When still barely into her twenties, Miss Borthwick spent a year documenting the latest episode in the interminable conflict between the Ottoman Empire and the Serbs. She did that in hundreds of still images, but in moving images too, and even though she had lied about her age and received only three days' training, she went everywhere the Bulgarian army went.

The gun was one she herself had taken off the dead body of a soldier, and in Adrianople she saw two men hang and then came down with cholera. Back home, her films were exhibited in Covent Garden, at the bare, expensive Scala theatre, and Jessica accompanied them with a lecture in which she attempted to do justice to everything she had heard, seen, and had to endure.

She next went to the Arctic, intending to set up a colony for the cure of consumption. There, in what she referred to as 'God's sanatorium', she farmed reindeer and hunted seals, but the film she had promised to make of all that never appeared. When war came, she drove an ambulance between Ypres, Diksmuide and Ghent, serving tea and Oxo to the wounded. She got shot at herself, and bombed at Oudekapelle, and she used her own little boat to bring the last refugees from Ostend. The Belgians made her an honorary corporal for that, another corporal cutting the stripes off his tunic so she could be decorated on the battlefield.

It wasn't just her exploits that aroused the interest of the press. The man from the *Bioscope* was taken with her voice as well, describing it as 'beautiful, deep and like a resonant organ note.' He had interviewed her in her South Kensington studio shortly after she came back from the Balkans, the two of them sitting next to the projector and screen that had turned the room into a temporary picture house. What she had made upon him, he conceded, was 'an immediate impression of great strength, both physical and mental.' 'Idealist, thinker, and practical woman of action,' he added:

> Miss Borthwick has a unique individuality, and the history of her life, short as it has been up to the present, is already a record such as few men of any age could match.

Later, during a brief respite from her ambulance duties, Jessica gave an interview to the *Daily News*, choosing on that occasion to report a grim incident in Flanders. 'It was a full moon and the country is flat,' she said, 'with very few trees left standing, most having been cut down for fuel.'

So, we had to lie flat and crawl along till we got to the trenches. The rifle firing was incessant, but we picked out men it was possible to move. That night, too, we had to burn piles of the German dead, for they had been throwing them in the river and spoiling the water.

When Jessica Borthwick gave her lecture, and showed her films, in Covent Garden, she did so under the title *The Aftermath of the Balkan War*. And yet, the report of the event that appeared in the *New York Times* was headed 'Horrors of War Seen by a Girl'.

Ethyle Batley was another woman who made films with her husband. She did so on her own account as well, however, and if Laura Bayley's close-ups are ignored, and Lizzie Le Blond's Alpine films, she might be said to have been the first woman director.

She began with the perhaps contentiously named *Peggy Gets Rid of the Baby*, in which a young girl, jealous of her new sibling, swaps it for a puppy. Ethyle's husband Ernest appeared in that film, alongside the couple's young daughter, Dorothy, and the child would feature in her mother's next film as well, putting on a Boy Scout uniform and trying to do good deeds. Ernest Batley, meanwhile, would be the father shown being rescued by his daughter at 3,000 feet. And he was also Napoleon in the Waterloo film lampooned by Pimple.

Ethyle's work was unpretentious, and it offered a distinctive, often humorous view of what she saw around her. Alongside the thieves, tramps and drunkards, there is unemployment, poverty and charity, imprisonment, inheritance, seduction, infidelity. There are orphans, blind girls, foundlings, waifs,

Mother Hubbard and *The Old Woman in the Shoe*. Children are crippled or borrowed or saved from gypsies, and they are shown reconciling their parents or crawling along telephone wires to escape a fire. There are £1 notes, a thieving Chinaman, a caravan in flames, and a gun for bringing down Zeppelins.

Like many of her contemporaries, and like her husband as well, Ethyle Batley was happy to contribute to the war effort. *Remember Belgium* was one of her films, its title echoing the call-to-arms on a well-known recruiting poster, and *The Pressure of the Poster* another. *Answering the Call* is about men who do precisely that, and *The Man Who Went* sees a wounded soldier come back to reclaim his girl. Dorothy Batley, meanwhile, would put on her brother's uniform again, most notably in *The Girl Boy Scout*, in which she apprehends an ice cream man who has been revealed to be German. She would also be seen in *An Englishman's Home*, the film that sees a pacifist reform when foreigners take over his house. It was directed by her father, Ernest, but Dorothy also starred in war films made by her mother, and *War is Hell* shows her actually shooting a German soldier.

51

A stern schoolmistress is brandishing a besom.

A winding country road can be glimpsed through the open door of a classroom.

There are girls in long frocks and white caps.

This too is an old film.

A new girl arrives. She seems very nervous. The black of her hat stands out against the white of the other girls' caps. The hat is tall as well as black, and undeniably pointed.

The other girls don't like the new one, that much is obvious, and for her part, the schoolmistress makes the sign of the cross.

The girl sits alone on a bench and finds herself being pelted with books. When she gets hit with the besom, she runs off, sobbing.

In the woods, an old woman proclaims 'Malediction!'

There is a flash of light, and girls are suddenly boys.

But then a match is made and everything is as it was.

Alice Melford called herself 'Jackeydawra', which was another of the names she had been given. It was the product of her father's fascination with the diligent, vicar-like birds of the English farmland and seacoast. They were thought to portend new life, or early death, or maybe rain, and to be so stupid as to risk starvation waiting for figs to become ripe. But Mark Melford called his house near Southampton the 'Jackdaw's Nest'. He set aside a room there for whatever wished to come in and roost, and he kept the windows open wide in every kind of weather.

A celebrated actor, writer and *farceur*, Mr Melford produced plays and music-hall sketches on murder, lunacy and kleptomania. He claimed to have sold one of them, about a broken promise of marriage, for what would now be £60,000. He was a freethinker, a supporter of suffragettes, and an advocate for animals. And when he prosecuted a showman who had been found mistreating elephants, he acknowledged the part his daughter had played. She was his 'spy-in-chief', he said.

Jackeydawra couldn't remember when the two of them first appeared on stage together, but after that she rarely left his side. He named a comic opera after her. He told everyone about the little bird she adopted, and how she would walk down to the river with it perched on top of her head. And though his career in films would be cruelly brief, she was his one trusted collaborator. The work they produced together was about Gretna Green and *The Land of Nursery Rhymes*, inconvenient meetings, errant vergers, and people who can't quite manage to kill themselves.

In *The Herncrake Witch*, Jackeydawra plays a character with a name similar to her own, the granddaughter of the old woman of the title, and it is her schoolmates who suddenly change sex and then change back again. The film took its cue from her father's opera, and Jackeydawra was not only its star, but also its producer. The *Cinema* was intrigued by that, and the magazine carried a long profile, commending her 'ease, repose, grace,' her technical proficiency, and her 'power of expression.'

But then, Mark Melford was gone, dead at barely sixty after a final, brave matinee put on by his daughter. That brought her to an important decision. 'She has never appeared in any company but her father's,' Jackeydawra wrote, of herself, in advertisements in the press. And she announced that she had retired from acting: 'Being now a perfect mistress of the camera, she will continue her recent successes as a cinematograph operator.' 'She will, we think, make a name in the cinema world,' the *Cinema* predicted, 'and "Jackeydawra" will become a household word.'

At the time of his death, Mark Melford had been working on a new film, *The Inn on the Heath*, and his daughter had been a key part of that project as well. Given the job of writing a screenplay, she scoured history books, visited museums, and even made a trip to York to see what vestiges of Dick Turpin she could find in the castle. The heroine she created falls in love with a highwayman in Georgian times, and saves him from prison and the hangman's rope.

Jackeydawra Melford worked hard to make sure *The Inn on the Heath* was completed, and she is now remembered as the film's producer, as well as its writer and, indeed, its star. She was also, however, the film's director, and by some people at least, she – and not Miss Bayley, Missus Batley or Miss Le Blond – is considered the first woman director. She even created her own company to promote *The Inn on the Heath*, giving it the name 'Jackdaw Films', and the effort must surely have seemed worthwhile. This was 'an extremely creditable production,' the *Bioscope* said, 'worthy of a place in most programmes.' The film's creator had displayed a 'firm grasp of picture-play technique' and 'real artistic sensibility.' 'Miss Melford's work is full of promise,' the magazine concluded. 'We shall look forward with real interest to her future doings.'

But neither that piece nor the one in the *Cinema* was Jackeydawra's first appearance in the press.

On a cold, wet January day, nearly a decade after Irene Miller did the same, a young woman rose to her feet in the police court in Westminster. The woman was accused not of using threatening language or breaching the peace, but of shooting bullets from a catapult. The man who accused her was Herbert Muskett, who had done the same to Ms Miller before she received her first sentence of imprisonment. This was the beginning of the year in which Will Barker turned out *Sixty Years A Queen* and his own version of *East Lynne*. The bullets had 'Votes for Women' cast into them.

The campaign for women's suffrage had lately become more urgent, with those 2,000 policemen coming onto the streets near Parliament, and those women with placards trudging around in the rain. The bullets were weighty ones, made of lead, and the target had been a luxurious hotel in Westminster. They struck with resounding force, a constable told the court, and then they dropped into the basement below. The hotel was the place where the National League for Opposing Women's Suffrage had been formed, and where that organisation, whose president was Elinor Glyn's friend Lord Curzon, had subsequently made a home.

The woman had fired the bullets from the top deck of a motor bus, and when she was arrested, she still had the catapult in her lap. As she was led away, several more bullets dropped from under her long skirt, fell onto the road, and began rolling around at her feet. In the police station, a second catapult was discovered on the chair where she had been sitting.

She had been detected in an extremely wicked act, Mr Muskett told the court; one that might have had the most serious consequences. 'This new warfare has taken place in different parts of the Metropolis for several days,' he said. It was regrettable that the penalty prescribed by law was so meagre.

The woman who stood up to answer the charge was, of course, Jackeydawra Melford. And though it is unclear whether she was able to display in court the ease, repose and grace that would be discerned by the *Cinema*, she was certainly a committed suffragette. She had several similar incidents on her record already.

The reports contain little of what Jackeydawra herself said during the hearing, and it was not she, but her father who would have the last word. Mark Melford conceded that the catapults were his; the bullets, too. He used them to kill rabbits in the fields around his home. But she must have taken them from him. (Mr Muskett again.) 'I don't blame her, it's her business.' But the bullets might have killed a man. 'I have no control over my daughter.' ('Laughter.')

Jackeydawra was told she could pay forty shillings or go to prison for a month. Her father said he would pay the fine right away.

52

Crimson

Under the hot planet Mars or the fierce harvest moon

Lonsdale is in a bedroom at home, lying on the bed, apparently asleep –

The great sacrifice.

Viola comes in, wearing a fur coat and hat, and she goes up to the bed, carrying a letter.

It must be the one she was writing before she got into that tussle with Lawton.

Viola strokes Lonsdale's face, kisses his forehead, and leaves the room.

She walks along a street and can then be seen putting the letter into a post box.

*

Lonsdale has come down for breakfast, wearing a dressing gown.

He walks over to the sideboard and picks up some letters that are lying there.

One of them seems to surprise him, and he opens it quickly –

'I am in awful trouble. Husband died. Me sent to 'Frisco to be sold. Please you buy me. 500 dollars to Mrs Hackett. Suzee.'

This must be the letter she was in such a hurry to post.

Lonsdale puts it down and picks up another one.

At first, the sight of this letter makes him smile. But then, as he reads it, his face falls –

'My dearest One, I must go from you.

'At the end of this miserable year I shall return to you and all my joy in life.

'Do not try to find me, but while I am away, you are free to follow whatever paths of pleasure open before you.

'Viola.'

Lonsdale is fully dressed now, and walking in a garden.

He sits down on a bench, takes some letters from his pocket, and looks at one he saw before –

'I am in awful trouble. Husband died. Me sent to 'Frisco to be sold. Please you buy me. 500 dollars to Mrs Hackett. Suzee.'

Lonsdale gets up off the bench.

*

Hop Lee appears – he hasn't died after all.

He is standing in front of the cabinet Suzee opened, having just discovered that she has robbed him.

From the look on his face, he is very angry.

*

Lonsdale is once again walking down narrow streets in a loose suit –

Lonsdale arrives at 'Frisco.

They are different streets this time, though, and Lonsdale is on his own –

In the heart of Chinatown.

He goes through a passage and up to a door, and he knocks on it several times.

A slot opens in the door and an old man peeps through, and when Lonsdale raises his hand, the door opens.

Lonsdale is sitting on a couch, with some women milling about.

Suzee comes in, and on seeing him she runs straight into his arms.

The two of them kiss.

She is still pecking at his face as he carries her out of the room, and as they pass an old black woman in the corner, Lonsdale tosses her some money.

He carries Suzee down a narrow passage, and he tosses some more money at the old man at the door.

Then, they're out on the street –

Lonsdale hears that Hop Lee is looking for his wife. He takes her to his hotel.

They are walking through the lobby of a swanky place, and several people turn their noses up as they pass.

*

Hop Lee, meanwhile, is with the old black woman.

He takes a pencil and a piece of paper from his pocket.

Then, without warning, he throws his pigtail around the woman's neck and starts to strangle her.

He is pulling quite a face –

'What have you done with Suzee? Write her address!'

The woman writes on the paper, Hop Lee reads what she has written, and then he takes the pigtail from around her neck and leaves the room.

*

Back at the hotel, Lonsdale and Suzee are sitting in a bedroom.

He gets up and kisses her, and then he leaves the room.

*

In another bedroom, a solemn man in a frock coat is standing at the head of the bed, with a woman dressed like a nurse at the foot.

There's a table with a top hat on it and a small leather bag.

It is Viola who is in the bed, and as she raises herself up, the nurse hands her a little child, dressed in long clothes.

Viola places the child in the bed beside her, and the man picks up his hat and bag and leaves the room.

*

Back in the first bedroom again – the one in the hotel in San Francisco – Suzee is sitting where Lonsdale left her.

She is looking out of the window when a waiter comes carrying a tray of dishes.

He takes the dishes off the tray and puts them on the table.

Suzee moves to a chair next to the table, and as the waiter turns away, she takes hold of his arm.

The man is surprised, and then he smiles, and Suzee pulls him towards her.

He sits on the arm of her chair and she strokes his face with both her hands.

They are kissing.

Lonsdale is walking down a corridor of the hotel with a small box in his hand.

When he comes into the bedroom, he sees Suzee and the waiter on the chair.

She is on the waiter's knee and they are still kissing.

Lonsdale is surprised at first, and he takes a step backwards. But then he recovers himself and punches the waiter, who falls to the floor and crawls away.

Lonsdale is angry with Suzee – but then she is sitting on his knee and they have themselves begun to cuddle and kiss.

*

It is later now, and darker.

The same hotel room can be seen, with another one

adjoining it – on the other side of a door no one has bothered to close.

Lonsdale is in bed, but his eyes are open.

And here is Hop Lee.

He is walking up some steps with a knife in his hand. It is a large knife and the steps are stone ones.

Hop Lee is climbing up a metal fire escape, the knife still in his hand.

Inside the bedroom, the lights are off.

There is a narrow bed, barely visible in the gloom – and a mirror that shows the adjoining bedroom.

That's where Suzee is on the bed, apparently asleep, and alone.

Hop Lee is climbing in through an open window.

It is Suzee's window!

He rushes at her, seizes her by the shoulders, and begins to shake her violently.

Lonsdale sees this happen from the next-door bedroom.

He leaps up, rushes through the open door, and grabs hold of Hop Lee.

There is a terrible commotion as they twist and turn.

The picture disappears, and when it comes back, Suzee is lying across the bed with her head lolling over the side.

Her face is turned upwards, towards the light, and it is the brightest thing in the room. But her eyes are closed and her mouth is shut.

Hop Lee is lying on the floor beside the bed, his face upwards too, but this time in shadow.

And Lonsdale is slumped on the floor near the mirror, his legs splayed, his torso upright against the wall.

His head is inclined towards Suzee, and his arm is raised from his side, as if he is seeking some unseen support.

The other arm is drawn across his body, over his chest, as if shielding it.

In his hand Lonsdale holds a pistol, which is pointing towards the floor, and his finger has slipped from the trigger.

The bedroom is a mess, with sheets and pillows everywhere.

Two policemen come in, and one of them walks over to Hop Lee, takes a look at him, and walks away.

There is a slight movement from Lonsdale, and the policeman goes over to him.

Lonsdale seems to have come round.

He leaves the room, half dragging himself – and as he goes past Suzee, he kisses her on the forehead.

53

'I think we can vouch for the paths of pleasure.'

But the witness wouldn't permit even this modest concession.

'I don't know that it reads exactly as that.'

'Come, Mr Stott.'

This was the Chief Constable's barrister, cross-examining the witness again, and he wasn't getting very far.

'I can't remember every title-card and every word that was on the film. It is impossible.'

'Perhaps it may be unimportant to you, Mr Stott, but suppose some young fellow or young woman reads this – "You are free to follow whatever paths of pleasure open before you." Perhaps your recollection of the screen is not very good?'

'Oh, yes. It is.'

'Do you remember that?'

'I can't remember it. Not word for word.'

'Take it that it is there. Is it a proper thing to see? Or do you think that clean-minded people might object to a wife, or mistress, leaving her husband with a letter saying, "You may go on whatever paths of pleasure you like"? Is that the sort of thing which a clean-minded man might or might not object to?'

'I don't see anything to object to.'

'You do not see anything to object to?'

'No.'

'What do you think it meant?'

'I have put no particular meaning to it.'

'What might be expected, or be understood, to be likely to follow when a wife does that, or a woman does that, and says "You may follow the paths of pleasure open before you"?'

'It isn't meant that way at all.'

'Not meant that way?'

'No.'

When it came to San Francisco and the goings-on there – the man with the pigtail, the old woman, the money being tossed around – some people were very critical. One of them was Charles C Charsley, the Chief Constable of Coventry. In his opinion, 'The scene in the Chinese den depicts an objectionable phase of life, without point or moral.'

That scene was brought up during the trial as well, with the court in Manchester fretting over Lonsdale's return visit to Suzee, and itself returning to a familiar question.

'He comes to a Chinese place apparently kept by an old mulatto?'

'Yes.'

'You can only get in by paying, apparently. You can only get out by paying. And when you are there, you have got to pay the woman. What sort of a place is that?'

'What sort of a place?' Mr Stott wanted to be sure he had the question right.

'Yes.'

'I do not know that there are any such places in existence.'

'What sort of place does it suggest?'

'Suggest?'

'Yes.'

'I can't say that it suggests any particular sort.'

'I am going to suggest that a clean-minded man might think it suggested it was a brothel.'

'Nothing of the kind.'

'What sort of a place is this?' This was the judge intervening. 'You must not mind me putting it to you. There are some young girls dressed in a fashionable Eastern way. They are locked up and there is an old black woman there, and the man comes there, and pays money, and takes a girl away. What sort of establishment is that?'

'I have no idea what they call them, my lord.'

'What would they call them in England?' This was the barrister again, but Mr Stott was standing firm.

'We have no such places.'

'Why not?'

'Why not? They would not allow such places.'

'Why would they not allow them in England?'

'They do not allow them.'

'Very well. Just one other word. In the description on page ten, this establishment is called "One of the many noisome dens that flourish in the city."'

The barrister was referring to the sumptuous brochure Barker had again put out to accompany its film. Like the one for *East Lynne*, it contained striking photographs, a *dramatis personae* and a summary of the plot. Its covers are deep green, the paper reassuringly thick, and gold is this time reserved for the border around the picture on the front, which shows a man and a woman in formal dress. The picture is mauve and grey in colour; ochre and maroon. The woman has a feather in her hair, and the man is holding her in a passionate embrace, his arms supporting her arched back, her head tipped right back. In the foreground there is a comfy settee that might even be a bed.

'Why "noisome"?' The barrister was again pressing the point.

'I don't know.'

'Where is that?' This was the judge. He had his own copy of the brochure, and he was waving it about vigorously, stirring up the chill air of the lofty courtroom.

'Page ten, my lord.' The barrister again, trying to be helpful. Then, reading: '"She fled to 'Frisco, where she found refuge in one of the many noisome dens that flourish in the city."'

'I thought I saw it described somewhere as a boarding house?'

'No, my lord. I do not see that. It is described as a "noisome den" here.'

'Yes, I thought I had marked it. That is the part I looked for as soon as I saw this book, because that particular scene impressed me very much. "Reaching San Francisco…"'

'Yes, my lord. "Reaching San Francisco, Lonsdale was directed to an unsavoury boarding house in Chinatown where Suzee received him with a squeal of wild delight, and kissed him rapturously with flaming lips as he took her tiny body in his arms and sank upon the grand divan that filled the centre of the room."'

When the judge offered the brochure to the witness, turning to one side and reaching out towards the witness box, it was already open at the relevant page.

'Just look at those words and tell us again what sort of a place you think that described.'

The barrister continued.

'You have read that before, have you not?'

'No.' Mr Stott was again emphatic.

'Well you have read it now?'

'I have read it now, yes.'

'Does it make a difference in your view?'

'No.'

'That is the book which apparently is sent out with the advertisements to persuade people to hire the film?'

'Yes.'

'What did you read before you showed the film?'

'What did I read?'

'Yes.'

'Nothing.'

'Did you see the film?'

'Yes.'

'Where?'

'In Manchester.'

'Before you hired it?'

'Yes.'

'This is what the producer suggests this means – "Reaching San Francisco, Lonsdale was directed to an unsavoury boarding house in Chinatown where Suzee received him with a squeal of wild delight, and kissed him rapturously with flaming lips as he took her tiny body in his arms and sank upon the grand divan that filled the centre of the room." He does take her tiny body in his arms, doesn't he?'

'Yes.'

'He does for a moment sink upon the divan?'

'Sits down.'

'He then rushes from the place, carrying her in his arms, carrying her you do not know where, till he emerges from that place, having paid the price the woman demanded? Now, what sort of a place is that?'

'It is referred to as a boarding house.'

'What did you call it?'

'A boarding house.'

'If I called it a bawdy house, would not that be better?'

'No.'

'Do you not think a clean-minded man would view it as such?'

'No.'

'Do you not think a clean-minded man would be horrified by it?'

'No.'

54

At her home in Alaska, Mary did all sorts of things to get by.

She went looking for gold herself, paying $15 for an old claim, hoping to find her fortune in a lode of quartz inside a lump of greywacke or granite. She had learned so much since coming to this place, and now, where Sawmill Creek ran into the sea at Sawmill Cove, she learned how to use powder to blast through solid rock. It was Mary's husband, the Scandinavian, Fred Johnson, who taught her that. He had been a miner himself, and the two of them would spend hours underground, crouching low, kneeling down, maybe wriggling on their bellies, wielding pickaxes by the light of a candle, hauling a wheelbarrow towards the light of day. None of this daunted her in the least, and when, as she often did, she received an injury, she always tried to make it good herself.

The mine also provided them with a ramshackle sort of home. It had to be sold after Mary struck her hand with a hammer and caused an injury no one could make good. But the $100 she received represented a reasonable profit, and it helped her buy a small farm. Trees were felled and land cleared, and shelter was provided for both humans and kine. But the place was cut off when the weather turned, and Mary's milk froze in the pail. After that, they farmed fox for a while, until poachers got the better of them. And then, they struck out for the wilderness that rose up all around them. It was nuggets, not lodes, they went looking for this time, dipping their pans into the freezing river. And if that rarely produced anything so much as dust, the mink they also went looking for proved less elusive, falling in large numbers upon traps set for them among the blueberry brush and willow, the salmonberry and devil's club.

When they turned to fishing, Mary and Fred took to different boats. The troller she had chosen for herself was long and open, its bait-bearing lines trailing out far behind, and she made a point of sailing it all alone. The first Sitka woman to do the job, she proved more than equal to it, paying little heed to the weather, putting out into the Gulf of Alaska when everyone else was turning round. And when she did finally get back to port, late at night, sodden and exhausted, her hands raw and her back aching, she flung down her catch on the spindly dock and sold it for three cents a pound.

Mary and Fred did that for years, making enough money to send her daughter Annie to college. But then Fred became ill and Mary nursed him until the end. It was too late to go back to sea after that, so she took on yet another job, becoming matron at the local jail, which stood on Lincoln Street, close to the Russian Orthodox cathedral, and shared its bare, rectilinear home with the courthouse and post office. She was still working there in her seventieth year.

Here is a final photograph of Mary. She is much older now, and that can be seen in her face. She is depicted from the side, almost in profile, one foot placed in front of the other. She is wearing a turban, which reveals the same broad forehead, together with a hint of eyebrow and a pale stripe of eyeshadow. And she is as composed as ever, her mouth closed as she gazes into the middle distance, beyond the edge of the photograph, once again.

Fashions have changed, and what enfolds Mary now is not silk or a cinched dress, but a dark overcoat, with a collar that is unmistakeably fur. It must be winter. The coat hangs well because her back is still straight and her shoulders are level. She has her hand in her pocket. She is wearing sensible shoes, but her socks are short and her shins are bare. She is standing on a quayside, or on the apron of an aerodrome somewhere. There is concrete beneath her feet. She is about to embark on another journey.

55

It became clear during the trial that a particular course would have to be adopted.

'I cannot conceive that the jury could better try this case by not seeing the film,' the judge said. That was early in the proceedings – on the first morning, in fact, as the barrister representing Walter Stott and Fred White was setting out their case – and arrangements therefore had to be made for another private viewing. *Five Nights* would be shown at the day's end, and when that was announced in court, Mr Justice Shearman came over quite giddy. 'I must send for the proper costume,' he said.

The barrister then turned to the film's contents. 'The play is a sort of exposition of the troubles a youthful artist gets into through being too ready to kiss one or two pretty girls...'

The artist's name is Lonsdale, and the scene opens with him and a friend of his sailing in a yacht into a harbour...

Then you get taken to the outside of the tea house, and together they enter into the tea room where there are two or three Chinese girls walking about...

Suzee kneels in front of Lonsdale in the way we are led to believe Chinese girls do...

She begins to – well, probably many people would describe it as 'giving him the glad eye'...

Suddenly, the husband parts the curtains and comes into the room. And then there is one of the scenes so common in cinema halls – a fight...

Then I think you have done for a time with Sitka...

And the next thing is you come to Lonsdale's home and his studio.

This was being done too slowly and in too much detail for the judge's liking. 'Is it necessary to go through the five nights?' he asked.

'My lord, I am just indicating the points members of the jury have specially to look at.'

'We are going to see it, and I thought the object of going to see it was to obviate spending five days in the description of the five nights.'

There was loud laughter in court.

As dusk settled on Manchester and a filthy rain fell, the parties, their lawyers, the judge, and the gentlemen of the jury filed out of the Assize Court and made their way to the Star Picture Palace across the road.

This was a narrow hall, in the middle of a terrace that dated from before Victoria was Queen. It was covered in grime and had hosiers and tailors for neighbours; beer-sellers, instrument-makers, hat-makers. Lang and Schneck were their names; Dooley, Higham, Hartley, Solomons. It was here that the showing which had so excited Tont Shearman would take place.

That was by no means the perfect solution, for *Five Nights* could be annoyingly oblique. People who had seen the film often found themselves disagreeing as to its precise contents, and no one who saw the version shown at the Star could be sure that it was identical to the version shown at the King's Palace in Preston. But if the film had somehow failed to speak for itself, what then? The judge and lawyers might turn to the promotional brochure with the thick green covers, but if still further elucidation was required, where might that be found? Might the jury go so far as to peer into the pages of the novel itself?

The court was forced to confront those questions when the subject of the dinner in the restaurant came up. That scene takes place early in *Five Nights*, of course, just before Lonsdale and Viola go back to his studio, and the Chief Constable's barrister was keen to establish the precise sequence of events. He picked up his own copy of the novel and began leafing through it in search of a particular passage. He cleared his throat and then, in a firm voice, began to read:

> They supped that night at a fashionable restaurant holding a tiny festival over the progress of their work. 'Twas a silent evening, a night of reverie, but ever and anon as Viola raised her eyes, she found her comrade regarding her intently. Love shone in his face. A love that she would now do nothing to repel. Their supper ended, she thanked him gently while he cloaked her to meet the evening air. But as he left her carriage door and bade goodnight a wave of wild abandonment overwhelmed her self-restraint. She called him back and whispered, while a flood of colour mounted to her brow – 'The picture! Let us go back to it, dearest!'

Next came the key question: 'Is it conceivable to your mind, Mr Stott, that anybody going there, with the cleanest mind in the world, must necessarily draw an inference from that scene that something went on in that studio?'

'Certainly not,' Walter replied.

'Then, what did they go back to the studio for? Is the suggestion left at large?'

'Yes, for clean-minded people.'

The barrister took the same approach with an even earlier scene: the one immediately before the dinner in the restaurant, in which Viola sheds her clothes.

'In the book,' he said, 'that is called the unrobing of Phryne?'

'Yes,' Mr Stott replied, his admitted lack of learning in mythology notwithstanding. 'I believe it is.'

'And that is a picture where a celebrated woman in Greek antiquity strips herself of all clothes to be judged of by a certain assembly?'

'No, I cannot say as to that.'

'However, she is supposed to strip herself naked in the original?'

'In the film, do you mean?'

'In the book.' The barrister's tone betrayed some impatience.

'Not that I know of.'

'I suggest that in the book she strips herself naked?'

'Yes, but we are not going to say the film is like the book.' Mr Stott had put his finger firmly on the key point.

'The film is founded on the book?'

'Well, I had nothing to do with the book.'

It was when this approach was applied to that early sketch that everything became too much for the judge.

'The sketch?' Tont asked. 'Which is that?'

It was the one shown to Suzee. The one which, in the words of the Chief Constable's barrister, 'made her put her hands before her face.' The one Lonsdale showed her in the tea house in Sitka.

'I do not take it,' the judge said, 'that he made that sketch at all there.'

'Well,' the barrister replied, 'the book says he makes a sketch.'

Tont was dismayed by this. 'We are not criticising the book,' he said. 'I cannot see the relevancy of the book at all.'

'The relevancy of it is this, my lord. At the beginning of the film, in conspicuous type across the screen, there appear first of all these words: "*Five Nights*. By Victoria Cross." My lord, that is a distinct reference to the book.'

'I cannot follow that it is of the least importance. What is in the book was not shown. There was a book, but I do not know what was in the book. I do not suppose now I ever shall know.'

'There is a dispute here as to whether a certain incident

263

appeared upon the screen. The film is suggested to be a film founded on the book in the advertisement by the authoress on the screen itself, and all I am asking is this…'

But the judge was firm:

I shall tell the jury the book has nothing to do with it. I am going to say as emphatically as I can to the jury to dismiss the book from their minds.

56

A young woman is alone in a dismal cell, where the debris on the floor might be plaster from the crumbling walls.

The woman looks bewildered, her long hair in disarray, and she rushes to the door and bangs on it time after time. When no one comes, she sinks to her knees, her arms raised, her hands clasped above her head.

This is Nina, and she is being held captive by Andrew.

In the room above, another man walks through the door. He is Nina's lover, and he confronts Andrew, each man levelling a pistol at the other.

Nina hears the commotion overhead and screams for help.

A trapdoor falls open and Andrew drops into Nina's cell. Then, a sheet drops into the cell as well, and as Nina climbs upwards, desperate to escape, Andrew shoots at her and she falls to the floor.

The lover comes in and Nina is still alive. Andrew takes aim once again, but there is a tussle, his gun goes off, and he is killed.

Nina is Danish, and all of this takes place in Salt Lake City, where Andrew had been a Mormon priest.

When *A Victim of the Mormons* came out, Denmark's movie industry could claim to be the strongest in the world. Dozens of films had already been made in the country, the first of them being shown in Copenhagen in the middle of summer, in a cheerful booth next to the place where the Town Hall would soon be built. Audiences could expect to be shown fire engines, people out shopping, and lives much resembling their own. There were dogs in Greenland, wrestlers, and King Christian welcoming the Tsar. The melodramas were particularly erotic, and received particular attention. There were circus folk and witches, and the tale of a woman awaiting execution for the murder of her children.

Captive women were a popular subject. *The White Slave Trade* showed a woman being liberated from a brothel by her fiancé and the police. The longest film yet made in Denmark, it did good business from the very start – such good business, in fact, that a virtual copy, with precisely the same title, was doing the rounds within weeks. It is the film the owner of the Savoy cinema complained about when *Sapho* was banned in Leeds.

A Danish film was another of those to come to the attention of William Larkin, Dublin's inveterate protester. *In the Shadow of the Throne* shows one nun celebrating mass and another falling into the arms of a handsome man. 'How long is Catholic Dublin going to stand for this sort of thing?' a letter in the *Freeman's Journal* asked, sparking a controversy that was sufficient to keep the film in the city for another week. And this time when Mr Larkin turned up it wasn't at the Bohemian, but at the brand-new Phibsborough Picture House. He rose to his feet at eight o'clock, shouted that his religion had been insulted, and called upon the Catholics present to leave the hall right away. 'Chuck him out!' someone replied, but then William threw some ink, a woman in the orchestra was hit, and pandemonium ensued. Before long, he would be locked up in Mountjoy Prison, only a few yards away.

Mormonism was also a popular subject in Denmark, where fears of abduction now combined with opposition to the practice of polygamy. The Church had found an early home in the country, taking 20,000 converts in return. A good half of those converts had subsequently made their way to Utah, leaving homes and families, and great consternation, behind. So great was the consternation, and so intense the public fascination, that actors in the Tivoli Gardens could be heard to sing:

I agree with the priests; the Mormons have to go.
They steal all of our girls, especially the pretty ones.

And:

Mormons, Mormons!
Yes, they must be persecuted, we must fight against
them.
But wife-swapping! Wife-swapping!
We have the right to do that here too!

And for all that the Church might claim to have abandoned polygamy, it continued to find controversy wherever it went. Its missionaries had fanned out in the nineteenth century – across Scandinavia, to Hamburg and into Prussia, the Netherlands, France, Switzerland – and they were soon turning up in the works of Conan Doyle and Mark Twain, and in the dime novels of less illustrious authors. There were rumours and insinuations and downright lies, and newspapers were full of urgent reports, in which the faith was forever being 'unveiled' or 'revealed'. Headlines spoke of *The Mysteries and Crimes of Mormonism* and *Perversion, or The Causes and Consequences of Infidelity: A Tale of the Times*. And there was *Wife No 19, or The Story of a Life in Bondage*, whose author had been married to the Church's President, Brigham Young.

Critics of the faith were as ubiquitous as its missionaries, and they too found a place in the public eye. Some were one-time believers who had recanted, and who now wandered Europe, occupying theatre stage and public lectern, as often standing on the backs of carts, giving talks, and handing out pamphlets, spreading pitiful tales, issuing warnings. There were plays, such as *The Mormon Peril*, to aid the cause, and illicit photographs taken inside the great temple itself. And there were also lots of painted glass slides:

Something New Under The Sun.
Jarman, Ex-Mormon Priest, from Salt Lake, will
Expose The Mormons and show his Wonderful
and Curious Scenes of Mormon Life.
600 Pictures Shown.
The Greatest & Most Curious Show on Earth.
Everybody Delighted With It.
Admission: Give What You Please. All Who Give
Silver Get Reserved Seats. Those who give Coppers
get seats behind the reserved seats.

Given these controversies, and the queues of people wanting to see the controversies played out on the screen, it isn't surprising that film people quickly discovered an interest in captive women and *outré* practices. Given the fascinations he had himself displayed, it isn't surprising that Fred White found his way into that company.

In the United States, *Traffic in Souls* was a sensation. It tells a melodramatic tale – of young women, fresh off the boat from Scandinavia, forced into white slavery; and of one woman in particular being rescued from degradation by a host of constables. Fast-paced and shot on location on Ellis Island and the Upper West Side, the film was banned in Brooklyn but shown widely across other boroughs of New York, and it ended up making eight times what it cost. When it came to Britain, though, it landed Mr White in court. He had acquired the rights and set about hawking the film around. But he promised it exclusively to the picture house in Porth having promised it to a place in Tonypandy as well, and a jury found that he was in breach of contract.

A Victim of the Mormons ran for nearly an hour and was almost the longest film yet produced. It made great claims for itself. 'Extraordinary Exposure of a Terrible Doctrine!' ran one advertisement. The Church, meanwhile, tried to have the film banned, and across Europe, missionaries handed out pamphlets of their own that claimed to expose its lies, and that offered large cash sums to anyone who could produce evidence of a real-life Nina. In Utah itself, the Governor said the producers of the film were 'only exceeded in their perversion of the truth by their absurdity,' and nationally, censors who had once seen nothing to complain about now demanded that changes be made.

This furore had a predictable effect. The *Motion Picture News* said that the film 'has no equal as a money maker,' while according to the *Bioscope*, 'the song of the shrewd successful showman is "The Mormons are coming, Hurrah! Hurrah!"'

In Britain, however, the reception wasn't always welcoming. The Church had established its very first overseas mission there, and taken half of all its converts from the country, but in Liverpool, a curious incident now took place. At the Picturedrome in Garston, as the lights went down and the darkness came in, a young man rose to his feet and shouted, 'I protest against this picture being shown in this hall tonight.' The man might have been an outraged Mormon, or he might have been connected to the film and keen to keep the furore going. No one seemed to know for sure, but either way, he was back out on the pavement before you could sing 'Hurrah! Hurrah!'

Within weeks, *A Victim of the Mormons* had been followed by a near-copy, also Danish, which also did terrific business. But while those films were set in the present day, there were others which looked backwards, to the very beginnings of the Church, and to mythical events from the Old West. They were called such things as *Mountain Meadows Massacre* and *Marriage or Death*, and they showed members of the faithful being cruel to apostates, collaborating with Red Indians, killing Red Indians, ambushing wagon trains to get themselves new wives, and ultimately being vanquished by cowboys. Harold Mitschke had already given the people of Hartlepool his lecture on Mormons and Mormonism, and when *Flower of the Mormon City* arrived at the Northern Pictures in the town, he made sure the fact was proclaimed in a large advertisement in a local newspaper.

The British writer Winifred Graham was a prominent and energetic campaigner against the Latter-day Saints. The play *Through Death Valley* came from her pen, as did an overheated, unreliable history of the Church, together with several novels that claimed to lay bare the Church's evils, and articles with titles such as *The Mormon Pass to Slavery* and *Orgies of the Mormons*. One of her novels, *The Love Story of a Mormon*, features a polygamist with mesmeric powers, who persuades young women in the maritime city of 'Riverpool' to follow him to Utah. The book was published in time for a crusade that would see large crowds gather in halls and market squares across the land.

That crusade began in the maritime city of Liverpool, where a public meeting called upon the Home Secretary, Winston Churchill, to 'safeguard English homes' from Mormonism. *Outré* practices were reported across the river in Birkenhead and Wallasey, and everywhere from Wakefield and Warwick to Chichester and Bognor Regis as well. There were pamphlets, petitions, and letters to editors, many of them anonymous and most utterly devoid of detail. Services were interrupted and participants harassed. Missionaries in Salford were pelted with clods of earth. And in Sheffield and Barnsley, public baths that had been used for baptisms for years were suddenly closed to all Mormon business.

Local worthies, churchmen as much as aldermen, called upon the working men of the country to rise up against this great threat. Winifred Graham had spoken of the Latter-day Saints 'infesting' Europe, and the vicar of Leamington now described them as 'a filthy, immoral sect,' and asked for volunteers to help him horsewhip them from their homes. (He did so during a Thursday evening meeting of Warwickshire's Sunday School teachers.) And back on the banks of the Mersey, the campaign grew louder and even uglier. In Liverpool, a Mormon home was violated by a man who said he had been sent by God, while in Birkenhead, a mob descended upon a building in use as a tabernacle. The mob had a brass band at its head, and policemen who tried to intervene were driven back under a hail of stones.

The government, not wishing to seem indifferent to the public mood, announced that the Church would be the subject of an inquiry by the Home Secretary, and Mr Churchill announced that he would even consider whether Mormons should be expelled from the country. This couldn't help but find an echo in picture houses. *A Study in Scarlet*, the first British film version of that early Conan Doyle tale, has Cheddar Gorge standing in for the Rocky Mountains, Southport sands for the Utah plains. The title of *Marriage or Death* encapsulates the stark choice afforded one young woman after she has been spirited away from her family. And *A Modern Don Juan* has a man join the Church simply so that he can woo several women at the same time.

Before all of that, however, and before even the first of the Danish films, the Hepworth company had produced a short piece that was as prescient as it was funny. Another in the ever-popular series, *Tilly and the Mormon Missionary* again features Alma Taylor in the title role. She and her friend Chrissie White are shown enduring a long sermon from the missionary in question, after he has turned up, quite uninvited, at their home. The girls are fidgeting and yawning, swapping wicked glances, and furtively looking away. And then they too find themselves clapped up in a dismal room, with the door locked and the window barred. They soon get out, of course – by climbing up the chimney – and when they encounter the missionary again, they do him a terrible mischief.

57

Walter Stott and Fred White were adamant that James Watson had defamed them over *Five Nights*, and in court, they said he had done so twice – first in the letter to William Broadhead, and then in what he said to the reporter during their conversation on the telephone. This was 'a gross abuse of Mr Watson's position as Chief Constable,' their barrister told the gentlemen of the jury.

After its one showing in Preston – at the Monday matinee, in front of Corporal Daggers, William Meagher, young Edward Bennett, Margaret Buck and many others – the film would not be seen in the town again, and Walter and Fred would never receive their £40 rent. If Leslie Knight is to be believed, they might easily have suffered an even greater loss.

Mr Knight was the manager of the Theatre Royal, a rival to the King's Palace, and the place where Franz Liszt had once performed and film of the Whit Monday procession had been shown.

Though new to the post, Leslie had already been praised for his acumen. His place was the first in Preston to show *The Battle of Waterloo*, and he had been careful to eschew the scabrous Pimple lampoon which followed. He had, however, shown *Three Weeks* and *A Modern Magdalen*, which left Dublin so inflamed. And he had staged a 'Grand Patriotic Concert' in the earliest days of the war, hanging up flags and bunting, putting on comedians, a ventriloquist, performing ponies and dogs. A local soprano gave 'Land of Hope and Glory', and the musicians he had taken on played the anthems of the Allied nations. Five of them were reported to have been so impressed by the event that they enlisted in the Army the very next day.

And even if his hall and theirs were rivals, Mr Knight did what he could to get on with other exhibitors. His geniality was something else for which he was praised, and he would become firm friends with Will Onda of the Prince's Theatre, and with Billy Boyle, the manager of the King's Palace. He shared a love of sport with Will and a splendid moustache with Billy, even if his friendship with Mr Boyle will have been tested by evidence he gave in the *Five Nights* trial.

When he was questioned by the barrister representing Walter Stott and Fred White, Leslie Knight said they had offered him the film for £75 a week. So was it simply the size of the fee that had led him to reject the offer? Leslie denied that. After he refused to pay the £75, he said, he had been invited to name his own price, but had declined to do so. And that was because he had heard that *Five Nights* 'was hardly a suitable picture for the Theatre Royal, Preston.' But the town was 'notorious for excessively puritanical views,' the barrister insisted. 'I hardly think so,' Mr Knight replied.

This case was about more than a single week's rent. When he himself gave evidence, Walter Stott told the court he had expected many exhibitors to come to the King's Palace to see *Five Nights*, and that he had hoped those who came would decide they must have the film for their own halls. 'The first week is the impression that people get,' he explained, 'and after that, the business comes.' Mr Stott said that if things had gone to plan, he would have taken twenty copies of *Five Nights*. As it was, the original six copies had been sufficient, and he had made less use of them than he had expected. He and Fred White would make a profit on the film only if it was still doing the rounds at Christmas. But after the trouble that began in Preston, demand had all but dried up by Bonfire Night.

This wasn't, however, the only account Walter Stott gave. The previous summer, shortly before *Five Nights* was released, he had been visited in Manchester by a reporter from the *Bioscope*. Walter had taken the man around his offices and put on a bit of a show. He had even brought out a saddle he said had once belonged to Broncho Billy. And when their conversation turned to the new film, his mood was optimistic. 'It is already fixed up right from September until March next year,' he said. 'That is *some* booking,' his visitor replied.

The Chief Constable did not dispute the arithmetic. That could be left to the jury, his barrister said, should the need arise. Where James Watson disagreed with Walter and Fred was in how he characterised what he had done, and in the fact that he considered it perfectly reasonable.

Mr Watson argued that his comments, both in the letter and in his conversation with the reporter, were fair comment on a matter of genuine public importance, and that the law therefore gave him a complete defence. And on the subject of the letter, the Chief Constable went further. He said it had been sent to someone – William Broadhead – with whom he shared a common interest. They would both wish to ensure that films were fit to be shown to the public, he argued, and what he had written was therefore subject to privilege. This meant that it was specially protected by law, and that too would give him a complete defence.

That the letter was privileged Walter and Fred did not deny. If they were to succeed in this aspect of their claim, therefore, they would have to show that the Chief Constable had been motivated by malice when he wrote what he did. And on that point, the judge was firm. At the end of the plaintiffs' case, during the second day of the trial, without hearing any evidence for the defence, Mr Justice Shearman ruled that while James Watson might have misremembered some details of the film, including some quite important ones, his words had not been malicious. The claim concerning the letter must therefore fail.

The words spoken on the telephone were, however, still in

issue, and they would have to be left to the jury.

Walter and Fred's barrister had been forthright on this point. For the Chief Constable to have said what he did to the reporter, the lawyer argued, 'knowing what he said would be spread throughout the district, was a most malicious and wicked thing to do.' But here too Tont Shearman was firm. The issue was not *Five Nights*, what it showed or did not show, and whether that was offensive or improper. The issue, he instructed the jury, was the precise words the Chief Constable had uttered about the film, and whether they went beyond fair comment. And even then, Mr Watson would be entitled to a good deal of latitude:

> As long as any reasonable man, however strong the language he uses, could have arrived at that opinion, he is protected.

With the clock showing nearly five, the jury was sent from the court into a room set aside for its deliberations. As the jurymen formed into a line and filed out, their foreman carried in his hand a single sheet of paper on which the words in question had been neatly typed out:

> I viewed the picture at a matinee, and at the conclusion I decided I could not approve it, because of its objectionable features.

'Gentlemen, those are the words,' the judge had told them, 'and those are the only words which you have to consider.' Their deliberations lasted for little more than an hour, and once they had filed back into court, their verdict was swiftly delivered: the Chief Constable's words were fair comment and nothing more. His defence had indeed proved a complete one, and the claim brought by Walter Stott and Fred White would have to be dismissed. The two men immediately announced that they would appeal.

Easter was as late as could be that year, and when it did finally arrive, Jack Johnson fought again. His opponent this time was Arthur Cravan, a *provocateur* from Lausanne, who had been born with a quite different name.

Arthur wrote intense poems, claimed Oscar Wilde as his uncle, and gave lectures that usually ended in fights. He lived on his wits and his belligerence, and he favoured what he took to be the American way: 'Chew, never speak, always look busy,' he told his followers, 'and above all else, crown yourself with arrogance.' That was advice he never failed to follow himself.

He was tall and lean, with obscene tattoos and a way that could sometimes be winning. He admitted to being 'the world's shortest-haired poet, boxer, hotel rat, muleteer, snake-charmer, chauffeur, ailurophile, gold prospector,' and let it be known that he had once fought a duel with Guillaume Apollinaire. He floated around Europe on dubious papers, sold equally dubious Manets and manuscripts he swore were Wilde's, made friends with hookers and got himself expelled from Berlin, worked as a stoker, sometimes stowed away, jumped ship on his way to the South Seas, and was the sort of man the only slightly more fictional *Sapho* might have sought out. He put out a scabrous magazine, which he hawked through the streets of Paris himself, on the back of a cart taken from a costermonger. His aim, he said, was to 'infuriate my colleagues, to get myself talked about, and to make a name for myself.' When people turned up for his talks, it was often because he had promised to kill himself, or because they thought he might shoot at them, or exhort them to rob the Louvre, or at least bare his arse.

Arthur Cravan's claim to be the champion of Europe was the flimsiest of all. The bout still went ahead, though, in Barcelona, on the 300th anniversary of the death of Cervantes, in a half-empty bullring, as a filthy rain fell. And if it ended precisely when Jack Johnson decided it should, that was in a manner that will have been to Arthur's liking: with boos and hissing, and chairs being thrown. Six cameras had been set up around the ring, but the film he insisted was taken of the event didn't even survive the day.

58

On the day the jury in Manchester returned its verdict in the *Five Nights* trial, councillors across the Pennines in Huddersfield found themselves discussing a related matter. The film was still playing there, even though the authorities had come out against it, and the Chief Constable, John Morton, had decided to make a stand. He should be congratulated for that, one of the councillors told the rest, because 'the whole tendency of the film is to fill the youthful mind with impurity.'

The week before, at a special session of the town's magistrates, Mr Morton had brought up the subject of the Olympia picture house. That was where the film was playing, and the Chief Constable felt it should now be the subject of decisive action.

The place was known to locals as the 'Rumble' because it stood so close to the railway line that every single train, including the one from Holmfirth, could be heard – and felt – as it thundered by. It also stood close to the rink named for the Duke of Albany, Queen Victoria's doomed youngest son, who would not live to marry Daisy Greville. The Albany Hall had an orchestrion made of walnut and brass, which piped and pounded, plinked and plonked, trilled and tinkled away for the skaters as they went round and round on the perfect maple floor.

Addressing the magistrates, Chief Constable Morton made a point of not referring to *Five Nights* by name. That was, however, the limit of his circumspection. He proclaimed that the film was suggestive of immorality all the way through, and that its showing at the Olympia demonstrated that the place was not being properly run. The licence for the place should be taken away, he said, and he was supported in that demand by not one, but two gentlemen of the cloth: the Vicar of Huddersfield and the leader of the Wesleyan Methodists in the town.

When the proprietor of the Olympia finally got his chance to speak, he argued that the merits or demerits of *Five Nights*, its virtues or vices, should have nothing to do with the question of the licence. He conceded, however, that he had carried on showing the film even after he had been asked not to do so. A councillor then told the court that he had himself seen it, at a private viewing, and that he knew for sure that it was immoral in the highest degree and suggestive from beginning to end.

By now, the magistrates were aware of James Watson's success in Manchester, and their deliberations lasted barely fifteen minutes. Once they had filed back into court, the chairman announced that they were in agreement with Mr Morton – the picture house had not been properly run; its licence would therefore be withdrawn.

Unable to do business any more, the Olympia closed its doors. When it reopened several months later, on Christmas Day, it had a different name. The old, derided proprietor was gone as well, and good riddance some said, for this wasn't the first time Walter Stott had come up before the Huddersfield bench.

59

In an office on the ground floor, a man is sitting behind a desk. It is a large desk, the office is small, and the man is in his forties. He is wearing a fashionable brown suit, the jacket of which is long and loose, woollen and much too warm.

This too is Walter Stott, and this the Olympia cinema as well. It is the evening of another hot August day, two years before *Five Nights*, and only a few days after that unfortunate business in Darlington with *Sapho* – the film Walter and his partner, Fred White, have been hawking around the North.

As well as being a renter of films, Walter is also the proprietor of several cinemas. This one was a toffee factory for years and now offers plush seating for a few hundred, with space, should the need arise, for a few more patrons on rough benches at the front, for which they will be charged only tuppence.

A second man now comes in. He is Arthur Preston, the manager of the Olympia, and by his side is a young woman, whose name is Dora, and who recently turned sixteen. Mr Preston introduces Dora to Walter and then leaves the room. The truth of what happened next will be known only to the two of them – and to the two young men who are, even now, watching from up above.

Mr Stott, it was alleged, behaved improperly that day, and without Dora's consent, and the queue that formed outside Huddersfield police court a few weeks later was much greater than any seen lately at the Olympia. She had been a cashier there, and she said she had tried to scream but been unable to.

Dora's mother, Clara Smith, appeared as a witness for the

prosecution. She worked at the Theatre Royal in Huddersfield, in the bar, and she said the manager of the Rumble had come looking for her. She had asked him whether anyone had given a thought to her daughter's honour, and he had replied:

> Let Stott buy you!
> I want you to let money buy you. He has plenty of it!
> Don't you think fifty or a hundred pounds would
> be better than going to the police?

At the end of the morning's proceedings, after Dora and Clara had returned home, a large crowd gathered outside their house and hooted and booed at them. So excited was the crowd that a little girl was knocked to the ground and had her arm broken, and the police had to escort the two women back to court. It was then that Walter gave evidence in his own defence.

He said he talked to Dora about her work in the pay box, and she told him she was going to Blackpool for a week and asked if he would like to go with her. 'You're a nice girl,' he said, and she sat on his knee and placed his arm around her neck. She was most certainly a consenting party to what happened next.

When Arthur Preston spoke, he said he suspected Dora made the first move, as she had told him that she liked the chap in the brown suit and asked if he had plenty of money. He had heard the door being closed behind him as he left the office, and when he came back, the young woman was very frank about what had happened. She was laughing, he said. She told him she might be going on holiday. And she asked if he thought Mr Stott would go with her.

Mr Preston agreed he had spoken to Dora's mother, but he said it was she who had brought up the money, and that she claimed she could get hundreds of pounds from Stott. Arthur had offered a tenner, the mother had asked for fifteen, and he had said he would see what he could do. But their discussions ended shortly afterwards when she went to see a solicitor.

And then it was the turn of the two young men. They were responsible for the machinery at the Olympia, and for cranking the films and making sure they showed up all right on the screen, and all of this had taken place just before the second house. The room they worked in was up a flight of stairs, and it gave a clear view through a fanlight into the office below. They had seen what happened between Dora and Walter. It all seemed to be with her consent, they said.

The magistrates were out for only five minutes, and when they came back, they dismissed the charge. The evidence against Mr Stott wasn't good enough, and there was no reasonable prospect of him being convicted if the case went ahead. That wasn't, though, the end of the matter.

The chairman of the bench felt duty-bound to comment upon the defendant's conduct. It had been disgraceful, he said, and reprehensible in every way. Applause ran round the court, and by the time Walter emerged, another large crowd had formed outside. The police were taking no chances with Dora, given what had happened earlier in the day, and she and her mother were hurried away down an underground corridor.

'You are not proud of what you did on this occasion?' Mr Stott was asked by a reporter. 'No,' he replied. 'I am very much ashamed of it.'

60

The picture houses of those days could be perilous places, once dark had fallen and the curtains drawn apart, and for audiences and members of staff alike there was a real risk that they might come to harm.

The risk, too often, was of unwanted physical contact, but the West Riding of Yorkshire wasn't the only place in which it might be encountered. In Cardiff, a man was convicted of molesting a woman who happened to sit down next to him, while at a hall in Devonport, a sailor indecently assaulted a girl of twelve. He was fined £1, the magistrate addressing him merely to enquire whether he would now lose his job.

But the risk didn't just come from other filmgoers. In Walton-on-Thames, down by the river, an attendant at the Picture Palace was charged with molesting another twelve-year-old girl. He had done it while the film was in progress, the prosecutor said, as the victim sat in the darkness, her friends and younger sister by her side. 'I may have tickled her about a bit,' the man said, when asked to explain himself, 'but there was no harm.' On Shepherd's Bush Green, an old man had his shoulder put out as he was being ejected from the King's Hall. (There was, admittedly, something confrontational about that place, where the leader of the orchestra had said that any pianist who claimed to be able to improvise was a liar and a charlatan.) In New Cross, meanwhile, a manager was fined for actually punching a member of his audience. 'The average picture patron not only wants a lot for his money,' the *Bioscope* noted, reflecting ruefully upon the case, 'he also demands considerable attention and forbearance.'

When it came to battery, it could just as easily be members of staff inflicting that upon each another. That was the case in Rotherham, where the manager of the Cinema House was sent for trial. His was a Moorish place, whose four striped towers each had its own cupola. And even though he was convicted of striking a projectionist, his punishment was modest. 'The bench considered there had been some provocation,' it was explained. But newspapers also told of attendants being beaten by customers. The culprit in Angus was the son of another old man who had been ejected, his frail body passed over the heads of the audience to be dumped unceremoniously in the street outside. A manager was hit with a stick in Birmingham, by a patron he had asked to sit down. And in Aberdeen, the victim was a doorman and the scene of the crime the Star picture house whose owner was Bert Gates.

In Conisbrough, two pit-hands were sent to prison for what they did in the Globe. Having set off some stink-bombs, they tried to escape over the seats, before punching the manager and a constable when they tried to apprehend them. The owner of a hall in Chester-le-Street was assaulted by two men, who had forced their way in and were only finally restrained by members of the audience. And in Bolsover, a man was convicted of beating the manager of the Picture Palace just as the first house was coming out. The aisles being crowded, he too had taken a more direct route, only to find himself seized by the lapels. There had been too much of this jumping over seats, the manager said, especially on Saturday nights, when a much rougher element had started turning up.

It was often on the way out that customers cut up rough. In Notting Hill, a sixteen-year-old boy followed an attendant into the foyer, challenged him to a fight, and then kicked him in the groin. While in Paddington, an attendant was slashed in the face by a youth he had asked to leave. The hall in which that happened had recently been the Ritz, and it would soon be the Coliseum. For now, though, and for the duration, it was the British Cinema.

On occasions, it was the ejected themselves who turned to the law, aiming not so much to secure punishment as to gain recompense. One gentleman was successful in his claim against a picture house in Kensington. He had become embroiled in a row with a lady attendant there over a sixpenny ticket she suspected he didn't have, and when he refused to move, he was unceremoniously hauled from his seat by the doorkeeper. That happened in full view of the rest of the audience, and a jury awarded the man a considerable sum. In Birmingham, meanwhile, two women also recovered damages. They had been shown to a private box in a hall in the city, and the row in their case was about a lamp they insisted should remain lit. When the women were asked to leave, they tarried a little too long, an attendant became impatient, and then he turned aggressive. 'Get out!' he shouted, over the noise of the supporting feature. 'We've had your sort in here before.' Then, seizing hold of the women, their furs, and a small box they had with them:

Out you go! Chocolates and all!

Whatever the nature of the parties, whether member of staff or valued customer, what often triggered confrontations was people standing in the aisles. It annoyed everyone, of course, and stopped them enjoying the film, but it was a particular concern for managers and proprietors. Picture houses were only permitted to admit so many, and an excess might cause someone's livelihood to be lost.

At the Empire in Chesterfield, the manager was assaulted not only by a customer he had asked to sit down, but also by the man's sister, who took exception to what was being done to her brother. 'She caused quite a scene,' the manager said in court, 'and everybody was getting on to the seats to see what was the matter.' Meanwhile, at a cinema in Holloway perhaps unwisely named the Ideal, a man paid for a threepenny ticket only to find that all the seats were full. He was told he couldn't remain in the sixpenny seats to which he removed himself, and when he went into the shilling seats he was asked to leave. There followed hot words, raised fists and a general melee. The manager's clothes were torn and a jewelled tiepin was lost. And then some constables arrived. The man was fined ten shillings and ordered to pay two guineas in costs.

But even if a seat could be found, and a decent view obtained, an evening at the pictures might still be a discomfiting experience, whether in the heart of London or elsewhere. On a winter's day back in the West Riding, in the cinema in Holmfirth of which Reggie Switz had made a home, a young boy fired a revolver at the screen. The boy was a Scout named Baden Powell Wimpenny, and when he appeared in court, he was wearing a uniform just like Winky's. The magistrates fined the boy £1 and instructed his father to stop it out of his pocket money.

In the West End, meanwhile, there was real trouble on the Strand and the manager of Terry's Theatre was hauled up before the bench. A constable who had visited the place several times claimed to have witnessed disorderly conduct in the gallery and the stalls. The culprits, he said, were 'colonial soldiers and women, several of the latter being of known bad character':

> There was a good deal of larking, kissing, cuddling and suchlike familiarities going on. Snatches of popular songs were being loudly sung. A good deal of obscene language was used. And no attention was given by these people to the exhibition of the films.

61

People standing up was a real problem, as films became more popular and competition for audiences grew more intense. For the authorities it meant that halls were full beyond their limit, and everyone was being put at greater and greater risk.

It was certainly a problem at the Picture House in Sunderland, which had a roof that could be drawn back, but usually wasn't, and which was known to locals as the 'Ranch', because of all the cowboy films it showed. When the man from the *Bioscope* arrived there, the seats were full and there were 200 people in the aisles. The problem was the same at the Empire in Wombwell, where the mosaics on the façade matched those in the foyer, but a constable found close to a hundred people on their feet. The owner said they had taken him by surprise, but this wasn't his first offence, and he was fined £3.

And while this sort of thing might have been a staple of the police courts, it didn't go unremarked in town halls. Middlesex councillors were informed that a half of all cinema inspections had revealed overcrowding, and an official who turned up at the Pavilion in Sheffield received a robust response. That place had pilasters on the front, tiled in bands of green, yellow, and white, and there were stained-glass windows in the veranda over the door. Inside, where it was all white and Tudor oak, the lights were actually lanterns, and there were more than 1,000 seats. A man could nevertheless be seen squatting on the floor with his wife and five children. He had paid for all their tickets, the man said, and they were damn well going to see the show.

More than a hundred people were found standing up at the Parkend Empire in Gloucester, nearly 200 at the Cinema

Theatre in Chiswick. And in Manchester, a man who went so far as to complain about the crush at the Deansgate Picture House was awarded damages. The woman in front of him had been poked in the chest by an attendant she asked to find her a seat, and when the man himself issued a stern rebuke, he had his spectacles knocked off and he was thrown out into the street.

The authorities took whatever action they thought they could. Councillors in Nottingham closed down the Parliament Street Picture House because of overcrowding, even though the manager said they had no power to do that, and complained he hadn't been allowed to give his side of the story. Usually, though, the people responsible were summonsed for failing to keep the gangways clear. When that happened to W Harold Speer, the proprietor of the Queen's Theatre in Brighton, he wasn't daunted in the least.

A journalist and publisher, who would go on to make and distribute films of his own, Mr Speer had already opened the first permanent cinema in the town. The Electric Bioscope had just thirty seats, and a projector Harold had to crank by hand, but it proved so successful that he was able to buy the shop next door, put in another 200 seats, and give the new place its illustrious name. The Queen's stood close to Bertie Smith's six leafy acres and chalybeate spring, and the two men shared a passion not only for filmmaking, but also for experimenting with the use of colour. Before long, they were rivals, and then they were adversaries, when Harold joined the legal proceedings that would see Bertie leave the business altogether. For now, though, he put a special notice up on the screen, making no bones about his summons and inviting patrons to 'attend the entertainment at Brighton police court next Tuesday.' What else was to be expected of the place given that a large hoarding across the front promised 'Mirth, Mystery, Comedy, Drama'?

Agnes Shand, in contrast, could do nothing but admit her guilt. She owned the West End Kinema in Dundee, which ran uphill along Shepherd's Loan, between the River Tay and a great grey church, where jute might still be found floating on the breeze. There were towers with cupolas here too, but the walls and roof were made of corrugated iron, and scores of people had been found standing in the aisles one Saturday night. Mrs Shand blamed it on a sudden storm, and on everyone wanting to get out of the rain, but she was fined £1, nonetheless. The film showing that night was *The Campbells Are Coming*, which dealt with the exploits of Highland regiments during the Indian Mutiny. There was a pipe band outside, kilted and skirling away. And Agnes was damned by the advertisement she had placed in a local newspaper. 'Come Early To Avoid The Crush!' the advertisement had said.

A summons was also received by the manager of the Picturedrome in Macclesfield, where the number in the aisles was not far short of the number in the seats. Things were difficult on Saturday nights, he said, because people still got in, no matter what he did to stop them. And most of them did in fact have seats, but had simply chosen to stand up to get a better view. The summons served on Rupert Whittaker received an equally fatalistic response. He was proprietor of the De Luxe Picturedrome in Nelson, where he also gave lectures to accompany the films, and where a hundred people had been discovered in the aisles. This was during an interval, Mr Whittaker said, when customers briefly vacated seats they most certainly possessed. But a constable who had been present told a different story. The seats were really just benches, he said, arranged around stoves that were the only source of heat, and the overcrowding had taken place in the dark, while the film was actually in progress. Rupert, when challenged, had said, 'What can I do?' and he had made no attempt to clear the place. He too was fined £1.

There had also been a hundred up on their feet at the Electric Theatre in Bloxwich. It was all the fault of the railways, the owner's solicitor said in court, because the main film had been delayed and people attending the first house had stayed on for the second house in order to see it. He urged the magistrates to take a broader view, for on some nights:

> ... there was hardly a picture theatre in the Midlands where it was possible to always keep the gangway clear. He had even been in the Royal Courts of Justice when it was next to impossible to move. (Laughter.)

Excesses were reported all over the country, and by no means small ones: thirty people in Harlesden and Acton, at the Cinematograph Theatre and the Crown; forty or fifty in Canning Town, and that number again in Chiswick; sixty people at the Alcazar in Hounslow; and eighty in West Drayton, where the manager said he considered it a kindness to let them come in out of the cold and the wet. A similar excess was reported at the Empire in Whitley Bay. There was space there for everyone, the manager assured the magistrates:

> ... but the people of the town were especially courteous and would not push past those who were sitting in order to get to the seats.

The excuses they came up with were invariably ingenious –

There were more free seats than people standing, or those people were simply looking for seats, or they had chosen to remain standing, even though there were seats, in the hope of being transferred to more expensive ones than those for which they had paid, or they weren't in any danger because, in an emergency, they would have been the first people out of the building, and the films being shown were patriotic ones, so the manager was actually doing work of national importance and was therefore to be congratulated, and certainly not fined.

In Aberdeen, Bert Gates was sued by a man who claimed to have been crushed against a door at the Star. The place was so full of people, the man said, that more attendants should have been provided. But Bert persuaded the court that he had tried to force his way in and was therefore the author of his own misfortune. In any case, he said, proprietors had a patriotic duty to overfill their picture houses, so that more takings could be generated, and more tax collected with which to aid the war effort.

The response the authorities received was often far from contrite. Inside the Electric Theatre in St Helens, a constable found a mass of people huddled together on the steps of the balcony. 'Oh, we generally let them sit there,' an attendant explained, and the manager, when challenged, said, 'They're doing no harm.' But there was also a bicycle blocking an exit. 'Yes, and it's going to stop there,' the manager continued. 'I'm not having it moved for the likes of you.'

And if the dangers of overcrowding were self-evident, they had merged in some minds with another, newer fear. The Mayor of East Ham was particularly emphatic. People should not be standing in the aisles, he told a meeting of the council, 'especially in view of the Zeppelin danger.'

For many people, though, there was a more immediate and even more terrible concern.

62

The Palace in Jarrow, which went up in flames under the stewardship of TV Padden, wasn't the only picture house to meet that fate at around the same time. Nor were the Wood Green Picture Palladium or the Imperial in Walsall.

There were many, many fires, and they usually began in the projection box. The celluloid film of those days was highly combustible – as combustible as the hydrogen inside a Zeppelin – and it often overheated in the projector, or was ignited in some other way as it spooled out onto the floor and settled in brittle coils around the projectionist's feet. And then there were all the discarded cigarettes to contend with.

The Borough Theatre in North Shields was badly burned. This was a large place, reputedly the largest in the town, but it was made of wood and corrugated iron. It stood where Alvo's Circus and a Novelty Hippodrome used to stand, and it was run for a while by Arthur Jefferson, whose son would become Stan Laurel. Under him, the place was a music hall and hosted Shakespeare, and then, under his successor, it started showing films.

It was films that were being shown at the Borough on the night in question, when the fire broke out just after the second house. Within moments, the place was an inferno, visible as a glare in the sky for miles around, and the huge crowd that gathered was kept back only by the intense heat. Flames licked at the surrounding buildings, doors caught alight and windows burst out, and firemen intent on rescue had to be doused from the hose first. The roof fell in just before midnight, followed by one of the walls. Wires and fuses were exposed, and vivid blue flashes could be seen going off everywhere. By dawn, the theatre was a mass of embers and twisted metal, the front gable end reduced to a vestige.

There were also fires –

In Teignmouth, at the impeccably classical Riviera.

In Rochdale, Bradford, and Dunoon.

At the Victoria Palace in Abercarn.

In Royston, in Hertfordshire, where several thousand feet went up.

In Huddersfield again, at the sometimes overcrowded Picturedrome in Golcar.

At the Gem in Maesteg, and in Slough, where the proprietor was given the Albert Medal for his efforts in rescuing a boy.

In Ancoats, during the first house, although the second house was able to go ahead without a hitch.

In Wallasey, at the Lyceum, on a number of occasions.

In Westminster, where a passing film crew filmed it.

At the Hippodrome in St Helens, which played its part in the Five Nights affair, and where the manager was had up for not taking proper precautions.

At Longton, in the Potteries, at what was now the Alexandra. (It had been the Panopticon before that, and a rink before anything else.)

At the Newington Electric Cinema, and in Launceston, during a benefit show for the manager.

In Blackpool, at the Grand Theatre, which had only just started showing films, and where the second house had to be abandoned.

At the Hall of the Good Templar in Arbroath, and the Electric Palace in Nelson. And in Portsmouth, while 2,000 people were watching scenes from the Coronation.

In Cleethorpes, where the cinema had just been given back by the military and was made of wood. And in Dundee, at the

Princess, where what wasn't wood was iron.

And in Bridgend, where the projectionist was overcome in his box and three men with hammers had to smash their way in from the balcony.

At Goole, meanwhile, the Picture Palace was hit by four fires in a single day, and the culprit turned out to be the projectionist himself. He had done it, he said, for ten shillings offered to him by the owner of a rival hall.

The fire at Riddell's Picturedrome in Fraserburgh came on the opening night and began at the same time as the film, but the pianist kept the audience calm by playing some lively airs. Down the road in Aberdeen, only a short while later, there was a fire at Dove Paterson's lovely vermillion hall. The cause this time was a paraffin lamp left unattended on a landing, and its consequence was panic in the gallery, and a broken leg for the woman who threw herself over a banister while trying to escape.

The damage these fires caused could be considerable. A fairground booth in Huddersfield was destroyed when flames that had already claimed the film quickly spread to the canvas roof. And in Thirsk, when a portable cinema went up, the owner refused to pay for the fire brigade, saying he hadn't been the person who called them out. Among places lost to the flames were the Palace in High Wycombe, the Gem in Hexham, Vint's Hippodrome in Neath, and the King's in Perth, where all the musicians' instruments went up as well. At the Brinksway Pictorium in Stockport, an explosion sent the manager flying down a flight of stairs, destroyed the projection box, and tore up the floor. But the pianist, Mrs Finney, told everyone there was nothing to fear, and she struck up a brisk march to prove the point.

Members of staff often came to grief, and the injuries they sustained could even be fatal. Many were burned on the hands and face as they attempted to save blazing film. That happened in Dudley, and also in Handsworth, where the manager and the projectionist were both disfigured. In Stockton-on-Tees, a projectionist died from his burns, while in Abercynon, the victim was a fifteen-year-old boy.

In Charing Cross, at the Cambridge Circus Cinematograph Theatre, it was a workman from outside who lost his life. He had been in the basement when films stored there went up, and the blaze was so fierce that it scorched trees on the other side of the road. The films were in tins the man had been soldering shut, and it was probably his iron that set them alight. The owner of the theatre, Montagu Pyke, had been hoping to export the films to France, but when a coroner's jury concluded that death was due to manslaughter, he found himself facing a criminal charge.

Mr Pyke had been a commercial traveller, like Will Barker, and after a spell prospecting for gold in the American West, he had peddled hair-restorer and patent medicines. He went bankrupt doing that, but after seeing a long queue for a shop-front cinematograph, he had his own hall in no time at all. Other halls followed one by one, with the Cambridge being at least the fourteenth in his chain. It had been done out in baronial style, with wood panelling, thick plush, and even a suit of armour. And, like the owner of the place behind the Red Cow in Salford, Montagu claimed to enjoy the patronage of Queen Alexandra.

On the morning of the trial, the prosecutor rose to address the court. The most that could be alleged against Mr Pyke, he said, was that he had been careless in the way he stored his films. But it wasn't that which had been fatal. There were the tins and the soldering iron to think about as well, and they had been the workman's responsibility. On reflection, it would not be proper to offer any evidence against the defendant, and he would have to be found not guilty. And with that concession made, Archibald Bodkin sat down again.

But this wasn't the end of Montagu's troubles, for he had been losing money for years and now owed three times what he was worth. There were too many picture houses, he said, when he appeared before the bankruptcy court, and his halls were way too small. And it didn't help that they weren't allowed to open on Sundays. Then there were the homes he had bought, and the motor car too, and all the jewellery he had given to his wife. And then she had divorced him, and that was going to cost a pretty penny. But the court wasn't ignorant of what he had achieved. 'You were the pioneer of cinematograph companies on a grand scale?' Montagu Pyke was asked. 'Yes,' he replied. 'I believe I was.'

There were fires overseas as well, with especially tragic ones in Porto Rico, Valence-sur-Rhône, Algeria, Java, the Aisne, Lisbon, Villa Real, New York, Flanders, Salerno, Charleroi. And the many deaths were usually attributed, in the British press at least, to a stampede that was itself the result of pure, blind panic.

The convention was different, though, in the aftermath of fires at home. When the Queen's in Walthamstow went up, a local paper assured its readers that it 'was cleared without the slightest panic,' even though egress was through the house next door. There was 'a complete absence of panic' at the Pavilion in North Ormesby. And in Tavistock, soldiers put out the flames and, the *Exeter & Plymouth Gazette* reported, 'Mrs Walford continued to play the piano.'

It was only much later that the truth came out, when a proper inquiry was held and evidence given on oath had to be reported in all its grim detail. The fire at the Imperial in Walsall had caused 'something of a panic,' it was revealed, as members of the audience rushed for the exits. And the items left behind included 'a few straw hats belonging to females' and 'a baby's odd shoe.' In Stoke-on-Trent, the cry of 'Fire!' might have been a false one, but the ensuing panic was all too real, 'and the corridors were packed with a mass of terror-stricken children, some of whom were knocked down and trampled upon.' There were fatalities in Horncastle, during a fire there. 'The din was great,' a witness said, 'and many older people showed little regard for children in their rush to the open street: several fell down and were trampled on.'

In Deptford, after another false alarm, four children were killed in the crush. And in Middlesbrough, what the coroner was told again gave the lie to earlier reports. The Picture Palace there had been close to full when news of the blaze was proclaimed. There was a rush for the aisles and the doors, an inquest was told, and 'People quite lost their heads.'

One woman fell about two seats from the bottom, and the rest fell on the top. There were about two dozen women and children on the floor near the exit, but the people still rushed on from behind.

Account after account suggested horrible chaos –

People fought madly to escape.

The people in the gallery rushed for the exits and struggled for freedom.

Men, women and children pushed and jostled, falling over one another in their frenzied rush, and the injured simply rolled down the tiers of the gallery.

They rolled into the gutter of the gallery, where at least one body was found. The body was that of a girl about sixteen years-of-age. The spectacle was sickening in the extreme.

They were fighting and jostling in the staircase without heed for sex or age in their mad desire to escape from the building. Children fared the worst and the staircase soon became choked with a seething mass of humanity.

I saw both men and women walk over a heap of injured.

Those on the lower tiers fought and struggled to get up to the exits, and many children were trampled upon and left behind.

I saw two young fellows walk right over the people on the floor.

I stooped down to pick the child up when someone took me by the hair and pulled me to the ground. When I got up, I had lost the child.

Men shouted. Women screamed hysterically.

Women shrieked their loudest and the pandemonium which ensued was unrelieved even when the lights were turned up.

While all this was happening, the orchestra played on and the manager went through the crowd, making announcements he hoped would prove reassuring. He even went up onto the stage to ask for calm, but it was all to no avail. 'My voice could scarcely be heard,' he said, and the noise of the instruments drowned out the moans of the injured and the shrieks of utter, utter panic.

Women, men, and also children, were struggling hatless and with torn clothes down the staircase into the street.

Hatless and breathless they poured through the opening, and the shrieks of hysterical women were mingled with the cries of the injured.

A huge crowd had gathered outside the hall, attracted by the commotion within, and the throng of bystanders and gawpers was swollen by scores of would-be rescuers. Truly pathetic scenes were witnessed:

… as parents having children at the performance came on the scene hatless and breathless to inquire for their little ones. Several fainted from excitement and anxiety, whilst others, securing their children in the crowd, became hysterical with joy and had to receive attention.

63

White

One of the Arctic nights

The room is familiar, and so is the man standing at the easel –
Lonsdale back in his studio in London.

He is painting. He must have recovered.

What Lonsdale is painting is a woman, and as she stands on the pedestal in front of him, she affects a rather exaggerated pose.

This is a new woman, and she has all her clothes on.

Lonsdale breaks off painting and walks up to her.

She smiles at him, comes closer, and tries to stroke his hand.

She even tries to kiss him, but Lonsdale wants none of that and he shows her the door.

The woman goes out of the studio, and when she comes back, she is wearing a coat and hat.

She passes into another room, where Lonsdale is waiting. He takes some money from a box and gives it to her, and the woman leaves.

Back in the studio, Lonsdale is very angry.

He seizes the canvas, pulls it off the easel, and dashes it repeatedly against the floor.

Once, twice…

Then, he goes to a cabinet and takes out a revolver.

He sits down and stares at the gun, and begins to run his hands over it.

He looks away several times, as if he has been distracted, but he always comes back to the gun –

At length one day, when Lonsdale had reached the depths of his abyss, a carriage halted at his door and Viola alighted.

Viola is in her carriage. She is dressed as she was when she left Lonsdale.

There is a young woman with her, obviously a nurse, and the young woman is carrying a baby swathed in baby clothes.

Viola arrives at Lonsdale's studio, and then she's in the entrance hall with the nurse and the child.

Lonsdale is looking at the revolver again, but then he seems to hear something.

The curtain across the door is pulled aside and Viola enters the studio –

The Model.

When Lonsdale sees Viola, he is confused and many different feelings seem to run across his face. But he puts the revolver down on the table.

Viola is smiling at him. Her head is tilted to one side and her eyes seem to glisten.

She and he draw close together, they embrace, and then they kiss, and kiss again.

In between kisses, Viola and Lonsdale talk excitedly.

Then, there is a pause, and she walks slowly out of the room.

When she comes back in, she has the baby in her arms.

Viola holds the baby out to Lonsdale. He looks at the baby, and then he looks at Viola, and she nods her head.

Lonsdale takes the baby in his arms – gingerly at first, as if afraid he might drop it – and then he kisses it.

He kisses Viola too, and it is plain that he and she are crying.

Viola speaks –

'I went away, dearest, in order that you might only know the perfect form which you have always held so sacred.'

Lonsdale leads Viola into a corner of the studio, where he positions her next to the easel.

Then, he steps back a little and cocks his head to the side, and Viola is seen, standing there with the little child in her arms –

His Masterpiece.

64

Many people criticised *Five Nights*, and while some of them singled out particular pieces of action, others made more general complaints about the film, and about the effect they feared it might have.

We have heard from some of those people already –

Of the five scenes of which it is composed there is little to choose between them in regard propriety and fitness for public exhibition. Here there is no question of any moral to be derived or useful lesson to be learned. Each of these scenes is simply the development of situations with adultery as the climax.

(William Patrick Meagher, Preston.)

The picture throughout was very suggestive, offensive, and objectionable. There was no moral good in it whatever. It is a dangerous exhibition to display and entirely unsuitable for young persons to see, for I am convinced the showing of it will have an immoral effect on the minds of young men and women who may unfortunately witness the exhibition of it.

The picture conveys to one's mind that the artist has had sexual intercourse with different women in five nights. From a police point of view, I consider the picture an improper one to display in any licensed theatre or music hall to a public audience.

(John Winstanley, Preston, Chief Inspector.)

There is no good moral or teaching in this film. It is indecent and suggestive and shows a continuation of instances which lead up to immoral conduct with the artist and the young woman. It is not a fit and proper picture to be shown to the public, especially to a mixed audience, as no doubt it would have a tendency to put evil thoughts into the minds of young people.

(James Williamson, Preston, Detective Inspector.)

In my opinion the picture is an immoral one. You cannot get away from it.

(Richard Dorricott, Manchester, Police Inspector.)

It was a very indecent and disgraceful picture all through, and I would not allow anyone belonging to me to see it if I could help it, as anyone could plainly see the immoral meaning from start to finish. I have never seen a picture half as bad as this one.

(Margaret Buck, Preston.)

It was vulgar and made you think bad things when you did not want to do so. The scenes are all in my opinion very vulgar and disgraceful to be shown in any picture palace, and not fit to be shown to any respectable person. It was a nasty picture and ought never to have been shown at all.

(Margaret Nickson, Preston.)

All the scenes in the picture were very objectionable, suggestive and indecent, and in my opinion it was not a fit picture to be shown to any young person, as no doubt it would affect their future morals, and young people can learn such things without being taught by such a rubbishy picture, as all through it indicated immoral conduct with the artist and the young women.

(Frederick Daggers, Preston.)

Several portions of the picture were most certainly indecent and offensive. I would not have liked any of my female relations or friends to have been with me when I saw it.

Although I am not an angel myself, the film as far as I saw it was disgusting to me.

I did not see the finish of the picture, but from what I saw I could plainly see that the subject of the picture was one likely to lead to immorality by those who saw it.

(Edward Bennett, Preston.)

My opinion on the film was that it was an extremely immoral and suggestive picture, and in my judgment entirely unfit to be exhibited to any audience.

I would not have liked to have taken my wife or daughter to see such a thing, and if any female had been in the theatre I would have walked out. Indeed, I should have been ashamed for anyone to have seen me in the place where it was being shown, and this apart from the fact that I am a public man and Mayor of the Borough.

(Benjamin Swanwick, Wallasey, Mayor.)

I cannot go into all the details of the film, but to my mind the whole thing is absolutely immoral.

(Edwin Peace, Wallasey, Councillor.)

In my opinion, there was an utterly immoral atmosphere about the film from beginning to end – in fact, the whole play would be utterly meaningless without the suggestion of immorality. This is based not so much on open indecency – there was nothing in the actual pictures which was indecent – as upon the general drift of the story. I do not think it a fit film to be shown to a mixed audience.

(Arthur Henry Arkle, Birkenhead, Mayor.)

In my opinion, after seeing the film, I considered it improper, especially so far as young people between 12 and 18 years of age. It is not so much what is shown as what is suggested. It was suggestive all the way through and was not ordinary love making, but sensual love making all the way through, and left the impression that every girl he came in contact with he would seduce if he could.

(George William Saville, Birkenhead.)

Altogether I formed the opinion that the film was of a sordid character, depicting scenes of a libertine's amours, which could be fairly considered licentious, and which portrayed no moral, and was neither entertaining nor instructive.

(Charles Christopher Charsley, Coventry.)

I consider it was a very disgraceful picture for any decent people to see, as anyone seeing it could plainly understand that the meaning of it was anything but good.

(May Fazackerley, Preston.)

Like those of everyone else here, May Fazackerley's observations were set out in a formal, written statement drawn up by Chief Constable Watson's lawyer. (That might explain why her words sometimes echo those of other witnesses, and why those witnesses sometimes echo each other.)

Though still young, May was already the mother of two

children, and she lived close to Margaret Buck, in another of the dark houses which confronted the King's Palace. The typescript of her statement contains a comment that suggests she was interviewed in person. It is written in pencil, in a rounded, flowing script. 'A bit deaf,' reads the comment. 'Not a regular picture goer. Only been about twice since.' At the end of the typescript, the same hand has added another comment:

I have never seen anything like it in my life before.

Few of the people who provided witness statements were afforded the opportunity to give evidence in court. They all turned up there, of course – May, Mr Meagher, the two Margarets, Fred, Eddie, and everyone else; housewives, projectionists, and policemen jostling sundry worships, worthies, and clergy. And all, doubtless, in their best bib and tucker.

That wasn't the fault of James Watson. His barrister had asked if he might be permitted to call them all, so that they could talk about their reactions to *Five Nights* and tell the gentlemen of the jury how outraged the film had made them feel. But the judge was not to be persuaded. 'One side might call fifty witnesses and the other a hundred,' Tont declared, 'but that wouldn't prove anything.'

65

After the trial, and despite its result, *Five Nights* could still be seen across the country.

In Bedford, where it was showing at the Empire, they called it: 'The greatest and most talked of film ever produced.' That place had grey and white walls, a carpet of blue, and deep-red seats. And though nothing more had been heard of the sovereign Will Barker offered at the first showing of *East Lynne*, there was still a band to be enjoyed, under the direction of Haydn Farnhill. He was a composer of music as well as a conductor; a choirmaster and a master of brass. And the *Bedfordshire Mercury* said that under his baton, 'the Empire Orchestra plays delightful and appropriate music all through the show.'

That spring, Zeppelins continued to harry England from the east. Coming in over the dark and brutal cliffs of Flamborough Head, with the worst of the weather behind them, they made for Hull once again. Snow had been falling there for hours, the pavements were several inches deep, and the roofs of the buildings glistened white under the stars.

The first of the intruders arrived after midnight, with a drone – or maybe a rattle or a throbbing – that was unmistakeable. Its arrival had been heralded by ships out at sea, and then by a riot of green flares that lit up the sky. But after that, the airship took its own terrible time. It floated above the city for an hour or more, moving this way and that as if choosing its targets with care, pausing every now and again, and sometimes coming down very low indeed. People ran into the streets to view the spectacle, many in their nightclothes, and when the bombardment began, some of them dropped to the ground.

The explosions were seen as a bright red flash. They ripped up tramlines and sewers, and sent masonry, stained glass and broken furniture hurtling through the air. The three maiden Ingamells sisters succumbed to a single bomb in Linnaeus Street, and a young mother was killed beside her four children. A picture house was pressed into service as a dressing station, and survivors were searched for under lanterns that made soft, shifting pools of gold on the white ground.

Save for a single searchlight, which briefly caused one of them to hide behind a cloud, the Zeppelins went unmolested, and when a minister expressed the government's sympathy, a local paper was unimpressed. 'A fig for sympathy!' it stormed. 'We want shells and aeroplanes in the air!' The raids were repeated further south as well, with East Anglia and the Home Counties targeted as they had been before. In Bury St Edmunds, another Zeppelin followed the course of Prussia Lane and destroyed the *King of Prussia* pub, stopping the clock at precisely 10.45.

There were still places, however, where the old nonchalance remained. The London Underground was one of them, at least on the evening Irene Miller made her visit. The celebrated suffragette, novelist, and film writer had been dining out when the sirens went off, and now she was on her way home. 'So I went into the Tube,' she wrote, in a private letter that somehow found its way into the *Illustrated London News*:

> There were a lot of people taking shelter there, sitting about on the steps and platforms, but hundreds more were just going home in the ordinary way...
>
> Lots of those taking shelter weren't really terrified. I know, for they were loving couples, making it a sort of Hampstead Heath on Bank Holiday. Each soldier and his girl spread a newspaper on the platform, sat down,

308

and leant against the wall with their arms around each other's neck and their heads on each other's shoulders (so to speak). There were little groups of such, on the giggle, and enjoying themselves immensely.

As the interlopers grew in confidence and stamina, sorties were made into previously unknown territory: Northamptonshire, Nottinghamshire, Lincolnshire, Rutland, Huntingdonshire. Scotland was reached before Easter, with attacks made on Edinburgh and the docks at Leith. And in Todmorden, what had once been nothing more than a way for Messrs Batty, Ogden and Spencer to drum up trade suddenly became a terrifying reality. The consequences of all this were less screamingly funny than the films, or the newspapers that wrote about the films, had made them seem. Damage worth £1m had been done and 300 people had been killed.

Among other Empires at which *Five Nights* could be seen was the one in Biggleswade.

This place had been built by a showman, on the meadow where his cheerful booths had once been pitched, next to the wooden pavilion he was surprised to find had now been put up by his great rival. It had been given a grand arch and a handsome iron canopy, and special double seats for courting couples. The words picked out in glass on the canopy promised that what went on inside would be both 'Educational' and 'Interesting.' And whatever that was, it would be accompanied by Horace Newman on piano and Gordon Rainbow on violin. Mr Newman was a stalwart of the town's Methodists and its Band of Hope, while Mr Rainbow had played at Temperance events across the county. 'He won golden opinions from his audience,' the *Biggleswade Chronicle* reported, and what the two men produced together at the Empire 'was at all times pleasing and gave additional charm to the pictures.'

The arrival of *Five Nights* in Biggleswade was heralded in the familiar fashion:

A romance of profound emotional appeal presented in a noble manner. An adaptation of the most talked of novel ever published. The most criticised photo-play ever produced.

And the people of the town could also watch a boxing match between Jack Johnson and Jess Willard:

The Greatest Fight Film Picture – World's Heavyweight Championship. Far away, above, beyond all other moving picture portrayals of similar or kindred athletic events. As yet the World's Sporting Masterpiece.

This was the contest in which the great champion, his bout with Pimple notwithstanding, finally succumbed. It took place in Havana, where Johnson was knocked to the canvas in the twenty-sixth round and later said he had taken a dive. 'If he was going to throw the fight,' Willard replied, 'I wish he'd done it sooner. It was hotter 'n hell out there.'

66

Another version of *Five Nights* would eventually appear in halls across the land. And though this one took the form a play, it was the success of Will Barker's film that made it inevitable. Unlike the film, however, this version was all the work of the novel's author.

At first, the Lord Chamberlain took a dim view. The play was not fit to be performed in public, he said, and there could be no question of a theatrical licence being granted. But then he received a revised script that was very different from its predecessor, together with an imploring note from Victoria Cross herself. 'As I understood you wished,' she wrote, 'I have tried to make the atmosphere of the play more serious and moral.' There had plainly been some horse-trading between them, and Miss Cross was keen to place on record the changes she had made. One of them had to do with the delicate question of costume. 'The heroine should pose for a draped picture instead of undraped,' she explained, and she tried to emphasise what she saw as the overall merit of the work:

> The moral is excellent, as Suzee pays with her life for her misdoing and Lonsdale only narrowly escapes.

This had the desired effect, and a licence was soon forthcoming. As a mark of her gratitude, Victoria Cross would make a Censor of Plays the romantic hero of one of her later books.

Then, it was on with the motley. There was an opening night in Camden, at the Bedford Theatre, the baroque-style gem that had enchanted Walter Sickert. An advertisement was placed in the *Stage*, making a virtue of necessity and announcing that the play had been 'specially re-written by its author to conform with the desires of the Lord Chamberlain.' And a portrait of Miss Cross was put on display in London and reproduced in the pages of the *Tatler* and the *Sketch*. The work of May Bridges Lee, a society painter who, like her subject, was a child of the Raj, it is an elegant portrait. But it certainly isn't demure: although Miss Cross is shown with her hair up and her mouth set in a firm line, the dress she is wearing leaves her arms and shoulders bare.

Several elaborate sets had meanwhile been constructed for the play – a tea house (or whatever it was) in Sitka, an artist's studio, Lonsdale's drawing room, and his bedroom in the hotel in San Francisco – and they were praised for their sumptuousness and detail. Special music had been composed to accompany the action, and a large cast assembled, whose members were versed in melodrama, mystery and farce. Two of them had even appeared on film: the actress playing Viola in *Lady Windermere's Fan*; the actor playing Lonsdale in *The Footballer's Honour*. (He turns down a bribe, gets kidnapped by crooks and rescued by his sweetheart, and arrives at the stadium just in time to score the winning goal.) Then, what was billed 'A Love Problem for All Ages' set out on tour.

Swansea saw the first provincial performances, with others following in Bournemouth, in front of what a newspaper described as a 'large and appreciative house.' ('Which reminds us,' the paper went on: '*Five Nights* is being given for six nights this week. This joke should make even Victoria Cross.') Audiences would see a prelude, three acts and an epilogue, each corresponding to one of the nights of the novel (and the film) and sharing its distinctive colour.

The atmosphere on stage was lighter, however, with more humour than many remembered. Characters who had merely been mentioned in print, and who had never appeared on screen, now had lines of their own. And the first performances received praise. Lonsdale was said to have been endowed with 'a romantic and living character' and Viola to be possessed of 'great charm and beautiful feeling,' while the young actress playing Suzee, who had come straight from pantomime, was declared 'as near perfection as can be.'

There were runs in Southampton and Northampton, Bedford and Reading; at the Pier Theatre in Eastbourne and on Brighton's West Pier. And there was a first London run at the Borough Theatre in Stratford. The play was reviewed there by the *Stage*. 'The notoriety achieved by Victoria Cross's novel of passion, and the further advertisement secured by the banning of the film version of the book, will doubtless stimulate many persons into going to see this play,' the newspaper predicted, 'but it may be said at once that they will be considerably disappointed.'

Across the Irish Sea, the official reception was poor. When *Five Nights* arrived in Belfast, the *Northern Whig* declared that it was:

> ... not so much a well-constructed story with a clean-cut plot as a series of loosely and rather clumsily connected episodes in the life of an artist, a study of his rather hectic emotional adventures, which is not in the real sense dramatic.

Several performances were, however, staged at the Grand Opera House, with eight more following at the Gaiety Theatre in Dublin.

The efforts of William Larkin and his confederates had begun to bear fruit in that city, where an official board of censors had now been installed. It comprised a magistrate of independent means, a local headmaster, and two female sanitary inspectors, and a complaint about *Five Nights* was one of the first it received. The complaint again came from the Dublin Vigilance Committee, but it was given short shrift, with the censors deciding that no further action was required.

The *Irish Independent* was as unimpressed with *Five Nights* as its northern rival had been. Lonsdale 'talks posh, paints pictures and messes about with his models,' it reported, before complaining that he and Viola 'feel they are above and beyond all other mere people.' And yet, as they had in towns throughout Britain, the people of Belfast and Dublin came out in their droves to see the play. Long queues snaked along Great Victoria Street and South King Street (and maybe around the corner into Glengall Street and Clarendon Row) and in only a fortnight, the takings from the two cities had grown to nearly £3,000.

In Scotland, *Five Nights* was performed in Edinburgh, and at the Pavilion in Glasgow, where it proved 'a signal success.' In Newcastle, it was hailed as a 'sex problem play of absorbing interest.' But when performances were advertised in the West Riding of Yorkshire, a firm letter landed on the Lord Chamberlain's desk.

The letter came from something calling itself the London Council for the Promotion of Public Morality. This claque of churchmen, teachers and doctors had long campaigned to rid the capital's streets and parks of prostitutes, itinerants and courting couples. Now, it warned that *Five Nights* had already corrupted Putney and Willesden, and that the play would have to be banned if Huddersfield wasn't to meet the same fate. The town was, of course, home to Dora, the young woman who had so enchanted Walter Stott. The play had been booked for the Theatre Royal, and it was there that Dora's mother, Clara, worked as a barmaid, and that Clara had said she would take £15 for her daughter's good name.

The play was performed across the Pennines in Nelson, and down the road in Burnley, where it was 'received with much enthusiasm by a crowded audience.' This was at the Victoria

Opera House and, the *Burnley News* decided, 'a tribute to the following which the novelist enjoys among all classes.' The newspaper was in a reflective mood:

> It would have been impossible a few years ago for a play on these lines to have been performed without strong criticism from a large section of the public, but the hearty reception given to this production seems significant of a change in popular opinion.

Praise was also forthcoming in Coventry, where the *Evening Telegraph* called it 'a most attractive play which was thoroughly enjoyed' at the Opera House. It was only a short stroll from there to the Globe picture house, where the management had been so proud of Signor Avanzi and his string band, and where Chief Constable Charsley had delivered his stern warning about the showing of the *Five Nights* film.

The newspaper went on to say that the killing of Hop Lee and Suzee, and the wounding of Lonsdale, 'made a strangely tragic scene, coming so suddenly after the humorous episode of Suzee appearing in European attire.' That episode had not been shown in the film, nor mentioned either in the brochure produced to promote the film, or in the witness statements drafted in anticipation of the trial. Its appearance in Coventry might be further evidence of the Lord Chamberlain's influence upon Miss Cross.

There were visits to two Grand Theatres. At the one in Croydon, the *Surrey Mirror* wrote, 'the daring nature of the performance attracts crowds and is enthusiastically applauded.' This town was one of several where the play was advertised as being 'For Adults Only'. The Grand Theatre in Derby, meanwhile, stood close to the place where the film of *Five Nights* was shown. But the *Derbyshire Advertiser and Journal* was critical of the play, and also of Lonsdale, whom it considered 'possessed of a rather questionable and peculiar perspective on moral obligations and principles.'

In Liverpool, *Five Nights* was presented at the Shakespeare Theatre, which locals couldn't help but call the 'Shakey'. The play arrived there just after *Three Weeks* had left, Elinor Glyn having been as successful as Victoria Cross in persuading the Lord Chamberlain to change his mind. Horse-trading had taken place here as well, with the gap between the age of 'The Lady' and that of her lover being greatly reduced. Just like Miss Cross, Ms Glyn had made a point of stressing the moral benefits of having her heroine killed off. But while the changes she had made might have satisfied the authorities, they did not make the play any more credible. 'The audience last night was inclined to take the whole affair as a joke,' the Lord Chamberlain's spy informed his master, 'and indeed the unconscious fun considerably relieved the boredom of it.'

The producers of *Five Nights* would eventually boast that it had been on the road continuously for more than two years. The play was performed in Aston and Bath, Leicester, Llanelli, Smethwick and Penge. In London, it appeared at the Borough Theatre again, and at the Royal Artillery Theatre in Woolwich. It was performed in Bognor Regis from Monday to Wednesday; while in Worthing, on Thursday, a special announcement was made from the stage of the New Theatre Royal – once Saturday's matinee was done, the play's female star would descend by parachute from the skies over the town.

It was in Yorkshire, however, that the reception proved most phlegmatic. The play had gone ahead in Huddersfield, despite the dire warnings of the Lord Chamberlain's correspondent, and there had been a good house on the opening night, despite some filthy weather. The town seemed to have come through the experience unscathed, and yet the *Huddersfield Daily Examiner* was unimpressed. 'Almost everyone in the drama is represented as showing highly developed amatory tendencies,' it noted, 'and the play therefore suffers in interest somewhat for want of greater contrast in mood.'

There had been good houses in Wakefield and Doncaster as well, even if the play had been pronounced 'as decorous as a tea party' in Leeds. But the people of Hull had been unimpressed by Lonsdale's killing of Hop Lee. 'It would have been more equitable,' a local paper said, 'if the Englishman had met that fate instead of the Chinaman.' And in Halifax, people were unimpressed with the whole wretched thing. 'Lonsdale is an artist of easy morals,' the local newspaper informed its readers:

> ... ready to flirt with anything presentable in the feminine line, and the majority of the women in the play are of similar type, and rave over this said artist in the most unmaidenly style.
>
> The whole atmosphere is calculated to appeal to the neurotic and shallow-pated but is likely to be dissipated by a good breath of Yorkshire common sense.

There were still places where the appetite for *Five Nights* could only be satisfied by the film itself. That was the case from Sittingbourne, Ramsgate and Haywards Heath all the way to Montrose, Musselburgh and Perth. A particularly strong impression had been made upon the people of Lincoln, where, long after the film was first shown, two new offerings at the Central Cinema were advertised as being 'a *Five Nights* type' of story and 'greater than *Five Nights*'.

When the showings finally began to dwindle, it was just as the performances were doing the same – nearly three years after the play had opened, and fully five years after the film had been seen so very briefly in Preston.

The play had visited that town in the autumn of its first year, and it had received rather more performances there than the film had had showings. The venue for those performances was the Empire Theatre, whose owner made a point of saying that he would present only 'clean, wholesome amusement.' And if, like people in Burnley, audiences couldn't help but recall what had gone on previously, that was only to be expected. 'The story is not a pretty one,' the *Lancashire Evening Post* wrote, 'though it is harmlessly worked out in this adaptation.' The paper revealed how Victoria Cross had given effect to another of the concessions the Lord Chamberlain had wrung out of her. During the play, readers were informed, Viola refuses to marry Lonsdale publicly for fear of impeding his artistic development. She and he have already been shown taking part in a clandestine ceremony, however, and though she believes that ceremony to have been a sham, she is mistaken – and:

As she is married to him at the start, and as the secret is well known to the audience, the conventions are duly respected.

67

Before long, Walter Stott and Fred White were in court again. They were, indeed, in the Manchester Assize Court again, standing under the great striped roof, on the floor of chocolates and cream. And they were the plaintiffs again, gazing up at the acanthus leaves, the great rose window, the carvings of punishments through the ages. Their opponent this time, however, was not a policeman, but a newspaper publisher.

The subject of the proceedings was the letter the *Bury Times* had published the previous year, while *Five Nights* was playing in the town; the one in which Reverend Glenday called the film 'notoriously suggestive and indecent,' and said that, in allowing it to be shown, councillors had 'outraged the sense of decency of every sober-minded citizen.' Walter and Fred again claimed that their good name had been tarnished, and they again demanded damages to compensate for their loss. They used the same lawyers they had used in their suit against James Watson, while the newspaper instructed the ones who had so successfully represented him. And, as the Chief Constable had done, the paper argued that the words in the clergyman's letter were nothing more than fair comment on a matter of public importance.

The trial again took two days, and the gentlemen of the jury again found themselves crossing the road and filing into the Star picture house to watch *Five Nights* for themselves. They too had been out for a couple of hours when their foreman rose to address the court. There was no prospect, he said, of a verdict ever being reached. The trial was therefore brought to an end, and Walter and Fred announced that they would let the matter drop.

But it was only the proceedings against the *Bury Times* that Walter and Fred let drop, for barely a fortnight later, they were back in court yet again. This time they were suing for damages from the magistrates of St Helens, who, in the very week of the vicar's letter, had banned *Five Nights* from being shown at the Hippodrome picture house in the town. Walter and Fred had failed in an earlier attempt to have the ban overturned, and now they sought to recover what they said the ban had cost them in lost rental fees.

The St Helens magistrates had certainly gone further than James Watson did in Preston, and Walter and Fred now alleged that they had also gone beyond their legal powers. The judge, however, did not agree. The licence for the Hippodrome stipulated that no film should be shown that was likely 'to educate the young in the wrong direction.' That objective was both reasonable and desirable, the judge said, and he ruled that the objective would be frustrated if *Five Nights* were shown. In doing that, he too went further than anyone before him. His ruling wasn't confined to a discrete comment and the question of whether or not the comment was fair; it was a verdict on the moral worth of the film itself.

Paula, too, was in court at this time, the Bamforth company having been accused of breaking promises made to the actress who took on the title role. Hetty Payne was her name, and she had been paid three guineas a week for her work on the company's first feature, as she strove to do justice to Victoria Cross's beautiful but doomed altruist. But Hetty claimed that she was also due a bonus, which might be worth as much as £100.

The claim was heard in the Strand, at the Royal Courts of Justice, where Hetty told the jury that she had worked on *Paula* for up to twelve hours a day, sometimes even on Sundays. She pushed herself so hard she became quite ill, she said, but then she received a letter saying her services were no longer required.

Hetty spoke quietly when recounting this tale – so quietly that the judge had difficulty hearing her. 'It is a good thing you play in cinema plays, and not in others,' he said.

Hetty Payne had, in fact, been playing in cinema plays for years, ever since she came to the attention of Cecil Hepworth and was given a job at his studio, down by the river in Walton-on-Thames. She might have been one of the women dancing behind the odd little man in *I Do Like to Be Where the Girls Are*, or chasing after Alma Taylor in *Tilly and the Fire Engines*. But she was over thirty now, and *Paula* was her first lead role. As well as the wage and the possible bonus, it brought her attention of a kind she hadn't known before. She had been born in Lambeth, the daughter of a housepainter, the granddaughter of a plumber and a coachman, and she had herself been in domestic service before going into films. Now, she would see herself mentioned alongside Eve Balfour in the pages of the *Daily Mirror*.

Her childhood had been marked by disruption and sadness, the product, most often, of her father's own troubles. Eber Payne had lost his job on the railway because of his drinking, and he was soon brought up before the police court, accused of neglecting Hetty, her siblings and their mother. He was no longer living with them, the court was told – in the small house they shared with thirteen other people – and he was most often to be found in pubs and beer shops. He had given his wife only five shillings in the last month, and she and the children had been forced to look to the parish for relief. But imprisonment would not be the end of his or his family's tribulations. Soon after Mr Payne's release, a rumour went round Lambeth, saying that he had drowned himself in the sea. The rumour persisted, even after the Chief Constable himself denied it, and when Eber's death was confirmed no one was greatly surprised. The death hadn't occurred in the sea, however, but in hospital; and its cause wasn't suicide, but fibrosis, a lung disease whose terrible effects Eber will have had to endure for many months.

When *Paula* came out, Hetty Payne's photograph, like the one of Sybil de Bray before her, appeared in the *Sketch*. It had been taken by a man who made portraits of Marie Lloyd and George Robey, and who had photographed Reginald Switz on stage before he became Winky. This photograph shows Hetty in a loose blouse with lace at the cuffs, and a long, full skirt. She is carrying a garland of flowers, as she engages the viewer with her dark, almost mournful eyes. Her hair is dark as well, short, and unquestionably tousled. And the caption makes sure to say that 'She has another important cinema engagement in hand.'

It was Bamforth's managing director who had sent Hetty the letter, and he said in court that he had known from the start that the film was bad – 'Very bad. Very bad indeed.' A review describing it as 'a tragedy with more laughter than tears' had shaken everyone up, and then there was all the expense: Victoria Cross had been paid £900 for the rights to her book; wages and overheads had been well over £2,000; and so far, little more than £100 had been recouped.

But that wasn't at all what had been predicted. Hetty told the court that, after an early showing, the managing director had patted her on the back and said, 'This film is going to be a great success.' Then, the company placed an advertisement in the press, saying, '*Paula* will go down as one of the greatest money-takers ever produced in Great Britain.' And the *Bioscope* called it, 'a picture which any exhibitor can put before his patrons with every confidence.' In Glasgow, the film was reported to be 'an immediate success,' and to have 'already been booked for numerous runs in the city.' It would be seen by audiences from Barnstaple to Shipley, and at Agnes Shand's place in Dundee. In Hastings, it was shown at the Central, where there was no sign, just a simple red light to bring in the customers, and Mrs Collins, who had a bus to catch, would close the lid of her piano at 10.30pm sharp, whether the film had finished or not. Business was so good, in fact, that at the end of the year, the *Bioscope* included the film on a list of those 'Still Winning Bread.'

Hetty Payne got married while she was waiting to have her day in court. It was a lovely ceremony, held in Dover, where her new husband was stationed. She wore a dress of crêpe de chine with a net of lavender tint. Her corsage was orange blossoms and white heather, and she carried a shower bouquet of pink and white carnations. And when the time came, the jury awarded her everything she had claimed.

The *Five Nights* film could be seen all that summer, fully a year after it had appeared so briefly in Preston. It was shown in South Shields again, at the Westoe Picture House this time, which some called the 'Chi', because it stood on Chichester Road. The place had a band, but no carpet, and wooden forms where seats ought to be. The film was also shown in Bo'ness, Burntisland, and Kilsyth, and in Port Brae, where the picture house was lapped by the grey waters of the Firth of Forth.

When *Five Nights* was shown in Dumfries, at the hall in the Mechanics Institute, the local paper was in two minds. 'As is only to be expected,' it wrote, 'the tone of the picture is not too high, but the photography is good.' A few weeks later, in the town's magistrates' court, the licence for the hall came up for renewal, and the Chief Constable had something to say. It wasn't so much about the film as about the handbills that had been passed around to advertise it. They were objectionable, he told the provost and bailies, and regrettably, they had come into the hands of children.

At a packed meeting, on another hot day in summer, the Mayor of Preston informed the town's councillors that legal proceedings against James Watson were now at an end. The appeal Walter Stott and Fred White had announced at the end of the *Five Nights* trial was not to be pursued after all. ('Hear,

hear!') The Mayor was in triumphal mood, and he didn't stop there. The Chief Constable's stance had been fully vindicated, he said, because it had brought the film to the attention of the authorities, and that was in the interests of good morals and the proper supervision of the kinema. Mr Watson's courage was to be praised. ('Applause.') And there was one final 'gratifying circumstance' to be considered: because of his victory, the Council had been awarded its legal costs and had actually ended up in profit. 'Litigation would be more popular if that result had been more often achieved,' the Mayor said. ('Laughter.')

Five Nights had been seen in many towns by now, but banned from many others, and its allure was finally starting to diminish. But while Walter Stott and Fred White had had their day in court – several days, in fact – they had failed to silence their critics, or to obtain a single penny in damages.

The *Preston Herald* now took time to consider what all this might mean…

68

This finally ends a case which had in it many interesting features, but in the trial of which some vital points were left unconsidered.

For example, we should all have liked a decision on the question of the right of the police to interfere with the public exhibition of films which have already been passed by the Censor... The question of competence or qualification of policemen to act as critics and to judge upon the artistic merits or moral qualities of films was also ignored, although to many the issue of the case would seem to have a bearing on this point.

These are points which will certainly have to be settled sooner or later...

Public exhibitors of films have nothing to gain by showing immoral films; on the contrary, they have thereby much to lose. They are not in business to present pictures which offend the sensitive mind and shock the moral feelings of religious people, nor yet to incur the displeasure of the police, and, in fact, bring them in open conflict with the authorities. Their business is to entertain the public in a sober and healthy fashion, and to place before them a respectable programme. Indecency doesn't pay them. They know it better than anyone else.

This fact admitted, they are at least entitled to ordinary consideration. They have invested their money in the picture business, and therefore should not be subject to unfair or capricious interference from the police or anyone else. So long as their shows are untainted and have been approved or passed by expert censors, it should not come within the purview or the functions of an ordinary policeman to exercise a ban or issue a threat.

It is not enough that the policeman might – however free from bias he might be – consider that a picture is indecent.

The question which arises is this – is he a competent person to judge artistically upon the merits of the film? Of nine out of every ten policemen, it may be answered, without the slightest disrespect, with an unqualified negative. We are not making any allegation or charge against the Preston police; they are as able and efficient as the best police force in the United Kingdom. Our remarks are intended to have a general application.

Meanwhile, as public opinion ripens, it has to be observed that both judge and jury approved of the action of our Chief Constable. It has also to be further observed that Mr Watson's action almost immediately set in motion the active surveillance of the police authorities throughout the country so far as this particular film was concerned, and the results which followed in other towns clearly showed that he was by no means alone in his judgment. His judgment, so to speak, has been largely endorsed.

We have no guarantee, however, that every policeman is as competent a judge upon films as Mr Watson, or that their judgment would withstand the crucial test through which he passed.

69

And in that way the *Five Nights* business came to an end; with a few carefully chosen words in a local newspaper, perhaps after an exchange of letters between the solicitors for each side. After all that upset, all those witness statements, all that money spent on legal fees. It wouldn't, though, be Walter or Fred's last time in the spotlight, nor would it be the end of their questionable, provocative dealings, or of solicitors' letters or long days spent in court.

Advertisements soon began appearing in the press for yet another bold new film. *Zepped!* was the title the advertisements proclaimed, before repeating it over and over again. And even if they didn't at first name the star, his identity cannot have been in doubt. Prominent in each advertisement was a caricature of a man with a bowler hat, a baggy suit, bow legs and a cane. Eventually, the advertisements stopped making any bones about it. 'The Great Chaplin Film' is what they proclaimed.

Beneath the title, alongside the caricature, there appeared a drawing of an airship caught in the glow of searchlights above the silhouette of a desperate town. 'Not a Cartoon, but a Real Zepp,' the advertisements promised. 'Actual Explosions and a Cast That Draws.' Each one occupied a double page. 'Come and View the film,' it said. 'It's a Scream!' 'Don't put off until tomorrow what your opposition can do today.'

Many picture house proprietors were persuaded by this, and the film was soon playing to audiences in Chichester, at the Corn Exchange, and in Bognor again, on the pier. It was playing in Leamington Spa and Rugby, in Batley, and in Wakefield as well, at the Hippodrome, where the supremely self-confident

Richard Lloyd Horner had once held court.

And *Zepped* could also be seen in places that had experienced the brutality of the Zeppelins for themselves. Walsall was one such place, Nottingham another. The film was shown there at the Goldsmith Picture House, which stood close to Victoria Station, where bombs had fallen on platform seven, and close to the Primitive Methodist chapel as well, which had been all but destroyed. In Hull, bombs had fallen only yards from the Tower Picture House, rattling the green and cream faience tiles of the façade.

Zepped was shown there, at what was, in truth, a marvel of the Edwardian baroque. The place had a broad, splayed entrance, with its name picked out in stained glass on the arched canopy above. A large lunette reposed on the first floor, inside a sunburst surround, behind columns and a wrought-iron balustrade. There were domes like onions at opposite ends of the roof, each covered in mosaic and gold. And a classical figure perched nervously – and perhaps unwisely – on the pediment between the domes, her breasts bared to friend and foe alike, and to everyone passing along Anlaby Road fifty feet below.

The film shows Charlie sitting beneath a tree in a beautiful park, reading a newspaper and apparently finding out what has been happening in the land of his birth. 'Zeppelin Brought Down', the headline says. 'Airship In Flames. Fell In Three Parts'. He raises an eyebrow and then lowers it, does that again, and comes over all wistful. *Oh! Take me back to dear old Blighty*, says a title-card, perhaps as a cue for the audience to sing along. Charlie dozes off in the sunshine, and when he wakes, he is in the middle of a fantastical flight – going up, up into the heavens, spinning down through the clouds, and gently coming to rest on top of a charming little church.

This scene is delivered in the sort of simple, staccato animation that was commonplace by now. A later one shows a fat sausage – tied off at both ends, with 'Made in Germany' written along it – spinning around as Charlie had, then splitting open to reveal another caricature – Kaiser Bill with a Pickelhaube on his head.

The Zeppelin, when it appears, is sailing serenely over some trees and the chimneys of a dark English house, and Charlie himself is gazing upwards and holding onto his girl. Then, he is calling for the police, spitting on his hands and rolling up his sleeves, clutching a rifle and loosing off bullets into the sky. There are constables everywhere, in fact – special ones, village ones, and a posse of comedy ones who will have been familiar to his many fans, and who charge this way and that, hither and yon. Sometimes the film is white and grey, sometimes turquoise or a sickly sort of yellow. The airship seems huge, and it too is pictured in the play of lights. And at the end, it can be seen crashing to the ground in a great ball of flame, and Charlie can be seen running away with the seat of his trousers on fire.

Or the film would have you believe it is Charlie doing those things. The airship looks real enough, but the footage might not show an actual Zeppelin, and it might have been filmed well before the war. And the sightings of the man himself are nothing but clips from his earlier films – *His New Profession*, *The Tramp*, *A Jitney Elopement*, *By the Sea* – put together now in the service of a quite different story. Night and day seem interchangeable here, and in the park, reading the newspaper, Charlie is sitting on a bench one minute and lying on the grass the next; his bow tie has suddenly become a necktie; and he is not looking wistful anymore, but very, very glum. While *Zepped* might suggest that he was finally doing something for the war effort, the man himself didn't shoot a single frame for the film. He probably didn't even know it was being made.

In the new advertisements, the men responsible for this great opportunistic exercise informed readers that it could be viewed twice a day at their business premises in Manchester. Those were, as it happens, the premises of Walter Stott and Fred White. And it was those men who added to the advertisements an exclamation mark that does not appear in the title on the film itself.

70

On a warm evening near the end of summer, a mob descended upon the Electric Palace in Notting Hill, hurling stones at the Spanish mahogany doors, and imperilling the lavish plasterwork that lay within. An explanation of sorts could be found in events of the previous night, when explosions had been felt in nearby streets and damage had reportedly been done to houses. Everyone said the culprit was a Zeppelin drawn in by lights for which the cinema's German manager was responsible.

The first film had been shown there several years before. It was *Henry VIII*, Will Barker's sumptuous but ephemeral masterpiece, and the threepence or sixpence patrons paid for admission bought them a bun and an orange as well.

The Electric Palace claimed to be the very first purpose-built picture house, and it had fruiterers for neighbours, cake-makers, butchers, and cheesemongers. It too bore traces of the baroque, with a cupola above those dark doors, a *trompe l'oeil* on the façade and *flambeaux* on the roof. A second cupola sat on top of the red and gold paybox, and the name of the place was picked out in blue on the tessellated floor. The ceiling of the auditorium was vaulted and coffered. There were pilasters and a cornice in ivory or white; garlands, cartouches, roundels. And what surrounded the screen wasn't so much a proscenium as a picture frame, surmounted by a globe in a golden arch.

The Notting Hill of those days was a disparate, restless place. Once known for its brick kilns and piggeries, and for a racecourse that became waterlogged much too easily, it was the place where Nehru and Thomas Hardy had lived as students. It had been a devotional place for Carmelites, Poor Clare's, and

Little Sisters of the Poor. And, after they were released from prison, it was the place where Emmeline Pankhurst and her daughter Christabel came looking for refuge. People connected with the Electric Palace had lately found it a discomfiting place.

There had already been a disturbance, when a large crowd gathered outside the hall and began disputing the finer points of the war. That was followed by a fire inside – the result, the management insisted, of utter negligence in the projection box. And now, there was the prospect of real competition. The Coronet, a beautiful theatre that stood not five minutes' walk away, had played host to Ellen Terry, *Sapho* and, inevitably, King Edward. It had been refurbished in a fashion the critics agreed was both beautiful and chaste, and advertisements in the better newspapers had proclaimed the coming of films. On opening night, 'God Save the King' was given by Mr Hayden Coffin, the audience couldn't help but join in, and footage was shown of the Zeppelin that had recently been shot down over Potters Bar.

The Zeppelin had been shot down barely a week before, with the loss of its entire crew. The commander – the infamous, charismatic Kapitänleutnant Heinrich Mathy – had taken part in the very first raid, and in more of the ones which followed than anyone else. He was, indeed, the man who had so nimbly navigated Prussia Lane in Bury St Edmunds and stopped the clock at the King of Prussia pub. He was a native not of Prussia, however, but of Baden-Württenberg, in Germany's South West. He had been born and educated in Mannheim, which, like Holmfirth, sits at the confluence of two fierce rivers. The city was famous for its courtly music, for motor cars made by Karl Benz, and for the many airships that were being cajoled out of their hangars close by.

Mathy was fond of making audacious claims, none more audacious than the claim that he had let his bombs fall on the Bank of England and Tower Bridge. Now, though, he had remained fixed in a lattice of searchlights for much too long, and a British pilot had been able to close on him and confront him in the clear, dark skies above North London. After some adroit manoeuvring of his own, Second Lieutenant Wulstan Tempest had even been able to fly under the belly of Mathy's craft and loose off several rounds. There was a great glowing within, as if from a Chinese lantern, Tempest would say; flames were spat out of the front; and the whole thing tipped finally downwards. A journalist remembered it as 'a ruined star falling slowly to earth,' and its burning was bright enough to illuminate bedrooms for miles around. It became perpendicular and then split in half, and the Commander chose to fling himself from the gondola before it smashed into the ground.

Doors and windows had been rattled, and cows gone berserk. Locals had come out into the streets to watch the terrible spectacle unfold, often in their nightclothes. None of them could know how it would end, or if they themselves would be safe, but as the behemoth finally succumbed, some of them started singing 'God Save the King'. The light was somehow lurid, an acrid smell filled the nostrils, and sparks and glowing splinters danced on the air.

The first people to reach the scene found an Iron Cross, a watch – stopped at 1.20 – and some pieces of black bread, which they shared out amongst themselves. They were soon joined by sightseers, some of them in evening dress, as if they had come straight from the West End. The cordon that had been thrown around the site proved a permeable affair, and souvenirs were to be had from soldiers for a few cigarettes or a bit of chocolate. The owner of an adjoining field allowed visitors to view the wreckage for a shilling a head.

One of the halves had fallen into a tree that would forever afterwards be known as the Zeppelin Oak. This portion appears in the film as a mess of twisted metal struts, still smoking the following day. The tree is terribly disturbed, and the struts don't repose in it so much as completely overwhelm it, like the nest of a massive, unruly bird. Soldiers can be seen milling about as the camera pans from left to right, chatting, shouldering arms, smoking cigarettes. There is a man in a bowler hat who might have come from the ministry. And in the background, onlookers with umbrellas are casually held back.

The body of Commander Mathy was found straight away, embedded in the soft earth, still clad in his dark uniform and the greatcoat with gold stripes on the sleeve. One of his arms was straight, the other crooked; one hand open, the other a fist. And still wound around his neck was the thick scarf that had been a present from his wife. A photographer made sure that the impression the body left behind was captured for the newspapers, and for all time.

The funeral took place four days later, with advertisements for the film of the wreckage already doing the rounds. Several hundred people crowded into the tiny churchyard on Mutton Lane. Many of them were soldiers, some invalids, but the ceremony was given only a bare minimum of military pomp. The remains of each crewman were placed in a coffin of Japanese ash, and Mathy's coffin, covered by a black pall, was carried to the graveside by officers of the Royal Flying Corps. A local vicar performed the obsequies, alongside an Army chaplain who found it impossible, when the Commander's body was committed to the earth, to acknowledge him in the traditional way as 'this our brother.'

The foreign connections of the Electric Palace had been known to the authorities for some time, and they were revealed to the British public in the same campaign that saw the *Evening News* call for a boycott of the West End Cinema.

One man was considered to be of particular concern. Alfred Liebmann had been a hop merchant before he went into films, working in his father's business. Like Heinrich Mathy, he was born and educated in Mannheim. He travelled in France and Belgium for a while, before the business brought him to Britain. He had lived in the country for more than twenty-five years, and had long ago swapped hops for celluloid, but his origins were enough, once hostilities began, to get his picture house licence taken away. Alfred was outraged by the decision, and determined to challenge it, but when he went to court, his case was dismissed. Three judges ruled that the licence had been lawfully taken away, and they even ordered Alfred to pay all the costs. One of the judges was Sir Montague Shearman, and the lawyer who persuaded him to make the ruling he did was Archibald Bodkin.

Alfred Liebmann was well known in London, in the picture house trade and the world of films. Like Oszkár Rausch, he was a leading light of the Selsior company, and the 'dancing films' were largely down to him. But that was no help when posters started appearing on walls around the Electric Palace. 'General Warning!' the posters warned:

German agents in England are engaged in collecting funds for the enemy by running a number of electric cinema shows…

Some of these capitalists are at this moment fighting with the Mad Kaiser's Army.

What will the British public now think of these cunning Germ-huns as soldiers or picture show proprietors?

Britons! Beat down your enemies!

Stand by your own people in their hour of peril!

Alfred thought he knew who was responsible for this, and he issued a writ for libel. And this time when he went to court, he came out on top. He was awarded damages of £25, and the posters were ordered to be taken down. But he wasn't able to savour his victory for long. In a matter of days, he was fighting for much more than his reputation.

Although Alfred had relinquished his German nationality many years before, he had never formally become British, and in official eyes, at least, that meant he was an enemy. The posters and the business with the licence had exposed a troubling lacuna, and the authorities plainly took the view that something must be done. A constable was therefore dispatched up Portobello Road, and soon, like Oszkár Rausch, Alfred Liebmann was languishing in a camp for aliens.

In Alfred's case, however, that camp wasn't situated on the Isle of Man, but in Wakefield, in West Yorkshire; a much less exposed or permeable place. He was still a man of means, at least for the time being, and he was entitled to be interned among the more privileged of the nation's supposed enemies. In exchange for a rent of ten shillings a week, he would have access to barbers' shops and tailors' shops, education classes, drama groups, and a library. For some men there was even the prospect of extra rations and a bottle or two of wine, and of visits from their wives, or from other women entirely.

Alfred appealed again, of course – doing so in the very week *Five Nights* should have been showing in Preston – but he was again unsuccessful. No evidence could be produced against him, but that wasn't sufficient to secure his release. His lawyer, changing tack, argued that the power of internment was nowhere mentioned in the law – not even in the hurriedly made law of which Anton Blazer had fallen foul. That might be so, the judge replied, but it was a power the monarch had enjoyed since time immemorial, and it was available to the government as well. If there were such a power, it could only be used against combatants, the lawyer insisted, and no one said Mr Liebmann was one of those. In response to this point, the judge broke new ground. 'This war is not being carried on by naval and military forces only,' he said:

Reports, rumours, intrigues play a large part. Methods

of communication with the enemy have been entirely altered and largely used. I need only refer to wireless telegraph, signalling by lights, and the employment, on a scale hitherto unknown, of carrier pigeons…

In these circumstances a German civilian in this country may be a danger in promoting unrest, suspicion, doubts of victory; in communicating intelligence; in assisting in the movement of submarines and Zeppelins – a far greater danger, indeed, than a German soldier or sailor.

The German people – the judge continued, drawing on evidence that surely cannot have been laid before the court – 'consider that the acceptance of hospitality connotes no obligation, and that no blow can be foul.' It would be folly, he said, 'to wait for proof of an overt act or for evidence of an evil intent.'

Whatever motivated the members of the mob that descended upon Notting Hill, whether it was the judge's words or prejudice of a less composed kind, they were sadly mistaken, even if their blood was up. The government had not been sated by Alfred Liebmann's internment, and it didn't rest, even when he was behind a fence. Steps had been taken to dispossess him of his lovely hall – steps that were as brutally effective as they were unimpeachably lawful. And the Electric Palace had for some time reposed in different, wholly British hands.

71

A young woman signals to her lover from the window of the room in which she is confined, and she is then rescued by him, and by another posse of constables and detectives, after a furious bout of hand-to-hand, toe-to-toe fighting. The woman is English, and her captor – once again a Mormon missionary – is once again mesmeric.

These are scenes from *Trapped by the Mormons*, and by the time that film came out, audiences were used to such things. They had seen adaptations of the books of Zane Grey, the Ohio dentist who eulogised the Old West to great commercial effect, and whose purple prose told of sequestered women and a city of sealed wives. They might have seen *A Mormon Maid*, billed as 'The most exciting and thrilling of all sensational feature screen dramas.' And if they saw *The Mormon Uncle*, they might also have seen film of Jack Dempsey's own 'Fight of the Century' with the European champion, Georges Carpentier.

Trapped by the Mormons was completed in only four weeks, and though that was largely thanks to its cast and crew, it was also thanks to Harry Parkinson, the industrious young man who had been the film's producer and director.

Harry came from Burnley, where he had become known for the wry stories he contributed to a local newspaper. He was also known for escorting groups of holidaymakers around the West Country, and for taking such good care of them that they showered him with gifts: a gold-mounted fountain pen one week, a gold-mounted umbrella the next. When he returned home, to his small house on the steep terrace that was Woodbine

Road, he used that pen to write about the sights he had seen. And he spoke about those sights as well, in lantern lectures at the Weavers' Institute –

The hills richly clad in fragrant verdure. Eucalyptus, almond, and venerable hawthorn trees. Tiers of pretty white villas rising up from the water's edge. Shady walks. Tennis lawns and golfing grounds, and concerts on the pier. The semi-circular bay. White-winged yachts skimming over an ultramarine sea. Steamships, pleasure craft, and trawlers with their red-brown leathery sails. The gardens full of aloe, agave, linum, orange, canna, dracaena, verbena, myrtle.

His career accelerated after he made the move into films. He took on one hall after another, spending his own money on some, bestowing the name 'Picturedrome' on most. These were fugitive affairs, in truth, appearing suddenly in one public building or another, and disappearing just as suddenly, in a welter of recriminations and writs. But for a while they could be found all over – from Retford to Bideford, from the Town Hall in Rotherham to Llanelli's elegant old Athenaeum Hall.

When Harry Parkinson went back to Burnley, it was as an employee. He had been appointed manager of Andrews' Pictures in the town, which stood barely a mile from Woodbine Road and only yards from the Weavers' Institute. He would be the person to make the place famous. He hired a ladies' choir to accompany the films, and singers, comedians and a banjoist to fill the gaps in between. He announced that 'dainty afternoon teas' would be served to anyone who had paid at least sixpence for their ticket. And he placed advertisements, proclaiming, 'Everybody who is anybody visits Andrews.' That must have done the trick, for subsequent advertisements reported, 'Hundreds turned away every night.'

The lecturer was Harry's idea as well. Frank Warner had followed him from an earlier hall and quickly won his own portion of praise. Mr Warner's 'choice diction' was noted by the press, together with his 'dignified eloquence, which invests the pictures with a deeper and subtler interest.' But that was only to be expected. 'He has an excellent education behind him,' the *Burnley Express* reported, 'and a vast amount of reading, so that his lecturing is cultured and eloquent.' When the subject of opium and opium dens came up, Frank 'gave a very instructive dissertation on the effects of this drug, not forgetting to mention Coleridge and De Quincey.' And though he might have been heard in silence while the film was in progress, the audience 'burst out into the most rapturous acclamations' when he was done. He even came to the attention of the *Stage*, which pronounced his lectures 'irreproachable throughout.'

Perhaps the most popular film Harry Parkinson showed in Burnley was *A Victim of the Mormons* – the early Danish epic, which featured Nina and the shooting of Andrew, the priest. And if the film's popularity in the town was largely thanks to its story – which 'held the audience breathless to the end' – it might also have been thanks to the supporting bill. The 'popular duettists' Desmond and Sterling did a turn, even though a shortage of time prevented them repeating it, and Frank Warner was soon stepping into the half-light again. 'The origin of the Mormon creed was explained by the lecturer,' the newspaper reported.

Harry Parkinson became so popular in Burnley that, when it was time to move on again, his colleagues presented him with a stout travelling bag. His hall was one of many on the Andrews circuit, and Harry had now been put in charge of them all. He would find himself trekking not just to nearby Colne, but also to Rochdale and Stalybridge, and to towns from Edmonton to Inverness.

Those Andrews places could also be found in public buildings. The one in Burnley had taken over the Church Institute, while the one in Colne was inside the Victoria Hall, above a draper's and a boot and shoe shop. In Northampton, it occupied the Temperance Hall, while in Edmonton it was tucked behind the King's Head. But the circuit was developing apace. The company's picture house in Plymouth had been purpose-built, and its home in Southsea, at another Victoria Hall, was especially grand. Films had been shown there since the very beginning, and roller skaters gone round and round even before that. The hall had seen suffragists protest and spiritualists conduct séances. It had also seen a terrible tragedy, when a false cry of 'Fire!' caused the death of an eleven-year-old boy. Talks had been given there, political meetings held, and dioramas put on show. And when Harry Parkinson departed, after a stint as stand-in manager, a leather attaché case is what he was given by his colleagues.

Harry departed the Andrews circuit at much the same time, bound for Brighton, where he had been appointed manager of the Academy Picture Palace. A Turkish bath for nearly fifty years, this place was Moorish in appearance, with pointed arches, horseshoe arches, and castellation. There were hot rooms, cooler rooms, and forty-five-foot-high cooling rooms; and in some of the rooms, men were diligently separated from women, the more wealthy customers from the less. When the place opened as a picture house, the films of GA Smith, a local resident, were the first ones shown, and Bertie himself made an appearance, reminiscing with the audience about his leafy acres and chalybeate spring, and about the audacious, brief career he had shared with Laura Bayley.

The Academy claimed, not unreasonably, to be loftier and airier than its competitors, and Harry Parkinson once again claimed a great success. He showed local cup matches on the very day they were played, and brought in a Ladies' Viennese Orchestra. And when he showed spy films, he had two men dress as Naval officers and march up and down on the pavement outside. He showed *Sapho* in his first week as manager, and *Pimple* as frequently as he could after that. And in his last week, as Britain declared war on Germany, he showed the Barker melodrama *In the Hands of the London Crooks*.

Harry Parkinson's next move was more than merely geographical: he quit Brighton all right, bound for London's West End; but he also quit the life of an exhibitor, becoming a producer of films instead. He had been appointed manager of International Exclusives Limited, the company that would soon provide the finance to make *Five Nights*, but that was for the moment operating a modest film rental business across the south-east of England.

Before long, Harry had acquired *Pimple's Three Weeks*, and once he had managed to distribute that troublesome film right across the capital, he was rewarded with a seat on the board. When International Exclusives Limited made its own move into film production, that will have been with his consent. The commissioning of *Five Nights* from Will Barker will have been Harry's decision, at least in part. And the renting out of the film to exhibitors not just in the Home Counties, but across the rest of the country will be what brought him into contact with Walter Stott and Fred White. It wouldn't be the last time he worked with Mr White.

But then, as suddenly as he had arrived in or departed from Retford or Rotherham, Harry Parkinson was on the move again. International Exclusives Limited was itself a thing of the past, and Harry was once again living on his wits. A decade after *Devonshire – A Trip to Sunshine Land* appeared in the *Burnley Express*, he had started producing films in his own name.

Trapped by the Mormons arrived in picture houses in Harry Parkinson's fourth year as a producer and director. And if the young Lancastrian had proved that he was industrious, he had also proved that he was versatile. There were biographies and melodramas to his credit already, together with adaptations of Dickens and Thackeray, and of the opulent, profligate Ouida. To his serial with familiar broad characters, he had added a series of films illustrating popular songs, such as *Home, Sweet Home* and *Won't You Buy My Pretty Flowers*. He had turned out another version of *Sapho*, and yet another version of *East Lynne*. And soon, he would turn out some old-time boxing stories.

Harry Parkinson directed most of the films in the *Romances of the Prize Ring* series, using modern-day fighters to recreate famous contests from the past. The series included *When Giants Fought* and *Gypsy Courage*, and one of its stars was Bombardier Billy Wells. After that unfortunate business with Jack Johnson, the Bombardier had twice been knocked out by Georges Carpentier with the European title at stake.

Harry would also be responsible for the score of remarkable travelogues that make up *Wonderful London*. Crisp, coloured and idiosyncratic, those films are full of barges and blooms, street life, Sunday life, the Thames in its upper reaches –

A *Punch & Judy* show in Shaftesbury Avenue. Acton's Lock. *A veritable oasis of colour in a desert of drabness.* Ye Olde Cheshire Cheese. 'F Richards. Cheapest and Best Funeral Furnisher in London.' Giant mixed Gloxinia and hybrid gesneras. *Here one's nostrils are assailed by the scent of the homely antirrhinum.* Jellied eels on Petticoat Lane. Scarlet godetia and the Star-of-the-Veldt. In Hyde Park, the Church Parade. Bookies and Salvationists. *Odd little bunches of loveliness – speaking mutely of a sunnier clime.* 'Ring-a-Roses' on Kinnerton Street. Swan River daisies. Riding out on Rotten Row. An old maid descending Essex Stairs. Larkspur and lavatera. Imortelles.

One film in the series takes a meandering stroll from Soho to Saffron Hill and beyond. *Cosmopolitan London* shows laundries and pharmacies, the Restaurant Salonika, and the Café Bar Conte. There are newspapers for sale – *Le Figaro*, *l'Humanité* – and Lascars in gala dress. And there is both a Scandinavian Mission Hall and a Scandinavian Temperance Home.

Near the end, finding itself out East, the film tarries in Limehouse Causeway. *Dim and mysterious is London's Chinatown*, a title-card says. *One gets the tang of betel-nut, of bhang, and of – Opium!* And if there is little to be seen of the denizens of this place, an explanation is forthcoming: *The Chink either slinks away at the sight of the camera or bursts into volleys of hysterical protest.*

But if Harry Parkinson was attracted by the lurid, the sentimental, and the sweat-drenched, what attracted him most were subjects he thought might sell. And to his travel films and boxing histories there must be added his films about Latter-day Saints. When *Trapped by the Mormons* was showing in Burnley, a local newspaper interviewed Harry at length. Perhaps with memories of *A Victim of the Mormons* in mind, Harry said that he had realised 'by the recent anti-Mormon campaign, that a film giving enlightenment on the real facts of the Mormon religion would do much to combat the danger.'

Trapped by the Mormons was based upon *The Love Story of a Mormon*: the overheated novel Winifred Graham had published at the beginning of an earlier anti-Mormon campaign. And wherever the film was shown, handbills were passed around like religious tracts. 'The honour of our womanhood is at stake,' said one. 'Shall all English girls be white slaves to Mormons?' The posters, meanwhile, were as big as a goal, and they spoke of 'An English girl's fight to save her honour.' In Nottingham, three of the Church's missionaries had themselves photographed in front of one such poster. They are done up against the weather, with overcoats and wide-brimmed hats. One man has a sheaf of what might be tracts in his hands, and each of them is smiling the broadest of smiles.

But while *Trapped by the Mormons* was largely the work of Harry Parkinson, the money to make it came from another man entirely. That man had a wealth of experience in the industry and had been putting out films on his own account for a good few years. He too had been involved in *Romances of the Prize Ring*, and lately, he had been hawking around *Where Are My Children?* This controversial American film argued against abortion, at least for the upper and middle classes, and in favour of birth control, at least for the lower classes. And though it was unsubtle and melodramatic, it had proved a sensation on the Eastern Seaboard and beyond.

The man in question had undergone something of a transformation, and where once he had been content to be known as plain Fred, he was now calling himself Frederick White. He had also parted company with Walter Stott, becoming principal instead of something that called itself 'The Frederick White Company'. Whether Mr White had also come to share the preoccupations that are threaded through his films is unclear, but he certainly hadn't become any more reticent with the passing of the years. Of late, indeed, he had taken to proclaiming himself 'Frederick the Great of Filmland'. (The original Frederick the Great, it will be remembered, had once proclaimed himself King of Prussia.)

72

One of the films Harry Parkinson must have hoped would sell was *The Life Story of Charles Chaplin*, which he had produced and directed, and indeed written, himself. The film was again made quickly, and it was announced with all the customary hoopla, the money behind it having come once again from Frederick White.

Mr White plainly hadn't given up on Charlie, whatever the fate of his earlier film with the airship. Nor had he abandoned the techniques that had been used to such curious effect in *Zepped*. The subject of the latest film again appeared in excerpts from others – *Tango Tangles, The Kid, The Pilgrim, Gold Rush* – and clips were even included from *The Circus*, which hadn't been finished yet.

There is, admittedly, some new material here, but it certainly doesn't show the man himself. It consists of footage of an obscure music-hall performer, made up to look like Charlie and filmed only at a distance or in poor light. The actor's name was Chick Wango, and he plays what was described as a 'shadow' part – dressing, walking, and larking about as Chaplin did. Or at least trying to do so.

For much of the near-forty minutes of this equally curious piece, the movie clips are interspersed with languorous shots of 'Charlie' wandering through streets south of the River Thames and gazing, again wistfully, at places he will have known as a boy –

East Street, Walworth, where he was born. East Lane market under naphtha lamps, where the people strolling about might easily be taken for him. Pownall Terrace, with that tiny, stinking flat. Walcot Mansions, where he first larked about on a makeshift stage. The foreshore at Lambeth (which will also have been known to Hetty Payne). The infants' school belonging to the workhouse, and the corporation baths where he swam second-class for threepence. St Mary-at-Lambeth, St Mary-the-Less. The National School there, and the boys' school on Hercules Road. Doulton's dock just up from the Archbishop's palace.

The film also shows people Charlie Chaplin knew then: his old landlady, a clogdancer who performed alongside him, and a man who watched him larking about on that long-ago makeshift stage. And there is newsreel footage of his return to all this, tanned and in triumph, a little while ago. Here he is in his beautiful suite at the Ritz, and standing at the window in a fine grey suit, bestowing carnation petals on the great crowd gathered beneath. Here is the beautiful home in Beverly Hills to which he will shortly return.

Frederick White promised Chaplin's people they would see the film before it appeared, but he didn't remain true to his word. Hundreds of exhibitors were summoned to a trade show in London, and more bold advertisements appeared in the press. 'The biggest box office attraction ever made,' they promised. 'The public will delight to welcome the opportunity of seeing the life story of Mr Chaplin portrayed on the screen.' Fred even put out a brochure containing still photographs from the film – or, at least, from the films from which this one had been assembled. But the photographs, too, were used without permission.

The great man was 'exceedingly annoyed and offended' by this, his lawyer said. And when a firm letter to Mr White received an equally firm reply, there was only one thing for it. A writ was issued in the High Court, the real Charlie Chaplin proving much less wistful than Chick Wango had led everyone to expect. The writ named not just Frederick White as a defendant, but Harry Parkinson as well.

These had been difficult days for Charlie, and he might, perhaps, have been forgiven for resorting to the law. His wife had walked out of the beautiful home in Beverly Hills, taking the couple's infant sons with her, and she had succeeded in obtaining a divorce that saw him branded cruel and inhumane in the popular press, and that would end up costing him a fortune. Filming had been suspended in the light of these events, which is why *The Circus* hadn't yet been finished. The beautiful home, meanwhile, had been built by studio carpenters more used to putting up temporary sets, and though Charlie had designed it himself, in a style he liked to call 'California Gothic', it had begun to fall apart.

Frederick and Harry had no right, of course, to use clips from Charlie Chaplin's films. Much was made of that in the claim, and the two men were accused of trying to take advantage of a name and a character that were his alone to exploit. They were 'damnifying the fame and goodwill enjoyed by Mr Chaplin,' his lawyer announced, even though his client must by now have grown used to being honoured only by his absence. The film was 'cheap and unauthenticated balderdash,' he said, and it couldn't possibly have cost more than £400. And poor though Chick Wango's impersonation was, renters, exhibitors and audiences might still be deceived into thinking that it was Chaplin himself up there on the screen; that he had authorised the film; and that the events portrayed were really ones from his life. A range of people, from cinema managers to motor engineers, lined up to say that as it happened, they had themselves been deceived.

Chaplin asked that the film be handed over to him, or better still destroyed, and he claimed damages to cover losses he said he had incurred. First, though, he demanded an injunction to prevent the wretched thing being shown to anyone at all.

The matter came to court only hours before the trade show was due to begin, and the hearing ended with Messrs White and Parkinson promising that the show would be postponed, and that the film would not be exhibited, at least for the duration of the case. Charlie's claim never did receive a final hearing, in fact, but the men's promise held good, nonetheless. The film into which Frederick had invested so much money, and Harry so much time and effort, never would be seen by a paying audience.

Nor was Charlie the only Chaplin to have his voice heard in this case. Aubrey was his first cousin, a licensed victualler, and the son of a licensed victualler, and he too was unhappy about what had been done. The film was one thing, of course, but he would have to concede some ambivalence about that. He now thought it 'a very ordinary affair' and said he could see why Charlie was so upset. But only a few weeks before, having met Harry Parkinson and been given a private viewing, he had called it 'a very nice and complimentary thing to have made.'

Aubrey Chaplin had gone further than that, in fact. He had said that the film surpassed all his expectations and he was sure his cousin would be delighted with it. He had said that to Harry Parkinson in person, but he had also said it in a letter the producer had helpfully typed out for him on headed notepaper. Aubrey asked for the letter back, of course, once he changed his mind, but that turned out to be impossible. The letter, he was told, to his great dismay, had passed into the hands of Frederick White, and that indefatigable impresario was now using it to drum up trade across the North of England.

73

Almost everyone had something to say about *Where Are My Children?* Editorials fulminated, the usual bold posters went up on walls, and when the advertisements appeared, they proclaimed it 'The Great National Film Concerning the Regeneration of the British Race.' In North Shields, where the film was to be shown at the now-restored Borough Theatre, the advertisements even promised that the film would be accompanied by a lecture from a man named Padden.

This wasn't, however, TV Padden, who had explained *Five Nights* at the Palace in Hartlepool; it was JC Padden. He had once been the manager of that theatre, and he happened to be Thomas Padden's brother. And he too had consented to be dazzled by the great beam of light.

James Clement Padden often used his middle name in preference to his first. He was a family man, married to a schoolteacher and the father of two daughters. Like his brother, he had been an engineer before going into films, but he was the first of them to make the change, and he would remain in the business much longer. The brothers were the sons of a policeman, who was himself descended from an Irishman who had fetched up in County Durham after leaving his homeland in search of work.

Clement Padden managed the Palace theatre in Jarrow before his brother did, and before it went up in flames. Then, in Hartlepool, he managed not only the Palace, but also its rival, the Empire. Films were not his only business, though, at least at first. They weren't even his main business, and for a long time in his halls, customers were as likely to be presented with variety turns –

Macintosh and Royal, the champion clog and big boot dancers. Madame Hengleur and her performing dogs. Mr JH McCann, the roller-skater ('He dances with the skates on.') The Misses Judge, with their famous collection of cockatoos, parrots, and macaws. Dumorski, the Apache Lady Violiniste. Charles Weimar, who had played his trumpet all along the doomed, dusty track from Kabul to Kandahar. Amandus, an impressionist. ('His representation of Mr Lloyd George is very good.') Miss Eugene, the lady singer with a male voice. Will Netta's Singing Jockeys.

Mr Padden had even presented his customers with Fred Evans. When the great comedian gave the audience his Apache Dance, the *Northern Daily Mail* said he was 'distinctly original in his novel absurdity.' But the turns were becoming steadily less popular, and people were far more interested in the films. When Clement moved to Monkwearmouth, he made a striking boast: 'We show the finest films in Sunderland,' he said, 'and the success of the hall tells its own tale. Slip in and have a chat with me.'

Doing as his brother had done, this affable man combined the duties of manager with those of lecturer. He brought great energy to the role, and displayed real panache, sometimes describing what he provided as a *feuilleton*. He might have to speak for an hour non-stop, and to do that twice in one night, but he did it so well that his fame quickly spread. He found himself travelling throughout the region in his brand-new car; not just to Jarrow, Hartlepool, and North Shields, but to South Shields too, and to Ashington, Byker and Berwick. He went to Manchester more than once, and was proclaimed 'England's Crack Lecturer.' And as war approached, he was booked for a fortnight in Middlesbrough. Standing in the wings at the Grand Opera House in the town, he will have been able to witness for himself the wonder that was Eric Williams and his speaking pictures.

In Hartlepool, Clement Padden lectured at the Empire while Harold Mitschke was doing the same at the Northerns. He lectured to *Burnt Wings*, the film in which Eve Balfour starred just after *Five Nights*. And when he lectured to *A Victim of the Mormons*, he did it so well that one newspaper went on calling him 'The Man Who Exposed the Mormons' for years afterwards. 'He has a natural gift for speaking,' the *Jarrow Express* said, 'and gives a very clear and lucid interpretation of the various scenes depicted upon the screen.' And his celebrity continued to grow and grow. Where once he had been merely 'the famous dramatic and humorous exponent,' he would eventually come to be billed as:

Padden – the man who makes the screen speak.

In places, there is even a hint that he sometimes went beyond his text – a hint that, like some *benshi* or *bonimenteur* of the Borough Theatre, he brought in material of his own. 'Mr Padden is an able lecturer,' the *Jarrow Express* informed its readers:

He has travelled and read a great deal. Consequently, he is able to give a clear and lucid explanation of each and every picture shown.

There is evidence, in fact, that Clement Padden sometimes went a long way beyond his text.

74

In one town, in particular, Clement Padden was hailed a star (even if only in advertisements he had placed himself) –

Mr JC Padden's Pilgrimage of Pure Entertainment continues.
Amazing scenes at Monkwearmouth.
Roker Avenue Besieged by Hundreds of Well-Dressed, Well-Behaved Women.

Mr Beaumont begs to announce that Mr Padden will lecture on his own immense Photo-Play entitled *Black Fear*.
Don't Miss It – Don't Miss It.
A Stupendous Kinematographic Triumph made into a gem of cleanliness and purity by the Invincible Padden.
Only At The Roker Theatre Can These Sights Be Witnessed.

Mr James C Padden (The Original) will give to the Splendid Characters in this Film Subject the very Potent Powers of Charm which characterise Presence, Personality and, above all, Voice.
Mr James C Padden (The Original) will add considerably to the Power of the Film as an Entertainment by actually speaking the words which proceed from line so fair and firm, and by interpreting the language of eyes so large, so tender and so beautiful.
Mr James C Padden (The Original) will adorn the

clever people on the Silent Stage with verbal jewels and witchery that will create more sighs and yearnings for the handsome and beautiful on the screen, not only from impressionable youth, but from their parents as well; and these devious loves, described by Mr Padden, will endure; aye, they'll not be easily forgotten.

Mr James C Padden. (The Original.)
Mr Padden's Moving Picture Lectures at the above theatre are features which never fail to attract all those thousands of the public who like to see and hear at the same time the Powerful Stories From Real Life which Mr James C Padden (The Original) Makes A Special Study Of And Speaks Upon In A Truthful, Fearless And Eloquent Fashion Every Night.

To-Night! To-Night! A Gripping Tale Of Jealousy.
Mr James C Padden (The Original) Visits The Roker Variety Theatre This Week With another Great Batch of New Film Subjects – Four in Number – and huge audiences will sit spellbound by his intense personality and verbal witchery as the astounding interpretations enter his mind every second of the time he occupies the darkened stage and cascades of truth flow from his mobile lips.

75

From the moment it was released, *Trapped by the Mormons* was a great success. Long, excited queues greeted the film in Glasgow. The Central in Portobello had to close its doors early. And in Thurnscoe, the Cinema House was filled to capacity throughout what was actually its opening week. Among the many people who flocked to the Electra Palace in Sheffield, some will have been attracted by the sandwich men who processed through the streets with a donkey at their head. And though *Variety* complained that the film's 'melodramatic properties smack somewhat of the screen's infancy,' everyone could see that Frederick White, and Harry Parkinson, still knew just what their audiences required.

For the second time in a decade, the country was said to be trembling in fear of the Latter-day Saints, and though the Church again offered £200 for evidence of even a single abduction, that didn't help. Windows were smashed again and tracts ripped up. The faithful were chased again, this time in Swindon, and they had stones thrown at them in Bristol. And in Plymouth, the crowd that pursued them was larger even than the one turned away from the Cinedrome. 'I do not advocate repressive measures,' the Bishop of Barking wrote, 'unless missionaries secure converts, in which case I support deportation.' And the *Daily Express* was in a similar mood. 'The public does not intend to have Mormons in England,' it announced. 'Fling them out!' The Home Secretary was again said to be inquiring into the situation. He spoke to some elders of the Church, who made him a gift of a hand-tooled Bible, and then in Parliament, he told Elinor Glyn's friend, Lord Curzon, that he was having them closely watched.

In Manchester, *Trapped by the Mormons* was shown at the Futurist cinema, which stood across from the Assize Court and had only recently changed its name from the Star. That hall was the one in which, during the *Five Nights* trial, Walter Stott, Fred White and Chief Constable Watson – together with the jury and, once he had secured the proper costume, the judge – had all attended a private viewing. The Mormon film could also be seen in the capital, not least at the Rivoli on Whitechapel Road, which was put up to replace a hall that had burned to the ground. This was the district in which Winston Churchill had been shown scowling in a top hat and Harry Parkinson had taken his cosmopolitan stroll; the one whose King the redoubtable Pimple had once set out to assassinate.

Wonderland, as the hall had been known, was a cavernous, rough-and-ready sort of a place, which conversed in Yiddish before anything else. A tavern for years, and then a music hall, it was home to wire walkers and waxworks after that; to snake charmers, ventriloquists, menageries. The Queen of the Midgets held court from the centre of the hall. There were performing dogs and talking donkeys, a man who would dive from the roof into four feet of water, and a woman with lobster claws instead of hands. ('She can sew, embroider, and play the piano.') But it was the boxing matches held on Mondays and Saturdays that were the biggest draw of all.

There might be 2,000 spectators in the hall on those nights, crammed in, cursing, sweating, smoking, baying. The lights hung low over their heads, arrayed on huge wheels depending from the roof, glowing brightly through plain glass shades. The curtains over the long windows were drawn closed, and the ring, raised up, was demarcated by gaudy ropes that resembled a barber's pole. Restless bookies would bob up and down, and vendors would thread their way through the crowd, holding aloft trays of cigarettes, stewed eels, soft drinks, and oranges in enamelled basins.

Wonderland's most notable son was probably Aschel 'Young' Josephs. He fought there more than seventy times, on the way to a European title he would eventually lose to Georges Carpentier. He was even filmed there by Will Barker, in a fight with another local favourite. The bouts Wonderland hosted were of undoubted quality. George Gunther, of course, fought there, before he turned to films and was given a job by Cecil Hepworth. The first black boxer to win a British title won it there. The Bombardier fought there on the way to his own title. And the Canadian boxer Tommy Burns defended his world title there, before he lost it to Jack Johnson.

Films had been shown in the hall from the very beginning, even if they were blurred and indistinct, and people started booing and hissing, and some of them had to be given their money back. There were those, indeed, who blamed an unattended film projector for the fire that eventually consumed the place. (Others, however, blamed the hall's two proprietors, and on the acrimonious falling out they had recently had.)

After the fire, the Rivoli was given arches, columns and pilasters that set it apart from its predecessor, and the front was covered in bright white tiles. The auditorium was huge and ornate, and there was a beautiful organ and a spacious café. And business was still good. When *Trapped by the Mormons* arrived, the *East London Observer* wrote that the management was 'hard-pressed to find seating accommodation for the huge numbers who made application for admission.'

The film was equally popular in Hull, where *Five Nights* had been well received, and where the *Daily Mail* now called Mormons 'devilish people who are unfit to be in any decent society.' 'The revelations which this picture gives,' the paper went on, 'will satisfy even the most doubtful that the religion of the Latter-day Saints is better left to devils.' There followed a woeful tale:

357

'Mormonism has wrecked my happiness and ruined my home.' This tragic declaration was made to me by Mr William Jenkins of Bridge Road, Southampton.

Mr Jenkins nine years ago was a prosperous businessman with a happy home, a wife and four children. Mormonism robbed him of his wife and four daughters, broke up his home and threw him on the world a grief-stricken and broken-hearted man.

Owing to the Mormon Propaganda operating in our large Cities today, It Is Your Duty To See This Picture.

And, in a development that will surely have gratified its creator, the film was also showing at the Andrews' Picture House in Burnley – the very hall of which Harry Parkinson had once been the manager. But although that place had been the first in the town to show films, it had long since acquired its share of competitors.

The Empire Theatre was only a short stroll away, and had been praised for its elegance and dainty ornamentation, while the Empress cinema had lately been made larger and more splendid. At the Royal, though, more than forty people had been found standing in the aisles on Christmas Day. The manager of the King's had been instructed to set the seats further apart, and to make sure they were properly screwed down. And the Pavilion was considered inadequate even by its own proprietors. This place had opened as a rink, and though it had remained one for barely two years, it still had wooden walls and a roof of corrugated tin. It also had its screen across the centre of the hall, and customers could pay half-price to watch the film the wrong way round.

When the *Burnley Express and Advertiser* reviewed *Trapped by the Mormons*, it had Mr Parkinson very much in mind. 'The ubiquitous film-maker is very much alive to the advantage that lies in catching the market,' the newspaper wrote, 'and when he gets the opportunity to be topical, he grasps it.' Overall, opinion in the town was favourable. 'Taken for what it is,' the paper added, 'the picture quite deserves applause.'

Back over the Pennines, *Trapped by the Mormons* was showing in Leeds, at a place that was almost new. The Crescent had its beautiful organ in common with the Rivoli in Whitechapel, and also its habit of calling itself a 'Super Cinema'.

The name, which was now becoming familiar across the country, was intended to convey to patrons not only the size of the hall, but also that it was luxurious to a degree they had never experienced before. 'The entrance doors are mahogany,' another of those places boasted, 'the exit and subsidiary doors polished teak,' and suddenly, it seemed that cornices and cartouches, swags and garlands might have had their day. 'All metal work is in oxidised silver' was yet another boast; 'the divan deluxe chairs in the balcony are the last word in comfort.' The golds and ivories of the old halls were giving way to mauves and greys, the deep plush to corduroy. 'A luncheon bar and an America bar' were among the new amenities; public telephones, concealed lighting, a Flugel soda fountain. And with only the most cursory of backwards glances, the Super Cinemas were declaring themselves to be fireproof and well ventilated, to have film projectors that were utterly flicker-less, and to be able to offer an uninterrupted view of the screen. One newspaper told its readers that in Nottingham, 'it is whispered that saxophones and other "jazz" instruments will have their place in the orchestra.' And the Crescent itself was said to have been 'conceived and executed in a style so magnificent that it is strangely unfamiliar to Leeds.'

In the South West, with memories still fresh of all the chasing and the stoning, the film could be seen at the King's Kinema in Gloucester. 'The incidents are well worked up to an exciting finish,' the *Citizen* reported, 'and although some are overdone, they make good if not altogether convincing melodrama.' The *Devon and*

Exeter Gazette told its readers that great credit was due to Harry Parkinson for having 'spared no effort to bring about the downfall of Mormonism.' And the *Wiltshire Times* hailed what it described as 'a super film in every sense of the word.' 'The activities of the Mormons in this county are now more conspicuous than ever they were,' the newspaper continued, in words resembling ones that had appeared on posters across the land:

> ... and this film, depicting an English girl's fight for her most precious possession, her honour, should serve as a warning to all right-thinking parents to safeguard their daughters from the ever-present menace.

Attention was as keen in the opposite corner of England, where the *Shields Daily News* promised its readers 'the very latest exposure of the Mormon Menace' at the Comedy Theatre. Inevitably, it also promised that 'JC Padden will lecture.' In the Midlands, however, a very different mood prevailed.

Even among the sumptuous picture houses of the time, the White Hall in Derby was a jewel. It too had a bright white façade, topped off with an angel holding up a globe, while inside, there were classical murals and a large foyer lit by chandeliers, which glittered and were glitteringly reflected in the mirrors that lined the walls. But all of this will have been lost on Mr Steven, for he was a worried man:

> Mormon Fury Roused By A Film.
> THEATRE MANAGER THREATENED.
> Unwelcome Truth.
> TROUBLE IS BREWING IN DERBY.
> Mr WE Steven, manager of the White Hall, has booked a film called *Trapped by the Mormons*, which will be shown next Tuesday, June 1st. He has been receiving threatening anonymous letters and telephonic menaces

from a voice with an accent familiar on the Santa Fe trail.

'Your film is a gross and wicked libel on the high and reputable church of the Latter-day Saints,' says one of the letter-writers, who posted his communication in Derby, 'and if you do not withdraw the film you personally will be held responsible.'

The voice on the telephone went further than this. It said bluntly: 'You will be shot before the week is out.' POLICE GUARD.

The White Hall manager sits with a life-preserver on his desk, and we understand is arranging for a couple of policemen to guard the entrance to the theatre.

76

The people of Scotland were particularly exercised by *Trapped by the Mormons*, and the film played to packed houses not just in Glasgow and Edinburgh, but in Bellshill and Wishaw as well. It could be seen everywhere from Selkirk to Fraserburgh, in fact, and from Motherwell to Dundee. It was proclaimed a 'startler' in Coatbridge, and in Airdrie, the conclusion of a local newspaper was firm:

> One can scarcely see how any representative of Utah can dare to walk with our people.

In Forfar, the mood was much the same. 'Every mother and every daughter should see this picture,' an advertisement exclaimed, when *Trapped by the Mormons* turned up at the Reid Hall. 'A Warning to us all. The Religion of Lust. Clear out the Mormons!'

Reference was also made to a recent incident in the capital, which had seen elders of the Church being confronted about their beliefs. The details of the incident seemed particularly cruel, especially when relayed in the jocular tone many newspapers chose to adopt. 'Students "Rag" Mormons,' ran one headline, 'Treacle for Mormons' another, above articles describing how two elderly men, a third man who had lost the use of an arm and a leg, and a young woman who had attempted to come to their aid were barracked by as many as forty young men who had lain in wait for them, before being knocked to the ground, daubed with a mixture of green paint, honey, engine oil, and animal blood, and left covered in feathers and down. 'Why do you do this?' someone had asked. 'You have taken away our sisters,' one of the students replied.

If that wasn't enough, a second film about the Church turned up barely a fortnight later. *Married to a Mormon* had the same leading lady as *Trapped by the Mormons*, and much the same cast. It ran for about as long and told a similar story. And it was again the work of Harry Parkinson, made with funds again provided by Frederick White. 'It gains a little spurious interest,' *The Times* wrote, 'owing to the fact that it is more or less topical.'

The two films did the rounds together, often appearing in the same place at more or less the same time. In Montrose and Luton, at the Empire and the Palace, *Trapped by the Mormons* was shown for the first half of the week and *Married to a Mormon* for the second. And each was sometimes described as the sequel to the other.

In Perth and Motherwell, meanwhile, audiences were once again being offered *A Victim of the Mormons*. 'Come and see how a simple, trusting girl was sacrificed to the will of a Mormon elder,' an advertisement proclaimed, of a film that had first seen the light of day more than a decade before.

And contained within the attention these films received was a measure of cynicism about their motive. 'There's money in anti-Mormonism,' the *Daily Herald* wrote, while the *Stage* noted that, 'a rush of Mormon screenplays seems sweeping into the kinemas':

> Already we have *Married to a Mormon* and *Trapped by the Mormons*. I expect we shall soon get *The Life of Brigham Young* – unless it might be considered too costly to have to engage thirty or forty leading actresses to play his many wives!

In the North East of England, *Married to a Mormon* was shown in Newcastle and Sunderland, Hartlepool and Chester-le-

Street. It was also shown in North Shields, at the Comedy Theatre, where an advertisement promised, 'a big, strong melodrama of suspense, heart-throbs, and action.' Inevitably, the advertisement also promised, 'Padden will Lecture.' And the following week, in proof of the great man's versatility, another advertisement for the theatre promised '*Cocaine* – Padden will Lecture.'

This was a reference to the film *Cocaine*, which was yet another of Harry Parkinson's productions. (And Mr Padden, it will be remembered, had been pronounced 'England's Crack Lecturer.') This film too was controversial, playing as it did on another current fear – that the country and the capital were being swamped with 'dope', and that immigrants were to blame. 'Sensation-mongering,' one trade paper called it, and there were stereotypical Chinese characters, played by actors who weren't even remotely Chinese. (One of the actors had played a Mormon elder in *Trapped by the Mormons*.)

Though the film did not ignore the harmful effects of the drug, the Censor was concerned that it might lure cinemagoers into a world of which they would otherwise have been blissfully unaware. The *Kinematograph Weekly* was, however, unabashed. 'Boom the title!' it advised:

> With interest being taken in the drug traffic at the moment, the title offers the best advertisement angle. Stress the moral of the tale, and its British origin.

Cocaine was banned at first, and Harry Parkinson got a taste of what his collaborator, Fred White, had experienced a few years before. But the ban was quickly overturned, once the title had been changed to *While London Sleeps*, councils in Coventry, Salford and Glasgow had decided to ignore the Censor, and large crowds had turned up at showings in Cardiff and Manchester. None of that impressed *Variety*, with the magazine, never easily impressed at the best of times, describing the film as 'bad melodrama of the type which may attract the coarser class of patrons to the cheaper kinema.'

Still bearing its old title, *Cocaine* arrived at the sumptuous White Hall in Derby just after *Trapped by the Mormons* had left, and with the threatening letters the manager, WE Steven, had received still sitting on his desk. It was almost the last film he showed there, in fact, for within a week Mr Steven was gone, his life-preserver doubtless tucked inside his jacket. The film with which his successor chose to open his own account was *Five Nights*.

It wasn't just cinemas and the people who ran them that profited from Harry and Frederick's Mormon films. When an elder of the Church wrote home from Hull, he could barely contain his glee. He had been standing with other Latter-day Saints outside cinemas where the films were playing, and now, he reported that they were, 'the best stroke of advertising that we have put forth since coming over here.'

> In three evenings, we let more people know that we are here than we could have done in three months at ordinary tracting from door to door.

There were others among the faithful who felt differently, however, and who gave the films a frosty reception. When *Married to a Mormon* was to be shown at the New Cinema in Nelson, the Church again registered its objections, and again asked that the film be withdrawn. And it again received short shrift. As the *Leader* reported:

> The management promptly informed it that such a course was impossible... and would not be keeping faith with the public, and that it was their intention to show the film no matter how many people objected to it.

365

But while the management might have been resolute, it certainly wasn't foolhardy. 'Steps have already been taken to ensure that the film will be shown,' the *Leader* said, 'extra staff having been engaged to cope with any attempt that may be made to stop the exhibition.' That was prudent, for even in Cheshire there had been violence:

MORMONS MOBBED.
PELTED WITH CLODS OF EARTH BY CROWD.
Five Mormon missionaries, who have been preaching in Sandbach for a week, were pelted with clods of earth by a crowd of a thousand people last night and advised by the police to leave the town.

The Mormons attended a kinema performance at which there was a film called *Trapped by the Mormons*. The crowd waited for the Mormons to come out of the picture house and surrounded them, many persons adopted a threatening attitude. Two policemen tried to persuade the Mormons to return to their lodgings, but instead the Mormons started to walk from the town, followed by the crowd throwing missiles.

They were pursued for a mile, and a police sergeant, who followed them on a buggie, urged them not to return to the town but to go on to Congleton, eight miles away, and leave their belongings at their lodgings. The crowd were then turned back by the police sergeant.

Sometime later, there was another curious development. It took place not in Cheshire, Derby, Edinburgh or Nelson, but in Kitale, a farming town in what was now the British Kenya colony.

This was a new place, built by white settlers high up in the Rift Valley. Those people were so numerous now that the area was known as the White Highlands. Many of them had been officers in the British Army, lured to East Africa by the promise of fertile pasture and a status they couldn't hope to be accorded back home. They were resourceful and determined people, but their town was isolated; still without a railway connection, and often reachable only by ox wagon. It was rife with infection as well, and lacking all basic utilities. And it was surrounded by grassland that was in truth the province of lions. For many years, it had been a waypoint on the slave route to Zanzibar and the Indian Ocean.

The settlers had become dissatisfied of late with the picture house in Kitale. The place wasn't being properly conducted, they said, and there was one film in particular which attracted their ire. Letters had been written and meetings held. Various religious folk had attempted to intercede. And before long, the settlers got their wish. Their position might easily be undermined by the film, the chief of police announced: *Trapped by the Mormons* must not be shown to Africans.

77

Clement Padden carried on lecturing until the demand fell away. The films had been getting longer and more complicated, and better at telling a story. And as the cinemas got bigger, it became even harder to fill them with one man's voice alone.

He took charge of one place after another, sometimes moving between rival chains, and eventually, he acquired a small chain of his own. His children had left home and, in his late fifties, he was living in County Durham with his wife and her sister. That is when the incident occurred that will have coloured the last quarter of his life.

Mr Padden's chain by now comprised three cinemas in the East Durham coalfields – in Blackhall and Horden, and, in Easington Colliery, the Rialto on Seaside Lane. A complaint was made about a member of staff there. Her name was Annie and she was nineteen years of age, and the complaint was that her dress was much too tight.

One evening, just before the second house, Annie was standing near the steps to the circle when she was told to go to the office. There she found Mr Padden, holding a piece of string, and in the moments that followed, he affected to measure her bust and hips, and maybe he touched her leg as well.

He said he had to do it, and that he'd done it in the usual way, but Annie said she didn't see why a dressmaker couldn't have done it. 'My measuring is as good as anyone's,' Clement told her, but when his hands went inside her clothes, she said she wouldn't stand for it.

'Why?' his barrister asked, sometime later.

'Because I am only a young girl,' she replied.

Padden had denied indecently assaulting Annie, and he continued to do so all the way to the Quarter Sessions in Durham.

Annie said he had called her plump and had used rather vulgar and rude language. Then, she said, he had asked her whether she was wearing a dress underneath. She told him she wasn't, but that hadn't been good enough. 'I'll have to make sure,' he had said, and placed his hand down the front.

'You are a little plump, are you not?' his barrister asked.

'Yes,' Annie replied.

'Don't you think you have made a great deal of fuss about nothing?'

'No, sir.'

'I suppose you have been measured for frocks before?'

'Yes, but not like that.'

But Clement and Annie had not been alone in the office. Another person, George Foggin, was also there, and he was the manager of the Rialto.

'It was all done so sharp in front of my eyes,' George said. When Annie went out of the office, he could see she was crying, and she asked if she could go home, and he said that she could.

Padden then said he was going to have twenty minutes' lie-down and he asked for a glass of whisky. Once he had downed that, he asked for another.

Why, the barrister was curious, had George not reported the incident himself?

'I did, in my statement to the police.'

But before that, on the day, did he say anything?

'I did not say anything. It was really done so quickly that I did not say anything. I was so much taken aback by Mr Padden's actions that I was speechless.'

'You played the part of a mouse rather than a man, didn't you?'

No reply.

George Foggin had been Padden's assistant for some years.

'How old are you?'

'Forty-six.'

'You have more than once told those who own these cinemas that if Mr Padden was out of the way you could manage them?'

This was denied.

Foggin was a miserable, cowardly wretch, the barrister told the court, and every word of his evidence should be rejected.

There was no need for the magistrates to retire. James Clement Padden was acquitted, with the chairman of the bench saying Mr Foggin was not a good witness.

If anything was said about the evidence Annie herself gave to the court, it has not been preserved.

78

It was almost Valentine's Day when the letters began to arrive. Their subject was a brand-new series of films, and they had been sent to the men responsible for the series, who were now doing everything they could to generate publicity.

In recent days, big, brassy advertisements had begun to appear in the press, promising 'Something New! Something Different! Something Original!' That something turned out to be *Secrets of Scotland Yard*, the very idea of which had caused the Metropolitan Police Commissioner concern. The advertisements promised that the series would offer 'Tales from the Life of a Great Detective,' and that there would be,

Revelations and the Sunshine and the Shadow.
The Smiles and Tears of a Great Detective's Life.

The films were again the work of The Frederick White Company, and one of the letters was therefore dispatched to the company's principal, at his offices in Manchester. Written in the name of the Commissioner, the letter had a legalistic tone its recipient cannot have failed to recognise. He was, after all, well used to such things.

The new series, Mr White was told, 'purports to reveal official secrets of Scotland Yard,' and:

... is calculated seriously to prejudice the Criminal Investigation Department of the Metropolitan Police Force in the estimation of the public, and to impede its work by destroying public confidence in it.

In case there was any doubt, the letter said that the films that had been advertised should now be withdrawn. Barely five years after the one in Preston, Frederick White was facing yet another police ban.

The great detective in question was Ernest Haigh, who had served in the Met for nearly thirty years, ultimately as a Chief Inspector in the CID. 'A terror to criminals of every type,' was how the advertisements described him, 'yet a man with a big human heart and a keen sense of humour.' Those qualities were about to be put to the test. Haigh was approaching fifty, and newly retired to Hampshire, where he was said to be living the life of a farmer. 'He has bought a freehold farm,' the *Evening Telegraph* reported, 'has modernised the house in many ways, and, with three acres, a cow and some pigs, is looking forward to a life of much contentment.'

Such was his experience and eminence that Mr Haigh had been involved in many celebrated cases. But it was his last case that had been the most celebrated of all. He had been a key witness in the trial of Harold Greenwood, a solicitor from Carmarthenshire who was charged with murder. Haigh had, indeed, been the man who arrested Greenwood, moments after a coroner's jury concluded that his wife had died from poisoning, and photographs immediately appeared in the press, showing him escorting his prisoner to the local police court.

Greenwood looks a treat in the photographs, with his walrus moustache, plus-fours and baggy cap, as he strides out in front of a crowd of women held back by a single, grim-faced constable. One of the women, in a cloche hat and a sensible skirt, is linking arms with the policeman, while another woman is holding back a third, who seems set on giving Greenwood a piece of her mind. Behind him, half hidden, is Haigh, his mouth firm under a walrus moustache of his own, his fingers just visible, keeping tight hold on Greenwood's arm. Half hidden Haigh may be, but inconspicuous he is not.

The trial which followed, in the Guild Hall in Carmarthen, lasted for a little over two days, and it ended in sensational style, with Greenwood being acquitted by a jury composed entirely of men. The flummery surrounding the proceedings featured prominently on the newsreel –

A carriage bowls out of the pale sunlight shining on the old gaol across the square and is followed by dozens of excited children. There are policemen on horses acting as escorts. People stand in lines, craning their necks for a better view, or on the upper floors of nearby buildings. They are wearing hats and bowler hats, and bonnets and flat caps, and among the men, only the youngest are clean-shaven. A horse can be seen to cough. Though some men wear overcoats, others, who seem to have just stepped out, are in aprons and shirtsleeves. There is jostling and badinage, and a flash as the brass on a shoulder strap is caught in the sunlight. Someone is filming from a first-floor window, one camera watching another.

The carriage pulls up under an old stone canopy, where two heralds are awaiting it. One of the heralds tips up his trumpet to clear it out. A handsome motor car arrives, and the page who greets it is all in velvet, with gloves, buckles and a bicorn hat. An elderly man steps out of the car, his moustache as white and dense as his wig. He is already gowned, and the tabs at his throat dance on the breeze. The man breaks his stride at the foot of the steps, looks up, says something without smiling, and moves on.

This is one of His Majesty's Judges. It is in fact the trial judge, Sir Montague Shearman, whom no one here, at least to his face, calls Tont.

What brought Ernest Haigh to Frederick White's attention was a clutch of articles he had written for the popular press. They were fresh, slangy, and light on their feet; pungent with his experiences in the Met. And that was the approach he now brought to the films. Before long, he had turned out *The Girl Who Came Back*; *Mother's Darling*; *Lost, Stolen or Strayed*; *The Lady in Black*; and *The Prodigal Son*.

The films tell of charming, discreet waiters and girls-gone-wrong; baby-stealers, baby-farmers, missing women; dubious women, and men who play too high; pigeons waiting to be plucked; and men, once something in the city, who are now, thanks to Haigh, something in the cells. And every film features an appearance by the great detective himself.

Haigh was promised £600 for his labours – the equivalent of more than £30,000 today – with half that sum to be paid up front and the remainder to follow. The films would not, however, be his responsibility alone, for the job of producing the series had again been entrusted to Harry Parkinson. He was the man who could turn out boxing films and melodramas, London films, cocaine films, anti-Mormon films, and Charlie Chaplin Zeppelin films; the collaborator with whom Frederick White shared a taste for the lurid and seamy, and for the indisputably commercial.

79

Another of the letters arrived at Ernest Haigh's farm in Hampshire. The Commissioner, it said, had noted from the advertisements that the former detective was among those associated with this new, objectionable series of films.

But although this letter resembled the one that had been sent to Frederick White, its conclusion went much further. It didn't just demand that *Secrets of Scotland Yard* be withdrawn; it also sought to remind Mr Haigh 'of the provisions relating to the forfeiture of pension contained in Section 8 of the Police Act 1890 as amended by section 5 of the Police (Superannuation) Act 1906.'

The implication was hard to miss: he stood to lose a great deal.

Ernest replied straight away. In an ordered, affable script, full of loops and tails and fully rounded o's, he assured the Commissioner that he had neither approved the advertisements nor known about their contents, and he said he would see to it that they never appeared again. 'I regret very much indeed that any cause of complaint should have arisen,' he wrote. 'That I should have been so easily enmeshed in trouble makes me ashamed.'

> To imagine that I should in any way bring discredit upon the work of the Service is awful to me to even contemplate, for I've loved the Service all my life and hate to think I should be deemed to have lowered it in any way.

The title of the series was, in any case, misleading, Mr Haigh added, because 'no secret of any sort' would be revealed. And the films:

> … are all clean, of good moral tone, do not depict sordid crimes or murders, and most certainly do not in any way prejudice the CID or tend in the slightest degree to destroy the public confidence that exists therein.

He had believed, he said, that 'whilst I wrote pure fiction I was not doing anything to jeopardise my pension,' and he enquired whether the Commissioner would have any objection to his 'working as a film artist in a series of stories, all pure fiction, without disclosing my former connection with the service.' He was, he confirmed, 'prepared to submit to your ruling in the matter.'

Ernest Haigh's response reveals that the life of much contentment envisaged at the time of his retirement had eluded him. Work on the house has cost too much, he writes, his livestock have been sold at a loss, and his savings are gone. His hopes have been confounded, and so: 'To lose my hard-earned pension in my earnest endeavours to provide for the education and needs of my family and their future would be a ghastly tragedy.'

When it came to his new career, Haigh was scathing. He would, he wrote, 'without hesitation' choose his pension over films, for 'I loathe the work I have so unwittingly accepted.' 'I trust that this explanation will clear the issue so far as I am concerned,' he concluded, 'for the worry of it all is having a terrible effect upon both my wife and I.' And he asked:

> Would it be possible to grant an interview with me and a representative of the firm responsible for the productions with a view to arrive at an amicable understanding?

The response the Commissioner received from Frederick White was altogether more robust. It came in a letter written on the company's own headed notepaper – 'The Frederick White Company, Proprietor Frederick White' – and its tone was unapologetic, even aggressive. 'We regret very much the conclusions you have come to on this matter,' Mr White wrote, 'and can only assume that you are not fully acquainted with the real facts and particulars.'

We assure you with every confidence, that in our opinion the effects of our endeavours in respect to this subject will reflect in a manner quite the contrary to the views expressed in your letter as far as the public and the CID are concerned.

The author of the letter signed it personally, with a great flourish that was positively baroque.

Ernest Haigh was granted the meeting he had requested. It took place on Valentine's Day, on the anniversary of the *Five Nights* trial, at Metropolitan Police headquarters in New Scotland Yard. Ernest was accompanied to the meeting by Harry Parkinson, but although Frederick White had also made the journey to London, he was told that he would have to wait outside.

Three men attended the meeting on behalf of the Commissioner. One of them was the Commissioner's secretary, WH Kendall, who had sent the letters to Mr White and Mr Haigh, while another one was Edmund Maddick. Well into his sixties by now, Major Maddick had trained as a doctor and once been Admiral Surgeon of the Fleet. And, like Daisy (Daisy) Greville, he had been a close friend of King Edward.

During the war, Edmund Maddick was put in charge of filming on the Western Front, and *The Battle of the Somme* was partly his work. That great propaganda piece received its premiere in Covent Garden, at the Scala theatre, where Jessica Borthwick had shown her films and Daisy Greville had her expectations confounded. It was a theatre Major Maddick happened to own and to have had built.

The Royal Family was said to be delighted with the film, and when the opportunity arose, the King presented Edmund with a handsome gold pin. The ceremony came not a moment too soon, for a telescope had been found at his home near the harbour in Portsmouth, there was talk of a transmitter on the roof, and Madame Mona, who he had always insisted was his housekeeper, had been given twenty-four hours to leave the country.

Whatever his achievements – and Edmund Maddick was also a Knight of the Crown of Italy and an expert on the urethra – he was not a policeman, nor in the employ of the Met. So why had he taken himself to Mr Kendall's office that Valentine's Day, when *Secrets of Scotland Yard* was to be discussed?

It can be no coincidence that the Major had recently completed another film. It went by the inelegant title *Scotland Yard 1921 – For the King, the Law, the People,* and it too aimed to put the Met on cinema screens across the land. The film took the form of a documentary, however, not a drama, and an official conceded that it was made to demonstrate that the police 'are the friends, and not the enemies, of the public.' It makes a fuss of some senior detectives; shows jemmies, hammers, and jewels in pieces of fruit. And constables can be seen dealing with demonstrators, and raiding opium and cocaine dens out in Chinatown.

This film, too, received a royal showing, and Mr Maddick felt able to boast that it was 'going with a fine swing... and drawing patrons from the official classes.' The Chief Constable, the Mayor, sundry magistrates, and forty constables turned up to see it in Manchester; while in Liverpool, the nearly 200 constables who turned up found themselves being serenaded by the police band.

And the film was different in another way from the ones Ernest Haigh and Frederick White proposed: it had been made with the full cooperation of the Commissioner and he, in return, had been promised a full share of any profits. That meant that his and the film's fortunes were bound up together, and that he and not just the Commissioner might be damaged by a rival film. And that is likely to be why, when Ernest entered Mr Kendall's office, he discovered that Edmund Maddick was already there.

The third man from the Met present that afternoon was Herbert Muskett. He was a solicitor, who had the Commissioner himself for a client, and he had for some years been a familiar feature in London's criminal courts.

When DH Lawrence's novel *The Rainbow* came out it was Mr Muskett who brought a summons against the publisher. There might not be a single obscene word anywhere in the book, he said, but it was still a mass of obscenity, thought, idea, and action. The summons was heard in the week John Rigg climbed into the dock in Preston, in the court where Jack Johnson had met Billy Wells. And it too had a dramatic conclusion: Lawrence's publisher, taking fright, agreed to withdraw the book, and the remaining copies were burned by the public hangman in a very public ceremony on the steps of the Royal Exchange.

Herbert Muskett was also the man who prosecuted Jackeydawra Melford for that unfortunate business with the catapult and the bullets. And he prosecuted Irene Miller not once, but twice, and made a point of seeing to it that she was put behind bars.

80

By the time the meeting began, Ernest Haigh was in a state of great and very obvious agitation.

Perching on the edge of a chair in Mr Kendall's office, the soft lights doing nothing to dispel the gloom, he began by repeating the account he had given in his ordered, affable letter. Then, he turned to the assurances – the sincere assurances – he had also given before. Ernest spoke slowly, pausing every now and then to assess the effect his words were having. But it quickly became too much. His shoulders fell as thoughts outpaced his grasp, and he asked that Harry Parkinson be permitted to speak on his behalf.

As might be expected from the man responsible for *The Fighting Gladiator*, Mr Parkinson was combative at first. The title *Secrets of Scotland Yard* was not new, he said – it had been used time and again on Ernest's articles in the popular press. But Kendall broke in and Harry was forced to concede, as Haigh had done, that the title was actually misleading in the extreme. The Commissioner simply could not countenance any use of the name 'Scotland Yard', Kendall told him, and Harry found himself promising that the advertisements would be stopped. As for the films themselves, he said that he and Ernest would give the matter careful thought.

The Commissioner's final word was contained in a letter Mr Kendall sent out the following day. Ernest Haigh would not be pursued further, the man himself was informed, and his pension would not be taken away, provided this business was not repeated. And Mr Haigh was left with another frosty note of caution:

You would be well advised to dissociate yourself entirely from any scheme which might be regarded as exploiting Scotland Yard, with which you were so long creditably connected.

Although the Haigh films did eventually appear, the name of the series was not the one Frederick White had announced. The Commissioner's warning had plainly had the desired effect, because *Leaves from My Life* was substituted for *Secrets of Scotland Yard*. The titles of the individual films did, however, remain unchanged, and other films soon followed, called such things as: *The Tables Turned, Something in the City, The Mystery of the Stolen Jewels, The Belle of the Gambling Den, The Notorious Mrs Fagin, A Case About a Packing Case, Love and Burglars, The Blackmailed Church Warden* and *The Man Who Came Back*.

They were all boomed with customary brio –

All True, Clean Real-life Stories… The Big, Outstanding Attraction of The Year… Featuring the Man of the Moment… The Big British Serial… No Sordid Crimes, No Murders, No Suicides, No Two Stories Are Alike, Each Episode Is Different… No More Fascinating Tales of a Detective's Life Have Ever Been Portrayed.

And –

Ernest Haigh Has Never Carried A Revolver, Or Even A Truncheon.
He has always relied on tact and two fists – coupled with a knowledge of ju-jitsu.

Each film did the rounds for a month a two, often turning up in places that had agreed to take all of them as a job-lot. They could be seen in Shipley and Dover, in former rinks in

Fraserburgh and Worthing, and in a hall in South Normanton where a man had dropped dead during a showing of Georges Carpentier's first feature. In Preston, where Frederick White's relationship with William Broadhead plainly hadn't been destroyed by the *Five Nights* affair, the films turned up at the King's Palace, alongside the latest Charlie Chaplin.

What little notice the press took was grudging. The acting was good in parts, the *Bioscope* said, and Haigh himself 'admirably natural.' But while the films 'should form a sound attraction in the industrial neighbourhoods,' they were long and gory and could be 'scarcely intended for better class houses.' The *Daily Telegraph* pronounced them inferior to recent Sherlock Holmes adaptations, whilst also implying that it knew something of what had happened to Ernest Haigh:

No doubt if he were absolved from the trammels of professional secrecy, and given a free hand, the man from Scotland Yard could also make our flesh creep. As it is, his stories appear tame and insipid.

Before sending out his threatening letters, the Commissioner had taken the precaution of seeking the opinion of some senior lawyers. Would it be possible, they were asked, for Frederick White to be sued for libel? The lawyers in question included Archibald Bodkin, who had made such a good job of defending the Electric Coliseum Cinema in Harringay, and who had lately been appointed Director of Public Prosecutions. Sir Archibald came to the same conclusion as the other lawyers consulted: nothing could be done in respect of *Secrets of Scotland Yard*, because Fred White and his comrades had not broken the law.

After his brief excursion into film, Ernest Haigh went back to journalism, writing a series of articles for *Detective Magazine*. The title of the first article, *Stories from My Notebook*, had a familiar ring, and the article itself appeared alongside others on topics such as forensic science, fingerprints, and blind trails. There was also a very dry effort, on the subject of the forgery of wills, whose author was Sir Archibald Bodkin.

The pieces Ernest published in the months that followed had titles such as:

Temptations of Detectives
Detectives' Daily Dangers
Surprises for Detectives
Detectives and Disappointments
An Error of Judgment

And:
If Only.

81

Among Archibald Bodkin's many *bêtes noires* was the novel *Ulysses*. He admitted having been able to make neither 'head nor tail' of James Joyce's masterpiece, but that didn't stop him announcing that it contained 'a great deal of unmitigated filth and obscenity'. Nor, when he became Director of Public Prosecutions, did it stop him banning the book outright. He also took against *The Well of Loneliness* and what he described as the 'filth' of Sigmund Freud. And he would live to see himself named the country's foremost suppressor of literature by Virginia Woolf.

The year James Joyce left his meagre house in Phibsborough was also the year he left Ireland. When he returned a few years later it was to set up the Cinematograph Volta – the city's, and the country's, first dedicated picture house. He had seen such things for himself, in Trieste, where he was living. His sister had made some encouraging remarks. And now here he was, having men paint the walls cream, buying wooden benches – and some Windsor chairs for the quality – and taking on string players for the augmented orchestra. Before the year was out, however, his interest had waned and he had left the country once again.

Harry Mitchelson, the young projectionist, died almost immediately he arrived on the Western Front. A cigarette case found in the pocket of his tunic was inscribed: 'With best wishes from the Proprietor and Staff of the Bohemian Picture Theatre, Dublin. September 11th, 1915.'

When Edmund Maddick was laid to rest, in the mausoleum he designed for himself, a gold pin was placed in his lapel. That was the one that had been presented to him by the King, after the special showing of *The Battle of the Somme*. The Major had recently married a woman half his age, whom he had once claimed to be his adopted daughter. And he had admitted lying about his house in Portsmouth, and about Madame Mona as well.

Herbert Muskett prosecuted DH Lawrence at least once more, over some paintings the writer exhibited in a gallery near Regent's Park. In a film of Lawrence's life, Mr Muskett was played by Sir John Gielgud.

Ernest Haigh enjoyed a reasonably long retirement, in Hampshire, on his farm. And it was there that he died, only a short time after Major Maddick.

A decade after its release, another secretary to the Metropolitan Police would write that the official Scotland Yard film 'was never regarded as a very successful or flattering production from our point of view.' 'The Commissioner thinks it is best forgotten,' he said.

82

Harry Parkinson, who made boxing films, London films, Mormon films and many other films besides, retired from all that to open a hotel next to the River Mersey.

When a copy of his Charlie Chaplin film turned up, it sold at auction for a tidy sum. But a copy of his cobbled-together Zeppelin film failed to reach its reserve.

Chick Wango, one of many people trying to be Charlie, never appeared on screen again.

Harold Speer's hall in Brighton had already been the Electric Bioscope, and after being the Queen's Theatre, it would be the Picturedrome, the Scala and the Regal. It would get a new art deco front and become the Curzon Kinema, but it would close for good not long after becoming the Classic.

Although the Rivoli – or Wonderland – in Whitechapel was destroyed by a second generation of German air-raiders, a single wall of the old place can still be seen. Not even five feet wide, sandwiched between a bookshop and a budget hotel, the end of the wall is still covered in the shimmering tiles that once ran across the whole façade.

Following his rapid exit from Britain, Anton Blazer returned to Rotterdam, where he became an eminent performer and composer of music.

Heinrich Feiler left Liverpool just as the *Five Nights* case came to an end. He and his wife lived in New York for a while, and then settled near Detroit. It was there, during the Twenties, while he was still working as a musician, that he became a US citizen.

The Electric Pavilion in Brixton, where Jean Michaud once played, eventually became the Ritzy. He, meanwhile, moved on to Islington, to the Carlton, which was brand new and quite as much Tutankhamen as Napoleon in style. 'In this orchestra will be included all the most modern instruments,' the *Era* wrote, 'and each one of these will be played by an expert':

From-week-to-week the orchestra will change not only its programmes, but its costumes.

Now it will be announced as *Johnny Mitchell and His All-Black Plantation Boys from Virginia in Modern American Jazz.*

Another time as *Jean Michaud and His Parisian Orchestra in French Jazz and Waltzes.*

And again it will appear as *Don Juan Michando and His Toreador Band from Barcelona in Spanish Dance Tunes and Songs.*

83

In Burnley, the Andrews' place became the Roxy and was given a huge, curved screen just in time to show Jane Russell. ('Mean... Moody... Magnificent!') It burned down in the Sixties, though, and was never rebuilt.

The Academy Picture Palace in Brighton proved a less fugitive place than others in which Harry Parkinson showed his films. When it finally closed, in 1973, the last picture shown there was *The Last Picture Show.*

Of other places where Andrews' Pictures were shown: the two Victoria Halls – in Colne and Southsea – closed in 1960, within a few weeks of each other; the one in Plymouth closed in 1930; and the one in Edmonton didn't even see out the Great War. In Northampton, though, they were still showing films at the Temperance Hall well into the Sixties, before the place finally went over to bingo.

The Premier Picture Hall, on Cheetham Hill Road in Manchester, also became a bingo hall. Among other places which did the same were –

The Salford Cinema, which was reopened by Ena Sharples from Coronation Street.

The Tower Picturedrome in Broughton.

The Picturedrome in Macclesfield, which had once been full to bursting.

The Hippodrome in St Helens, which someone had once called 'the Dottydrome'.

The Crescent Super Cinema in Leeds.

The Northerns in Hartlepool and the Empire in Whitley Bay. The Globe in Coventry.

The Alexandra in Longton, the Picture Palace in Goole, and the Pavilion in North Ormesby, all of which had once gone up in flames.

The Pavilion in Sheffield and the Empire in Wombwell.

The Cinema House in Rotherham, where everything Moorish was then effaced.

The Regent Street Picture House in Weston-super-Mare, where the first sign of trouble over Five Nights was detected.

The Imperial in Walsall, which, when it closed to bingo, was turned into a pub named 'The Imperial'.

The replacement for the picture house that belonged to Montagu Pyke was also turned into a pub, named 'The Montagu Pyke'.

The hard, bare Cupid's Cinema in Leicester Square was a Palm Court for a while, and then became a pub named 'The Moon Under Water'. The pub in what was the Deansgate Picture House in Manchester also has that name, which was suggested by George Orwell in one of his essays.

After the Grosvenor in Manchester closed, and bingo came and went, snooker took over. But modern-day visitors to the place can see quite a bit of what it used to be.

The Cinema House in Thurnscoe also became a snooker hall after it was a bingo hall.

Among several Temperance Billiard Halls that became pubs are the ones in Clapham and Chorlton-cum-Hardy, and also the one on Fulham High Street, which called itself 'The Temperance'.

Jack Johnson did eventually get to fight another Englishman, even if it was in Nuevo Laredo, on the Mexican border, and even if the victory he won was only on points.

It may be that Arthur Cravan died in Mexico, or in the sea just off the coast. He went missing from a fishing boat, and it was recorded that he had drowned. But people, being what they are, said he had faked his own death – which, ironically, is just what Arthur had been saying about his uncle for years.

Whatever struck those houses near the Electric Palace in Notting Hill, it didn't come from a Zeppelin.

Heinrich Mathy now lies buried with other members of his crew, alongside the crews of other Zeppelins downed in Britain, at the German Military Cemetery in Cannock Chase. The field in which he died is criss-crossed by roads with names such as Wulstan Park and Tempest Avenue.

To the DSO that Wulstan Tempest was awarded after the encounter over Potters Bar would be added a Military Cross, and he would end the Great War with the rank of Major. His downing of Commander Mathy came only days after he learned that his own brother had been killed in action.

The raids on Britain ended on the evening of another warm day in August, in the sky over Great Yarmouth, where they had first begun.

The unimpeachably British hands into which the Electric Palace was placed were those of Mark Wolfe. He had once been accused of charging extortionate rates of interest, and of leading minors into debt. And he would later be convicted of showing far too few British films.

The Zeppelin Oak, by then bare and withered, was cut down in the Thirties.

The King of Prussia is now a house.

The Belmont Road Picture House in Liverpool was, for a while, the Wookey Hollow.

The Pavilion Theatre in Musselburgh became Arcadia.

The De Luxe Picturedrome in Nelson was found to be too dangerous to be granted a licence, and it was promptly knocked down.

The Electric Theatre in Folkestone, where the costermonger film *Fog* had proved so popular, would later be the scene of a curious, touching incident.

Shortly after the end of the Great War, during the showing of a comedy film, a young man named Charlie Noakes got up from his seat and began to cause a commotion. He had been struck dumb by his experiences on the Western Front, and forced to communicate using a slate and chalk. But now, Charlie had found himself laughing loudly at the antics on the screen.

'I have regained my speech, thank God,' he exclaimed to a bewildered hall, before dropping to his knees in the aisle and beginning to pray.

'China Mary' lived out her days in a neat house on Baranof Street in Sitka, up by the creek, with the Gyldeneges, the Ozawas, and the Rezeks for neighbours. She grew huge raspberries there, the moss being no impediment, and she watched them like a hawk. When she died, in the Pioneer Home, Alaska was about to join the Union. She had been a citizen for a good few years by then, and 'Mrs Mary Johnson' for a few years more.

84

Jackeydawra Melford married and raised a family, and when she died, at almost one hundred years of age, she left behind some tapes on which she talks at length about her father and their work together. If she made any films of her own after completing his last one, they have still to be found.

Laura Bayley died at home, in Hove, two decades before her husband, Bertie. By the time of his death, the colour films he had tried so hard to master could be seen just about anywhere.

Mrs Aubrey Le Blond would receive the *Croix de Guerre* and survive a total of four husbands. Among her many books is an autobiography, in which she talks about her mountain-climbing and magic lantern lectures, but never once mentions that she used to make films.

Jessica Borthwick opened a factory in Chelsea, where she trained the wounded to make the fine children's toys that just couldn't be had from Germany. Then, she changed her name, took up sculpture and was praised by Rodin.

Ethyle Batley died when she was only forty. It was her husband, Ernest, who made George Robey into an anarchist (although the great comedian's attack on Parliament didn't prevent him being given a knighthood). Dorothy Batley eventually returned to films and went into television. She even had a part in *The Blue Lagoon*.

Nellie Lucoque wrote several films after Will Barker's *She*, most of them for the company set up by her husband, Lisle. He worked with Rider Haggard again, even going to South Africa to film a new version of the book, but his health deteriorated, he met with one misfortune after another, and ultimately, he took his own life. Nellie didn't write a film for anyone else after that.

Nearly all of Irene Miller's work was done for the Barker company. Then, she let it be known that she was giving it all up to live in a caravan and write a book about classical Greece. She had gone into films 'full of enthusiasm,' she said, but she had received one rejection too many, and now, she was 'sick of it all'.

Cecil Hepworth went bankrupt in the Twenties, and his films were melted down for their silver. Blanche MacIntosh didn't write for anyone else after that. She died within sight of the old studio in Walton-on-Thames.

May Clark, cinema's very first Alice, went on to marry the Mad Hatter.

When Charles Christopher Charsley retired as Chief Constable of Coventry, he moved to Weston-super-Mare and turned his hand to writing stories, some of which were based upon his exploits in the police. He died in the town just before his eightieth birthday, a few days after his wife.

Reverend EA Glenday, the author of that letter to the *Bury Times*, lost two nephews in the Great War. Ferdinand and Alexander had lived with their uncle for more than a decade. Alexander fell at the battle of Loos, and the Reverend Glenday's letter, which landed the newspaper in court and must have caused him great anguish, was written just after he had learned that Ferdinand too was dead.

Pimple – Fred Evans – claimed to have produced more than 200 films at his studio in the middle of the Thames. His popularity declined, however, and by the time the last film came out, *Trapped by the Mormons* was all the rage. Bankrupt by now, Fred went back on the stage, appearing in revues, circuses, and a puppet show. Shortly before he died, at his caravan in Cornwall, he had been wrestling with a three-foot-tall marionette. His wife died the following day. And in no time at all, the Rolling Stones were playing in the place they had once called home.

Reggie Switz was finished with films by the second Christmas of the war. He changed his surname to Sheridan, his mother's maiden name, perhaps to avoid being thought German. He went back to being Reginald as well, and he also went back into musical theatre. Sometimes, he appeared with Lily Ward, whom he had first met in Holmfirth. And if she was lower down the bill, it wasn't by much and it wasn't for long. Reginald eventually married Lily, having fought Alf Scott for her affections in real life as well as on film. They moved to Australia, where they lived out their days together.

The Holme Valley Theatre in Holmfirth was another picture house that went over to bingo (although it went back to films after that).

Bamforth's stopped making films during the Great War, celluloid having become scarce and several cameramen having decamped to a rival. The firm devoted itself to postcards after that, and they gradually became saucier and saucier, and were themselves mentioned by George Orwell. The feature film *Paula* proved much more popular than the firm had been willing to admit, and it was still playing in Moscow during the last days of the Tsar.

When Hannah Hinchliffe arrived in New York, as a witness in James Bamforth's case, she told her family that she wanted to stay there. Eventually, however, she was persuaded to return to Holmfirth, and it is there that she married Fred Taylor, who ran a garage.

The firm's postcards were rediscovered in the Seventies, and Marion Leake became something of a celebrity, getting interviewed by newspapers and even appearing on the BBC. A film about her, *Marion at Bamforth's*, is held in the National Film Archive.

85

Montague Shearman died at his home in London, just as the Talkies were coming in. 'As a judge,' it was said, 'he was eminently fair, good-tempered and moderate, seldom coming into collision with witnesses or opposing counsel.'

Shortly after the *Five Nights* affair, Mr Justice Shearman sat on the official inquiry into the Easter Rising. And after the business with the poison in Carmarthen, he presided over of the trial of Edith Thompson and Edward Bywaters for the murder of her husband Percy. He received fierce criticism for his pains. The case against Thompson rested chiefly upon letters she had sent to Bywaters – ones in which, Sir Montague instructed the jury, she revealed herself to be deceitful and an adulterer. His obvious disapproval was thought to be the reason Thompson as well as Bywaters was convicted. Both hanged, she at Holloway prison, when she was practically unconscious and probably pregnant.

Terry's, where larking, kissing, and cuddling wasn't nearly the end of it, had been a theatre for years before it became a picture house, but it was pulled down so they could widen The Strand.

In Nottingham, the Parliament Street Picture House became the Odd Hour Cinema.

The Electric Theatre in St Helens became the Scala.

In Bedford, the Empire became known for its 'X' films. The son of Haydn Farnhill, who had been the cinema's musical director, joined the Navy, eventually became an Admiral, and was for a while the keeper of Britain's official secrets.

The 'Chi' in South Shields still didn't have a carpet or proper seats by the time it closed.

When times changed and the largest cinema orchestra in Leeds was disbanded, one musician gave an interview to the *Yorkshire Evening Post*. 'These Talkies are only a craze at present,' he said, 'and personally, I don't see they are here to stop.'

But Gwen Berry was less confident. She played her cello in cinemas around Birmingham, most often at the Grand on Alum Rock Road. 'We have been about seven miles to do seven minutes playing,' she wrote in her diary, as the Thirties dawned. 'Soon, I suppose they won't want us at all. At least I hope we won't go on like this – it's too unsettling.'

Dove Paterson died after a swimming accident, just before the Battle of the Somme, and whatever business he had built up in Aberdeen soon fell away. It was then that an advertisement appeared in the classifieds: 'Mrs Dove Paterson, widow of the late Dove Paterson, disengaged for speaking picture artist, management or cinema artist, thoroughly experienced in all lines.'

Thanks to Bert and Nellie Gates, though, the peculiar practice that had been developed in the city continued right up to the coming of the Talkies.

Harold Mitschke died suddenly, at the height of what a newspaper in Hartlepool would call 'his wonderful elocutionary powers'.

In Horden, as the years went by, Bert Velma took to keeping a revolver in his office.

One day, in North Shields, advertisements began appearing for a special event at the Borough Theatre. 'Jubilee Anniversary Programme,' they promised:

Old-Time Silent Pictures...
Old-Time Variety Turns...
Old-Time Orchestra and many other interesting items...
Don't Miss The Show Which Will Recall Happy Memories.
With JC Padden as Lecturer.

The Manchester Assize Court was badly damaged by bombs in the Second World War, and what remained was pulled down in the Fifties.

The Futurist cinema, which stood across the road from the court and had once been the Star, was home for a while to the Manchester & Salford Workers' Film Society. It was levelled in the same raid that did for the court, and after its remains had been swept away, a tax office was put up in their place.

The former Pankhurst Hall was subsequently the Marlborough, the New Marlborough, and the Embassy, but it had become the Astor by the time it closed. Yet another bingo hall after that, it was demolished after succumbing to a serious fire. It isn't known precisely when Sylvia's elegant murals were effaced, but effaced they certainly were.

Within walking distance of the Assize Court –

The Shakespeare became the Continental and announced it would now be a home for 'classy' European films. It was showing blue films within the year, however, and it closed for good with a Japanese monster movie.

The Market Street Picture House took a similar course, its final film being *Where Are You Going All Naked?*

The Victoria was redesigned, with a Jacobean-style café, but it closed when trade dropped off because the houses all around it had been knocked down.

The Tower Picturedrome became a cabaret after the bingo, and the Empire Electric *Jump-in Jacks*.

The Salford Cinema, which had once been a church, became a church again once the bingo was done.

The Temple, which had never been a temple, closed one Christmas with *Sex in a Women's Prison*.

86

The Palladium in Brighton went all art deco and became an Odeon, but it reverted to its old name when a different Odeon opened up around the corner.

In Hartlepool, the Palace became the Gaiety but had gone before long, and Jayne Mansfield proved all too much for the Pavilion in Hawick.

In Darlington, where *Sapho* had also proved too much, at least for some, the Alhambra Palace closed on the day after Valentine's. There was a 'Gaumont' sign hanging outside by then, but 'Alhambra' was still carved in stone over the door.

Although the Rialto in Easington Colliery closed in the Seventies, it would eventually make an appearance of its own on the silver screen, when its boarded-up doors featured in a few frames of *Billy Elliot*.

Kitty Marion was force-fed more than 200 times. She emigrated to the United States after that, where she argued for birth control and carried on getting arrested.

Christabel Pankhurst came back to England and served thirty days of a three-year prison sentence. Eventually, she too went to the United States, where she became an Adventist.

Sylvia Pankhurst opposed the war, broke from her mother and sister, and became involved in left-wing politics. She made a friend of Haile Selassie and moved to Ethiopia, writing a book about the country, and dying in Addis Ababa, where she was given a state funeral.

Hetty Payne died a few days short of her ninety-third birthday, more than forty years after the young man she had married in Dover during the war while she was awaiting her day in court.

Of picture houses that went up in flames –

That proved to be the end for the Brinksway Pictorium in Stockport, and also for the Lyceum in Wallasey.

The Forum in Hexham superseded the Gem; the Windsor, in Neath, Vint's Hippodrome.

In Stockton-on-Tees, the Globe was replaced by another Globe, and then by a third.

Hove Town Hall, which in successive weeks hosted *Attack on a China Mission* and Lizzie Le Blond, also burned to the ground.

Chrissie White's biggest successes were after *Five Nights*, and they were very big indeed. For a while, in the Twenties, she and her husband, Henry Edwards, were the country's most talked-about celebrity couple. But she made only two Talkies and her career was over by the time she was forty. She lived out her days in Surrey, at Gracious Pond, in an old house with a beautiful garden, where she liked to sit quite still and allow birds to alight upon her outstretched arms.

Alma Taylor would go on to receive even greater acclaim, being named Britain's favourite film star by another magazine. And she too would be with Cecil Hepworth until the very end, featuring in his final film, *Comin' Thro' the Rye*.

That film can be seen in another, much later one. *The Smallest Show on Earth* is about a run-down old cinema next to a rumbling railway line, and about the elderly staff and their memories of happier, silent days. As the earlier film is being shown, a pianist can be seen, playing along from beneath the screen, and carefully watching the two lovers as they part. (*The rye will all be harvested before you come back* – a title-card reads

– and the field will be as empty as my heart.) Alma Taylor plays one of the lovers, in a beautiful crinoline, at a country gate in the very height of summer. But she is present in the later film as well, sitting in the middle of the audience, in a tailored jacket and a chignon.

87

William Broadhead rejected an offer of £250,000 from someone who wanted to turn his theatres into full-time cinemas. He died soon after the Talkies arrived. His business fell apart and his chain was dismantled. But the King's Palace in Preston stayed in the family.

The Royal Osborne became a rink of the 'roller-disco' variety, while the Empress, near the Tripe Colony, went up in flames and then fell down while everyone was trying to decide what to do with it.

A good few of Mr Broadhead's halls were destroyed by fire, in fact, including the ones in Bury and Longsight.

Nearly all of the halls have been demolished, and of the few that haven't, most are in a terrible state of repair. The Winter Gardens in Morecambe is opening its doors once again, though, for ghost tours and the occasional old film.

Mr Broadhead's two Pavilions went over to bingo, and some of his Hippodromes took a turn for the titillating. The one in Harpurhey offered dancers a ten-shilling bonus to take off their bras, while the one in Hulme gave a home to Pauline Penny and her 'Nud-E-Ville' show.

After the Junction – also in Hulme – became the Playhouse, it was a home for the BBC and hosted the likes of Jimmy Clitheroe, Les Dawson, and Ken Dodd. It was where the Beatles first recorded for the radio, and, after the Beeb had gone, a place where Nina Simone performed.

Billy Boyle eventually left the King's Palace – and Preston and William Broadhead. He was the man who received the letter that sparked the whole *Five Nights* affair, but when he returned to the town it was as the manager of a rival theatre.

Walter Stott spent the latter part of the Great War working nights in a munitions factory. And then, in a club for cinema executives, with a wager of £1 on the table, he ate twelve Eccles cakes at a single sitting. The Olympia cinema in Huddersfield went on just fine without him. Damaged by fire on the day the Second World War broke out, it would be renamed and again remodelled, this time in the art deco style.

Mr Stott's companies continued renting out films right up to the war and beyond. And his other cinemas continued showing films as well. That was the case at the Majestic Picture Palace on Whitworth Street in Manchester. Through the years, pressed up against another rumbling railway line, that place would be the Kinemacolor Palace, the Electric Theatre, the News Theatre, the Essoldo, the Classic, and the Tatler. It would be converted to sound, and then into a furniture warehouse, and it ended up as just another place showing blue movies. After that, though, and for a good few years, it was the truly majestic Cornerhouse.

88

At a Preston Council by-election held a few months after the end of the Great War, Leslie Knight defeated the only other candidate, his good friend Hugh Rain (or Will Onda). The ward he was elected to serve was the one in which his own Theatre Royal was situated, and he became its second Conservative councillor, its first being the redoubtable John Rigg.

Dr Rigg, who thought so little of the tram conductors and old soldiers of Preston, died in the town between the two world wars, only weeks after his wife of almost fifty years.

Of the film *Attack on a China Mission*, about half survives.

George Oakey, Dr Rigg's adversary in Preston, survived him by five years.

On the occasion of their golden wedding, William Meagher and his wife received a telegram of congratulation and blessing from His Holiness, Pope Pius XI.

Hugh Rain now shares the grave he made for his wife, next to which there is a granite vase with the words 'My Sweetheart' written on the front.

After *Five Nights*, Eve Balfour appeared in some more British films, and in *Fantômas*, the American crime serial that created a stir but has now been lost. She went to Broadway and was painted by Augustus John, but her production company only ever made that one film.

Tom Coventry featured in only one more Barker film after *Five Nights*, and his co-star, Thomas H MacDonald, was gone from the company within weeks.

The film was Sybil de Bray's second, and also her last.

It was almost the last one Bert Haldane directed for Barker.

Rowland Talbot died on the Western Front, only days before the end of the Great War. To his credit there stands a body of more than a hundred films, and much else besides.

After being beaten by Jack Dempsey, Georges Carpentier never again fought for the world title. A distinguished aviator and a recipient of the *Croix de Guerre*, he turned to song and dance, wrote a novel, and appeared in more films than the one that proved fatal in Derbyshire.

Billy Wells, twice bested by Carpentier, worked for other directors as well as Harry Parkinson. They include King Vidor and Alfred Hitchcock, and another of his films – *Kent, the Fighting Man* – was written by Rowland Talbot. 'Bombardier Wells shows himself to be possessed of histrionic gifts in no way inferior to his great physical advantages,' the *Bioscope* wrote. He died in Ealing, not far from the studios, but he can still be seen banging the gong at the beginning of many J Arthur Rank films.

The Bombardier never got to fight for the world title. He did, however, defend his British title time and time again, and he was the first heavyweight to be awarded the belt named for Lord Lonsdale, who had gone to so much trouble to prevent his bout with Jack Johnson.

Kent, the Fighting Man was the 'important cinema engagement' Hetty Payne had in hand when she was pictured in the *Sketch*. Apart from *Paula*, it would be her only film, though she did go on advertising her acting services in the *Bioscope* for a little while afterwards.

The Yellow Earl won the St Leger but rarely attended the House of Lords. He spent freely, even after his money ran out, and when he died, at close to ninety, it was in much reduced circumstances.

After the Earl's Court debacle, no white man fought a black man in a British boxing ring until long after the Second World War.

What was once the Premier Electric Theatre in Harringay celebrated its ninetieth birthday with a showing of Alma Taylor – and Virginia McKenna and Bill Travers, and Margaret Rutherford and Peter Sellers – in *The Smallest Show on Earth*.

When the Walpole Picture Theatre in Ealing was knocked down, the tiled frontage was put back up a short distance away.

The Bijou in Bexhill-on-Sea was among the first places to show Talkies, and after being the St George's, it became the Savoy.

The Cinema House in Sheffield, meanwhile, was among the last of the old places to begin showing Talkies.

George Redford, who gave *Five Nights* its certificate and then spoke up for the film when the row was at its fiercest, was dead in little more than a year.

Every local authority is still its own censor of films. Most choose to accept the decision of what was the British Board of Film Censors, of course, but it remains their choice to make. David Cronenberg's *Crash* was banned in Westminster even though it was shown in next-door Camden; while *Monty Python's Life of Brian* appeared in Bournemouth only many years after it had been seen just about everywhere else.

Victoria Cross was well into her eighties when she died. She had carried on writing novels for two decades after the *Five Nights* film, albeit with diminishing success. She lived in India, in London, the New Forest, Malvern, and Brighton, and in warm and watery places around Europe.

Eventually, she settled in Geneva, and it was there that she fell for the American diplomat from whom her executors would later demand the return of £100,000. He claimed she gave him the money in gratitude when he saved her from suicide. She left her estate to a diamond dealer from Milan and is buried just outside that city, her beloved uncle by her side.

Elinor Glyn, too, wrote many more books. After reporting on the Versailles peace conference for the *News of the World*, she fetched up in Hollywood, where she charmed William Randolph Hearst and produced scripts for Gloria Swanson and Rudolph Valentino, turning Clara Bow into the very first 'It' girl on the way. Returning to England, Ms Glyn also returned to books, after losing money making films of her own. She died in London during the Second World War.

A copy of *Three Weeks* appears in many films of the Twenties and Thirties, not least *The Shindig*, which starred Mickey Mouse and Clarabelle the cow. She can be seen reading one such copy in her byre, and then hiding it under a pile of straw when a visitor arrives.

Will Barker announced his retirement from films the day after the Armistice. He made the occasional documentary after that, just for the newsreels, and he filmed the Prince of Wales on a tour of what was still the Empire. He died in Wimbledon, on the day after Bonfire Night.

Films continued to be made in the Ealing studio Mr Barker founded, and the comedies were especially popular. And not all of his *Henry VIII* is lost. Four frames are kept in a strong box in the National Archives, all of them tinted but only one whole. There are also rumours of a single, complete copy of the film, which was given to Sir Herbert as a memento and has yet to be found.

A fragment is also all that remains of *Sixty Years A Queen*.

89

In Preston, the Marathon cinema never made it to the Talkies, and the Picture Palace didn't even survive the Great War. Fleckie Bennett's place, meanwhile, became the Dominion and then the Rex, but by the time it closed people were calling it the 'Laugh and Scratch'.

The Alexander was turned into a dance hall, the Cosy succumbed early in the Fifties, and the Picturedrome closed a decade later, even though it had set aside a room in which customers could listen to gramophone records while they waited for the second house.

Leslie Knight's Theatre Royal became the ABC, before it was forced to make way for another ABC, opened by Richard Todd. It lost its stalls to a public bar – the 'Painted Wagon' – and finally closed its doors after a double bill of 'X' films. The Queen's Hall also went blue, and changed its name to the Continental to mark the event, but after that it became a Sikh temple.

The Prince's Theatre, which had once been owned by Will Onda (or Hugh Rain), was demolished to make way for a shopping arcade and a bingo hall, and the Palladium was knocked down soon after. The Empire, where the play of *Five Nights* was performed, was the last theatre in the town to become a full-time cinema, and it too ended up as a bingo hall. Opened by Elsie Tanner from *Coronation Street*, the hall closed for good after only a few years.

The King's Palace, where all of this began, alternated films with theatre for a while, and it played host to Harry Lauder, George Formby senior and George Formby junior. It became a rink again after that, but then it stood unused and unloved for years. There was talk of using it as a theatre again, but the final straw was a series of fires, started by children with nothing better to do. Developers moved in before the Sixties had properly begun to swing, and the place was hauled down and replaced by shops that are themselves now vacant.

Frederick White, the man who brought Bombardier Billy Wells to the screen, died at ringside during a bout in Harringay, in what had once been a rink. He also brought *Zepped* and some of those Mormon films to the screen, and, not yet sixty, he had been working with Harry Parkinson again. He was a keen sportsman, the papers said, but he had a bad heart, and though he often went to the boxing with friends, he died quite alone.

His company had merged with others by then, but when he spoke to the press, he said he had always made a point of creating box office pictures of nationwide appeal. And he told potential investors that the films of which he was most proud were *Sapho*, *Secrets of Scotland Yard* (as he insisted upon calling it) and *Five Nights*.

Fred had only recently moved to London, where his home was called 'The Rosary'. That was also the name of the film he had been renting out just after the *Five Nights* business and his sundering from Walter Stott. After his death, he was taken back to the place he was born. That was the town of Preston, where they had known him by a different name.

That was also when James Watson retired as Chief Constable of the town. He had served for more than forty years, and he was awarded a pension of more than £500. He was honoured with the King's Police Medal, having received the congratulations of the borough for his part in the Guild festivities.

Mr Watson died in Eastbourne, four years after his retirement, having caught a chill when visiting his daughter. 'Under his direction, the Preston constabulary increased in efficiency,' an obituary in the *Lancashire Daily Post* said. He was sympathetic to special constables, improved traffic lights, one-way streets, and road safety, and 'gave support to all organisations inculcating high standards of citizenship.' His pension would be paid up to the end of the month.

90

What remains of *Five Nights* may be found in Preston.

It is kept in a stout box on a long shelf under a harsh light.

It isn't much – just a piece of celluloid barely two inches square, showing all the signs of having been hardened by the years.

There are two frames of a film on this fragment, one above the other, both tinted pink, with perforations running down either side.

There aren't quite two frames, in fact, because the bottom one has been sheared through below the middle.

What they show, though, is unmistakeable: two people – a man and a woman – sitting side-by-side.

The man has his arms around the woman, and the woman has her arms around the man.

And though each frame captures only a splinter of time, and a lost splinter at that, it is unimpeachable evidence of an act that still goes on –

The simple act of kissing.

Sources

The newsreel referred to at the beginning of this book is *Gaumont Graphic* number 462, which came out on 26 August 1915. The Charlie Chaplin film is *A Film Johnnie* (1914, US) and the Broncho Billy film is *His Regeneration* (1915, US).

More details about other films mentioned here can be found at the Internet Movie Database, or on the website of the British Film Institute.

Among old films that can still be seen, either at the BFI website or elsewhere, are –

Cliff Climbing, Herring Harvest at Yarmouth, East Lynne, Jane Shore, Women's Rights, Did'ums Diddles the P'liceman, Tilly and the Fire Engines, The Herncrake Witch, A Victim of the Mormons, Trapped by the Mormons.

At least two versions of *The Kiss in the Tunnel* are still available, together with several Pimple films, some other Tilly films, one or two Winky films, and a portion of *Heart of a Coster*. But none of the Selsior dancing films is known to have survived.

The story of the early days of cinema, or a version of that story at least, is told in Rachel Low's *The History of the British Film 1919–1929* (1971, George Allen and Unwin). A rather more generous account is given by Matthew Sweet in his marvellous collection of memories, *Shepperton Babylon* (2005, Faber). I have drawn upon both those books, and also upon two essays by Luke McKernan: '"Only the screen was silent…": Memories of children's cinema-going in London before the First World War', *Film Studies*, Issue 10, Spring 2007; and 'Diverting Time: London's cinemas and their audiences, 1906–1914', *The London Journal*, volume 32, number 2, July 2007, pages 125–

144. Reference might also be made to: IS Hunter, Laraine Porter, Justin Smith (editors) *The Routledge Companion to British Cinema History* (2017, Routledge). (What Gwen Berry wrote in her diary as the Thirties dawned is quoted in Neil Brand's essay in that book.)

The vanished cinemas of Preston, and of Britain more generally, are remembered on the Cinema Treasures website, the vanished theatres on the Arthur Lloyd website.

In writing about the town of Preston, I have drawn upon three studies by David Hindle: *From a 'Gin Palace' to a 'King's Palace'? The Evolution of the Music Hall in Preston c 1840–1914* (2006, University of Central Lancashire, unpublished MA thesis); *From a Gin Palace to a King's Palace: Provincial Music Hall in Preston* (2007, Tempus); and *Life in Victorian Preston* (2014, Amberley). I have also drawn on Keith Johnson's book *Preston Remembered* (2011, The History Press). And my summary of the life and times of William Broadhead borrows from the work of Victoria Garlick, and in particular from *Quick, clean, smart, bright* (2015, University of Manchester, unpublished PhD thesis).

The *Five Nights* affair is described in some detail in two articles by David Williams: 'The Five Nights Affair' (2000) 3 *Journal of Popular British Cinema*; and 'What Made Victoria Cross?' in Alan Burton and Laraine Porter, *Scene-stealing: Sources for British Cinema Before 1930* (2003, Flicks Books). The affair is also discussed in the *Preston Herald* of 10, 17, 20 & 27 March 1915; 7 April 1915; 5, 6, 19 & 22 May 1915; 3, 4, 5 & 7 September 1915; 5 & 20 November 1915; and 19 February 1916. And it was reported in the *Daily Sketch* of 1 September 1915 and the *Manchester Evening News* of 7 September 1915.

The passage that the *Preston Herald* took from John Ruskin appears in *Sesame and Lilies* (1865, John Wiley & Son). He argues that women should be the moral guardians of men, and that girls should be educated with that purpose in mind. The considered view in Dumfries was set out in the *Dumfries &*

Galloway Standard of 7 February 1917, while the business about the handbills was discussed in that paper's edition of 19 May 1917.

My reconstruction of the five nights of the film is based upon *Five Nights: The Story of the Film* by James L Pollitt, a copy of which may be found in the Lancashire Archives in Preston (CBP/ACC 11945/1-6), and upon other documents held there. (This is the sumptuous promotional brochure to which the court also, briefly, had recourse.) What I have said about the trial is based upon the official transcript, and about the wider case upon witness statements, correspondence, and newspaper articles. A copy of James Watson's original inflammatory letter is also held in the archive, as is the fragment containing all that remains of the film itself.

What was said about *Five Nights* before it arrived in Preston was said in the *Preston Herald* of 25 & 28 August 1915, the *Midland Daily Telegraph* of 28 August 1915, and the *Derbyshire Advertiser* of 28 August 1915. Other helpful material was contained in the *Fulham Chronicle* of 3 September 1915, the *Western Daily Press* of 4 September 1915, the *Western Mail* of 4 September 1915, the *Edinburgh Evening News* of 6 September 1915, the *Leven Advertiser and Wemyss Gazette* of 9 September 1915, the *Motherwell Times* of 17 September 1915, the *Lincolnshire Chronicle* of 18 September 1915, the *Lincolnshire Echo* of 21 September 1915, the *West London Press* of 24 September 1915, and (in Hull) the *Daily Mail* of 27 September 1915.

Some details of the life, career and death of James Watson also come from records held at the Lancashire Archives (PLA 51/7) or the Cumbria Archives in Barrow (BSBP/11/1). Other details come from the *Preston Herald* of 10, 13, 17 & 20 March 1915; 7 April 1915; 1, 5 & 6 May 1915; 11 September 1915; and 24 December 1915. While yet others come from the *Lancashire Daily Post* of 19 & 25 January 1916, 2 February 1916, and

4 December 1941. In writing about Mr Watson, I have also drawn upon Census returns, and upon births, marriages and deaths records obtained from the General Register Office. I have done the same in writing about Ernest Haigh, Walter Stott and Fred White, and about some other people mentioned in this book, including John Rigg, William Meagher, Frederick Daggers, Margaret Buck, Hetty Payne and Winky. Details about the life and career of Mr Watson's predecessor, Captain John Unett, have come from a number of sources, including editions of the *Preston Herald* for 8 June 1912 and 20 February 1915.

Information about entertainments available in Preston immediately before the arrival of *Five Nights* has been taken from: the *Preston Herald* of 4, 7, 11, 18, 21, 25 & 28 August 1915, and 4 September 1915; the *Bioscope* of 11 March 1915, 1 April 1915, 6 May 1915, and 3 June 1915; and the *Devon and Exeter Gazette* of 9 March 1915, the *Leven Advertiser and Wemyss Gazette* of 19 August 1915, and the *Sheffield Daily Telegraph* of 26 August 1915. Entertainment available immediately afterwards, at least in the Broadhead empire, is described in the *Manchester Evening News* of 4 & 7 September 1915, and 15 February 1916; the *Preston Herald* of 1 & 4 September 1915; the *Liverpool Echo* of 4 September 1915; and the *Manchester Courier* of 7 September 1915.

The travails of Dr Rigg are recounted at length in editions of the *Preston Herald* dated 28 February 1914; 26 January 1915; 19 May 1915; 17, 20 & 27 November 1915; and 24 December 1915. His memoir of China appears in the preface to Mary E Darley's book *The Light of the Morning* (1902, Church of England Zenana Missionary Society). George Oakey was the subject of an article in the *Preston Herald* on 25 January 1913, and of articles in the *Lancashire Daily Post* of 25 September 1934, and 11, 12 & 13 July 1935.

Details of the life of Billy Boyle have been taken from articles in the *Preston Herald* of 6 September 1913, the *Lancashire Daily Post* of 18 May 1920, and the *Bioscope* of 20 May 1920.

In writing about Leslie Knight and the Theatre Royal in Preston, I have drawn upon articles in the *Preston Herald* of 9 August 1913; 6 & 27 September 1913; 9 May 1914; 9, 12 & 16 September 1914; 20 February 1915; 5 June 1915; 31 July 1915; and 19 February 1916. I have also drawn upon articles in the *Bioscope* of 5 June 1913 and the *Lancashire Evening Post* of 15 October 1919.

That Will Onda's son was among the soldiers he filmed at Preston station is apparent from an article in the *Preston Herald* of 17 July 1915. A film of what seems likely to be that event is another of those which may be found on the BFI website.

Walter Stott's appearances before the Huddersfield magistrates in 1916 are reported in the *Daily Mail* of 11 February, the *Leeds Mercury* of that date and 9 March, and the *Huddersfield Daily Examiner* of 17 February. The ones in 1913 are reported in the *Sheffield Daily Telegraph* of 9 October, the *Manchester Courier* of that date and 10 October, and the *Yorkshire Post* of the latter date. Other details of the Mr Stott's life were gleaned from the *Era* of 11 June 1910 and 1 January 1936, the *Bioscope* of 29 July 1915, and the *News* of 3 February 1937. The story of the Rumble is told in the third part of Gordon & Enid Minter's marvellous *Discovering Old Huddersfield* (1998, 2010, Huddersfield Local History Society).

Frederick White's experiences when he struck out on his own are recorded in the *Western Mail* of 13 April 1915 and the *Bioscope* of 21 August 1919. The libel action he and Mr Stott brought against the *Bury Times*, and the letter which provoked that action, are the subject of pieces in the *Manchester Evening News* of 18 & 19 May 1916. And more information about Charlie Chaplin's legal case against Mr White may be found in an article by David Lister in the *Independent* of 18 November 1997 (*Found: film Chaplin didn't find funny*). Papers from the case, including the writ, affidavits and transcripts, may be viewed on the website of the Charlie Chaplin Archive.

The early life and career of Harry Parkinson is described in the *Bioscope* of 14 October 1909, 20 January 1910, 31 March 1910, 19 May 1910, 25 August 1910, 9 May 1912, 3 & 31 July 1913, 5 February 1914, 2 April 1914, 6 & 13 August 1914, 2 September 1915, and 1 March 1917. It is also described in the *Burnley Express* of 6 July 1901; 24 September 1904; 15 October 1904; 1 July 1905; 13 & 20 April 1907; 5 June 1907; 7 March 1908; 16 December 1911; 14, 17 21, 24 & 28 February 1912; 27 March 1912; and 10 & 27 April 1912; and in the *Burnley Gazette* of 5 & 12 August 1908, and 11 May 1912.

Something, at least, about the life and career of Charles Charsley, the Chief Constable of Coventry, may be found in the *Birmingham Daily Post* of 30 August 1915, the *Coventry Standard* of 3 September 1915, and the *Coventry Herald* of 3/4 September 1915.

Zepped – or *Zepped!* – was advertised in editions of *Film-Renter* magazine dated 23 & 30 December 1916, and details of what the film contained have been taken from a review that appeared in the second of them. What the film was and was not, and whether the title should have had an exclamation mark, may also be deduced from an article by Kaleem Aftab that was published in the *Independent* of 6 November 2009 (*Lost Chaplin film discovered in $5 can bought on eBay*). What became of the film can be read on the BBC News website, in an article posted on 30 June 2011 (*Rare Charlie Chaplin film fails to sell*). Showings of the film in Hull are recorded in editions of that city's *Daily Mail* newspaper for 7 August 1917 and 20 November 1917, and showings elsewhere in the *Chichester Observer* of 6 & 13 June 1917, the *Wakefield Advertiser and Gazette* of 21 August 1917, the *Leeds Mercury* of 20 November 1917, the *Rugby Advertiser* of 10 August 1918, the *Nottingham Journal & Express* of 13 August 1918, and the *Walsall Observer* of 7 September 1918.

The Zeppelin raids on Britain are described in *The War in the Air* by HA Jones (1935, Oxford University Press). Details of the first of them are taken from the *Nottingham Evening Post* of 20 January 1915, and those of the others are set out on Ian Castle's website. Mention should also be made of his indispensable book *Zeppelin Onslaught: The Forgotten Blitz 1914–1915* (2018, Frontline Books).

William Gedge's memories of the very first raid can be heard on the website of the Imperial War Museum. The other memories referred to here are those of Samuel Uttin, Olive Smith and Jack Leader. They are contained in the BBC East documentary *Zeppelins*, which was first shown in 1972 and may now be seen on the website of the East Anglian Film Archive. James Watson's edict to the people of Preston, his activities between the *Five Nights* film and the beginning of the trial, and his comments on crime and the town hall clock, were reported in the *Lancashire Daily Post* of 3 & 19 January 1916, and 11 February 1916; and in the *Preston Herald* of 25 September 1915 and 12 February 1916. Victoria Cross's Zeppelin poem also appeared in that newspaper, on 25 September 1915.

The comments of the Chief Constable of King's Lynn on the very first Zeppelin raid were reported in the *Penrith Observer* of 26 January 1915. The results of other raids are set out in the *Bioscope* of 28 January 1915, 22 & 29 April 1915, 10 June 1915, 1 July 1915, 23 September 1915, and 30 December 1915, and in the edition of 12 October 1916; and in the *Shields Daily News* of 16 April 1915, the *District News* (in Todmorden) of 31 March 1916, the *Yorkshire Evening Post* of 13 October 1916, and the *Newcastle Daily Journal* of 26 September 1917. The aftermath of the Zeppelin raid on Ramsgate was shown in edition number 323b of the British Pathé newsreel in May 1916. The damage done to the roller-skating rink in the Aldwych is recorded in a painting by Emily M Paterson that may, again, be found on the website of the Imperial War Museum. And the photographs in the *Daily Sketch* appeared in editions of 17 April 1915, 3 & 15 February 1916, 5 April 1916, and 4 September 1916. The summary of *Britons Awake!* is taken from the *Banbury Guardian* of 17 May 1917.

The snowy Zeppelin attack on Hull was reported in the *Daily Mail* of that city on 2, 7 & 8 March 1916, and in the *Lancashire Daily Post* of 7 March 1916, the *Yorkshire Evening Post* of the same date, and the *Manchester Evening News* of the following day. The journalist who wrote about the downing of Heinrich Mathy by Wulstan Tempest was Michael MacDonagh, and the book in which he did so was *In London During the Great War: The Diary of a Journalist* (1935, Eyre and Spottiswoode). That event and its aftermath was described in the *Dundee Evening Telegraph and Post* of 2 October 1916, the *Falkirk Herald* of 4 October 1916, the *Daily Mirror* of 6 October 1916, the *Hendon and Finchley Times* of 6 October 1916, the *Mansfield Reporter and Sutton Times* of 6 October 1916, the *East London Observer* of 7 October 1916, the *Bury Free Press* of 7 October 1916, the *People's Journal* (in Dundee) of 7 October 1916, the *Daily Mail* (in Hull) of 10 October 1916, and the *Looker-On* (in Cheltenham) of 14 October 1916.

The advertisement for *Pimple's Zeppelin Scare* is taken from the *Bioscope* of 6 April 1916, while the reception the film received is described in the *Shields Daily News* of 29 August 1916, the *Sheffield Daily Independent* of 13 April 1916, the *Bournemouth Graphic* of 8 December 1916, and the *Bioscope* of 23 March 1916. It is also described in the *Western Daily Press* of 5 May 1917.

My account of the reception accorded *Pimple's Battle of Waterloo* is drawn from the *Bioscope* of 10 July 1913, the *Folkestone, Hythe, Sandgate and Cheriton Herald* of 30 August 1913, the *Bedfordshire Times and Independent* of 19 September 1913, the *Bexhill-on-Sea Observer* of 11 October 1913, the *Surrey Standard and Kent Mail* of 17 October 1913, and the *Todmorden Advertiser* of 16 January 1914.

The case against Pimple in respect of *Three Weeks* was reported as *Glyn v Weston Feature Film Company and George Black* [1916] 1 Ch 261. It is described by Stacy Gillis in 'Pimple's Three Weeks (without the option) with apologies to Elinor Glyn' (2014) 12(3) *Early Popular Visual Culture*, pages 378–391, and by Jeremy Phillips in 'Elinor Glyn and the "Three Weeks" Litigation' (1982) 12 *European Intellectual Property Review*, pages 336–340. The urgent advertisement for the film appeared in the *Bioscope* on 29 April 1915, while that magazine's kind words appeared in the edition of 22 January 1914. Ms Glyn's encounters with Mark Twain are described in Michael Shelden's book, *Mark Twain: Man in White* (2010, Random House), and in an article by Charles Henry Meltzer that appeared in the *New York American* of 27 September 1908 ('Twain Says He Told Her "Book a Mistake"'). I have also been assisted by Vincent L Barnett and Alexis Weedon, *Elinor Glyn as Novelist, Moviemaker, Glamour Icon and Businesswoman* (2016, Routledge); and by ES Turner, 'Shopping in Lucerne', *London Review of Books*, volume 16 number 11, 9 June 1994. My sketch of Lord Curzon draws upon an article by Simon Schama that appeared in the *New Yorker* of 9 June 2003 (*Superior Reason: Curzon in India*), one by Amanda Foreman in the *New York Times* of 29 June 2003 ('To The Imperial Manner Born'), and one by Megan McKinney on the *Classic Chicago* website ('Lord Curzon after Mary: Chicago's British Aristocracy', posted 21 August 2016).

The encounter between Joe Evans and the woman who said that Pimple owed her a guinea, and the police court case that was its result, was reported in the *Middlesex Chronicle* of 23 May 1914. The seamy side of life on Eel Pie Island was revealed by articles in the *Westminster Gazette* of 13 September 1910, the *Globe* of 7 December 1911, and the *Middlesex Chronicle* of 6 June 1914, and 14 & 28 August 1915.

The sudden rise and fall of rinking is described in the *Yorkshire Post* of 19 August 1909 and 18 October 1909; the

Luton Reporter of 2 September 1909 and 4 November 1909; the *Folkestone, Hythe, Sandgate and Cheriton Herald* of 18 & 25 December 1909; the *Tottenham and Edmonton Weekly Herald* of 7 October 1910 and 9 February 1912; the *Staffordshire Sentinel* of 5 January 1911 and 22 March 1911; the *Daily Mail* (in Hull) of 11 January 1911 and 22 January 1912; the *Perthshire Advertiser and Strathmore Journal* of 18 February 1911 and 9 August 1911; the *Evening Telegraph and Post* (in Dundee) of 12 July 1911 and 29 May 1914; and the *Music Hall and Theatre Review* of 30 November 1911 and 14 December 1911; and in the *Yarmouth Independent* of 26 December 1908, the *Courier* (in Dundee) of 6 February 1909, the *Daily News* of 10 March 1909, the *Lancashire Daily Post* of 25 May 1909, the *Era* of 5 June 1909, the *Burnley Express* of 28 August 1909, the *Sheffield Daily Telegraph* of 11 September 1909, the *Yorkshire Evening Post* of 8 October 1909, the *Buchan Observer and East Aberdeenshire Advertiser* of 2 November 1909, the *Beds Advertiser and Luton Times* of 5 November 1909, the *Melton Mowbray Mercury and Oakham & Uppingham News* of 2 December 1909, the *Observer and West Sussex Recorder* of 29 June 1910, the *Windsor, Eton & Slough Express* of 14 January 1911, the *Daily Express* (in Dublin) of 20 January 1911, the *Daily News* of 15 February 1911, the *Jarrow Express & Tyneside Advertiser* of 28 April 1911, the *Daily Mercury* (in Leeds) of 24 June 1911, the *Echo* (in Gloucestershire) of 12 September 1911, the *Pall Mall Gazette* of 19 September 1911, the *West London Observer* of 23 August 1912, the *Leicester Chronicle and Leicestershire Mercury* of 8 March 1913, the *Bath Chronicle* of 3 May 1913, the *Courier* (in Kent and Sussex) of 27 September 1913, and the *Cornishman* of 23 April 1914.

In writing about James Bamforth, I have drawn, in particular, upon: Ludwig Maria Vogl-Bierek, "'From life': The use of the magic lantern in nineteenth century social work', in Andreas Gestrich, Steven King and Lutz Raphael (editors), *Being Poor in Modern Europe: Historical Perspectives 1800–1940* (2006,

Peter Lang AG); Allan T Sutherland, 'The Yorkshire Pioneers', in John L Fell (editor), *Film Before Griffith* (1983, University of California Press); and Robert McMillan, 'James Bamforth', The *New Magic Lantern Journal*, volume 1, number 2 (February 1979) pages 12–15. The article in the *Huddersfield Chronicle* was in the edition of 20 January 1899.

The beautiful magic lantern slides of the Bamforth company are listed, and many of them are displayed in all their glory, at LUCERNA, the Magic Lantern Web Resource. Information about Marion Leake, Hannah Hinchliffe and some of the other life models who appear on those slides may be found in Hazel Wheeler, *First of the Summer Wine* (2004, MRM Associates).

Information about *Paula*, the company's only feature film, has been taken from articles in the *Bioscope* of 13 & 20 January 1916, 15 & 22 June 1916, and 21 December 1916. It has also been taken from the *Dover Express and East Kent News* of 25 August 1916, the *Globe* of 17 October 1916, the *Liverpool Echo* of 17 October 1916, the *Pall Mall Gazette* of 17 October 1916, the *Hastings & St Leonards Observer* of 25 November 1916, the *Airdrie and Coatbridge Advertiser* of 24 February 1917, the *Devon and Exeter Gazette* of 24 April 1917, the *Dorking and Leatherhead Advertiser* of 19 May 1917, the *Fifeshire Advertiser* of 29 September 1917, and the *Kirkintilloch Herald* of 14 November 1917.

The approving comments about Reginald Switz's prowess as a stage performer were contained in the *Eastbourne Gazette* of 23 August 1905, the *Burnley Gazette* of 20 September 1905, the *Evening Telegraph and Post* (of Dundee) for 8 October 1907, and the *Era* of 20 February 1909. The letter proclaiming his essential Englishness was published in the *Bioscope* of 24 December 1914, and his credentials were set out in editions of the same journal published on 28 May 1914 and 8 April 1915, and in the *Evening Chronicle*, in Newcastle, on 5 December 1914. Information about Winky's grandfather, and his brush with the law, comes from the *Morning Chronicle* of 24 November 1859.

A short film about the life of 'China Mary' – *Golden Mountain: Mary Bong* – which was made by Blair Brown in 1995 as part of the *Nobody's Girls* series for the Great Plains National Instructional Television Library, may be found in the New York Public Library. (*Variety* said the film was 'a tedious feminist tract masquerading as entertainment,' but that, as we have seen, is *Variety* for you.) My account of her life is based upon one that can be found on the Chinese Women in the Northwest website; upon the entry written by Judy Yung for the *Biographical Dictionary of Chinese Women: The Qing Period, 1644–1911*, Clara Wing-chung Ho (editor) (1998, Routledge); and upon an article by Bob DeArmond that appeared in the *Daily Sitka Sentinel* on 22 April 1992 (*Around & About Alaska*). The first photograph of Mary Bong may be found in the portrait collection at the library of the University of Washington (Collection number PH Coll 563, negative number UW6943, order number SOC 0261). My description of the Sitka Mary will have known is taken from a number of sources, not least the *Report on Population and Resources of Alaska: Eleventh Census: 1890* (1893, US Department of the Interior), and Adolph Knopf's report on *The Sitka Mining District, Alaska* (1912, United States Geological Survey, Bulletin 504).

The lives and work of many early female film directors and writers are discussed on the website of the Women Film Pioneers Project. That is especially so of Jackeydawra Melford, although details of her appearance in the Westminster police court come from the *Morning Post* of 28 January 1913, and the profile of her in the *Cinema* from the edition of 19 March 1913. Her father's words, meanwhile, are chiefly taken from his autobiography *Life in a Booth* (1913, Hendersons). The interview Jessica Borthwick gave to the *Bioscope* appeared in the edition of 7 May 1914, under the heading 'A Girl Cinematographer at the Balkan War', while what she told the *Daily News* was then repeated in the suffragist journal the *Common Cause* of 24 December 1914.

Frances 'Daisy' Greville's comments on films were set out in *A Woman and the* War (1916, George H Dorian Co), while those on the suffragettes appeared in *Answers* on 11 January 1908. The edition of the *Bioscope* in which she announced her plans is the one dated 18 September 1913. And information about Mrs Aubrey Le Blond is contained in an article by Dr Anne Rosenbusch in the *Irish Times* of 12 July 2016 ('Greystones woman climbed mountains in a skirt so not to offend').

The personal information vouchsafed by Alice de Winton was reported in the *Scottish Referee* of 23 March 1914 and the *Bioscope* of 24 October 1918. And details of the life and exploits of Irene Miller have been taken from: the *Vote* of 25 June 1910, 20 November 1917, 10 May 1918, and 4 July 1930; the *Globe* of 21 May 1908 and 6 December 1911; and the *Shields Daily News* of 12 June 1908 and 25 March 1922; and from the *Standard* of 10 March 1906, the *Edinburgh Evening News* of 27 April 1906, the *Morning Post* of 27 April 1906, the *Sheffield Daily Telegraph* of 25 October 1906, the *Leeds and Yorkshire Mercury* of 26 October 1906, the *Daily News* of 6 November 1906, the *Eastern Daily Press* of 26 November 1906, the *Yorkshire Evening Post* of 15 November 1907, the *Yorkshire Telegraph and* Star of 25 November 1907, the *Westminster Gazette* 21 May 1908, the *Eastern Evening News* of 21 May 1908, the *Western Daily Press* of 22 May 1908, the *Manchester Courier* of 22 May 1908, the *Western Chronicle* of 12 June 1908, the *Grantham Journal* of 13 June 1908, the *Newcastle Daily Chronicle* of 22 June 1908, the *Pall Mall Gazette* of 15 June 1912, the *Kinematograph and Lantern Weekly* of 7 September 1916, the *Arbroath Herald* of 8 September 1916, the *Dover Express and East Kent News* of 13 October 1916, the *Illustrated London News* of 9 February 1918, and *Motion Picture Studio* of 1 April 1922.

The life of Alma Taylor is discussed in Jonathan Burrows's essay in *British Stars and Stardom – from Alma Taylor to Sean Connery*, Bruce Babington (editor) (2001, Manchester

University Press), and in an article about her that appeared in *Pictures and the Picturegoer* on 4 July 1914. The results of that magazine's poll are contained in the edition of 3 July 1915. Cecil Hepworth's comments about his own films were made in *Came the Dawn: Memoirs of a Film Pioneer* (1951, Phoenix House). The reception afforded *Annie Laurie* is reported in the *Bioscope* of 20 January 1916 and 14 December 1916, the *Bradford Weekly Telegraph* of 3 March 1916, and the *Shipley Times and Express* of 17 November 1916.

The British Pathé newsreel film of the 1910 march is properly entitled *Scenes in the Record Demonstration of Suffragettes*. The large photographs the *Daily Sketch* published of Eve Balfour appeared in the edition of 15 September 1915.

The *Topical Budget* featuring Sybil de Bray is number 127–1. It was shown in 1914 and is entitled *Afternoon in the Clouds*, and it too survives. Ms de Bray's appearance and charms were noted in the *Sketch* of 25 June 1913 and 21 January 1914, the *Illustrated Sporting & Dramatic News* of 5 July 1913 and 16 May 1914, the *Tatler* of 28 May 1913, the *Bioscope* of 9 October 1913, the *Western Mail* of 13 December 1913, the *Era* of 7 January 1914, and the *Scotsman* of 9 February 1915.

Hetty Payne's turn in the *Sketch* came on 1 March 1916, and other details of her life have been taken from the *Norwood News* of 14 February 1891 and 4 July 1891, the *Daily Mirror* of 28 June 1916, the *Dover Express and East Kent News* of 25 August 1916, the *Sheffield Daily Telegraph* of 18 October 1916, the *Era* of 25 October 1916, the *Hastings and St Leonards Observer* of 25 November 1916, and the *Motherwell Times* of 29 December 1916.

Information about the Marchioness of Townshend has been taken from her autobiography, *It Was – and it Wasn't* (1937, John Long Ltd), from a fawning interview with her published in the *Bioscope* on 30 July 1914, and from a rather more hard-nosed piece in the *New York Times* on 16 October 1910. Her own unfavourable opinion of cinema pianists was quoted in the St Andrews newspaper the *Citizen* on 18 October 1913. That of 'EN', meanwhile, appeared in the *Birmingham Post* of 28 June 1915, and those of the correspondent of the *Bioscope* – on pianists, but also on the performance and correct placement of orchestras – appeared in the 18 November 1915, 24 February 1916, and 28 March 1918 editions of that magazine.

The reception the stage version of *Five Nights* received is described by Padraig Yeates in his book *A City in Wartime: Dublin 1914–1918* (2011, Gill & Macmillan). Other information about that play has been taken from the *Bournemouth Guardian* of 6 & 13 April 1918, the *Daily Record and Mail* of 10 & 13 August 1918, the *Lincolnshire Echo* of 10 December 1923 and 24 November 1925, the *Tatler* of 3 April 1918, the *Hastings and St Leonard's Observer* of 11 May 1918, the *Sketch* of 29 May 1918, the *Stage* of 13 June 1918, the *Huddersfield Daily Examiner* of 10 September 1918, the *Surrey Mirror* of 4 October 1918, the *Yorkshire Evening Post* of 17 June 1919, the *Daily Mail* of 1 July 1919, the *Halifax Evening Courier* of 26 August 1919, the *Worthing Gazette* of 23 June 1920, and the *Biggleswade Chronicle* of 7 April 1922.

In writing about what might have been heard alongside early movies – words as well as tunes – I have drawn upon Ben Model's *The Music of the Silent Films* (2015, Wise Publications), and upon Julie Brown & Annette Davison's *The Sounds of the Silents in Britain* (2013, Oxford University Press).

Information about Clement Padden comes from the *Bioscope* of 18 June 1914, 8 October 1914, and 15 April 1915. The hyperbolic descriptions of his prowess as a film lecturer all appeared in the *Sunderland Daily Echo*, in the editions of 24 February 1920, and 3 & 4 May 1920. His appearance before the Durham Quarter Sessions was reported in that same newspaper, in the edition of 4 January 1938, and in the *Northern Daily Mail* of the same date.

Dove Paterson's words on the demands of lecturing were published in the *Kinematograph and Lantern Weekly* of 2 July 1905, and those of Leslie Paget in the *Bioscope* of 23 March 1916. What happened to lecturers who were not Paddens is revealed in the following editions of that journal – 27 January 1910, 10 & 17 October 1912, 26 June 1913, 11 September 1913, 13 November 1913, 9 March 1914, 7 & 28 May 1914, 17 September 1914, 17 December 1914, 23 February 1915, 8 April 1915, 26 August 1915, 9 September 1915, 28 October 1915, 20 January 1916, 9 & 23 March 1916, 4 & 11 May 1916, 22 June 1916, and 31 January 1918. It is also revealed in the *Manchester Evening News* of 9 July 1914, 22 August 1914 and 16 February 1916; the *Sunderland Daily Echo* of 18 January 1915 and 19 February 1915; the *Northampton Daily Echo* of 30 October 1916 and 14 November 1916; and the *Aberdeen Journal* of 4 March 1898, the *Kinematograph and Lantern Weekly* of 2 July 1908, the *Todmorden and District News* of 22 March 1912, the *Shields Daily News* of 24 January 1913, the *Whitstable Times and Tankerton Press* of 7 June 1913, the *Berwick Advertiser* of 30 January 1914, the *Era* of 29 July 1914, the *Hawick News* of 4 December 1914, the *Newcastle Daily Journal* of 27 February 1915, the *Middlesex Chronicle* of 20 March 1915, the *Birmingham Daily Mail* of 30 October 1915, the *Scotsman* of 3 March 1916, the *Rochdale Observer* of 15 April 1916, and the *Western Mail* of 1 June 1916.

The story of Richard Lloyd Horner is told in the *Bioscope* of 23 September 1915 and 10 February 1916; the *Yorkshire Evening Post* of 3 February 1916, 30 April 1919, and 2 May 1919; the *Yorkshire Post* of 22 January 1916; and the *Northern Daily Mail* of 1 May 1919. Rupert Whittaker's run-in with the justices of Nelson was reported in the *Burnley Express* of 14 April 1915 and the *Bioscope* of 3 June 1915. And Harold Mitschke's story may be gleaned from the *Northern Daily Mail* of 27 November 1890, 1 August 1910, 4 May 1912, 28 September 1912, 31 October

1912, 1 February 1913, 28 June 1913, 9 May 1914, 2 June 1914, 11 & 18 March 1916, 6, 13 & 16 September 1916, 21 October 1916, 7 November 1916, 12 & 18 December 1916, 2 June 1917, and 1 March 1921. My account of the career of Frank Warner, meanwhile, is taken from articles in the *Bioscope* of 31 March 1910 and 14 February 1912; in the *Burnley Express* of 10 & 17 January 1912, and 21 February 1912; and in the *Stage* of 11 January 1912. And Bert Velma's gun is the subject of an article in the *Northern Daily Mail* of 8 October 1921.

The world of elocutionists and the *benshi* is described in: Rick Altman, *Silent Film Sound* (2004, Columbia University Press); Aaron Gerow, *Visions of Japanese Modernity: Articulations of Cinema, Nation and Spectatorship, 1895–1925* (2010, University of California Press); Charles Musser, *Before the Nickelodeon* (1991, University of California Press); Jeffrey Klenotic, *'The Sensational Acme of Realism': 'Talker' Pictures as Early Cinema Sound Practice*, in Richard Abel & Rick Altman (editors), *The Sounds of Early Cinema* (2001, Indiana University Press); Tomoko Shimoda, 'Rediscovering Benshi: Narration in the Japanese Silent Film Era', *Electronic Journal of Japanese Studies*, Volume 5, Issue 2 (November 2005); Jeffrey A Dym, 'Benshi and the Introduction of Motion Pictures to Japan', *Monumenta Nipponica*, Volume 55, Number 4 (Winter 2000) pages 509–536; Charles M Berg, 'The Human Voice and the Silent Cinema', a paper presented at the Society for Cinema Studies Conference (New York City, April 1975); 'The Tale of Benshi: The Forgotten Heritage of Japanese Silent Cinema', on the Facets Feature blog, post of 25 October 2012; Jasper Sharp and Michael Arnold, 'Forgotten Fragments: an Introduction to Japanese Silent Cinema', on the Midnight Eye website, post of 16 July 2002; Max Nelson, 'Speaking Pictures: Tokyo Chorus and the History of the Benshi in Japanese Cinema', on the Reverse Shot website, post of 6 November 2015. It is also described in an article Sidney Wise wrote for the *Motion*

Picture World of 22 August 1908 ('How Motion Pictures are Made').

The innovations and experiences of Dove and Marie Patterson, and Bert and Nellie Gates, are described in Trevor Griffiths, *The Cinema and Cinema-going in Scotland, 1896–1950* (2012, Edinburgh University Press); in the *Bioscope* of 7 October 1909, 15 & 22 September 1910, 17 November 1910, 5 January 1911, 23 February 1911, 7 May 1914, 13 April 1916, and 2 November 1916; in the *Aberdeen Daily Journal* of 23 June 1911, 13 & 21 September 1911, 6 October 1911, 17 May 1912, 2 May 1913 and 11 February 1914; and in the *Royal Leamington Spa Courier* of 19 August 1910, and the *Press and Journal* of 24 April 1972.

The approving comments in the *Era* about Miss Caicedo were made in the edition of 12 March 1913, and the others appeared in the *Music Hall and Theatre Review* of 27 June 1912. And other information about her is taken from the *Western Mail* of 9 December 1912. The comments about cannibals in Bexhill-on-Sea appeared in that town's *Observer* newspaper on 18 October 1919. And the praise 'A Sapper' lavished on the Picturedrome in Bedford was set out in the *Bedfordshire Times and Independent* of 5 January 1917.

The various categories of music that might be played in cinemas are taken from Erno Rapée's mammoth *Encyclopedia of Music for Pictures* (1925, Belwin). The interview with Jean Michaud appeared in the *Bioscope* of 31 January 1918, while the story of Winne and the piano she played from behind a curtain, under a barrage, may be found in the *Wymondham and Attleborough Mercury* of 23 May 2018. The reception *Ragtime à la Carte* received on Tottenham Court Road was described in *Cinema* on 9 April 1913; the words of praise for *Tango Waltz* are taken from the *Bioscope* of 10 July 1913; and the Selsior company's concern for *Society Tango* was expressed in that journal on 8 January 1914. Information about the various

Tango films has been taken from a number of sources, including editions of the *Bioscope* dated 18 December 1913, 19 February 1914, and 3 December 1914.

Anton Blazer's career and early success in Britain is described in the *Clifton Society* of 17 April 1913 and the *Horfield and Bishopston Record and Montpelier and District Free Press* of two days later. Information about Henry Feiler comes from the *Liverpool Echo* of 25 May 1914 and 2 September 1914, and from the *Stage* of 10 September 1914.

The story of Oszkár Rausch was told in an essay by Stephen Bottomore that appears in Julie Brown & Annette Davison's book, while conditions at the Knockaloe camp are described in Stefan Manz & Panikos Panayi, *Enemies in the Empire: Civilian Internment in the British Empire During the First World War* (2020, Oxford University Press). Representations made on behalf of Mr Rausch by the Imperial and Royal Ministry of Foreign Affairs in Vienna may be found in the National Archives (FO 383/114). And what happened to Alfred Liebmann was set out in editions of the *Bioscope* for 2 December 1914, 18 & 25 February 1915, and 10 June 1915. Mr Liebmann's attempt to secure his liberty was noted in the *East London Observer* of 11 September 1915. While his legal case, which was reported as *R v Superintendent of Vine Street Police Station* [1916] 1 KB 268, is the subject of a masterful analysis by Rachel Vorspan in 'Law and War: Individual Rights, Executive Authority, and Judicial Power in England during World War I', a paper that was first published in the *Vanderbilt Journal of Transnational Law* (number 2 of volume 38, March 2005). Some idea of the conditions at the Wakefield internment camp may be gleaned from the recollections of Paul Cohen-Portheim, published in David Cesarani and Tony Kushner (editors), *The Internment of Aliens in Twentieth Century Britain* (1993, Routledge); from the Parliamentary debate on 26 July 1915 reported in *Hansard*, volume 7, column 1963; and from articles in the *Westminster*

Gazette of 19 June 1918 and the *People* of 30 June 1918.

Descriptions of the Electric Palace in Notting Hill may be found in the *Bioscope* of 23 February 1911 and the *Westminster Gazette* of 12 February 1915; and of the Coronet Theatre in the *Globe* of 4 & 9 October 1916, the *Sporting Times* of 7 & 14 October 1916, *The Era* of 18 October 1916, the *Bioscope* of 26 October 1916, and the *West London Observer* of 17 November 1916. Details of the career of Mark Wolfe have been taken from the *Cambridge Independent Press* of 17 October 1913, the *Evening Dispatch* of 27 March 1915, the *Pall Mall Gazette* of 19 April 1919, and the *Daily Herald* of 9 July 1930.

My description of the reception for Will Barker's *Henry VIII*, and of what it looked like when that film went up in flames, is taken from articles in the *Bioscope* of 20 April 1911, and 11 & 25 May 1911; and in the *Harrow Observer* of 17 March 1911, the *Folkestone Express, Sandgate, Shorncliffe and Hythe Advertiser* of 1 April 1911, the *Luton Reporter* of 6 April 1911, and the *Referee* of 16 April 1911. The facts of Mr Barker's life are taken from the biography of him that appears on the BFI website, and from a talk he gave in February 1936, which was entitled 'Before 1910: Kinematograph Experiences', and which may be found in number 38 of the *Proceedings of the British Kinematographic Society*.

Sixty Years A Queen is the subject of a fascinating chapter by Jude Cowan Montague in Mandy Merck (editor) *The British Monarchy on Screen* (2016, Manchester University Press). That and other Barker films, including *East Lynne*, *She* and *Jane Shore*, is also described in the *Bioscope* of 5 & 26 June 1913, and 11 & 25 December 1913; the *Whitstable Times and Tankerton Press* of 3 May 1913 and 12 August 1916; the *Bexhill-on-Sea Observer* of 16 & 23 August 1913; and the *Yorkshire Telegraph & Star* of 23 December 1913 and 7 June 1916; and in the *Era* of 7 May 1913, the *Daily Mail* (in Hull) of 4 June 1913, the *Derbyshire Advertiser* of 28 June 1913, the *Western Mail* of 9 August 1913, the *Wigan Observer and District Advertiser* of 23 August 1913, the *Whitby Gazette* of 5 September 1913, the *Bedfordshire Times and Independent* of 12 September 1913, the *Courier* (in Tunbridge Wells) of 26 September 1913, the *Harrow Observer* of 24 October 1913, the *Staffordshire Advertiser* of 22 November 1913, the *Citizen* (in St Andrews) of 29 November 1913, the *Pall Mall Gazette* of 10 December 1913, the *Westminster Gazette* of 9 December 1913, the *Middlesex County Times* of 8 May 1915, the *Courier* (in Taunton) of 5 April 1916, the *Bournemouth Graphic* of 8 April 1916, the *Sporting Times* of 15 April 1916, the *Chronicle* (in Chester) of 6 May 1916, the *Nottingham Evening Post* of 29 May 1916, the *Midland Daily Telegraph* of 5 June 1916, the *Sheffield Independent* of 6 June 1916, the *Liverpool Echo* of 20 June 1916, the *Dumfries and Galloway Saturday Standard* of 7 October 1916, the *Thanet Advertiser and Echo* of 4 November 1916, the *Evening News and Southern Daily Mail* of 9 November 1916, the *Fifeshire Advertiser* of 11 November 1916, and the *Buckingham Advertiser and North Bucks Free Press* of 4 August 1917.

The story of Nellie and Lisle Lucoque is told in the *Bioscope* of 27 October 1921, 10 August 1922, 31 May 1923, 15 January 1925, 15 October 1925, and 5 November 1925; in the *Bath Chronicle and Herald* of 29 October 1921 and 5 December 1925; and in the Chester newspaper the *Chronicle* of 20 April 1916.

Information about the Temperance Billiard Halls has been gathered from a number of sources, not least articles in the *Rochdale Observer* of 21 March 1914, the *Manchester Courier* of 4 April 1913 and 1 October 1915, and the *Manchester Evening News* of 8 February 1919.

It was in 1911 editions of the British Pathé newsreel that Lord Lonsdale was shown with the costermonger, and that the Siege of Sidney Street was portrayed. The latter event also appears in an edition of the *Gaumont Graphic* put out in January of the year, and in a rare newsreel made by the Andrews company.

What I have written about costermongers and their escapades is taken from articles in the *Bioscope* of 10 June 1909, 12 May 1910, 5 January 1911, 7 March 1912, 20 February 1913, 24 April 1913, 25 February 1915, and 20 March 1919; and in the *Leigh Chronicle* of 26 June 1908, the *Taunton Courier* of 13 April 1910, the *Bedfordshire Times and Independent* of 8 July 1910, the *Burnley Express* of 23 November 1910, the *Worthing Gazette* of 22 May 1912, the *Burnley Gazette* of 21 August 1912, the *Folkestone, Hythe, Sandgate and Cheriton Herald* of 10 May 1913, the *Daily Mail* (in Hull) of 27 May 1914, and the *Banbury Advertiser* of 15 March 1917.

Information about Jack Johnson's fight with Jim Jeffries, and its aftermath, has been taken from an article by Wayne Rozen in the *New York Times* of 3 July 2010 (*Great White Hope: Not Great, No Hope*), and from: Dan Streible, *Fight Pictures: A History of Boxing and Early Cinema* (2008, University of California Press); Kendall R Phillips, *Controversial Cinema: The Films that Outraged America* (2008, Greenwood Publishing Group); and Barak Y Orbach (2010) 'The Johnson-Jeffries Fight and Censorship of Black Supremacy', 5 *NYU Journal of Law & Liberty*, 270.

Johnson's run-in with the Home Secretary, when he thought he would be facing the Bombardier, is described in detail in Jeffrey Green's marvellous, infuriating essay 'Boxing and the "Colour Question" in Edwardian Britain: the "White Problem" of 1911' (1988) 5 *International Journal of the History of Sport*, Number 1, pages 115–119. Film of his drive through Charing Cross can be seen on the British Pathé website, and of his trip to Manchester docks on the BFI website. His harsh words on the subject of the British are quoted in Theresa Runstedtler's book *Jack Johnson, Rebel Sojourner: Boxing in the Shadow of the Global Colour Line* (2012, University of California Press). And his views on suffragists were reported in the *Clarence and Richmond Examiner* of 10 August 1911.

The brief, full life of Arthur Cravan is summarised in two marvellous pieces: one by Edward White on the website of the *Paris Review* ('Arthur Cravan, the Original Troll', posted 5 January 2018); the other by Graham Parker in the *Guardian* of 22 April 2016 ('The forgotten story of Jack Johnson's fight with Oscar Wilde's poet nephew').

Information about Wonderland in Whitechapel, and the wonders to be observed there, has been taken from Robert Machray's book *The Night Side of London* (1902, JB Lippincott), and from an article that appeared in the *Era* on 16 May 1896. The impact George Gunther made in that place is evident from a piece that appeared in the *Sporting Life* on 10 January 1910. His controversial fight with William Whitehead is the subject of a fascinating article by Heidi Bakk-Hansen that may be found on the Zenith City Online website (*Rumble on the St Louis River*), and of pieces in the *Duluth Evening Herald* of 20 & 21 September 1909 ('Black Men Battle on the Historic St Louis and Gunther Plays in Hard Luck'.) The film Mr Gunther made with Cecil Hepworth is described in the *Bioscope* of 11 November 1915, the *Cambridge Independent Press* of 12 May 1916, the *Leven Advertiser & Wemyss Gazette* of 8 June 1916, the *Ripley & Heanor News* of 7 July 1916, the Aberdeen *Evening Express* of 5 August 1916, the *Luton Reporter* of 25 September 1916, and the *Forfar Dispatch* of 26 October 1916.

The fire at the Imperial in Walsall was reported in the *Walsall Advertiser* of 13 February 1909, and the one at the Borough Theatre in North Shields in the *Shields Daily Gazette* of 9 April 1910. The one in the Picture Palace in Middlesbrough in 1911 was described in the *Courier* (in Dundee) of 5 April, in the *Stage* of 6 April, and in the *Leeds Mercury* of 12 April. Details of the fire at the Wood Green Picture Palladium may be found in the *Globe* of 9 April 1915, the *Scotsman* of 10 April 1915, and the *Bioscope* of 16 September 1915, and of what happened when the place was convicted of opening on a Sunday in the *Bioscope* of 11

March 1915. The merits and demerits of Burnley's various halls were reported in the *Burnley Express* of 13 September 1911, 6 April 1912, and 19 February 1921.

William Larkin's protests are the subject of an article by Maurice Walsh in the *Irish Times* of 18 November 2015 (*Ireland before the Rising: From Gallipoli to the Little Tramp*), and of reports in the *Freeman's Journal* and Dublin's *The Daily Express*, both for 6 June 1914, and in the former newspaper for 12 October 1915. The context for the protests is explained in Denis Condon, "'Offensive and Riotous Behaviour"? Performing the Role of an Audience in Irish Cinema of the mid-1910s,' in Kaveh Askari et al, *Performing New Media 1890–1915* (2015, Indiana University Press). It is also explained in several of Mr Condon's posts on the Early Irish Cinema blog.

What I have said about James Joyce was said first by Richard Ellmann in *James Joyce* (1959, Oxford University Press), while Harry Mitchelson, the projectionist at the Bohemian Picture House in Dublin, is mentioned in a piece by Harry Mount that appeared in the *Spectator* on 19 March 2016 (*Rebel Angels*).

L'affaire *Sapho* is described in the *Bioscope* of 6 March 1913, 24 July 1913, and 10 June 1915; the *Yorkshire Evening Post* of 31 March 1913 and 16 April 1913; and the *Shipley Times* of 18 April 1913, the *Harrow Observer* of 27 March 1914, *The Fife Free Press* of 16 May 1914, the *Forfar Herald and Kirriemuir Advertiser* of 11 September 1914, and the *Guardian* (in Runcorn) of 23 April 1915.

The fuss in Harringay about Sunday opening was described in editions of the *Bioscope* for 13 February 1913, 1 October 1914, and 5 November 1914. And details of the colourful life of Montagu Pyke have been taken from Luke McKernan's essays; from editions of the *Bioscope* for 16 September 1915, 7 October 1915, and 23 December 1915; and from the *Globe* of 7 September 1915.

The man who died in South Normanton was Alfred Best, and his last moments – in the Picture Palace, during a matinee –

were described in the *Derby Daily Telegraph* of 9 March 1921 and the *Nottingham Evening Post* of the following day. The Georges Carpentier film – *The Wonder Man* – featured spies, derring-do, and a bit of boxing. It was, the *Staffordshire Advertiser* wrote, 'a brilliant drama of love, mystery and gloves.'

The Mormon movie that featured Tilly was described in the *Bioscope* of 3 August 1911, and its reception was reported in the *Gloucester Journal* of 18 August 1911, the *Northern Daily Mail* of 29 August 1911, and the *Linlithgowshire Gazette* of 31 May 1912.

The reception afforded *Trapped by the Mormons* and *Married to a Mormon* is described in the *Bellshill Speaker* of 19 May 1922 and 9 June 1922, the *Shields Daily News* of 9 June 1922 and 12 July 1922, the *Burnley News* of 10 June 1922 and 16 February 1924, the *Courier* (in Dundee) of 19 June 1922 and 18 July 1922, and the *Forfar Dispatch* of 22 June 1922 and 3 August 1922; and in the *East London Observer* of 18 March 1922, the *Stage* of 16 March 1922, the *Burnley Express* of 8 April 1922, the *Airdrie & Coatbridge Advertiser* of 6 May 1922, the *Citizen* (in Gloucester) of 9 May 1922, the *Coatbridge Express* of 10 May 1922, the *Aberdeen Journal* of 13 May 1922, the *Devon and Exeter Gazette* of 16 May 1922, the *Bedfordshire Times and Independent* of 2 June 1922, the *Perthshire Advertiser* of 3 June 1922, the *Fraserburgh Herald and Northern Counties' Advertiser* of 6 June 1922, the *Wiltshire Times* of 10 June 1922, the *Devon and Exeter Gazette* of 19 June 1922, the *Shields Daily News* of 20 June 1922, the *Yorkshire Post* of 20 June 1922, the *Motherwell Times* of 7 July 1922, the *Newsman* (in Essex) of 8 July 1922, the *Kilmarnock Herald* of 28 July 1922, the *Newcastle Daily Chronicle* of 29 August 1922, the *Midlothian Journal* of 1 September 1922, the *Southern Reporter* of 14 September 1922, the *Motherwell Times* of 15 September 1922, the *Wishaw Press and Advertiser* of 15 September 1922, the *Musselburgh News* of 22 September 1922, and the *Montrose, Arbroath, and Brechin Review* of 12 January 1923.

The threats the unfortunate Mr Steven received when he was manager of the White Hall in Derby were reported in editions of the *Derbyshire Advertiser* of 26 May 1922 and 9 June 1922, and in the *Derby Daily Telegraph* of 12 June 1922. The warning to the people of Ripley was printed in the *Ripley & Heanor News* of 16 June 1922. The cautionary tale about the Mormons in Sandbach was set out in the *Lancashire Daily Post* of 25 June 1926. The ban imposed in Kitale on *Trapped by the Mormons* was reported in the *Daily Mail* (in Hull) of 30 December 1927. And details about the life and campaigns of Winifred Graham have been taken from a number of sources, including: Malcolm R Thorp, *Winifred Graham and the Mormon Image in England* (1979) Journal of Mormon History, volume 6, pages 107–121.

The arrival of the Super Cinemas was chronicled in the *Bioscope* for 14 October 1920; 24 February 1921, 17 March 1921, 30 June 1921, and 1 September 1921; and 5 January 1922, 30 March 1922, 1 June 1922, and 3 August 1922. It was also the subject of articles in the *Nottingham Evening Post* of 20 August 1921, the *Bath Chronicle* of 5 November 1921, the *Leeds Mercury* of 18 January 1922, the *Burnley News* of 21 January 1922, the *Gazette* (in Ealing) of the same date, the *Pall Mall Gazette* of 1 May 1922, the *Daily Mail* (in Hull) of 13 May 1922, the *West London Observer* of 2 June 1922, and the *Evening Telegraph* (in Dundee) of 3 July 1922.

The trial of Harold Greenwood is the subject of a book of its own, edited by Winifred Duke and published in 1930, which forms part of the *Notable British Trials* series. (It is also from there that the obituary of Sir Montague Shearman is taken.) The *Gaumont Graphic* featuring Mr Greenwood is number 982, of November 1920.

What happened to *The Rainbow* in 1915 is described in *The Times* of 15 November and the *New Statesman* of 20 November. The similar fate of *The Yoke* is recounted in the *Globe* of 14 December 1908. And the critical comment Virginia Woolf made about Sir Archibald Bodkin was contained in *A Room of One's Own* (1929, Hogarth Press). Sir Archibald's prowess in cinema cases is recorded in editions of the *Bioscope* for 18 April 1912, 3 December 1914, 11 November 1915, and 2 December 1915.

Documents detailing Ernest Haigh's – and Frederick White's – run-in with the Metropolitan Police Commissioner may be found in the National Archives (MEPO 2/7442/1A-12A). They include letters and copy letters, memoranda and advertisements. Descriptions of the making of the Haig films, meanwhile, appeared in the *Bioscope* on 22 & 29 September 1921.

The inaugural edition of the *Detective Magazine*, in which Mr Haigh shared space with Sir Archibald Bodkin, is dated 24 November 1922. And something, at least, of the colourful life of Edmund Maddick may be learned from articles in the *Pall Mall Gazette* of 7 December 1917 and the *Nottingham Evening Post* of 21 August 1939, and from a piece by his great-grandson, Chris Byng-Maddick, in the newsletter of the Friends of West Norwood Cemetery (Number 35, of May 1999). Information about the *Scotland Yard 1921* film was contained in Gloucestershire's the *Echo* newspaper, in the edition for 12 March 1921, in the *Sheffield Daily Telegraph* of 19 March 1921, and in the *Bioscope* of 24 March 1921.

The title of the first, Gold night is the product of my imagination, and the same is true of what I have described Thomas and Clement Padden saying to their respective audiences.

Little else, though, has been made up…

Not Norwood Suffling, The Queen of the Midgets, or Elijah Waddilove's lemonade.

Not the corsage of orange blossoms and white heather.

Not *Hold me tighter, Willie dear!*

Not Will Barker's leather whip or Broncho Billy's saddle.

Not Monsieur Louis Pingen, Baden Powell Wimpenny, or Miss Hilda Merrilees.

Not the ceiling of pressed tin or the determined tattoo that was beaten on the First Lord's Knocker.

Not *Too Much Sausage.*

Not Will Netta's Singing Jockeys.

Not *Archibald in a Tangle* or the tang of bhang and betel-nut.

Not Red Cow, 'Malediction!' or *Charlie on the Brain.*

And certainly not the finches that alighted upon Chrissie White, or whatever flew in to roost on top of Jackeydawra's head.

Acknowledgements

I should like to thank my wife, Leigh, who has again been tireless in her support of me and the book, and just plain sensible.

I must also thank Marion Hartley of the Lancashire Record Office, Susan Benson of the Cumbria Archive Service, Alison Depledge of the West Yorkshire Archive Service, Katina Bill of Kirklees Museums and Galleries, Tony Lees of Manchester Archives, Mike Hill and Michelle Blade of the *Lancashire Post*, Gill Johnson of the *Lancashire Telegraph*, and Marion Hewitt of the North West Film Archives. Their assistance has made this a much richer book than it would otherwise have been.

I knew Edith and Mary for only a short time, and that is something I now regret.